Data Protection Act 2018

ISBN: 9798834857730

WESTMINSTER
LEGAL PUBLISHING, LONDON

PART 1 Preliminary

PART 2 General processing

CHAPTER 1 Scope and definitions

CHAPTER 2 The UK GDPR

Meaning of certain terms used in the UK GDPR

Lawfulness of processing

Special categories of personal data

Rights of the data subject

Exemptions etc

Certification

CHAPTER 3 Exemptions for manual unstructured processing and for national security and defence purposes

PART 3 Law enforcement processing

CHAPTER 1 Scope and definitions

CHAPTER 2 Principles

CHAPTER 3 Rights of the data subject

Overview and scope

Information: controller's general duties

Data subject's right of access

Data subject's rights to rectification or erasure etc

Automated individual decision-making

Supplementary

CHAPTER 4 Controller and processor

Overview and scope

General obligations

Obligations relating to security

Obligations relating to personal data breaches

Data protection officers

CHAPTER 5 Transfers of personal data to third countries etc

Overview and interpretation

General principles for transfers

CHAPTER 6 Supplementary

PART 4 Intelligence services processing

CHAPTER 1 Scope and definitions
Scope

Definitions

CHAPTER 2 Principles
Overview

The data protection principles

CHAPTER 3 Rights of the data subject

PART 5 The Information Commissioner

PART 6 Enforcement

PART 7 Supplementary and final provision

Data Protection Act 2018

2018 CHAPTER 12

An Act to make provision for the regulation of the processing of information relating to individuals; to make provision in connection with the Information Commissioner's functions under certain regulations relating to information; to make provision for a direct marketing code of practice; and for connected purposes.
                                                    [23rd May 2018]

B E IT ENACTED by the Queen's most Excellent Majesty, by and with the advice and consent of the Lords Spiritual and Temporal, and Commons, in this present Parliament assembled, and by the authority of the same, as follows: —

PART 1

PRELIMINARY

1   Overview

(1)   This Act makes provision about the processing of personal data.

(2)   Most processing of personal data is subject to the GDPR.

(3)   Part 2 supplements the GDPR (see Chapter 2) and applies a broadly equivalent regime to certain types of processing to which the GDPR does not apply (see Chapter 3).

(4)   Part 3 makes provision about the processing of personal data by competent authorities for law enforcement purposes and implements the Law Enforcement Directive.

(5)   Part 4 makes provision about the processing of personal data by the intelligence services.

(6)   Part 5 makes provision about the Information Commissioner.

(7)   Part 6 makes provision about the enforcement of the data protection legislation.

(8) Part 7 makes supplementary provision, including provision about the application of this Act to the Crown and to Parliament.

2 Protection of personal data

(1) The GDPR, the applied GDPR and this Act protect individuals with regard to the processing of personal data, in particular by —

    (a) requiring personal data to be processed lawfully and fairly, on the basis of the data subject's consent or another specified basis,

    (b) conferring rights on the data subject to obtain information about the processing of personal data and to require inaccurate personal data to be rectified, and

    (c) conferring functions on the Commissioner, giving the holder of that office responsibility for monitoring and enforcing their provisions.

(2) When carrying out functions under the GDPR, the applied GDPR and this Act, the Commissioner must have regard to the importance of securing an appropriate level of protection for personal data, taking account of the interests of data subjects, controllers and others and matters of general public interest.

3 Terms relating to the processing of personal data

(1) This section defines some terms used in this Act.

(2) "Personal data" means any information relating to an identified or identifiable living individual (subject to subsection (14)(c)).

(3) "Identifiable living individual" means a living individual who can be identified, directly or indirectly, in particular by reference to —

    (a) an identifier such as a name, an identification number, location data or an online identifier, or

    (b) one or more factors specific to the physical, physiological, genetic, mental, economic, cultural or social identity of the individual.

(4) "Processing", in relation to information, means an operation or set of operations which is performed on information, or on sets of information, such as —

    (a) collection, recording, organisation, structuring or storage,

    (b) adaptation or alteration,

    (c) retrieval, consultation or use,

    (d) disclosure by transmission, dissemination or otherwise making available,

    (e) alignment or combination, or

    (f) restriction, erasure or destruction,

(subject to subsection (14)(c) and sections 5(7), 29(2) and 82(3), which make provision about references to processing in the different Parts of this Act).

(5) "Data subject" means the identified or identifiable living individual to whom personal data relates.

(6) "Controller" and "processor", in relation to the processing of personal data to which Chapter 2 or 3 of Part 2, Part 3 or Part 4 applies, have the same meaning as in that Chapter or Part (see sections 5, 6, 32 and 83 and see also subsection (14)(d)).

(7) "Filing system" means any structured set of personal data which is accessible according to specific criteria, whether held by automated means or manually and whether centralised, decentralised or dispersed on a functional or geographical basis.

(8) "The Commissioner" means the Information Commissioner (see section 114).

(9) "The data protection legislation" means —
   (a) the GDPR,
   (b) the applied GDPR,
   (c) this Act,
   (d) regulations made under this Act, and
   (e) regulations made under section 2(2) of the European Communities Act 1972 which relate to the GDPR or the Law Enforcement Directive.

(10) "The GDPR" means Regulation (EU) 2016/679 of the European Parliament and of the Council of 27 April 2016 on the protection of natural persons with regard to the processing of personal data and on the free movement of such data (General Data Protection Regulation).

(11) "The applied GDPR" means the GDPR as applied by Chapter 3 of Part 2.

(12) "The Law Enforcement Directive" means Directive (EU) 2016/680 of the European Parliament and of the Council of 27 April 2016 on the protection of natural persons with regard to the processing of personal data by competent authorities for the purposes of the prevention, investigation, detection or prosecution of criminal offences or the execution of criminal penalties, and on the free movement of such data, and repealing Council Framework Decision 2008/977/JHA.

(13) "The Data Protection Convention" means the Convention for the Protection of Individuals with regard to Automatic Processing of Personal Data which was opened for signature on 28 January 1981, as amended up to the day on which this Act is passed.

(14) In Parts 5 to 7, except where otherwise provided —
   (a) references to the GDPR are to the GDPR read with Chapter 2 of Part 2 and include the applied GDPR read with Chapter 3 of Part 2;
   (b) references to Chapter 2 of Part 2, or to a provision of that Chapter, include that Chapter or that provision as applied by Chapter 3 of Part 2;
   (c) references to personal data, and the processing of personal data, are to personal data and processing to which Chapter 2 or 3 of Part 2, Part 3 or Part 4 applies;
   (d) references to a controller or processor are to a controller or processor in relation to the processing of personal data to which Chapter 2 or 3 of Part 2, Part 3 or Part 4 applies.

(15) There is an index of defined expressions in section 206.

4   Processing to which this Part applies

(1)   This Part is relevant to most processing of personal data.

(2)   Chapter 2 of this Part—
  (a)   applies to the types of processing of personal data to which the GDPR applies by virtue of Article 2 of the GDPR, and
  (b)   supplements, and must be read with, the GDPR.

(3)   Chapter 3 of this Part—
  (a)   applies to certain types of processing of personal data to which the GDPR does not apply (see section 21), and
  (b)   makes provision for a regime broadly equivalent to the GDPR to apply to such processing.

5   Definitions

(1)   Terms used in Chapter 2 of this Part and in the GDPR have the same meaning in Chapter 2 as they have in the GDPR.

(2)   In subsection (1), the reference to a term's meaning in the GDPR is to its meaning in the GDPR read with any provision of Chapter 2 which modifies the term's meaning for the purposes of the GDPR.

(3)   Subsection (1) is subject to any provision in Chapter 2 which provides expressly for the term to have a different meaning and to section 204.

(4)   Terms used in Chapter 3 of this Part and in the applied GDPR have the same meaning in Chapter 3 as they have in the applied GDPR.

(5)   In subsection (4), the reference to a term's meaning in the applied GDPR is to its meaning in the GDPR read with any provision of Chapter 2 (as applied by Chapter 3) or Chapter 3 which modifies the term's meaning for the purposes of the applied GDPR.

(6)   Subsection (4) is subject to any provision in Chapter 2 (as applied by Chapter 3) or Chapter 3 which provides expressly for the term to have a different meaning.

(7)   A reference in Chapter 2 or Chapter 3 of this Part to the processing of personal data is to processing to which the Chapter applies.

(8)   Sections 3 and 205 include definitions of other expressions used in this Part.

CHAPTER 2

THE GDPR

Meaning of certain terms used in the GDPR

6   Meaning of "controller"

(1)   The definition of "controller" in Article 4(7) of the GDPR has effect subject to —
   (a)   subsection (2),
   (b)   section 209, and
   (c)   section 210.

(2)   For the purposes of the GDPR, where personal data is processed only —
   (a)   for purposes for which it is required by an enactment to be processed, and
   (b)   by means by which it is required by an enactment to be processed,
   the person on whom the obligation to process the data is imposed by the enactment (or, if different, one of the enactments) is the controller.

7   Meaning of "public authority" and "public body"

(1)   For the purposes of the GDPR, the following (and only the following) are "public authorities" and "public bodies" under the law of the United Kingdom —
   (a)   a public authority as defined by the Freedom of Information Act 2000,
   (b)   a Scottish public authority as defined by the Freedom of Information (Scotland) Act 2002 (asp 13), and
   (c)   an authority or body specified or described by the Secretary of State in regulations,
   subject to subsections (2), (3) and (4).

(2)   An authority or body that falls within subsection (1) is only a "public authority" or "public body" for the purposes of the GDPR when performing a task carried out in the public interest or in the exercise of official authority vested in it.

(3)   The references in subsection (1)(a) and (b) to public authorities and Scottish public authorities as defined by the Freedom of Information Act 2000 and the Freedom of Information (Scotland) Act 2002 (asp 13) do not include any of the following that fall within those definitions —
   (a)   a parish council in England;
   (b)   a community council in Wales;
   (c)   a community council in Scotland;
   (d)   a parish meeting constituted under section 13 of the Local Government Act 1972;
   (e)   a community meeting constituted under section 27 of that Act;
   (f)   charter trustees constituted —
      (i)   under section 246 of that Act,
      (ii)   under Part 1 of the Local Government and Public Involvement in Health Act 2007, or
      (iii) by the Charter Trustees Regulations 1996 (S.I. 1996/263).

(4)   The Secretary of State may by regulations provide that a person specified or described in the regulations that is a public authority described in subsection (1)(a) or (b) is not a "public authority" or "public body" for the purposes of the GDPR.

(5)   Regulations under this section are subject to the affirmative resolution procedure.

Lawfulness of processing

8   Lawfulness of processing: public interest etc

In Article 6(1) of the GDPR (lawfulness of processing), the reference in point (e) to processing of personal data that is necessary for the performance of a task carried out in the public interest or in the exercise of the controller's official authority includes processing of personal data that is necessary for—

(a)   the administration of justice,

(b)   the exercise of a function of either House of Parliament,

(c)   the exercise of a function conferred on a person by an enactment or rule of law,

(d)   the exercise of a function of the Crown, a Minister of the Crown or a government department, or

(e)   an activity that supports or promotes democratic engagement.

9   Child's consent in relation to information society services

In Article 8(1) of the GDPR (conditions applicable to child's consent in relation to information society services)—

(a)   references to "16 years" are to be read as references to "13 years", and

(b)   the reference to "information society services" does not include preventive or counselling services.

Special categories of personal data

10   Special categories of personal data and criminal convictions etc data

(1)   Subsections (2) and (3) make provision about the processing of personal data described in Article 9(1) of the GDPR (prohibition on processing of special categories of personal data) in reliance on an exception in one of the following points of Article 9(2)—

(a)   point (b) (employment, social security and social protection);

(b)   point (g) (substantial public interest);

(c)   point (h) (health and social care);

(d)   point (i) (public health);

(e)   point (j) (archiving, research and statistics).

(2)   The processing meets the requirement in point (b), (h), (i) or (j) of Article 9(2) of the GDPR for authorisation by, or a basis in, the law of the United Kingdom or a part of the United Kingdom only if it meets a condition in Part 1 of Schedule 1.

(3) The processing meets the requirement in point (g) of Article 9(2) of the GDPR for a basis in the law of the United Kingdom or a part of the United Kingdom only if it meets a condition in Part 2 of Schedule 1.

(4) Subsection (5) makes provision about the processing of personal data relating to criminal convictions and offences or related security measures that is not carried out under the control of official authority.

(5) The processing meets the requirement in Article 10 of the GDPR for authorisation by the law of the United Kingdom or a part of the United Kingdom only if it meets a condition in Part 1, 2 or 3 of Schedule 1.

(6) The Secretary of State may by regulations —
    (a) amend Schedule 1 —
        (i) by adding or varying conditions or safeguards, and
        (ii) by omitting conditions or safeguards added by regulations under this section, and
    (b) consequentially amend this section.

(7) Regulations under this section are subject to the affirmative resolution procedure.

11 Special categories of personal data etc: supplementary

(1) For the purposes of Article 9(2)(h) of the GDPR (processing for health or social care purposes etc), the circumstances in which the processing of personal data is carried out subject to the conditions and safeguards referred to in Article 9(3) of the GDPR (obligation of secrecy) include circumstances in which it is carried out —
    (a) by or under the responsibility of a health professional or a social work professional, or
    (b) by another person who in the circumstances owes a duty of confidentiality under an enactment or rule of law.

(2) In Article 10 of the GDPR and section 10, references to personal data relating to criminal convictions and offences or related security measures include personal data relating to —
    (a) the alleged commission of offences by the data subject, or
    (b) proceedings for an offence committed or alleged to have been committed by the data subject or the disposal of such proceedings, including sentencing.

Rights of the data subject

12 Limits on fees that may be charged by controllers

(1) The Secretary of State may by regulations specify limits on the fees that a controller may charge in reliance on —
    (a) Article 12(5) of the GDPR (reasonable fees when responding to manifestly unfounded or excessive requests), or
    (b) Article 15(3) of the GDPR (reasonable fees for provision of further copies).

(2) The Secretary of State may by regulations —

    (a)   require controllers of a description specified in the regulations to produce and publish guidance about the fees that they charge in reliance on those provisions, and

    (b)   specify what the guidance must include.

(3)   Regulations under this section are subject to the negative resolution procedure.

13   Obligations of credit reference agencies

(1)   This section applies where a controller is a credit reference agency (within the meaning of section 145(8) of the Consumer Credit Act 1974).

(2)   The controller's obligations under Article 15(1) to (3) of the GDPR (confirmation of processing, access to data and safeguards for third country transfers) are taken to apply only to personal data relating to the data subject's financial standing, unless the data subject has indicated a contrary intention.

(3)   Where the controller discloses personal data in pursuance of Article 15(1) to (3) of the GDPR, the disclosure must be accompanied by a statement informing the data subject of the data subject's rights under section 159 of the Consumer Credit Act 1974 (correction of wrong information).

14   Automated decision-making authorised by law: safeguards

(1)   This section makes provision for the purposes of Article 22(2)(b) of the GDPR (exception from Article 22(1) of the GDPR for significant decisions based solely on automated processing that are authorised by law and subject to safeguards for the data subject's rights, freedoms and legitimate interests).

(2)   A decision is a "significant decision" for the purposes of this section if, in relation to a data subject, it—

    (a)   produces legal effects concerning the data subject, or

    (b)   similarly significantly affects the data subject.

(3)   A decision is a "qualifying significant decision" for the purposes of this section if—

    (a)   it is a significant decision in relation to a data subject,

    (b)   it is required or authorised by law, and

    (c)   it does not fall within Article 22(2)(a) or (c) of the GDPR (decisions necessary to a contract or made with the data subject's consent).

(4)   Where a controller takes a qualifying significant decision in relation to a data subject based solely on automated processing—

    (a)   the controller must, as soon as reasonably practicable, notify the data subject in writing that a decision has been taken based solely on automated processing, and

    (b)   the data subject may, before the end of the period of 1 month beginning with receipt of the notification, request the controller to—

        (i)   reconsider the decision, or

        (ii) take a new decision that is not based solely on automated processing.

(5)   If a request is made to a controller under subsection (4), the controller must, within the period described in Article 12(3) of the GDPR—

    (a)   consider the request, including any information provided by the data subject that is relevant to it,

    (b)   comply with the request, and

    (c)   by notice in writing inform the data subject of—

        (i)   the steps taken to comply with the request, and

        (ii)   the outcome of complying with the request.

(6)   In connection with this section, a controller has the powers and obligations under Article 12 of the GDPR (transparency, procedure for extending time for acting on request, fees, manifestly unfounded or excessive requests etc) that apply in connection with Article 22 of the GDPR.

(7)   The Secretary of State may by regulations make such further provision as the Secretary of State considers appropriate to provide suitable measures to safeguard a data subject's rights, freedoms and legitimate interests in connection with the taking of qualifying significant decisions based solely on automated processing.

(8)   Regulations under subsection (7)—

    (a)   may amend this section, and

    (b)   are subject to the affirmative resolution procedure.

Restrictions on data subject's rights

15   Exemptions etc

(1)   Schedules 2, 3 and 4 make provision for exemptions from, and restrictions and adaptations of the application of, rules of the GDPR.

(2)   In Schedule 2—

    (a)   Part 1 makes provision adapting or restricting the application of rules contained in Articles 13 to 21 and 34 of the GDPR in specified circumstances, as allowed for by Article 6(3) and Article 23(1) of the GDPR;

    (b)   Part 2 makes provision restricting the application of rules contained in Articles 13 to 21 and 34 of the GDPR in specified circumstances, as allowed for by Article 23(1) of the GDPR;

    (c)   Part 3 makes provision restricting the application of Article 15 of the GDPR where this is necessary to protect the rights of others, as allowed for by Article 23(1) of the GDPR;

    (d)   Part 4 makes provision restricting the application of rules contained in Articles 13 to 15 of the GDPR in specified circumstances, as allowed for by Article 23(1) of the GDPR;

    (e)   Part 5 makes provision containing exemptions or derogations from Chapters II, III, IV, V and VII of the GDPR for reasons relating to freedom of expression, as allowed for by Article 85(2) of the GDPR;

    (f)   Part 6 makes provision containing derogations from rights contained in Articles 15, 16, 18, 19, 20 and 21 of the GDPR for scientific or historical research purposes, statistical purposes and archiving purposes, as allowed for by Article 89(2) and (3) of the GDPR.

(3)   Schedule 3 makes provision restricting the application of rules contained in Articles 13 to 21 of the GDPR to health, social work, education and child abuse data, as allowed for by Article 23(1) of the GDPR.

(4)   Schedule 4 makes provision restricting the application of rules contained in Articles 13 to 21 of the GDPR to information the disclosure of which is prohibited or restricted by an enactment, as allowed for by Article 23(1) of the GDPR.

(5)   In connection with the safeguarding of national security and with defence, see Chapter 3 of this Part and the exemption in section 26.

16   Power to make further exemptions etc by regulations

(1)   The following powers to make provision altering the application of the GDPR may be exercised by way of regulations made by the Secretary of State under this section —

    (a)   the power in Article 6(3) for Member State law to lay down a legal basis containing specific provisions to adapt the application of rules of the GDPR where processing is necessary for compliance with a legal obligation, for the performance of a task in the public interest or in the exercise of official authority;

    (b)   the power in Article 23(1) to make a legislative measure restricting the scope of the obligations and rights mentioned in that Article where necessary and proportionate to safeguard certain objectives of general public interest;

    (c)   the power in Article 85(2) to provide for exemptions or derogations from certain Chapters of the GDPR where necessary to reconcile the protection of personal data with the freedom of expression and information.

(2)   Regulations under this section may —

    (a)   amend Schedules 2 to 4 —

        (i)   by adding or varying provisions, and

        (ii)   by omitting provisions added by regulations under this section, and

    (b)   consequentially amend section 15.

(3)   Regulations under this section are subject to the affirmative resolution procedure.

Accreditation of certification providers

17   Accreditation of certification providers

(1)   Accreditation of a person as a certification provider is only valid when carried out by —

    (a)   the Commissioner, or

    (b)   the national accreditation body.

(2)   The Commissioner may only accredit a person as a certification provider where the Commissioner —

    (a)   has published a statement that the Commissioner will carry out such accreditation, and

    (b)   has not published a notice withdrawing that statement.

(3)   The national accreditation body may only accredit a person as a certification provider where the Commissioner —

> (a) has published a statement that the body may carry out such accreditation, and
>
> (b) has not published a notice withdrawing that statement.

(4) The publication of a notice under subsection (2)(b) or (3)(b) does not affect the validity of any accreditation carried out before its publication.

(5) Schedule 5 makes provision about reviews of, and appeals from, a decision relating to accreditation of a person as a certification provider.

(6) The national accreditation body may charge a reasonable fee in connection with, or incidental to, the carrying out of the body's functions under this section, Schedule 5 and Article 43 of the GDPR.

(7) The national accreditation body must provide the Secretary of State with such information relating to its functions under this section, Schedule 5 and Article 43 of the GDPR as the Secretary of State may reasonably require.

(8) In this section—

> "certification provider" means a person who issues certification for the purposes of Article 42 of the GDPR;
>
> "the national accreditation body" means the national accreditation body for the purposes of Article 4(1) of Regulation (EC) No 765/2008 of the European Parliament and of the Council of 9 July 2008 setting out the requirements for accreditation and market surveillance relating to the marketing of products and repealing Regulation (EEC) No 339/93.

Transfers of personal data to third countries etc

18 Transfers of personal data to third countries etc

(1) The Secretary of State may by regulations specify, for the purposes of Article 49(1)(d) of the GDPR—

> (a) circumstances in which a transfer of personal data to a third country or international organisation is to be taken to be necessary for important reasons of public interest, and
>
> (b) circumstances in which a transfer of personal data to a third country or international organisation which is not required by an enactment is not to be taken to be necessary for important reasons of public interest.

(2) The Secretary of State may by regulations restrict the transfer of a category of personal data to a third country or international organisation where—

> (a) the transfer is not authorised by an adequacy decision under Article 45(3) of the GDPR, and
>
> (b) the Secretary of State considers the restriction to be necessary for important reasons of public interest.

(3) Regulations under this section—

> (a) are subject to the made affirmative resolution procedure where the Secretary of State has made an urgency statement in respect of them;
>
> (b) are otherwise subject to the affirmative resolution procedure.

(4) For the purposes of this section, an urgency statement is a reasoned statement that the Secretary of State considers it desirable for the regulations to come into force without delay.

Specific processing situations

19 Processing for archiving, research and statistical purposes: safeguards

(1) This section makes provision about—

    (a) processing of personal data that is necessary for archiving purposes in the public interest,

    (b) processing of personal data that is necessary for scientific or historical research purposes, and

    (c) processing of personal data that is necessary for statistical purposes.

(2) Such processing does not satisfy the requirement in Article 89(1) of the GDPR for the processing to be subject to appropriate safeguards for the rights and freedoms of the data subject if it is likely to cause substantial damage or substantial distress to a data subject.

(3) Such processing does not satisfy that requirement if the processing is carried out for the purposes of measures or decisions with respect to a particular data subject, unless the purposes for which the processing is necessary include the purposes of approved medical research.

(4) In this section—

    "approved medical research" means medical research carried out by a person who has approval to carry out that research from—

        (a) a research ethics committee recognised or established by the Health Research Authority under Chapter 2 of Part 3 of the Care Act 2014, or

        (b) a body appointed by any of the following for the purpose of assessing the ethics of research involving individuals—

            (i) the Secretary of State, the Scottish Ministers, the Welsh Ministers, or a Northern Ireland department;

            (ii) a relevant NHS body;

            (iii) United Kingdom Research and Innovation or a body that is a Research Council for the purposes of the Science and Technology Act 1965;

            (iv) an institution that is a research institution for the purposes of Chapter 4A of Part 7 of the Income Tax (Earnings and Pensions) Act 2003 (see section 457 of that Act);

    "relevant NHS body" means—

        (a) an NHS trust or NHS foundation trust in England,

        (b) an NHS trust or Local Health Board in Wales,

        (c) a Health Board or Special Health Board constituted under section 2 of the National Health Service (Scotland) Act 1978,

        (d) the Common Services Agency for the Scottish Health Service, or

        (e) any of the health and social care bodies in Northern Ireland falling within paragraphs (a) to (e) of section 1(5) of the Health and Social Care (Reform) Act (Northern Ireland) 2009 (c. 1 (N.I.)).

(5) The Secretary of State may by regulations change the meaning of "approved medical research" for the purposes of this section, including by amending subsection (4).

(6)   Regulations under subsection (5) are subject to the affirmative resolution procedure.

Minor definition

20   Meaning of "court"

Section 5(1) (terms used in this Chapter to have the same meaning as in the GDPR) does not apply to references in this Chapter to a court and, accordingly, such references do not include a tribunal.

CHAPTER 3

OTHER GENERAL PROCESSING

Scope

21   Processing to which this Chapter applies

(1)   This Chapter applies to the automated or structured processing of personal data in the course of —

    (a)   an activity which is outside the scope of European Union law, or

    (b)   an activity which falls within the scope of Article 2(2)(b) of the GDPR (common foreign and security policy activities),

provided that the processing is not processing by a competent authority for any of the law enforcement purposes (as defined in Part 3) or processing to which Part 4 (intelligence services processing) applies.

(2)   This Chapter also applies to the manual unstructured processing of personal data held by an FOI public authority.

(3)   This Chapter does not apply to the processing of personal data by an individual in the course of a purely personal or household activity.

(4)   In this section —

    "the automated or structured processing of personal data" means —

        (a)   the processing of personal data wholly or partly by automated means, and

        (b)   the processing otherwise than by automated means of personal data which forms part of a filing system or is intended to form part of a filing system;

    "the manual unstructured processing of personal data" means the processing of personal data which is not the automated or structured processing of personal data.

(5)   In this Chapter, "FOI public authority" means —

    (a)   a public authority as defined in the Freedom of Information Act 2000, or

    (b)   a Scottish public authority as defined in the Freedom of Information (Scotland) Act 2002 (asp 13).

(6)   References in this Chapter to personal data "held" by an FOI public authority are to be interpreted —

(a) in relation to England and Wales and Northern Ireland, in accordance with section 3(2) of the Freedom of Information Act 2000, and

(b) in relation to Scotland, in accordance with section 3(2), (4) and (5) of the Freedom of Information (Scotland) Act 2002 (asp 13),

but such references do not include information held by an intelligence service (as defined in section 82) on behalf of an FOI public authority.

(7) But personal data is not to be treated as "held" by an FOI public authority for the purposes of this Chapter, where—

(a) section 7 of the Freedom of Information Act 2000 prevents Parts 1 to 5 of that Act from applying to the personal data, or

(b) section 7(1) of the Freedom of Information (Scotland) Act 2002 (asp 13) prevents that Act from applying to the personal data.

Application of the GDPR

22 Application of the GDPR to processing to which this Chapter applies

(1) The GDPR applies to the processing of personal data to which this Chapter applies but as if its Articles were part of an Act extending to England and Wales, Scotland and Northern Ireland.

(2) Chapter 2 of this Part applies for the purposes of the applied GDPR as it applies for the purposes of the GDPR.

(3) In this Chapter, "the applied Chapter 2" means Chapter 2 of this Part as applied by this Chapter.

(4) Schedule 6 contains provision modifying—

(a) the GDPR as it applies by virtue of subsection (1) (see Part 1);

(b) Chapter 2 of this Part as it applies by virtue of subsection (2) (see Part 2).

(5) A question as to the meaning or effect of a provision of the applied GDPR, or the applied Chapter 2, is to be determined consistently with the interpretation of the equivalent provision of the GDPR, or Chapter 2 of this Part, as it applies otherwise than by virtue of this Chapter, except so far as Schedule 6 requires a different interpretation.

23 Power to make provision in consequence of regulations related to the GDPR

(1) The Secretary of State may by regulations make provision in connection with the processing of personal data to which this Chapter applies which is equivalent to that made by GDPR regulations, subject to such modifications as the Secretary of State considers appropriate.

(2) In this section, "GDPR regulations" means regulations made under section 2(2) of the European Communities Act 1972 which make provision relating to the GDPR.

(3) Regulations under subsection (1) may apply a provision of GDPR regulations, with or without modification.

(4) Regulations under subsection (1) may amend or repeal a provision of—

(a) the applied GDPR;

(b) this Chapter;

(c) Parts 5 to 7, in so far as they apply in relation to the applied GDPR.

(5) Regulations under this section are subject to the affirmative resolution procedure.

Exemptions etc

24 Manual unstructured data held by FOI public authorities

(1) The provisions of the applied GDPR and this Act listed in subsection (2) do not apply to personal data to which this Chapter applies by virtue of section 21(2) (manual unstructured personal data held by FOI public authorities).

(2) Those provisions are—
   (a) in Chapter II of the applied GDPR (principles)—
      (i)   Article 5(1)(a) to (c), (e) and (f) (principles relating to processing, other than the accuracy principle),
      (ii) Article 6 (lawfulness),
      (iii) Article 7 (conditions for consent),
      (iv) Article 8(1) and (2) (child's consent),
      (v)   Article 9 (processing of special categories of personal data),
      (vi) Article 10 (data relating to criminal convictions etc), and
      (vii) Article 11(2) (processing not requiring identification);
   (b) in Chapter III of the applied GDPR (rights of the data subject)—
      (i)   Article 13(1) to (3) (personal data collected from data subject: information to be provided),
      (ii) Article 14(1) to (4) (personal data collected other than from data subject: information to be provided),
      (iii) Article 20 (right to data portability), and
      (iv) Article 21(1) (objections to processing);
   (c) in Chapter V of the applied GDPR, Articles 44 to 49 (transfers of personal data to third countries or international organisations);
   (d) sections 170 and 171 of this Act;
   (see also paragraph 1(2) of Schedule 18).

(3) In addition, the provisions of the applied GDPR listed in subsection (4) do not apply to personal data to which this Chapter applies by virtue of section 21(2) where the personal data relates to appointments, removals, pay, discipline, superannuation or other personnel matters in relation to—
   (a) service in any of the armed forces of the Crown;
   (b) service in any office or employment under the Crown or under any public authority;
   (c) service in any office or employment, or under any contract for services, in respect of which power to take action, or to determine or approve the action taken, in such matters is vested in—
      (i)   Her Majesty,
      (ii) a Minister of the Crown,
      (iii) the National Assembly for Wales,
      (iv) the Welsh Ministers,
      (v)   a Northern Ireland Minister (within the meaning of the Freedom of Information Act 2000), or

          (vi)   an FOI public authority.

(4) Those provisions are —
- (a) the remaining provisions of Chapters II and III (principles and rights of the data subject);
- (b) Chapter IV (controller and processor);
- (c) Chapter IX (specific processing situations).

(5) A controller is not obliged to comply with Article 15(1) to (3) of the applied GDPR (right of access by the data subject) in relation to personal data to which this Chapter applies by virtue of section 21(2) if —
- (a) the request under that Article does not contain a description of the personal data, or
- (b) the controller estimates that the cost of complying with the request so far as relating to the personal data would exceed the appropriate maximum.

(6) Subsection (5)(b) does not remove the controller's obligation to confirm whether or not personal data concerning the data subject is being processed unless the estimated cost of complying with that obligation alone in relation to the personal data would exceed the appropriate maximum.

(7) An estimate for the purposes of this section must be made in accordance with regulations under section 12(5) of the Freedom of Information Act 2000.

(8) In subsections (5) and (6), "the appropriate maximum" means the maximum amount specified by the Secretary of State by regulations.

(9) Regulations under subsection (8) are subject to the negative resolution procedure.

25 Manual unstructured data used in longstanding historical research

(1) The provisions of the applied GDPR listed in subsection (2) do not apply to personal data to which this Chapter applies by virtue of section 21(2) (manual unstructured personal data held by FOI public authorities) at any time when —
- (a) the personal data —
  - (i) is subject to processing which was already underway immediately before 24 October 1998, and
  - (ii) is processed only for the purposes of historical research, and
- (b) the processing is not carried out —
  - (i) for the purposes of measures or decisions with respect to a particular data subject, or
  - (ii) in a way that causes, or is likely to cause, substantial damage or substantial distress to a data subject.

(2) Those provisions are —
- (a) in Chapter II of the applied GDPR (principles), Article 5(1)(d) (the accuracy principle), and
- (b) in Chapter III of the applied GDPR (rights of the data subject) —
  - (i) Article 16 (right to rectification), and
  - (ii) Article 17(1) and (2) (right to erasure).

(3) The exemptions in this section apply in addition to the exemptions in section 24.

26 National security and defence exemption

(1) A provision of the applied GDPR or this Act mentioned in subsection (2) does not apply to personal data to which this Chapter applies if exemption from the provision is required for—

    (a) the purpose of safeguarding national security, or

    (b) defence purposes.

(2) The provisions are—

    (a) Chapter II of the applied GDPR (principles) except for—

        (i) Article 5(1)(a) (lawful, fair and transparent processing), so far as it requires processing of personal data to be lawful;

        (ii) Article 6 (lawfulness of processing);

        (iii) Article 9 (processing of special categories of personal data);

    (b) Chapter III of the applied GDPR (rights of data subjects);

    (c) in Chapter IV of the applied GDPR—

        (i) Article 33 (notification of personal data breach to the Commissioner);

        (ii) Article 34 (communication of personal data breach to the data subject);

    (d) Chapter V of the applied GDPR (transfers of personal data to third countries or international organisations);

    (e) in Chapter VI of the applied GDPR—

        (i) Article 57(1)(a) and (h) (Commissioner's duties to monitor and enforce the applied GDPR and to conduct investigations);

        (ii) Article 58 (investigative, corrective, authorisation and advisory powers of Commissioner);

    (f) Chapter VIII of the applied GDPR (remedies, liabilities and penalties) except for—

        (i) Article 83 (general conditions for imposing administrative fines);

        (ii) Article 84 (penalties);

    (g) in Part 5 of this Act—

        (i) in section 115 (general functions of the Commissioner), subsections (3) and (8);

        (ii) in section 115, subsection (9), so far as it relates to Article 58(2)(i) of the applied GDPR;

        (iii) section 119 (inspection in accordance with international obligations);

    (h) in Part 6 of this Act—

        (i) sections 142 to 154 and Schedule 15 (Commissioner's notices and powers of entry and inspection);

        (ii) sections 170 to 173 (offences relating to personal data);

    (i) in Part 7 of this Act, section 187 (representation of data subjects).

27 National security: certificate

(1) Subject to subsection (3), a certificate signed by a Minister of the Crown certifying that exemption from all or any of the provisions listed in section 26(2) is, or at any time was, required in relation to any personal data for the purpose of safeguarding national security is conclusive evidence of that fact.

(2)   A certificate under subsection (1) —

    (a)   may identify the personal data to which it applies by means of a general description, and

    (b)   may be expressed to have prospective effect.

(3)   Any person directly affected by a certificate under subsection (1) may appeal to the Tribunal against the certificate.

(4)   If, on an appeal under subsection (3), the Tribunal finds that, applying the principles applied by a court on an application for judicial review, the Minister did not have reasonable grounds for issuing a certificate, the Tribunal may —

    (a)   allow the appeal, and

    (b)   quash the certificate.

(5)   Where, in any proceedings under or by virtue of the applied GDPR or this Act, it is claimed by a controller that a certificate under subsection (1) which identifies the personal data to which it applies by means of a general description applies to any personal data, another party to the proceedings may appeal to the Tribunal on the ground that the certificate does not apply to the personal data in question.

(6)   But, subject to any determination under subsection (7), the certificate is to be conclusively presumed so to apply.

(7)   On an appeal under subsection (5), the Tribunal may determine that the certificate does not so apply.

(8)   A document purporting to be a certificate under subsection (1) is to be —

    (a)   received in evidence, and

    (b)   deemed to be such a certificate unless the contrary is proved.

(9)   A document which purports to be certified by or on behalf of a Minister of the Crown as a true copy of a certificate issued by that Minister under subsection (1) is —

    (a)   in any legal proceedings, evidence of that certificate;

    (b)   in any legal proceedings in Scotland, sufficient evidence of that certificate.

(10)   The power conferred by subsection (1) on a Minister of the Crown is exercisable only by —

    (a)   a Minister who is a member of the Cabinet, or

    (b)   the Attorney General or the Advocate General for Scotland.

28   National security and defence: modifications to Articles 9 and 32 of the applied GDPR

(1)   Article 9(1) of the applied GDPR (prohibition on processing of special categories of personal data) does not prohibit the processing of personal data to which this Chapter applies to the extent that the processing is carried out —

    (a)   for the purpose of safeguarding national security or for defence purposes, and

    (b)   with appropriate safeguards for the rights and freedoms of data subjects.

(2) Article 32 of the applied GDPR (security of processing) does not apply to a controller or processor to the extent that the controller or the processor (as the case may be) is processing personal data to which this Chapter applies for—

    (a) the purpose of safeguarding national security, or

    (b) defence purposes.

(3) Where Article 32 of the applied GDPR does not apply, the controller or the processor must implement security measures appropriate to the risks arising from the processing of the personal data.

(4) For the purposes of subsection (3), where the processing of personal data is carried out wholly or partly by automated means, the controller or the processor must, following an evaluation of the risks, implement measures designed to—

    (a) prevent unauthorised processing or unauthorised interference with the systems used in connection with the processing,

    (b) ensure that it is possible to establish the precise details of any processing that takes place,

    (c) ensure that any systems used in connection with the processing function properly and may, in the case of interruption, be restored, and

    (d) ensure that stored personal data cannot be corrupted if a system used in connection with the processing malfunctions.

PART 3

LAW ENFORCEMENT PROCESSING

CHAPTER 1

SCOPE AND DEFINITIONS

Scope

29   Processing to which this Part applies

(1) This Part applies to—

    (a) the processing by a competent authority of personal data wholly or partly by automated means, and

    (b) the processing by a competent authority otherwise than by automated means of personal data which forms part of a filing system or is intended to form part of a filing system.

(2) Any reference in this Part to the processing of personal data is to processing to which this Part applies.

(3) For the meaning of "competent authority", see section 30.

Definitions

30   Meaning of "competent authority"

(1) In this Part, "competent authority" means—

    (a) a person specified or described in Schedule 7, and

20   *Data Protection Act 2018 (c. 12)*
Part 3 – Law enforcement processing
Chapter 1 – Scope and definitions

   (b) any other person if and to the extent that the person has statutory functions for any of the law enforcement purposes.

 (2) But an intelligence service is not a competent authority within the meaning of this Part.

 (3) The Secretary of State may by regulations amend Schedule 7 —

   (a) so as to add or remove a person or description of person;

   (b) so as to reflect any change in the name of a person specified in the Schedule.

 (4) Regulations under subsection (3) which make provision of the kind described in subsection (3)(a) may also make consequential amendments of section 73(4)(b).

 (5) Regulations under subsection (3) which make provision of the kind described in subsection (3)(a), or which make provision of that kind and of the kind described in subsection (3)(b), are subject to the affirmative resolution procedure.

 (6) Regulations under subsection (3) which make provision only of the kind described in subsection (3)(b) are subject to the negative resolution procedure.

 (7) In this section —

   "intelligence service" means —

     (a) the Security Service;

     (b) the Secret Intelligence Service;

     (c) the Government Communications Headquarters;

   "statutory function" means a function under or by virtue of an enactment.

31 "The law enforcement purposes"

For the purposes of this Part, "the law enforcement purposes" are the purposes of the prevention, investigation, detection or prosecution of criminal offences or the execution of criminal penalties, including the safeguarding against and the prevention of threats to public security.

32 Meaning of "controller" and "processor"

 (1) In this Part, "controller" means the competent authority which, alone or jointly with others —

   (a) determines the purposes and means of the processing of personal data, or

   (b) is the controller by virtue of subsection (2).

 (2) Where personal data is processed only —

   (a) for purposes for which it is required by an enactment to be processed, and

   (b) by means by which it is required by an enactment to be processed,

  the competent authority on which the obligation to process the data is imposed by the enactment (or, if different, one of the enactments) is the controller.

 (3) In this Part, "processor" means any person who processes personal data on behalf of the controller (other than a person who is an employee of the controller).

Data Protection Act 2018 (c. 12)
Part 3 — Law enforcement processing
Chapter 1 — Scope and definitions

21

33 Other definitions

(1) This section defines certain other expressions used in this Part.

(2) "Employee", in relation to any person, includes an individual who holds a position (whether paid or unpaid) under the direction and control of that person.

(3) "Personal data breach" means a breach of security leading to the accidental or unlawful destruction, loss, alteration, unauthorised disclosure of, or access to, personal data transmitted, stored or otherwise processed.

(4) "Profiling" means any form of automated processing of personal data consisting of the use of personal data to evaluate certain personal aspects relating to an individual, in particular to analyse or predict aspects concerning that individual's performance at work, economic situation, health, personal preferences, interests, reliability, behaviour, location or movements.

(5) "Recipient", in relation to any personal data, means any person to whom the data is disclosed, whether a third party or not, but it does not include a public authority to whom disclosure is or may be made in the framework of a particular inquiry in accordance with the law.

(6) "Restriction of processing" means the marking of stored personal data with the aim of limiting its processing for the future.

(7) "Third country" means a country or territory other than a member State.

(8) Sections 3 and 205 include definitions of other expressions used in this Part.

CHAPTER 2

PRINCIPLES

34 Overview and general duty of controller

(1) This Chapter sets out the six data protection principles as follows —
   (a) section 35(1) sets out the first data protection principle (requirement that processing be lawful and fair);
   (b) section 36(1) sets out the second data protection principle (requirement that purposes of processing be specified, explicit and legitimate);
   (c) section 37 sets out the third data protection principle (requirement that personal data be adequate, relevant and not excessive);
   (d) section 38(1) sets out the fourth data protection principle (requirement that personal data be accurate and kept up to date);
   (e) section 39(1) sets out the fifth data protection principle (requirement that personal data be kept for no longer than is necessary);
   (f) section 40 sets out the sixth data protection principle (requirement that personal data be processed in a secure manner).

(2) In addition —
   (a) each of sections 35, 36, 38 and 39 makes provision to supplement the principle to which it relates, and
   (b) sections 41 and 42 make provision about the safeguards that apply in relation to certain types of processing.

22   *Data Protection Act 2018 (c. 12)*
Part 3 — Law enforcement processing
Chapter 2 — Principles

(3)   The controller in relation to personal data is responsible for, and must be able to demonstrate, compliance with this Chapter.

35   The first data protection principle

(1)   The first data protection principle is that the processing of personal data for any of the law enforcement purposes must be lawful and fair.

(2)   The processing of personal data for any of the law enforcement purposes is lawful only if and to the extent that it is based on law and either—

    (a)   the data subject has given consent to the processing for that purpose, or

    (b)   the processing is necessary for the performance of a task carried out for that purpose by a competent authority.

(3)   In addition, where the processing for any of the law enforcement purposes is sensitive processing, the processing is permitted only in the two cases set out in subsections (4) and (5).

(4)   The first case is where—

    (a)   the data subject has given consent to the processing for the law enforcement purpose as mentioned in subsection (2)(a), and

    (b)   at the time when the processing is carried out, the controller has an appropriate policy document in place (see section 42).

(5)   The second case is where—

    (a)   the processing is strictly necessary for the law enforcement purpose,

    (b)   the processing meets at least one of the conditions in Schedule 8, and

    (c)   at the time when the processing is carried out, the controller has an appropriate policy document in place (see section 42).

(6)   The Secretary of State may by regulations amend Schedule 8—

    (a)   by adding conditions;

    (b)   by omitting conditions added by regulations under paragraph (a).

(7)   Regulations under subsection (6) are subject to the affirmative resolution procedure.

(8)   In this section, "sensitive processing" means—

    (a)   the processing of personal data revealing racial or ethnic origin, political opinions, religious or philosophical beliefs or trade union membership;

    (b)   the processing of genetic data, or of biometric data, for the purpose of uniquely identifying an individual;

    (c)   the processing of data concerning health;

    (d)   the processing of data concerning an individual's sex life or sexual orientation.

36   The second data protection principle

(1)   The second data protection principle is that—

    (a)   the law enforcement purpose for which personal data is collected on any occasion must be specified, explicit and legitimate, and

    (b)   personal data so collected must not be processed in a manner that is incompatible with the purpose for which it was collected.

(2) Paragraph (b) of the second data protection principle is subject to subsections (3) and (4).

(3) Personal data collected for a law enforcement purpose may be processed for any other law enforcement purpose (whether by the controller that collected the data or by another controller) provided that—

   (a) the controller is authorised by law to process the data for the other purpose, and

   (b) the processing is necessary and proportionate to that other purpose.

(4) Personal data collected for any of the law enforcement purposes may not be processed for a purpose that is not a law enforcement purpose unless the processing is authorised by law.

37   The third data protection principle

The third data protection principle is that personal data processed for any of the law enforcement purposes must be adequate, relevant and not excessive in relation to the purpose for which it is processed.

38   The fourth data protection principle

(1) The fourth data protection principle is that—

   (a) personal data processed for any of the law enforcement purposes must be accurate and, where necessary, kept up to date, and

   (b) every reasonable step must be taken to ensure that personal data that is inaccurate, having regard to the law enforcement purpose for which it is processed, is erased or rectified without delay.

(2) In processing personal data for any of the law enforcement purposes, personal data based on facts must, so far as possible, be distinguished from personal data based on personal assessments.

(3) In processing personal data for any of the law enforcement purposes, a clear distinction must, where relevant and as far as possible, be made between personal data relating to different categories of data subject, such as—

   (a) persons suspected of having committed or being about to commit a criminal offence;

   (b) persons convicted of a criminal offence;

   (c) persons who are or may be victims of a criminal offence;

   (d) witnesses or other persons with information about offences.

(4) All reasonable steps must be taken to ensure that personal data which is inaccurate, incomplete or no longer up to date is not transmitted or made available for any of the law enforcement purposes.

(5) For that purpose—

   (a) the quality of personal data must be verified before it is transmitted or made available,

   (b) in all transmissions of personal data, the necessary information enabling the recipient to assess the degree of accuracy, completeness and reliability of the data and the extent to which it is up to date must be included, and

24   *Data Protection Act 2018 (c. 12)*
Part 3 – Law enforcement processing
Chapter 2 – Principles

    (c)   if, after personal data has been transmitted, it emerges that the data was incorrect or that the transmission was unlawful, the recipient must be notified without delay.

39   The fifth data protection principle

(1)   The fifth data protection principle is that personal data processed for any of the law enforcement purposes must be kept for no longer than is necessary for the purpose for which it is processed.

(2)   Appropriate time limits must be established for the periodic review of the need for the continued storage of personal data for any of the law enforcement purposes.

40   The sixth data protection principle

The sixth data protection principle is that personal data processed for any of the law enforcement purposes must be so processed in a manner that ensures appropriate security of the personal data, using appropriate technical or organisational measures (and, in this principle, "appropriate security" includes protection against unauthorised or unlawful processing and against accidental loss, destruction or damage).

41   Safeguards: archiving

(1)   This section applies in relation to the processing of personal data for a law enforcement purpose where the processing is necessary —
    (a)   for archiving purposes in the public interest,
    (b)   for scientific or historical research purposes, or
    (c)   for statistical purposes.

(2)   The processing is not permitted if —
    (a)   it is carried out for the purposes of, or in connection with, measures or decisions with respect to a particular data subject, or
    (b)   it is likely to cause substantial damage or substantial distress to a data subject.

42   Safeguards: sensitive processing

(1)   This section applies for the purposes of section 35(4) and (5) (which require a controller to have an appropriate policy document in place when carrying out sensitive processing in reliance on the consent of the data subject or, as the case may be, in reliance on a condition specified in Schedule 8).

(2)   The controller has an appropriate policy document in place in relation to the sensitive processing if the controller has produced a document which —
    (a)   explains the controller's procedures for securing compliance with the data protection principles (see section 34(1)) in connection with sensitive processing in reliance on the consent of the data subject or (as the case may be) in reliance on the condition in question, and
    (b)   explains the controller's policies as regards the retention and erasure of personal data processed in reliance on the consent of the data subject or (as the case may be) in reliance on the condition in question, giving an indication of how long such personal data is likely to be retained.

(3) Where personal data is processed on the basis that an appropriate policy document is in place, the controller must during the relevant period—

    (a) retain the appropriate policy document,

    (b) review and (if appropriate) update it from time to time, and

    (c) make it available to the Commissioner, on request, without charge.

(4) The record maintained by the controller under section 61(1) and, where the sensitive processing is carried out by a processor on behalf of the controller, the record maintained by the processor under section 61(3) must include the following information—

    (a) whether the sensitive processing is carried out in reliance on the consent of the data subject or, if not, which condition in Schedule 8 is relied on,

    (b) how the processing satisfies section 35 (lawfulness of processing), and

    (c) whether the personal data is retained and erased in accordance with the policies described in subsection (2)(b) and, if it is not, the reasons for not following those policies.

(5) In this section, "relevant period", in relation to sensitive processing in reliance on the consent of the data subject or in reliance on a condition specified in Schedule 8, means a period which—

    (a) begins when the controller starts to carry out the sensitive processing in reliance on the data subject's consent or (as the case may be) in reliance on that condition, and

    (b) ends at the end of the period of 6 months beginning when the controller ceases to carry out the processing.

CHAPTER 3

RIGHTS OF THE DATA SUBJECT

Overview and scope

43 Overview and scope

(1) This Chapter—

    (a) imposes general duties on the controller to make information available (see section 44);

    (b) confers a right of access by the data subject (see section 45);

    (c) confers rights on the data subject with respect to the rectification of personal data and the erasure of personal data or the restriction of its processing (see sections 46 to 48);

    (d) regulates automated decision-making (see sections 49 and 50);

    (e) makes supplementary provision (see sections 51 to 54).

(2) This Chapter applies only in relation to the processing of personal data for a law enforcement purpose.

(3) But sections 44 to 48 do not apply in relation to the processing of relevant personal data in the course of a criminal investigation or criminal proceedings, including proceedings for the purpose of executing a criminal penalty.

(4) In subsection (3), "relevant personal data" means personal data contained in a judicial decision or in other documents relating to the investigation or

26

Data Protection Act 2018 (c. 12)
Part 3 — Law enforcement processing
Chapter 3 — Rights of the data subject

proceedings which are created by or on behalf of a court or other judicial authority.

(5)   In this Chapter, "the controller", in relation to a data subject, means the controller in relation to personal data relating to the data subject.

Information: controller's general duties

44   Information: controller's general duties

(1)   The controller must make available to data subjects the following information (whether by making the information generally available to the public or in any other way) —

    (a)   the identity and the contact details of the controller;

    (b)   where applicable, the contact details of the data protection officer (see sections 69 to 71);

    (c)   the purposes for which the controller processes personal data;

    (d)   the existence of the rights of data subjects to request from the controller —

        (i)   access to personal data (see section 45),

        (ii)   rectification of personal data (see section 46), and

        (iii)   erasure of personal data or the restriction of its processing (see section 47);

    (e)   the existence of the right to lodge a complaint with the Commissioner and the contact details of the Commissioner.

(2)   The controller must also, in specific cases for the purpose of enabling the exercise of a data subject's rights under this Part, give the data subject the following —

    (a)   information about the legal basis for the processing;

    (b)   information about the period for which the personal data will be stored or, where that is not possible, about the criteria used to determine that period;

    (c)   where applicable, information about the categories of recipients of the personal data (including recipients in third countries or international organisations);

    (d)   such further information as is necessary to enable the exercise of the data subject's rights under this Part.

(3)   An example of where further information may be necessary as mentioned in subsection (2)(d) is where the personal data being processed was collected without the knowledge of the data subject.

(4)   The controller may restrict, wholly or partly, the provision of information to the data subject under subsection (2) to the extent that and for so long as the restriction is, having regard to the fundamental rights and legitimate interests of the data subject, a necessary and proportionate measure to —

    (a)   avoid obstructing an official or legal inquiry, investigation or procedure;

    (b)   avoid prejudicing the prevention, detection, investigation or prosecution of criminal offences or the execution of criminal penalties;

    (c)   protect public security;

    (d)   protect national security;

Data Protection Act 2018 (c. 12)
Part 3 — Law enforcement processing
Chapter 3 — Rights of the data subject

27

    (e)   protect the rights and freedoms of others.

(5)   Where the provision of information to a data subject under subsection (2) is restricted, wholly or partly, the controller must inform the data subject in writing without undue delay—

    (a)   that the provision of information has been restricted,

    (b)   of the reasons for the restriction,

    (c)   of the data subject's right to make a request to the Commissioner under section 51,

    (d)   of the data subject's right to lodge a complaint with the Commissioner, and

    (e)   of the data subject's right to apply to a court under section 167.

(6)   Subsection (5)(a) and (b) do not apply to the extent that complying with them would undermine the purpose of the restriction.

(7)   The controller must—

    (a)   record the reasons for a decision to restrict (whether wholly or partly) the provision of information to a data subject under subsection (2), and

    (b)   if requested to do so by the Commissioner, make the record available to the Commissioner.

Data subject's right of access

45   Right of access by the data subject

(1)   A data subject is entitled to obtain from the controller—

    (a)   confirmation as to whether or not personal data concerning him or her is being processed, and

    (b)   where that is the case, access to the personal data and the information set out in subsection (2).

(2)   That information is—

    (a)   the purposes of and legal basis for the processing;

    (b)   the categories of personal data concerned;

    (c)   the recipients or categories of recipients to whom the personal data has been disclosed (including recipients or categories of recipients in third countries or international organisations);

    (d)   the period for which it is envisaged that the personal data will be stored or, where that is not possible, the criteria used to determine that period;

    (e)   the existence of the data subject's rights to request from the controller—

        (i)   rectification of personal data (see section 46), and

        (ii)   erasure of personal data or the restriction of its processing (see section 47);

    (f)   the existence of the data subject's right to lodge a complaint with the Commissioner and the contact details of the Commissioner;

    (g)   communication of the personal data undergoing processing and of any available information as to its origin.

(3)   Where a data subject makes a request under subsection (1), the information to which the data subject is entitled must be provided in writing —

    (a)   without undue delay, and

28   *Data Protection Act 2018 (c. 12)*
                                          Part 3 — Law enforcement processing
                                          Chapter 3 — Rights of the data subject

      (b)   in any event, before the end of the applicable time period (as to which see section 54).

(4)   The controller may restrict, wholly or partly, the rights conferred by subsection (1) to the extent that and for so long as the restriction is, having regard to the fundamental rights and legitimate interests of the data subject, a necessary and proportionate measure to—

      (a)   avoid obstructing an official or legal inquiry, investigation or procedure;

      (b)   avoid prejudicing the prevention, detection, investigation or prosecution of criminal offences or the execution of criminal penalties;

      (c)   protect public security;

      (d)   protect national security;

      (e)   protect the rights and freedoms of others.

(5)   Where the rights of a data subject under subsection (1) are restricted, wholly or partly, the controller must inform the data subject in writing without undue delay—

      (a)   that the rights of the data subject have been restricted,

      (b)   of the reasons for the restriction,

      (c)   of the data subject's right to make a request to the Commissioner under section 51,

      (d)   of the data subject's right to lodge a complaint with the Commissioner, and

      (e)   of the data subject's right to apply to a court under section 167.

(6)   Subsection (5)(a) and (b) do not apply to the extent that the provision of the information would undermine the purpose of the restriction.

(7)   The controller must—

      (a)   record the reasons for a decision to restrict (whether wholly or partly) the rights of a data subject under subsection (1), and

      (b)   if requested to do so by the Commissioner, make the record available to the Commissioner.

Data subject's rights to rectification or erasure etc

46 Right to rectification

(1)   The controller must, if so requested by a data subject, rectify without undue delay inaccurate personal data relating to the data subject.

(2)   Where personal data is inaccurate because it is incomplete, the controller must, if so requested by a data subject, complete it.

(3)   The duty under subsection (2) may, in appropriate cases, be fulfilled by the provision of a supplementary statement.

(4)   Where the controller would be required to rectify personal data under this section but the personal data must be maintained for the purposes of evidence, the controller must (instead of rectifying the personal data) restrict its processing.

Data Protection Act 2018 (c. 12)
Part 3 − Law enforcement processing
Chapter 3 − Rights of the data subject

29

47   Right to erasure or restriction of processing

(1)   The controller must erase personal data without undue delay where —

    (a)   the processing of the personal data would infringe section 35, 36(1) to (3), 37, 38(1), 39(1), 40, 41 or 42, or

    (b)   the controller has a legal obligation to erase the data.

(2)   Where the controller would be required to erase personal data under subsection (1) but the personal data must be maintained for the purposes of evidence, the controller must (instead of erasing the personal data) restrict its processing.

(3)   Where a data subject contests the accuracy of personal data (whether in making a request under this section or section 46 or in any other way), but it is not possible to ascertain whether it is accurate or not, the controller must restrict its processing.

(4)   A data subject may request the controller to erase personal data or to restrict its processing (but the duties of the controller under this section apply whether or not such a request is made).

48   Rights under section 46 or 47: supplementary

(1)   Where a data subject requests the rectification or erasure of personal data or the restriction of its processing, the controller must inform the data subject in writing —

    (a)   whether the request has been granted, and

    (b)   if it has been refused —

        (i)   of the reasons for the refusal,

        (ii)   of the data subject's right to make a request to the Commissioner under section 51,

        (iii) of the data subject's right to lodge a complaint with the Commissioner, and

        (iv)   of the data subject's right to apply to a court under section 167.

(2)   The controller must comply with the duty under subsection (1) —

    (a)   without undue delay, and

    (b)   in any event, before the end of the applicable time period (see section 54).

(3)   The controller may restrict, wholly or partly, the provision of information to the data subject under subsection (1)(b)(i) to the extent that and for so long as the restriction is, having regard to the fundamental rights and legitimate interests of the data subject, a necessary and proportionate measure to —

    (a)   avoid obstructing an official or legal inquiry, investigation or procedure;

    (b)   avoid prejudicing the prevention, detection, investigation or prosecution of criminal offences or the execution of criminal penalties;

    (c)   protect public security;

    (d)   protect national security;

    (e)   protect the rights and freedoms of others.

(4)   Where the rights of a data subject under subsection (1) are restricted, wholly or partly, the controller must inform the data subject in writing without undue delay —

30   *Data Protection Act 2018 (c. 12)*
                                       Part 3 — Law enforcement processing
                                       Chapter 3 — Rights of the data subject

     (a)   that the rights of the data subject have been restricted,

     (b)   of the reasons for the restriction,

     (c)   of the data subject's right to lodge a complaint with the Commissioner, and

     (d)   of the data subject's right to apply to a court under section 167.

(5)   Subsection (4)(a) and (b) do not apply to the extent that the provision of the information would undermine the purpose of the restriction.

(6)   The controller must—

     (a)   record the reasons for a decision to restrict (whether wholly or partly) the provision of information to a data subject under subsection (1)(b)(i), and

     (b)   if requested to do so by the Commissioner, make the record available to the Commissioner.

(7)   Where the controller rectifies personal data, it must notify the competent authority (if any) from which the inaccurate personal data originated.

(8)   In subsection (7), the reference to a competent authority includes (in addition to a competent authority within the meaning of this Part) any person that is a competent authority for the purposes of the Law Enforcement Directive in a member State other than the United Kingdom.

(9)   Where the controller rectifies, erases or restricts the processing of personal data which has been disclosed by the controller—

     (a)   the controller must notify the recipients, and

     (b)   the recipients must similarly rectify, erase or restrict the processing of the personal data (so far as they retain responsibility for it).

(10) Where processing is restricted in accordance with section 47(3), the controller must inform the data subject before lifting the restriction.

Automated individual decision-making

49 Right not to be subject to automated decision-making

(1)   A controller may not take a significant decision based solely on automated processing unless that decision is required or authorised by law.

(2)   A decision is a "significant decision" for the purpose of this section if, in relation to a data subject, it—

     (a)   produces an adverse legal effect concerning the data subject, or

     (b)   significantly affects the data subject.

50 Automated decision-making authorised by law: safeguards

(1)   A decision is a "qualifying significant decision" for the purposes of this section if—

     (a)   it is a significant decision in relation to a data subject, and

     (b)   it is required or authorised by law.

(2)   Where a controller takes a qualifying significant decision in relation to a data subject based solely on automated processing—

Data Protection Act 2018 (c. 12)
Part 3 — Law enforcement processing
Chapter 3 — Rights of the data subject

31

> (a) the controller must, as soon as reasonably practicable, notify the data subject in writing that a decision has been taken based solely on automated processing, and
>
> (b) the data subject may, before the end of the period of 1 month beginning with receipt of the notification, request the controller to—
>
>> (i) reconsider the decision, or
>>
>> (ii) take a new decision that is not based solely on automated processing.

(3) If a request is made to a controller under subsection (2), the controller must, before the end of the period of 1 month beginning with receipt of the request—

> (a) consider the request, including any information provided by the data subject that is relevant to it,
>
> (b) comply with the request, and
>
> (c) by notice in writing inform the data subject of—
>
>> (i) the steps taken to comply with the request, and
>>
>> (ii) the outcome of complying with the request.

(4) The Secretary of State may by regulations make such further provision as the Secretary of State considers appropriate to provide suitable measures to safeguard a data subject's rights, freedoms and legitimate interests in connection with the taking of qualifying significant decisions based solely on automated processing.

(5) Regulations under subsection (4)—

> (a) may amend this section, and
>
> (b) are subject to the affirmative resolution procedure.

(6) In this section "significant decision" has the meaning given by section 49(2).

Supplementary

51   Exercise of rights through the Commissioner

(1) This section applies where a controller—

> (a) restricts under section 44(4) the information provided to the data subject under section 44(2) (duty of the controller to give the data subject additional information),
>
> (b) restricts under section 45(4) the data subject's rights under section 45(1) (right of access), or
>
> (c) refuses a request by the data subject for rectification under section 46 or for erasure or restriction of processing under section 47.

(2) The data subject may—

> (a) where subsection (1)(a) or (b) applies, request the Commissioner to check that the restriction imposed by the controller was lawful;
>
> (b) where subsection (1)(c) applies, request the Commissioner to check that the refusal of the data subject's request was lawful.

(3) The Commissioner must take such steps as appear to the Commissioner to be appropriate to respond to a request under subsection (2) (which may include the exercise of any of the powers conferred by sections 142 and 146).

(4) After taking those steps, the Commissioner must inform the data subject—

32   *Data Protection Act 2018 (c. 12)*
Part 3 — Law enforcement processing
Chapter 3 — Rights of the data subject

       (a)   where subsection (1)(a) or (b) applies, whether the Commissioner is satisfied that the restriction imposed by the controller was lawful;

       (b)   where subsection (1)(c) applies, whether the Commissioner is satisfied that the controller's refusal of the data subject's request was lawful.

(5)   The Commissioner must also inform the data subject of the data subject's right to apply to a court under section 167.

(6)   Where the Commissioner is not satisfied as mentioned in subsection (4)(a) or (b), the Commissioner may also inform the data subject of any further steps that the Commissioner is considering taking under Part 6.

52   Form of provision of information etc

(1)   The controller must take reasonable steps to ensure that any information that is required by this Chapter to be provided to the data subject is provided in a concise, intelligible and easily accessible form, using clear and plain language.

(2)   Subject to subsection (3), the information may be provided in any form, including electronic form.

(3)   Where information is provided in response to a request by the data subject under section 45, 46, 47 or 50, the controller must provide the information in the same form as the request where it is practicable to do so.

(4)   Where the controller has reasonable doubts about the identity of an individual making a request under section 45, 46 or 47, the controller may —

       (a)   request the provision of additional information to enable the controller to confirm the identity, and

       (b)   delay dealing with the request until the identity is confirmed.

(5)   Subject to section 53, any information that is required by this Chapter to be provided to the data subject must be provided free of charge.

(6)   The controller must facilitate the exercise of the rights of the data subject under sections 45 to 50.

53   Manifestly unfounded or excessive requests by the data subject

(1)   Where a request from a data subject under section 45, 46, 47 or 50 is manifestly unfounded or excessive, the controller may —

       (a)   charge a reasonable fee for dealing with the request, or

       (b)   refuse to act on the request.

(2)   An example of a request that may be excessive is one that merely repeats the substance of previous requests.

(3)   In any proceedings where there is an issue as to whether a request under section 45, 46, 47 or 50 is manifestly unfounded or excessive, it is for the controller to show that it is.

(4)   The Secretary of State may by regulations specify limits on the fees that a controller may charge in accordance with subsection (1)(a).

(5)   Regulations under subsection (4) are subject to the negative resolution procedure.

Data Protection Act 2018 (c. 12)
Part 3 — Law enforcement processing
Chapter 3 — Rights of the data subject

33

54   Meaning of "applicable time period"

(1)   This section defines "the applicable time period" for the purposes of sections 45(3)(b) and 48(2)(b).

(2)   "The applicable time period" means the period of 1 month, or such longer period as may be specified in regulations, beginning with the relevant time.

(3)   "The relevant time" means the latest of the following —
    (a)   when the controller receives the request in question;
    (b)   when the controller receives the information (if any) requested in connection with a request under section 52(4);
    (c)   when the fee (if any) charged in connection with the request under section 53 is paid.

(4)   The power to make regulations under subsection (2) is exercisable by the Secretary of State.

(5)   Regulations under subsection (2) may not specify a period which is longer than 3 months.

(6)   Regulations under subsection (2) are subject to the negative resolution procedure.

CHAPTER 4

CONTROLLER AND PROCESSOR

Overview and scope

55   Overview and scope

(1)   This Chapter —
    (a)   sets out the general obligations of controllers and processors (see sections 56 to 65);
    (b)   sets out specific obligations of controllers and processors with respect to security (see section 66);
    (c)   sets out specific obligations of controllers and processors with respect to personal data breaches (see sections 67 and 68);
    (d)   makes provision for the designation, position and tasks of data protection officers (see sections 69 to 71).

(2)   This Chapter applies only in relation to the processing of personal data for a law enforcement purpose.

(3)   Where a controller is required by any provision of this Chapter to implement appropriate technical and organisational measures, the controller must (in deciding what measures are appropriate) take into account —
    (a)   the latest developments in technology,
    (b)   the cost of implementation,
    (c)   the nature, scope, context and purposes of processing, and
    (d)   the risks for the rights and freedoms of individuals arising from the processing.

34   *Data Protection Act 2018 (c. 12)*
                                        Part 3 — Law enforcement processing
                                        Chapter 4 — Controller and processor

General obligations

56   General obligations of the controller

(1)   Each controller must implement appropriate technical and organisational measures to ensure, and to be able to demonstrate, that the processing of personal data complies with the requirements of this Part.

(2)   Where proportionate in relation to the processing, the measures implemented to comply with the duty under subsection (1) must include appropriate data protection policies.

(3)   The technical and organisational measures implemented under subsection (1) must be reviewed and updated where necessary.

57   Data protection by design and default

(1)   Each controller must implement appropriate technical and organisational measures which are designed —
    (a)   to implement the data protection principles in an effective manner, and
    (b)   to integrate into the processing itself the safeguards necessary for that purpose.

(2)   The duty under subsection (1) applies both at the time of the determination of the means of processing the data and at the time of the processing itself.

(3)   Each controller must implement appropriate technical and organisational measures for ensuring that, by default, only personal data which is necessary for each specific purpose of the processing is processed.

(4)   The duty under subsection (3) applies to —
    (a)   the amount of personal data collected,
    (b)   the extent of its processing,
    (c)   the period of its storage, and
    (d)   its accessibility.

(5)   In particular, the measures implemented to comply with the duty under subsection (3) must ensure that, by default, personal data is not made accessible to an indefinite number of people without an individual's intervention.

58   Joint controllers

(1)   Where two or more competent authorities jointly determine the purposes and means of processing personal data, they are joint controllers for the purposes of this Part.

(2)   Joint controllers must, in a transparent manner, determine their respective responsibilities for compliance with this Part by means of an arrangement between them, except to the extent that those responsibilities are determined under or by virtue of an enactment.

(3)   The arrangement must designate the controller which is to be the contact point for data subjects.

Data Protection Act 2018 (c. 12)
Part 3 — Law enforcement processing
Chapter 4 — Controller and processor

35

59   Processors

(1)   This section applies to the use by a controller of a processor to carry out processing of personal data on behalf of the controller.

(2)   The controller may use only a processor who provides guarantees to implement appropriate technical and organisational measures that are sufficient to secure that the processing will—

(a)   meet the requirements of this Part, and

(b)   ensure the protection of the rights of the data subject.

(3)   The processor used by the controller may not engage another processor ("a sub-processor") without the prior written authorisation of the controller, which may be specific or general.

(4)   Where the controller gives a general written authorisation to a processor, the processor must inform the controller if the processor proposes to add to the number of sub-processors engaged by it or to replace any of them (so that the controller has the opportunity to object to the proposal).

(5)   The processing by the processor must be governed by a contract in writing between the controller and the processor setting out the following—

(a)   the subject-matter and duration of the processing;

(b)   the nature and purpose of the processing;

(c)   the type of personal data and categories of data subjects involved;

(d)   the obligations and rights of the controller and processor.

(6)   The contract must, in particular, provide that the processor must—

(a)   act only on instructions from the controller,

(b)   ensure that the persons authorised to process personal data are subject to an appropriate duty of confidentiality,

(c)   assist the controller by any appropriate means to ensure compliance with the rights of the data subject under this Part,

(d)   at the end of the provision of services by the processor to the controller—

(i)   either delete or return to the controller (at the choice of the controller) the personal data to which the services relate, and

(ii)   delete copies of the personal data unless subject to a legal obligation to store the copies,

(e)   make available to the controller all information necessary to demonstrate compliance with this section, and

(f)   comply with the requirements of this section for engaging sub-processors.

(7)   The terms included in the contract in accordance with subsection (6)(a) must provide that the processor may transfer personal data to a third country or international organisation only if instructed by the controller to make the particular transfer.

(8)   If a processor determines, in breach of this Part, the purposes and means of processing, the processor is to be treated for the purposes of this Part as a controller in respect of that processing.

36   *Data Protection Act 2018 (c. 12)*
                                        Part 3 — Law enforcement processing
                                        Chapter 4 — Controller and processor

60   Processing under the authority of the controller or processor

A processor, and any person acting under the authority of a controller or processor, who has access to personal data may not process the data except —

    (a)   on instructions from the controller, or

    (b)   to comply with a legal obligation.

61   Records of processing activities

(1)   Each controller must maintain a record of all categories of processing activities for which the controller is responsible.

(2)   The controller's record must contain the following information —

    (a)   the name and contact details of the controller;

    (b)   where applicable, the name and contact details of the joint controller;

    (c)   where applicable, the name and contact details of the data protection officer;

    (d)   the purposes of the processing;

    (e)   the categories of recipients to whom personal data has been or will be disclosed (including recipients in third countries or international organisations);

    (f)   a description of the categories of —

        (i)   data subject, and

        (ii)   personal data;

    (g)   where applicable, details of the use of profiling;

    (h)   where applicable, the categories of transfers of personal data to a third country or an international organisation;

    (i)   an indication of the legal basis for the processing operations, including transfers, for which the personal data is intended;

    (j)   where possible, the envisaged time limits for erasure of the different categories of personal data;

    (k)   where possible, a general description of the technical and organisational security measures referred to in section 66.

(3)   Each processor must maintain a record of all categories of processing activities carried out on behalf of a controller.

(4)   The processor's record must contain the following information —

    (a)   the name and contact details of the processor and of any other processors engaged by the processor in accordance with section 59(3);

    (b)   the name and contact details of the controller on behalf of which the processor is acting;

    (c)   where applicable, the name and contact details of the data protection officer;

    (d)   the categories of processing carried out on behalf of the controller;

    (e)   where applicable, details of transfers of personal data to a third country or an international organisation where explicitly instructed to do so by the controller, including the identification of that third country or international organisation;

    (f)   where possible, a general description of the technical and organisational security measures referred to in section 66.

Data Protection Act 2018 (c. 12)
Part 3 – Law enforcement processing
Chapter 4 – Controller and processor

37

(5) The controller and the processor must make the records kept under this section available to the Commissioner on request.

62 Logging

(1) A controller (or, where personal data is processed on behalf of the controller by a processor, the processor) must keep logs for at least the following processing operations in automated processing systems—
   (a) collection;
   (b) alteration;
   (c) consultation;
   (d) disclosure (including transfers);
   (e) combination;
   (f) erasure.

(2) The logs of consultation must make it possible to establish—
   (a) the justification for, and date and time of, the consultation, and
   (b) so far as possible, the identity of the person who consulted the data.

(3) The logs of disclosure must make it possible to establish—
   (a) the justification for, and date and time of, the disclosure, and
   (b) so far as possible—
      (i) the identity of the person who disclosed the data, and
      (ii) the identity of the recipients of the data.

(4) The logs kept under subsection (1) may be used only for one or more of the following purposes—
   (a) to verify the lawfulness of processing;
   (b) to assist with self-monitoring by the controller or (as the case may be) the processor, including the conduct of internal disciplinary proceedings;
   (c) to ensure the integrity and security of personal data;
   (d) the purposes of criminal proceedings.

(5) The controller or (as the case may be) the processor must make the logs available to the Commissioner on request.

63 Co-operation with the Commissioner

Each controller and each processor must co-operate, on request, with the Commissioner in the performance of the Commissioner's tasks.

64 Data protection impact assessment

(1) Where a type of processing is likely to result in a high risk to the rights and freedoms of individuals, the controller must, prior to the processing, carry out a data protection impact assessment.

(2) A data protection impact assessment is an assessment of the impact of the envisaged processing operations on the protection of personal data.

(3) A data protection impact assessment must include the following—
   (a) a general description of the envisaged processing operations;
   (b) an assessment of the risks to the rights and freedoms of data subjects;

38   *Data Protection Act 2018 (c. 12)*
                                         Part 3 — Law enforcement processing
                                         Chapter 4 — Controller and processor

(c)   the measures envisaged to address those risks;

(d)   safeguards, security measures and mechanisms to ensure the protection of personal data and to demonstrate compliance with this Part, taking into account the rights and legitimate interests of the data subjects and other persons concerned.

(4)   In deciding whether a type of processing is likely to result in a high risk to the rights and freedoms of individuals, the controller must take into account the nature, scope, context and purposes of the processing.

65   Prior consultation with the Commissioner

(1)   This section applies where a controller intends to create a filing system and process personal data forming part of it.

(2)   The controller must consult the Commissioner prior to the processing if a data protection impact assessment prepared under section 64 indicates that the processing of the data would result in a high risk to the rights and freedoms of individuals (in the absence of measures to mitigate the risk).

(3)   Where the controller is required to consult the Commissioner under subsection (2), the controller must give the Commissioner —

(a)   the data protection impact assessment prepared under section 64, and

(b)   any other information requested by the Commissioner to enable the Commissioner to make an assessment of the compliance of the processing with the requirements of this Part.

(4)   Where the Commissioner is of the opinion that the intended processing referred to in subsection (1) would infringe any provision of this Part, the Commissioner must provide written advice to the controller and, where the controller is using a processor, to the processor.

(5)   The written advice must be provided before the end of the period of 6 weeks beginning with receipt of the request for consultation by the controller or the processor.

(6)   The Commissioner may extend the period of 6 weeks by a further period of 1 month, taking into account the complexity of the intended processing.

(7)   If the Commissioner extends the period of 6 weeks, the Commissioner must —

(a)   inform the controller and, where applicable, the processor of any such extension before the end of the period of 1 month beginning with receipt of the request for consultation, and

(b)   provide reasons for the delay.

Obligations relating to security

66   Security of processing

(1)   Each controller and each processor must implement appropriate technical and organisational measures to ensure a level of security appropriate to the risks arising from the processing of personal data.

(2)   In the case of automated processing, each controller and each processor must, following an evaluation of the risks, implement measures designed to—

Data Protection Act 2018 (c. 12)
Part 3 — Law enforcement processing
Chapter 4 — Controller and processor

39

    (a)   prevent unauthorised processing or unauthorised interference with the systems used in connection with it,

    (b)   ensure that it is possible to establish the precise details of any processing that takes place,

    (c)   ensure that any systems used in connection with the processing function properly and may, in the case of interruption, be restored, and

    (d)   ensure that stored personal data cannot be corrupted if a system used in connection with the processing malfunctions.

Obligations relating to personal data breaches

67   Notification of a personal data breach to the Commissioner

(1)   If a controller becomes aware of a personal data breach in relation to personal data for which the controller is responsible, the controller must notify the breach to the Commissioner—

    (a)   without undue delay, and

    (b)   where feasible, not later than 72 hours after becoming aware of it.

(2)   Subsection (1) does not apply if the personal data breach is unlikely to result in a risk to the rights and freedoms of individuals.

(3)   Where the notification to the Commissioner is not made within 72 hours, the notification must be accompanied by reasons for the delay.

(4)   Subject to subsection (5), the notification must include—

    (a)   a description of the nature of the personal data breach including, where possible, the categories and approximate number of data subjects concerned and the categories and approximate number of personal data records concerned;

    (b)   the name and contact details of the data protection officer or other contact point from whom more information can be obtained;

    (c)   a description of the likely consequences of the personal data breach;

    (d)   a description of the measures taken or proposed to be taken by the controller to address the personal data breach, including, where appropriate, measures to mitigate its possible adverse effects.

(5)   Where and to the extent that it is not possible to provide all the information mentioned in subsection (4) at the same time, the information may be provided in phases without undue further delay.

(6)   The controller must record the following information in relation to a personal data breach—

    (a)   the facts relating to the breach,

    (b)   its effects, and

    (c)   the remedial action taken.

(7)   The information mentioned in subsection (6) must be recorded in such a way as to enable the Commissioner to verify compliance with this section.

(8)   Where a personal data breach involves personal data that has been transmitted by or to a person who is a controller under the law of another member State, the information mentioned in subsection (6) must be communicated to that person without undue delay.

40   *Data Protection Act 2018 (c. 12)*
                                      Part 3 — Law enforcement processing
                                      Chapter 4 — Controller and processor

(9)   If a processor becomes aware of a personal data breach (in relation to personal data processed by the processor), the processor must notify the controller without undue delay.

68   Communication of a personal data breach to the data subject

(1)   Where a personal data breach is likely to result in a high risk to the rights and freedoms of individuals, the controller must inform the data subject of the breach without undue delay.

(2)   The information given to the data subject must include the following —
   (a)   a description of the nature of the breach;
   (b)   the name and contact details of the data protection officer or other contact point from whom more information can be obtained;
   (c)   a description of the likely consequences of the personal data breach;
   (d)   a description of the measures taken or proposed to be taken by the controller to address the personal data breach, including, where appropriate, measures to mitigate its possible adverse effects.

(3)   The duty under subsection (1) does not apply where —
   (a)   the controller has implemented appropriate technological and organisational protection measures which were applied to the personal data affected by the breach,
   (b)   the controller has taken subsequent measures which ensure that the high risk to the rights and freedoms of data subjects referred to in subsection (1) is no longer likely to materialise, or
   (c)   it would involve a disproportionate effort.

(4)   An example of a case which may fall within subsection (3)(a) is where measures that render personal data unintelligible to any person not authorised to access the data have been applied, such as encryption.

(5)   In a case falling within subsection (3)(c) (but not within subsection (3)(a) or (b)), the information mentioned in subsection (2) must be made available to the data subject in another equally effective way, for example, by means of a public communication.

(6)   Where the controller has not informed the data subject of the breach the Commissioner, on being notified under section 67 and after considering the likelihood of the breach resulting in a high risk, may —
   (a)   require the controller to notify the data subject of the breach, or
   (b)   decide that the controller is not required to do so because any of paragraphs (a) to (c) of subsection (3) applies.

(7)   The controller may restrict, wholly or partly, the provision of information to the data subject under subsection (1) to the extent that and for so long as the restriction is, having regard to the fundamental rights and legitimate interests of the data subject, a necessary and proportionate measure to —
   (a)   avoid obstructing an official or legal inquiry, investigation or procedure;
   (b)   avoid prejudicing the prevention, detection, investigation or prosecution of criminal offences or the execution of criminal penalties;
   (c)   protect public security;
   (d)   protect national security;
   (e)   protect the rights and freedoms of others.

Data Protection Act 2018 (c. 12)
Part 3 — Law enforcement processing
Chapter 4 — Controller and processor

41

(8) Subsection (6) does not apply where the controller's decision not to inform the data subject of the breach was made in reliance on subsection (7).

(9) The duties in section 52(1) and (2) apply in relation to information that the controller is required to provide to the data subject under this section as they apply in relation to information that the controller is required to provide to the data subject under Chapter 3.

Data protection officers

69   Designation of a data protection officer

(1) The controller must designate a data protection officer, unless the controller is a court, or other judicial authority, acting in its judicial capacity.

(2) When designating a data protection officer, the controller must have regard to the professional qualities of the proposed officer, in particular —

   (a) the proposed officer's expert knowledge of data protection law and practice, and

   (b) the ability of the proposed officer to perform the tasks mentioned in section 71.

(3) The same person may be designated as a data protection officer by several controllers, taking account of their organisational structure and size.

(4) The controller must publish the contact details of the data protection officer and communicate these to the Commissioner.

70   Position of data protection officer

(1) The controller must ensure that the data protection officer is involved, properly and in a timely manner, in all issues which relate to the protection of personal data.

(2) The controller must provide the data protection officer with the necessary resources and access to personal data and processing operations to enable the data protection officer to —

   (a) perform the tasks mentioned in section 71, and

   (b) maintain his or her expert knowledge of data protection law and practice.

(3) The controller —

   (a) must ensure that the data protection officer does not receive any instructions regarding the performance of the tasks mentioned in section 71;

   (b) must ensure that the data protection officer does not perform a task or fulfil a duty other than those mentioned in this Part where such task or duty would result in a conflict of interests;

   (c) must not dismiss or penalise the data protection officer for performing the tasks mentioned in section 71.

(4) A data subject may contact the data protection officer with regard to all issues relating to —

   (a) the processing of that data subject's personal data, or

   (b) the exercise of that data subject's rights under this Part.

42

Data Protection Act 2018 (c. 12)
Part 3 — Law enforcement processing
Chapter 4 — Controller and processor

(5) The data protection officer, in the performance of this role, must report to the highest management level of the controller.

71 Tasks of data protection officer

(1) The controller must entrust the data protection officer with at least the following tasks —

    (a) informing and advising the controller, any processor engaged by the controller, and any employee of the controller who carries out processing of personal data, of that person's obligations under this Part,

    (b) providing advice on the carrying out of a data protection impact assessment under section 64 and monitoring compliance with that section,

    (c) co-operating with the Commissioner,

    (d) acting as the contact point for the Commissioner on issues relating to processing, including in relation to the consultation mentioned in section 65, and consulting with the Commissioner, where appropriate, in relation to any other matter,

    (e) monitoring compliance with policies of the controller in relation to the protection of personal data, and

    (f) monitoring compliance by the controller with this Part.

(2) In relation to the policies mentioned in subsection (1)(e), the data protection officer's tasks include —

    (a) assigning responsibilities under those policies,

    (b) raising awareness of those policies,

    (c) training staff involved in processing operations, and

    (d) conducting audits required under those policies.

(3) In performing the tasks set out in subsections (1) and (2), the data protection officer must have regard to the risks associated with processing operations, taking into account the nature, scope, context and purposes of processing.

CHAPTER 5

TRANSFERS OF PERSONAL DATA TO THIRD COUNTRIES ETC

Overview and interpretation

72 Overview and interpretation

(1) This Chapter deals with the transfer of personal data to third countries or international organisations, as follows —

    (a) sections 73 to 76 set out the general conditions that apply;

    (b) section 77 sets out the special conditions that apply where the intended recipient of personal data is not a relevant authority in a third country or an international organisation;

    (c) section 78 makes special provision about subsequent transfers of personal data.

Data Protection Act 2018 (c. 12)
Part 3 — Law enforcement processing
Chapter 5 — Transfers of personal data to third countries etc

43

(2) In this Chapter, "relevant authority", in relation to a third country, means any person based in a third country that has (in that country) functions comparable to those of a competent authority.

General principles for transfers

73 General principles for transfers of personal data

(1) A controller may not transfer personal data to a third country or to an international organisation unless —

    (a) the three conditions set out in subsections (2) to (4) are met, and

    (b) in a case where the personal data was originally transmitted or otherwise made available to the controller or another competent authority by a member State other than the United Kingdom, that member State, or any person based in that member State which is a competent authority for the purposes of the Law Enforcement Directive, has authorised the transfer in accordance with the law of the member State.

(2) Condition 1 is that the transfer is necessary for any of the law enforcement purposes.

(3) Condition 2 is that the transfer —

    (a) is based on an adequacy decision (see section 74),

    (b) if not based on an adequacy decision, is based on there being appropriate safeguards (see section 75), or

    (c) if not based on an adequacy decision or on there being appropriate safeguards, is based on special circumstances (see section 76).

(4) Condition 3 is that —

    (a) the intended recipient is a relevant authority in a third country or an international organisation that is a relevant international organisation, or

    (b) in a case where the controller is a competent authority specified in any of paragraphs 5 to 17, 21, 24 to 28, 34 to 51, 54 and 56 of Schedule 7 —

        (i) the intended recipient is a person in a third country other than a relevant authority, and

        (ii) the additional conditions in section 77 are met.

(5) Authorisation is not required as mentioned in subsection (1)(b) if —

    (a) the transfer is necessary for the prevention of an immediate and serious threat either to the public security of a member State or a third country or to the essential interests of a member State, and

    (b) the authorisation cannot be obtained in good time.

(6) Where a transfer is made without the authorisation mentioned in subsection (1)(b), the authority in the member State which would have been responsible for deciding whether to authorise the transfer must be informed without delay.

(7) In this section, "relevant international organisation" means an international organisation that carries out functions for any of the law enforcement purposes.

44

Data Protection Act 2018 (c. 12)
Part 3 — Law enforcement processing
Chapter 5 — Transfers of personal data to third countries etc

74   Transfers on the basis of an adequacy decision

A transfer of personal data to a third country or an international organisation is based on an adequacy decision where—

    (a)   the European Commission has decided, in accordance with Article 36 of the Law Enforcement Directive, that—

        (i)   the third country or a territory or one or more specified sectors within that third country, or

        (ii)   (as the case may be) the international organisation,

        ensures an adequate level of protection of personal data, and

    (b)   that decision has not been repealed or suspended, or amended in a way that demonstrates that the Commission no longer considers there to be an adequate level of protection of personal data.

75   Transfers on the basis of appropriate safeguards

(1)   A transfer of personal data to a third country or an international organisation is based on there being appropriate safeguards where—

    (a)   a legal instrument containing appropriate safeguards for the protection of personal data binds the intended recipient of the data, or

    (b)   the controller, having assessed all the circumstances surrounding transfers of that type of personal data to the third country or international organisation, concludes that appropriate safeguards exist to protect the data.

(2)   The controller must inform the Commissioner about the categories of data transfers that take place in reliance on subsection (1)(b).

(3)   Where a transfer of data takes place in reliance on subsection (1)—

    (a)   the transfer must be documented,

    (b)   the documentation must be provided to the Commissioner on request, and

    (c)   the documentation must include, in particular—

        (i)   the date and time of the transfer,

        (ii)   the name of and any other pertinent information about the recipient,

        (iii)   the justification for the transfer, and

        (iv)   a description of the personal data transferred.

76   Transfers on the basis of special circumstances

(1)   A transfer of personal data to a third country or international organisation is based on special circumstances where the transfer is necessary—

    (a)   to protect the vital interests of the data subject or another person,

    (b)   to safeguard the legitimate interests of the data subject,

    (c)   for the prevention of an immediate and serious threat to the public security of a member State or a third country,

    (d)   in individual cases for any of the law enforcement purposes, or

    (e)   in individual cases for a legal purpose.

(2)   But subsection (1)(d) and (e) do not apply if the controller determines that fundamental rights and freedoms of the data subject override the public interest in the transfer.

Data Protection Act 2018 (c. 12)
Part 3 — Law enforcement processing
Chapter 5 — Transfers of personal data to third countries etc

45

(3) Where a transfer of data takes place in reliance on subsection (1) —
  (a) the transfer must be documented,
  (b) the documentation must be provided to the Commissioner on request, and
  (c) the documentation must include, in particular —
      (i) the date and time of the transfer,
      (ii) the name of and any other pertinent information about the recipient,
      (iii) the justification for the transfer, and
      (iv) a description of the personal data transferred.

(4) For the purposes of this section, a transfer is necessary for a legal purpose if —
  (a) it is necessary for the purpose of, or in connection with, any legal proceedings (including prospective legal proceedings) relating to any of the law enforcement purposes,
  (b) it is necessary for the purpose of obtaining legal advice in relation to any of the law enforcement purposes, or
  (c) it is otherwise necessary for the purposes of establishing, exercising or defending legal rights in relation to any of the law enforcement purposes.

Transfers to particular recipients

77 Transfers of personal data to persons other than relevant authorities

(1) The additional conditions referred to in section 73(4)(b)(ii) are the following four conditions.

(2) Condition 1 is that the transfer is strictly necessary in a specific case for the performance of a task of the transferring controller as provided by law for any of the law enforcement purposes.

(3) Condition 2 is that the transferring controller has determined that there are no fundamental rights and freedoms of the data subject concerned that override the public interest necessitating the transfer.

(4) Condition 3 is that the transferring controller considers that the transfer of the personal data to a relevant authority in the third country would be ineffective or inappropriate (for example, where the transfer could not be made in sufficient time to enable its purpose to be fulfilled).

(5) Condition 4 is that the transferring controller informs the intended recipient of the specific purpose or purposes for which the personal data may, so far as necessary, be processed.

(6) Where personal data is transferred to a person in a third country other than a relevant authority, the transferring controller must inform a relevant authority in that third country without undue delay of the transfer, unless this would be ineffective or inappropriate.

(7) The transferring controller must —
  (a) document any transfer to a recipient in a third country other than a relevant authority, and
  (b) inform the Commissioner about the transfer.

46

Data Protection Act 2018 (c. 12)
Part 3 — Law enforcement processing
Chapter 5 — Transfers of personal data to third countries etc

(8) This section does not affect the operation of any international agreement in force between member States and third countries in the field of judicial co-operation in criminal matters and police co-operation.

Subsequent transfers

78   Subsequent transfers

(1) Where personal data is transferred in accordance with section 73, the transferring controller must make it a condition of the transfer that the data is not to be further transferred to a third country or international organisation without the authorisation of the transferring controller or another competent authority.

(2) A competent authority may give an authorisation under subsection (1) only where the further transfer is necessary for a law enforcement purpose.

(3) In deciding whether to give the authorisation, the competent authority must take into account (among any other relevant factors) —

    (a) the seriousness of the circumstances leading to the request for authorisation,

    (b) the purpose for which the personal data was originally transferred, and

    (c) the standards for the protection of personal data that apply in the third country or international organisation to which the personal data would be transferred.

(4) In a case where the personal data was originally transmitted or otherwise made available to the transferring controller or another competent authority by a member State other than the United Kingdom, an authorisation may not be given under subsection (1) unless that member State, or any person based in that member State which is a competent authority for the purposes of the Law Enforcement Directive, has authorised the transfer in accordance with the law of the member State.

(5) Authorisation is not required as mentioned in subsection (4) if —

    (a) the transfer is necessary for the prevention of an immediate and serious threat either to the public security of a member State or a third country or to the essential interests of a member State, and

    (b) the authorisation cannot be obtained in good time.

(6) Where a transfer is made without the authorisation mentioned in subsection (4), the authority in the member State which would have been responsible for deciding whether to authorise the transfer must be informed without delay.

CHAPTER 6

SUPPLEMENTARY

79   National security: certificate

(1) A Minister of the Crown may issue a certificate certifying, for the purposes of section 44(4), 45(4), 48(3) or 68(7), that a restriction is a necessary and proportionate measure to protect national security.

(2) The certificate may —

    (a)   relate to a specific restriction (described in the certificate) which a controller has imposed or is proposing to impose under section 44(4), 45(4), 48(3) or 68(7), or

    (b)   identify any restriction to which it relates by means of a general description.

(3)   Subject to subsection (6), a certificate issued under subsection (1) is conclusive evidence that the specific restriction or (as the case may be) any restriction falling within the general description is, or at any time was, a necessary and proportionate measure to protect national security.

(4)   A certificate issued under subsection (1) may be expressed to have prospective effect.

(5)   Any person directly affected by the issuing of a certificate under subsection (1) may appeal to the Tribunal against the certificate.

(6)   If, on an appeal under subsection (5), the Tribunal finds that, applying the principles applied by a court on an application for judicial review, the Minister did not have reasonable grounds for issuing the certificate, the Tribunal may —

    (a)   allow the appeal, and

    (b)   quash the certificate.

(7)   Where in any proceedings under or by virtue of this Act, it is claimed by a controller that a restriction falls within a general description in a certificate issued under subsection (1), any other party to the proceedings may appeal to the Tribunal on the ground that the restriction does not fall within that description.

(8)   But, subject to any determination under subsection (9), the restriction is to be conclusively presumed to fall within the general description.

(9)   On an appeal under subsection (7), the Tribunal may determine that the certificate does not so apply.

(10)   A document purporting to be a certificate under subsection (1) is to be —

    (a)   received in evidence, and

    (b)   deemed to be such a certificate unless the contrary is proved.

(11)   A document which purports to be certified by or on behalf of a Minister of the Crown as a true copy of a certificate issued by that Minister under subsection (1) is —

    (a)   in any legal proceedings, evidence of that certificate, and

    (b)   in any legal proceedings in Scotland, sufficient evidence of that certificate.

(12)   The power conferred by subsection (1) on a Minister of the Crown is exercisable only by —

    (a)   a Minister who is a member of the Cabinet, or

    (b)   the Attorney General or the Advocate General for Scotland.

(13)   No power conferred by any provision of Part 6 may be exercised in relation to the imposition of —

    (a)   a specific restriction in a certificate under subsection (1), or

    (b)   a restriction falling within a general description in such a certificate.

80   Special processing restrictions

(1)   Subsections (3) and (4) apply where, for a law enforcement purpose, a controller transmits or otherwise makes available personal data to an EU recipient or a non-EU recipient.

(2)   In this section —

"EU recipient" means —

(a)   a recipient in a member State other than the United Kingdom, or

(b)   an agency, office or body established pursuant to Chapters 4 and 5 of Title V of the Treaty on the Functioning of the European Union;

"non-EU recipient" means —

(a)   a recipient in a third country, or

(b)   an international organisation.

(3)   The controller must consider whether, if the personal data had instead been transmitted or otherwise made available within the United Kingdom to another competent authority, processing of the data by the other competent authority would have been subject to any restrictions by virtue of any enactment or rule of law.

(4)   Where that would be the case, the controller must inform the EU recipient or non-EU recipient that the data is transmitted or otherwise made available subject to compliance by that person with the same restrictions (which must be set out in the information given to that person).

(5)   Except as provided by subsection (4), the controller may not impose restrictions on the processing of personal data transmitted or otherwise made available by the controller to an EU recipient.

(6)   Subsection (7) applies where —

(a)   a competent authority for the purposes of the Law Enforcement Directive in a member State other than the United Kingdom transmits or otherwise makes available personal data to a controller for a law enforcement purpose, and

(b)   the competent authority in the other member State informs the controller, in accordance with any law of that member State which implements Article 9(3) and (4) of the Law Enforcement Directive, that the data is transmitted or otherwise made available subject to compliance by the controller with restrictions set out by the competent authority.

(7)   The controller must comply with the restrictions.

81   Reporting of infringements

(1)   Each controller must implement effective mechanisms to encourage the reporting of an infringement of this Part.

(2)   The mechanisms implemented under subsection (1) must provide that an infringement may be reported to any of the following persons —

(a)   the controller;

(b)   the Commissioner.

(3)   The mechanisms implemented under subsection (1) must include —

      (a)   raising awareness of the protections provided by Part 4A of the Employment Rights Act 1996 and Part 5A of the Employment Rights (Northern Ireland) Order 1996 (S.I. 1996/1919 (N.I. 16)), and

      (b)   such other protections for a person who reports an infringement of this Part as the controller considers appropriate.

(4)   A person who reports an infringement of this Part does not breach—

      (a)   an obligation of confidence owed by the person, or

      (b)   any other restriction on the disclosure of information (however imposed).

(5)   Subsection (4) does not apply if or to the extent that the report includes a disclosure which is prohibited by any of Parts 1 to 7 or Chapter 1 of Part 9 of the Investigatory Powers Act 2016.

(6)   Until the repeal of Part 1 of the Regulation of Investigatory Powers Act 2000 by paragraphs 45 and 54 of Schedule 10 to the Investigatory Powers Act 2016 is fully in force, subsection (5) has effect as if it included a reference to that Part.

PART 4

INTELLIGENCE SERVICES PROCESSING

CHAPTER 1

SCOPE AND DEFINITIONS

Scope

82   Processing to which this Part applies

(1)   This Part applies to—

      (a)   the processing by an intelligence service of personal data wholly or partly by automated means, and

      (b)   the processing by an intelligence service otherwise than by automated means of personal data which forms part of a filing system or is intended to form part of a filing system.

(2)   In this Part, "intelligence service" means—

      (a)   the Security Service;

      (b)   the Secret Intelligence Service;

      (c)   the Government Communications Headquarters.

(3)   A reference in this Part to the processing of personal data is to processing to which this Part applies.

Definitions

83   Meaning of "controller" and "processor"

(1)   In this Part, "controller" means the intelligence service which, alone or jointly with others—

      (a)   determines the purposes and means of the processing of personal data, or

50   *Data Protection Act 2018 (c. 12)*
                              Part 4 — Intelligence services processing
                                    Chapter 1 — Scope and definitions

     (b)   is the controller by virtue of subsection (2).

(2)   Where personal data is processed only —

     (a)   for purposes for which it is required by an enactment to be processed, and

     (b)   by means by which it is required by an enactment to be processed,

the intelligence service on which the obligation to process the data is imposed by the enactment (or, if different, one of the enactments) is the controller.

(3)   In this Part, "processor" means any person who processes personal data on behalf of the controller (other than a person who is an employee of the controller).

84   Other definitions

(1)   This section defines other expressions used in this Part.

(2)   "Consent", in relation to the processing of personal data relating to an individual, means a freely given, specific, informed and unambiguous indication of the individual's wishes by which the individual, by a statement or by a clear affirmative action, signifies agreement to the processing of the personal data.

(3)   "Employee", in relation to any person, includes an individual who holds a position (whether paid or unpaid) under the direction and control of that person.

(4)   "Personal data breach" means a breach of security leading to the accidental or unlawful destruction, loss, alteration, unauthorised disclosure of, or access to, personal data transmitted, stored or otherwise processed.

(5)   "Recipient", in relation to any personal data, means any person to whom the data is disclosed, whether a third party or not, but it does not include a person to whom disclosure is or may be made in the framework of a particular inquiry in accordance with the law.

(6)   "Restriction of processing" means the marking of stored personal data with the aim of limiting its processing for the future.

(7)   Sections 3 and 205 include definitions of other expressions used in this Part.

CHAPTER 2

PRINCIPLES

Overview

85   Overview

(1)   This Chapter sets out the six data protection principles as follows —

     (a)   section 86 sets out the first data protection principle (requirement that processing be lawful, fair and transparent);

     (b)   section 87 sets out the second data protection principle (requirement that the purposes of processing be specified, explicit and legitimate);

(c)   section 88 sets out the third data protection principle (requirement that personal data be adequate, relevant and not excessive);

(d)   section 89 sets out the fourth data protection principle (requirement that personal data be accurate and kept up to date);

(e)   section 90 sets out the fifth data protection principle (requirement that personal data be kept for no longer than is necessary);

(f)   section 91 sets out the sixth data protection principle (requirement that personal data be processed in a secure manner).

(2)   Each of sections 86, 87 and 91 makes provision to supplement the principle to which it relates.

The data protection principles

86   The first data protection principle

(1)   The first data protection principle is that the processing of personal data must be—

(a)   lawful, and

(b)   fair and transparent.

(2)   The processing of personal data is lawful only if and to the extent that—

(a)   at least one of the conditions in Schedule 9 is met, and

(b)   in the case of sensitive processing, at least one of the conditions in Schedule 10 is also met.

(3)   The Secretary of State may by regulations amend Schedule 10—

(a)   by adding conditions;

(b)   by omitting conditions added by regulations under paragraph (a).

(4)   Regulations under subsection (3) are subject to the affirmative resolution procedure.

(5)   In determining whether the processing of personal data is fair and transparent, regard is to be had to the method by which it is obtained.

(6)   For the purposes of subsection (5), data is to be treated as obtained fairly and transparently if it consists of information obtained from a person who—

(a)   is authorised by an enactment to supply it, or

(b)   is required to supply it by an enactment or by an international obligation of the United Kingdom.

(7)   In this section, "sensitive processing" means—

(a)   the processing of personal data revealing racial or ethnic origin, political opinions, religious or philosophical beliefs or trade union membership;

(b)   the processing of genetic data for the purpose of uniquely identifying an individual;

(c)   the processing of biometric data for the purpose of uniquely identifying an individual;

(d)   the processing of data concerning health;

(e)   the processing of data concerning an individual's sex life or sexual orientation;

(f)   the processing of personal data as to—

      (i)   the commission or alleged commission of an offence by an individual, or

      (ii)   proceedings for an offence committed or alleged to have been committed by an individual, the disposal of such proceedings or the sentence of a court in such proceedings.

87   The second data protection principle

(1)   The second data protection principle is that—

    (a)   the purpose for which personal data is collected on any occasion must be specified, explicit and legitimate, and

    (b)   personal data so collected must not be processed in a manner that is incompatible with the purpose for which it is collected.

(2)   Paragraph (b) of the second data protection principle is subject to subsections (3) and (4).

(3)   Personal data collected by a controller for one purpose may be processed for any other purpose of the controller that collected the data or any purpose of another controller provided that—

    (a)   the controller is authorised by law to process the data for that purpose, and

    (b)   the processing is necessary and proportionate to that other purpose.

(4)   Processing of personal data is to be regarded as compatible with the purpose for which it is collected if the processing—

    (a)   consists of—

      (i)   processing for archiving purposes in the public interest,

      (ii)   processing for the purposes of scientific or historical research, or

      (iii) processing for statistical purposes, and

    (b)   is subject to appropriate safeguards for the rights and freedoms of the data subject.

88   The third data protection principle

The third data protection principle is that personal data must be adequate, relevant and not excessive in relation to the purpose for which it is processed.

89   The fourth data protection principle

The fourth data protection principle is that personal data undergoing processing must be accurate and, where necessary, kept up to date.

90   The fifth data protection principle

The fifth data protection principle is that personal data must be kept for no longer than is necessary for the purpose for which it is processed.

91   The sixth data protection principle

(1)   The sixth data protection principle is that personal data must be processed in a manner that includes taking appropriate security measures as regards risks that arise from processing personal data.

(2)   The risks referred to in subsection (1) include (but are not limited to) accidental or unauthorised access to, or destruction, loss, use, modification or disclosure of, personal data.

CHAPTER 3

RIGHTS OF THE DATA SUBJECT

Overview

92   Overview

(1)   This Chapter sets out the rights of the data subject as follows—
   (a)   section 93 deals with the information to be made available to the data subject;
   (b)   sections 94 and 95 deal with the right of access by the data subject;
   (c)   sections 96 and 97 deal with rights in relation to automated processing;
   (d)   section 98 deals with the right to information about decision-making;
   (e)   section 99 deals with the right to object to processing;
   (f)   section 100 deals with rights to rectification and erasure of personal data.

(2)   In this Chapter, "the controller", in relation to a data subject, means the controller in relation to personal data relating to the data subject.

Rights

93   Right to information

(1)   The controller must give a data subject the following information—
   (a)   the identity and the contact details of the controller;
   (b)   the legal basis on which, and the purposes for which, the controller processes personal data;
   (c)   the categories of personal data relating to the data subject that are being processed;
   (d)   the recipients or the categories of recipients of the personal data (if applicable);
   (e)   the right to lodge a complaint with the Commissioner and the contact details of the Commissioner;
   (f)   how to exercise rights under this Chapter;
   (g)   any other information needed to secure that the personal data is processed fairly and transparently.

(2)   The controller may comply with subsection (1) by making information generally available, where the controller considers it appropriate to do so.

(3)   The controller is not required under subsection (1) to give a data subject information that the data subject already has.

(4)   Where personal data relating to a data subject is collected by or on behalf of the controller from a person other than the data subject, the requirement in

54

Data Protection Act 2018 (c. 12)
Part 4 — Intelligence services processing
Chapter 3 — Rights of the data subject

subsection (1) has effect, in relation to the personal data so collected, with the following exceptions —

    (a)   the requirement does not apply in relation to processing that is authorised by an enactment;

    (b)   the requirement does not apply in relation to the data subject if giving the information to the data subject would be impossible or involve disproportionate effort.

94 Right of access

(1)   An individual is entitled to obtain from a controller —

    (a)   confirmation as to whether or not personal data concerning the individual is being processed, and

    (b)   where that is the case —

        (i)   communication, in intelligible form, of the personal data of which that individual is the data subject, and

        (ii)   the information set out in subsection (2).

(2)   That information is —

    (a)   the purposes of and legal basis for the processing;

    (b)   the categories of personal data concerned;

    (c)   the recipients or categories of recipients to whom the personal data has been disclosed;

    (d)   the period for which the personal data is to be preserved;

    (e)   the existence of a data subject's rights to rectification and erasure of personal data (see section 100);

    (f)   the right to lodge a complaint with the Commissioner and the contact details of the Commissioner;

    (g)   any information about the origin of the personal data concerned.

(3)   A controller is not obliged to provide information under this section unless the controller has received such reasonable fee as the controller may require, subject to subsection (4).

(4)   The Secretary of State may by regulations —

    (a)   specify cases in which a controller may not charge a fee;

    (b)   specify the maximum amount of a fee.

(5)   Where a controller —

    (a)   reasonably requires further information —

        (i)   in order that the controller be satisfied as to the identity of the individual making a request under subsection (1), or

        (ii)   to locate the information which that individual seeks, and

    (b)   has informed that individual of that requirement,

the controller is not obliged to comply with the request unless the controller is supplied with that further information.

(6)   Where a controller cannot comply with the request without disclosing information relating to another individual who can be identified from that information, the controller is not obliged to comply with the request unless —

    (a)   the other individual has consented to the disclosure of the information to the individual making the request, or

Data Protection Act 2018 (c. 12)
Part 4 — Intelligence services processing
Chapter 3 — Rights of the data subject

55

(b)   it is reasonable in all the circumstances to comply with the request without the consent of the other individual.

(7)   In subsection (6), the reference to information relating to another individual includes a reference to information identifying that individual as the source of the information sought by the request.

(8)   Subsection (6) is not to be construed as excusing a controller from communicating so much of the information sought by the request as can be communicated without disclosing the identity of the other individual concerned, whether by the omission of names or other identifying particulars or otherwise.

(9)   In determining for the purposes of subsection (6)(b) whether it is reasonable in all the circumstances to comply with the request without the consent of the other individual concerned, regard must be had, in particular, to—

    (a)   any duty of confidentiality owed to the other individual,
    (b)   any steps taken by the controller with a view to seeking the consent of the other individual,
    (c)   whether the other individual is capable of giving consent, and
    (d)   any express refusal of consent by the other individual.

(10)   Subject to subsection (6), a controller must comply with a request under subsection (1)—

    (a)   promptly, and
    (b)   in any event before the end of the applicable time period.

(11)   If a court is satisfied on the application of an individual who has made a request under subsection (1) that the controller in question has failed to comply with the request in contravention of this section, the court may order the controller to comply with the request.

(12)   A court may make an order under subsection (11) in relation to a joint controller whose responsibilities are determined in an arrangement under section 104 only if the controller is responsible for compliance with the obligation to which the order relates.

(13)   The jurisdiction conferred on a court by this section is exercisable by the High Court or, in Scotland, by the Court of Session.

(14)   In this section—

    "the applicable time period" means—
        (a)   the period of 1 month, or
        (b)   such longer period, not exceeding 3 months, as may be specified in regulations made by the Secretary of State,
        beginning with the relevant time;
    "the relevant time", in relation to a request under subsection (1), means the latest of the following—
        (a)   when the controller receives the request,
        (b)   when the fee (if any) is paid, and
        (c)   when the controller receives the information (if any) required under subsection (5) in connection with the request.

(15)   Regulations under this section are subject to the negative resolution procedure.

56   *Data Protection Act 2018 (c. 12)*
                                                 Part 4 — Intelligence services processing
                                                    Chapter 3 — Rights of the data subject

95   Right of access: supplementary

(1)   The controller must comply with the obligation imposed by section 94(1)(b)(i) by supplying the data subject with a copy of the information in writing unless—

    (a)   the supply of such a copy is not possible or would involve disproportionate effort, or

    (b)   the data subject agrees otherwise;

and where any of the information referred to in section 94(1)(b)(i) is expressed in terms which are not intelligible without explanation the copy must be accompanied by an explanation of those terms.

(2)   Where a controller has previously complied with a request made under section 94 by an individual, the controller is not obliged to comply with a subsequent identical or similar request under that section by that individual unless a reasonable interval has elapsed between compliance with the previous request and the making of the current request.

(3)   In determining for the purposes of subsection (2) whether requests under section 94 are made at reasonable intervals, regard must be had to—

    (a)   the nature of the data,

    (b)   the purpose for which the data is processed, and

    (c)   the frequency with which the data is altered.

(4)   The information to be supplied pursuant to a request under section 94 must be supplied by reference to the data in question at the time when the request is received, except that it may take account of any amendment or deletion made between that time and the time when the information is supplied, being an amendment or deletion that would have been made regardless of the receipt of the request.

(5)   For the purposes of section 94(6) to (8), an individual can be identified from information to be disclosed to a data subject by a controller if the individual can be identified from—

    (a)   that information, or

    (b)   that and any other information that the controller reasonably believes the data subject making the request is likely to possess or obtain.

96   Right not to be subject to automated decision-making

(1)   The controller may not take a decision significantly affecting a data subject that is based solely on automated processing of personal data relating to the data subject.

(2)   Subsection (1) does not prevent such a decision being made on that basis if—

    (a)   the decision is required or authorised by law,

    (b)   the data subject has given consent to the decision being made on that basis, or

    (c)   the decision is a decision taken in the course of steps taken—

        (i)   for the purpose of considering whether to enter into a contract with the data subject,

        (ii)   with a view to entering into such a contract, or

        (iii)   in the course of performing such a contract.

Data Protection Act 2018 (c. 12)
Part 4 — Intelligence services processing
Chapter 3 — Rights of the data subject

57

(3)   For the purposes of this section, a decision that has legal effects as regards an individual is to be regarded as significantly affecting the individual.

97   Right to intervene in automated decision-making

(1)   This section applies where —
    (a)   the controller takes a decision significantly affecting a data subject that is based solely on automated processing of personal data relating to the data subject, and
    (b)   the decision is required or authorised by law.

(2)   This section does not apply to such a decision if —
    (a)   the data subject has given consent to the decision being made on that basis, or
    (b)   the decision is a decision taken in the course of steps taken —
        (i)   for the purpose of considering whether to enter into a contract with the data subject,
        (ii)   with a view to entering into such a contract, or
        (iii)   in the course of performing such a contract.

(3)   The controller must as soon as reasonably practicable notify the data subject that such a decision has been made.

(4)   The data subject may, before the end of the period of 1 month beginning with receipt of the notification, request the controller —
    (a)   to reconsider the decision, or
    (b)   to take a new decision that is not based solely on automated processing.

(5)   If a request is made to the controller under subsection (4), the controller must, before the end of the period of 1 month beginning with receipt of the request —
    (a)   consider the request, including any information provided by the data subject that is relevant to it, and
    (b)   by notice in writing inform the data subject of the outcome of that consideration.

(6)   For the purposes of this section, a decision that has legal effects as regards an individual is to be regarded as significantly affecting the individual.

98   Right to information about decision-making

(1)   Where —
    (a)   the controller processes personal data relating to a data subject, and
    (b)   results produced by the processing are applied to the data subject,
the data subject is entitled to obtain from the controller, on request, knowledge of the reasoning underlying the processing.

(2)   Where the data subject makes a request under subsection (1), the controller must comply with the request without undue delay.

99   Right to object to processing

(1)   A data subject is entitled at any time, by notice given to the controller, to require the controller —
    (a)   not to process personal data relating to the data subject, or

58   *Data Protection Act 2018 (c. 12)*
                     Part 4 — Intelligence services processing
                     Chapter 3 — Rights of the data subject

(b)   not to process such data for a specified purpose or in a specified manner,

on the ground that, for specified reasons relating to the situation of the data subject, the processing in question is an unwarranted interference with the interests or rights of the data subject.

(2)   Where the controller —

    (a)   reasonably requires further information —

        (i)   in order that the controller be satisfied as to the identity of the individual giving notice under subsection (1), or

        (ii)   to locate the data to which the notice relates, and

    (b)   has informed that individual of that requirement,

the controller is not obliged to comply with the notice unless the controller is supplied with that further information.

(3)   The controller must, before the end of 21 days beginning with the relevant time, give a notice to the data subject —

    (a)   stating that the controller has complied or intends to comply with the notice under subsection (1), or

    (b)   stating the controller's reasons for not complying with the notice to any extent and the extent (if any) to which the controller has complied or intends to comply with the notice under subsection (1).

(4)   If the controller does not comply with a notice under subsection (1) to any extent, the data subject may apply to a court for an order that the controller take steps for complying with the notice.

(5)   If the court is satisfied that the controller should comply with the notice (or should comply to any extent), the court may order the controller to take such steps for complying with the notice (or for complying with it to that extent) as the court thinks fit.

(6)   A court may make an order under subsection (5) in relation to a joint controller whose responsibilities are determined in an arrangement under section 104 only if the controller is responsible for compliance with the obligation to which the order relates.

(7)   The jurisdiction conferred on a court by this section is exercisable by the High Court or, in Scotland, by the Court of Session.

(8)   In this section, "the relevant time", in relation to a notice under subsection (1), means —

    (a)   when the controller receives the notice, or

    (b)   if later, when the controller receives the information (if any) required under subsection (2) in connection with the notice.

100   Rights to rectification and erasure

(1)   If a court is satisfied on the application of a data subject that personal data relating to the data subject is inaccurate, the court may order the controller to rectify that data without undue delay.

(2)   If a court is satisfied on the application of a data subject that the processing of personal data relating to the data subject would infringe any of sections 86 to 91, the court may order the controller to erase that data without undue delay.

Data Protection Act 2018 (c. 12) 59
Part 4 — Intelligence services processing
Chapter 3 — Rights of the data subject

(3) If personal data relating to the data subject must be maintained for the purposes of evidence, the court may (instead of ordering the controller to rectify or erase the personal data) order the controller to restrict its processing without undue delay.

(4) If —
   (a) the data subject contests the accuracy of personal data, and
   (b) the court is satisfied that the controller is not able to ascertain whether the data is accurate or not,
   the court may (instead of ordering the controller to rectify or erase the personal data) order the controller to restrict its processing without undue delay.

(5) A court may make an order under this section in relation to a joint controller whose responsibilities are determined in an arrangement under section 104 only if the controller is responsible for carrying out the rectification, erasure or restriction of processing that the court proposes to order.

(6) The jurisdiction conferred on a court by this section is exercisable by the High Court or, in Scotland, by the Court of Session.

CHAPTER 4

CONTROLLER AND PROCESSOR

Overview

101 Overview

This Chapter sets out —
   (a) the general obligations of controllers and processors (see sections 102 to 106);
   (b) specific obligations of controllers and processors with respect to security (see section 107);
   (c) specific obligations of controllers and processors with respect to personal data breaches (see section 108).

General obligations

102 General obligations of the controller

Each controller must implement appropriate measures —
   (a) to ensure, and
   (b) to be able to demonstrate, in particular to the Commissioner,
   that the processing of personal data complies with the requirements of this Part.

103 Data protection by design

(1) Where a controller proposes that a particular type of processing of personal data be carried out by or on behalf of the controller, the controller must, prior to the processing, consider the impact of the proposed processing on the rights and freedoms of data subjects.

60

Data Protection Act 2018 (c. 12)
Part 4 — Intelligence services processing
Chapter 4 — Controller and processor

(2) A controller must implement appropriate technical and organisational measures which are designed to ensure that—
   (a) the data protection principles are implemented, and
   (b) risks to the rights and freedoms of data subjects are minimised.

104 Joint controllers

(1) Where two or more intelligence services jointly determine the purposes and means of processing personal data, they are joint controllers for the purposes of this Part.

(2) Joint controllers must, in a transparent manner, determine their respective responsibilities for compliance with this Part by means of an arrangement between them, except to the extent that those responsibilities are determined under or by virtue of an enactment.

(3) The arrangement must designate the controller which is to be the contact point for data subjects.

105 Processors

(1) This section applies to the use by a controller of a processor to carry out processing of personal data on behalf of the controller.

(2) The controller may use only a processor who undertakes—
   (a) to implement appropriate measures that are sufficient to secure that the processing complies with this Part;
   (b) to provide to the controller such information as is necessary for demonstrating that the processing complies with this Part.

(3) If a processor determines, in breach of this Part, the purposes and means of processing, the processor is to be treated for the purposes of this Part as a controller in respect of that processing.

106 Processing under the authority of the controller or processor

A processor, and any person acting under the authority of a controller or processor, who has access to personal data may not process the data except—
   (a) on instructions from the controller, or
   (b) to comply with a legal obligation.

Obligations relating to security

107 Security of processing

(1) Each controller and each processor must implement security measures appropriate to the risks arising from the processing of personal data.

(2) In the case of automated processing, each controller and each processor must, following an evaluation of the risks, implement measures designed to—
   (a) prevent unauthorised processing or unauthorised interference with the systems used in connection with it,
   (b) ensure that it is possible to establish the precise details of any processing that takes place,

Data Protection Act 2018 (c. 12)
Part 4 – Intelligence services processing
Chapter 4 – Controller and processor

61

(c) ensure that any systems used in connection with the processing function properly and may, in the case of interruption, be restored, and

(d) ensure that stored personal data cannot be corrupted if a system used in connection with the processing malfunctions.

Obligations relating to personal data breaches

108 Communication of a personal data breach

(1) If a controller becomes aware of a serious personal data breach in relation to personal data for which the controller is responsible, the controller must notify the Commissioner of the breach without undue delay.

(2) Where the notification to the Commissioner is not made within 72 hours, the notification must be accompanied by reasons for the delay.

(3) Subject to subsection (4), the notification must include—

(a) a description of the nature of the personal data breach including, where possible, the categories and approximate number of data subjects concerned and the categories and approximate number of personal data records concerned;

(b) the name and contact details of the contact point from whom more information can be obtained;

(c) a description of the likely consequences of the personal data breach;

(d) a description of the measures taken or proposed to be taken by the controller to address the personal data breach, including, where appropriate, measures to mitigate its possible adverse effects.

(4) Where and to the extent that it is not possible to provide all the information mentioned in subsection (3) at the same time, the information may be provided in phases without undue further delay.

(5) If a processor becomes aware of a personal data breach (in relation to data processed by the processor), the processor must notify the controller without undue delay.

(6) Subsection (1) does not apply in relation to a personal data breach if the breach also constitutes a relevant error within the meaning given by section 231(9) of the Investigatory Powers Act 2016.

(7) For the purposes of this section, a personal data breach is serious if the breach seriously interferes with the rights and freedoms of a data subject.

CHAPTER 5

TRANSFERS OF PERSONAL DATA OUTSIDE THE UNITED KINGDOM

109 Transfers of personal data outside the United Kingdom

(1) A controller may not transfer personal data to—

(a) a country or territory outside the United Kingdom, or

(b) an international organisation,

unless the transfer falls within subsection (2).

62

Data Protection Act 2018 (c. 12)
Part 4 — Intelligence services processing
Chapter 5 — Transfers of personal data outside the United Kingdom

(2) A transfer of personal data falls within this subsection if the transfer is a necessary and proportionate measure carried out—

    (a) for the purposes of the controller's statutory functions, or

    (b) for other purposes provided for, in relation to the controller, in section 2(2)(a) of the Security Service Act 1989 or section 2(2)(a) or 4(2)(a) of the Intelligence Services Act 1994.

CHAPTER 6

EXEMPTIONS

110 National security

(1) A provision mentioned in subsection (2) does not apply to personal data to which this Part applies if exemption from the provision is required for the purpose of safeguarding national security.

(2) The provisions are—

    (a) Chapter 2 (the data protection principles), except section 86(1)(a) and (2) and Schedules 9 and 10;

    (b) Chapter 3 (rights of data subjects);

    (c) in Chapter 4, section 108 (communication of a personal data breach to the Commissioner);

    (d) in Part 5—

        (i) section 119 (inspection in accordance with international obligations);

        (ii) in Schedule 13 (other general functions of the Commissioner), paragraphs 1(a) and (g) and 2;

    (e) in Part 6—

        (i) sections 142 to 154 and Schedule 15 (Commissioner's notices and powers of entry and inspection);

        (ii) sections 170 to 173 (offences relating to personal data);

        (iii) sections 174 to 176 (provision relating to the special purposes).

111 National security: certificate

(1) Subject to subsection (3), a certificate signed by a Minister of the Crown certifying that exemption from all or any of the provisions mentioned in section 110(2) is, or at any time was, required for the purpose of safeguarding national security in respect of any personal data is conclusive evidence of that fact.

(2) A certificate under subsection (1)—

    (a) may identify the personal data to which it applies by means of a general description, and

    (b) may be expressed to have prospective effect.

(3) Any person directly affected by the issuing of a certificate under subsection (1) may appeal to the Tribunal against the certificate.

(4) If on an appeal under subsection (3), the Tribunal finds that, applying the principles applied by a court on an application for judicial review, the Minister did not have reasonable grounds for issuing the certificate, the Tribunal may—

    (a) allow the appeal, and

(b)   quash the certificate.

(5)   Where, in any proceedings under or by virtue of this Act, it is claimed by a controller that a certificate under subsection (1) which identifies the personal data to which it applies by means of a general description applies to any personal data, another party to the proceedings may appeal to the Tribunal on the ground that the certificate does not apply to the personal data in question.

(6)   But, subject to any determination under subsection (7), the certificate is to be conclusively presumed so to apply.

(7)   On an appeal under subsection (5), the Tribunal may determine that the certificate does not so apply.

(8)   A document purporting to be a certificate under subsection (1) is to be —
    (a)   received in evidence, and
    (b)   deemed to be such a certificate unless the contrary is proved.

(9)   A document which purports to be certified by or on behalf of a Minister of the Crown as a true copy of a certificate issued by that Minister under subsection (1) is —
    (a)   in any legal proceedings, evidence of that certificate, and
    (b)   in any legal proceedings in Scotland, sufficient evidence of that certificate.

(10)   The power conferred by subsection (1) on a Minister of the Crown is exercisable only by —
    (a)   a Minister who is a member of the Cabinet, or
    (b)   the Attorney General or the Advocate General for Scotland.

112   Other exemptions

Schedule 11 provides for further exemptions.

113   Power to make further exemptions

(1)   The Secretary of State may by regulations amend Schedule 11 —
    (a)   by adding exemptions from any provision of this Part;
    (b)   by omitting exemptions added by regulations under paragraph (a).

(2)   Regulations under this section are subject to the affirmative resolution procedure.

PART 5

THE INFORMATION COMMISSIONER

The Commissioner

114   The Information Commissioner

(1)   There is to continue to be an Information Commissioner.

(2)   Schedule 12 makes provision about the Commissioner.

General functions

115 General functions under the GDPR and safeguards

(1) The Commissioner is to be the supervisory authority in the United Kingdom for the purposes of Article 51 of the GDPR.

(2) General functions are conferred on the Commissioner by —
    (a) Article 57 of the GDPR (tasks), and
    (b) Article 58 of the GDPR (powers),
(and see also the Commissioner's duty under section 2).

(3) The Commissioner's functions in relation to the processing of personal data to which the GDPR applies include —
    (a) a duty to advise Parliament, the government and other institutions and bodies on legislative and administrative measures relating to the protection of individuals' rights and freedoms with regard to the processing of personal data, and
    (b) a power to issue, on the Commissioner's own initiative or on request, opinions to Parliament, the government or other institutions and bodies as well as to the public on any issue related to the protection of personal data.

(4) The Commissioner's functions under Article 58 of the GDPR are subject to the safeguards in subsections (5) to (9).

(5) The Commissioner's power under Article 58(1)(a) of the GDPR (power to require a controller or processor to provide information that the Commissioner requires for the performance of the Commissioner's tasks under the GDPR) is exercisable only by giving an information notice under section 142.

(6) The Commissioner's power under Article 58(1)(b) of the GDPR (power to carry out data protection audits) is exercisable only in accordance with section 146.

(7) The Commissioner's powers under Article 58(1)(e) and (f) of the GDPR (power to obtain information from controllers and processors and access to their premises) are exercisable only —
    (a) in accordance with Schedule 15 (see section 154), or
    (b) to the extent that they are exercised in conjunction with the power under Article 58(1)(b) of the GDPR, in accordance with section 146.

(8) The following powers are exercisable only by giving an enforcement notice under section 149 —
    (a) the Commissioner's powers under Article 58(2)(c) to (g) and (j) of the GDPR (certain corrective powers);
    (b) the Commissioner's powers under Article 58(2)(h) to order a certification body to withdraw, or not to issue, a certification under Articles 42 and 43 of the GDPR.

(9) The Commissioner's powers under Articles 58(2)(i) and 83 of the GDPR (administrative fines) are exercisable only by giving a penalty notice under section 155.

(10) This section is without prejudice to other functions conferred on the Commissioner, whether by the GDPR, this Act or otherwise.

116 Other general functions

(1) The Commissioner —
    (a) is to be the supervisory authority in the United Kingdom for the purposes of Article 41 of the Law Enforcement Directive, and
    (b) is to continue to be the designated authority in the United Kingdom for the purposes of Article 13 of the Data Protection Convention.

(2) Schedule 13 confers general functions on the Commissioner in connection with processing to which the GDPR does not apply (and see also the Commissioner's duty under section 2).

(3) This section and Schedule 13 are without prejudice to other functions conferred on the Commissioner, whether by this Act or otherwise.

117 Competence in relation to courts etc

Nothing in this Act permits or requires the Commissioner to exercise functions in relation to the processing of personal data by —
    (a) an individual acting in a judicial capacity, or
    (b) a court or tribunal acting in its judicial capacity,
(and see also Article 55(3) of the GDPR).

International role

118 Co-operation and mutual assistance

(1) Articles 60 to 62 of the GDPR confer functions on the Commissioner in relation to co-operation and mutual assistance between, and joint operations of, supervisory authorities under the GDPR.

(2) References to the GDPR in subsection (1) do not include the applied GDPR.

(3) Article 61 of the applied GDPR confers functions on the Commissioner in relation to co-operation with other supervisory authorities (as defined in Article 4(21) of the applied GDPR).

(4) Part 1 of Schedule 14 makes provision as to the functions to be carried out by the Commissioner for the purposes of Article 50 of the Law Enforcement Directive (mutual assistance).

(5) Part 2 of Schedule 14 makes provision as to the functions to be carried out by the Commissioner for the purposes of Article 13 of the Data Protection Convention (co-operation between parties).

119 Inspection of personal data in accordance with international obligations

(1) The Commissioner may inspect personal data where the inspection is necessary in order to discharge an international obligation of the United Kingdom, subject to the restriction in subsection (2).

(2) The power under subsection (1) is exercisable only if the personal data —
    (a) is processed wholly or partly by automated means, or
    (b) is processed otherwise than by automated means and forms part of a filing system or is intended to form part of a filing system.

(3)   The power under subsection (1) includes power to inspect, operate and test equipment which is used for the processing of personal data.

(4)   Before exercising the power under subsection (1), the Commissioner must by written notice inform the controller and any processor that the Commissioner intends to do so.

(5)   Subsection (4) does not apply if the Commissioner considers that the case is urgent.

(6)   It is an offence—

     (a)   intentionally to obstruct a person exercising the power under subsection (1), or

     (b)   to fail without reasonable excuse to give a person exercising that power any assistance the person may reasonably require.

(7)   Paragraphs (c) and (d) of section 3(14) do not apply to references in this section to personal data, the processing of personal data, a controller or a processor.

120   Further international role

(1)   The Commissioner must, in relation to third countries and international organisations, take appropriate steps to—

     (a)   develop international co-operation mechanisms to facilitate the effective enforcement of legislation for the protection of personal data;

     (b)   provide international mutual assistance in the enforcement of legislation for the protection of personal data, subject to appropriate safeguards for the protection of personal data and other fundamental rights and freedoms;

     (c)   engage relevant stakeholders in discussion and activities aimed at furthering international co-operation in the enforcement of legislation for the protection of personal data;

     (d)   promote the exchange and documentation of legislation and practice for the protection of personal data, including legislation and practice relating to jurisdictional conflicts with third countries.

(2)   Subsection (1) applies only in connection with the processing of personal data to which the GDPR does not apply; for the equivalent duty in connection with the processing of personal data to which the GDPR applies, see Article 50 of the GDPR (international co-operation for the protection of personal data).

(3)   The Commissioner must carry out data protection functions which the Secretary of State directs the Commissioner to carry out for the purpose of enabling Her Majesty's Government in the United Kingdom to give effect to an international obligation of the United Kingdom.

(4)   The Commissioner may provide an authority carrying out data protection functions under the law of a British overseas territory with assistance in carrying out those functions.

(5)   The Secretary of State may direct that assistance under subsection (4) is to be provided on terms, including terms as to payment, specified or approved by the Secretary of State.

(6)   In this section—

     "data protection functions" means functions relating to the protection of individuals with respect to the processing of personal data;

> "mutual assistance in the enforcement of legislation for the protection of personal data" includes assistance in the form of notification, complaint referral, investigative assistance and information exchange;
>
> "third country" means a country or territory that is not a member State.

(7) Section 3(14)(c) does not apply to references to personal data and the processing of personal data in this section.

Codes of practice

121 Data-sharing code

(1) The Commissioner must prepare a code of practice which contains —

    (a) practical guidance in relation to the sharing of personal data in accordance with the requirements of the data protection legislation, and

    (b) such other guidance as the Commissioner considers appropriate to promote good practice in the sharing of personal data.

(2) Where a code under this section is in force, the Commissioner may prepare amendments of the code or a replacement code.

(3) Before preparing a code or amendments under this section, the Commissioner must consult the Secretary of State and such of the following as the Commissioner considers appropriate —

    (a) trade associations;

    (b) data subjects;

    (c) persons who appear to the Commissioner to represent the interests of data subjects.

(4) A code under this section may include transitional provision or savings.

(5) In this section —

> "good practice in the sharing of personal data" means such practice in the sharing of personal data as appears to the Commissioner to be desirable having regard to the interests of data subjects and others, including compliance with the requirements of the data protection legislation;
>
> "the sharing of personal data" means the disclosure of personal data by transmission, dissemination or otherwise making it available;
>
> "trade association" includes a body representing controllers or processors.

122 Direct marketing code

(1) The Commissioner must prepare a code of practice which contains —

    (a) practical guidance in relation to the carrying out of direct marketing in accordance with the requirements of the data protection legislation and the Privacy and Electronic Communications (EC Directive) Regulations 2003 (S.I. 2003/2426), and

    (b) such other guidance as the Commissioner considers appropriate to promote good practice in direct marketing.

(2) Where a code under this section is in force, the Commissioner may prepare amendments of the code or a replacement code.

(3)   Before preparing a code or amendments under this section, the Commissioner must consult the Secretary of State and such of the following as the Commissioner considers appropriate —

    (a)   trade associations;

    (b)   data subjects;

    (c)   persons who appear to the Commissioner to represent the interests of data subjects.

(4)   A code under this section may include transitional provision or savings.

(5)   In this section —

    "direct marketing" means the communication (by whatever means) of advertising or marketing material which is directed to particular individuals;

    "good practice in direct marketing" means such practice in direct marketing as appears to the Commissioner to be desirable having regard to the interests of data subjects and others, including compliance with the requirements mentioned in subsection (1)(a);

    "trade association" includes a body representing controllers or processors.

123   Age-appropriate design code

(1)   The Commissioner must prepare a code of practice which contains such guidance as the Commissioner considers appropriate on standards of age-appropriate design of relevant information society services which are likely to be accessed by children.

(2)   Where a code under this section is in force, the Commissioner may prepare amendments of the code or a replacement code.

(3)   Before preparing a code or amendments under this section, the Commissioner must consult the Secretary of State and such other persons as the Commissioner considers appropriate, including —

    (a)   children,

    (b)   parents,

    (c)   persons who appear to the Commissioner to represent the interests of children,

    (d)   child development experts, and

    (e)   trade associations.

(4)   In preparing a code or amendments under this section, the Commissioner must have regard —

    (a)   to the fact that children have different needs at different ages, and

    (b)   to the United Kingdom's obligations under the United Nations Convention on the Rights of the Child.

(5)   A code under this section may include transitional provision or savings.

(6)   Any transitional provision included in the first code under this section must cease to have effect before the end of the period of 12 months beginning when the code comes into force.

(7)   In this section —

"age-appropriate design" means the design of services so that they are appropriate for use by, and meet the development needs of, children;

"information society services" has the same meaning as in the GDPR, but does not include preventive or counselling services;

"relevant information society services" means information society services which involve the processing of personal data to which the GDPR applies;

"standards of age-appropriate design of relevant information society services" means such standards of age-appropriate design of such services as appear to the Commissioner to be desirable having regard to the best interests of children;

"trade association" includes a body representing controllers or processors;

"the United Nations Convention on the Rights of the Child" means the Convention on the Rights of the Child adopted by the General Assembly of the United Nations on 20 November 1989 (including any Protocols to that Convention which are in force in relation to the United Kingdom), subject to any reservations, objections or interpretative declarations by the United Kingdom for the time being in force.

124 Data protection and journalism code

(1) The Commissioner must prepare a code of practice which contains—

    (a) practical guidance in relation to the processing of personal data for the purposes of journalism in accordance with the requirements of the data protection legislation, and

    (b) such other guidance as the Commissioner considers appropriate to promote good practice in the processing of personal data for the purposes of journalism.

(2) Where a code under this section is in force, the Commissioner may prepare amendments of the code or a replacement code.

(3) Before preparing a code or amendments under this section, the Commissioner must consult such of the following as the Commissioner considers appropriate—

    (a) trade associations;

    (b) data subjects;

    (c) persons who appear to the Commissioner to represent the interests of data subjects.

(4) A code under this section may include transitional provision or savings.

(5) In this section—

"good practice in the processing of personal data for the purposes of journalism" means such practice in the processing of personal data for those purposes as appears to the Commissioner to be desirable having regard to—

    (a) the interests of data subjects and others, including compliance with the requirements of the data protection legislation, and

    (b) the special importance of the public interest in the freedom of expression and information;

"trade association" includes a body representing controllers or processors.

125 Approval of codes prepared under sections 121 to 124

(1) When a code is prepared under section 121, 122, 123 or 124 —
    (a) the Commissioner must submit the final version to the Secretary of State, and
    (b) the Secretary of State must lay the code before Parliament.

(2) In relation to the first code under section 123 —
    (a) the Commissioner must prepare the code as soon as reasonably practicable and must submit it to the Secretary of State before the end of the period of 18 months beginning when this Act is passed, and
    (b) the Secretary of State must lay it before Parliament as soon as reasonably practicable.

(3) If, within the 40-day period, either House of Parliament resolves not to approve a code prepared under section 121, 122, 123 or 124, the Commissioner must not issue the code.

(4) If no such resolution is made within that period —
    (a) the Commissioner must issue the code, and
    (b) the code comes into force at the end of the period of 21 days beginning with the day on which it is issued.

(5) If, as a result of subsection (3), there is no code in force under section 121, 122, 123 or 124, the Commissioner must prepare another version of the code.

(6) Nothing in subsection (3) prevents another version of the code being laid before Parliament.

(7) In this section, "the 40-day period" means —
    (a) if the code is laid before both Houses of Parliament on the same day, the period of 40 days beginning with that day, or
    (b) if the code is laid before the Houses of Parliament on different days, the period of 40 days beginning with the later of those days.

(8) In calculating the 40-day period, no account is to be taken of any period during which Parliament is dissolved or prorogued or during which both Houses of Parliament are adjourned for more than 4 days.

(9) This section, other than subsections (2) and (5), applies in relation to amendments prepared under section 121, 122, 123 or 124 as it applies in relation to codes prepared under those sections.

126 Publication and review of codes issued under section 125(4)

(1) The Commissioner must publish a code issued under section 125(4).

(2) Where an amendment of a code is issued under section 125(4), the Commissioner must publish —
    (a) the amendment, or
    (b) the code as amended by it.

(3) The Commissioner must keep under review each code issued under section 125(4) for the time being in force.

(4) Where the Commissioner becomes aware that the terms of such a code could result in a breach of an international obligation of the United Kingdom, the

Commissioner must exercise the power under section 121(2), 122(2), 123(2) or 124(2) with a view to remedying the situation.

127 Effect of codes issued under section 125(4)

(1) A failure by a person to act in accordance with a provision of a code issued under section 125(4) does not of itself make that person liable to legal proceedings in a court or tribunal.

(2) A code issued under section 125(4), including an amendment or replacement code, is admissible in evidence in legal proceedings.

(3) In any proceedings before a court or tribunal, the court or tribunal must take into account a provision of a code issued under section 125(4) in determining a question arising in the proceedings if—

    (a) the question relates to a time when the provision was in force, and

    (b) the provision appears to the court or tribunal to be relevant to the question.

(4) Where the Commissioner is carrying out a function described in subsection (5), the Commissioner must take into account a provision of a code issued under section 125(4) in determining a question arising in connection with the carrying out of the function if—

    (a) the question relates to a time when the provision was in force, and

    (b) the provision appears to the Commissioner to be relevant to the question.

(5) Those functions are functions under—

    (a) the data protection legislation, or

    (b) the Privacy and Electronic Communications (EC Directive) Regulations 2003 (S.I. 2003/2426).

128 Other codes of practice

(1) The Secretary of State may by regulations require the Commissioner—

    (a) to prepare appropriate codes of practice giving guidance as to good practice in the processing of personal data, and

    (b) to make them available to such persons as the Commissioner considers appropriate.

(2) Before preparing such codes, the Commissioner must consult such of the following as the Commissioner considers appropriate—

    (a) trade associations;

    (b) data subjects;

    (c) persons who appear to the Commissioner to represent the interests of data subjects.

(3) Regulations under this section—

    (a) must describe the personal data or processing to which the code of practice is to relate, and

    (b) may describe the persons or classes of person to whom it is to relate.

(4) Regulations under this section are subject to the negative resolution procedure.

(5) In this section—

"good practice in the processing of personal data" means such practice in the processing of personal data as appears to the Commissioner to be desirable having regard to the interests of data subjects and others, including compliance with the requirements of the data protection legislation;

"trade association" includes a body representing controllers or processors.

Consensual audits

129   Consensual audits

(1)   The Commissioner's functions under Article 58(1) of the GDPR and paragraph 1 of Schedule 13 include power, with the consent of a controller or processor, to carry out an assessment of whether the controller or processor is complying with good practice in the processing of personal data.

(2)   The Commissioner must inform the controller or processor of the results of such an assessment.

(3)   In this section, "good practice in the processing of personal data" has the same meaning as in section 128.

Records of national security certificates

130   Records of national security certificates

(1)   A Minister of the Crown who issues a certificate under section 27, 79 or 111 must send a copy of the certificate to the Commissioner.

(2)   If the Commissioner receives a copy of a certificate under subsection (1), the Commissioner must publish a record of the certificate.

(3)   The record must contain—
    (a)   the name of the Minister who issued the certificate,
    (b)   the date on which the certificate was issued, and
    (c)   subject to subsection (4), the text of the certificate.

(4)   The Commissioner must not publish the text, or a part of the text, of the certificate if—
    (a)   the Minister determines that publishing the text or that part of the text—
        (i)   would be against the interests of national security,
        (ii)   would be contrary to the public interest, or
        (iii)   might jeopardise the safety of any person, and
    (b)   the Minister has notified the Commissioner of that determination.

(5)   The Commissioner must keep the record of the certificate available to the public while the certificate is in force.

(6)   If a Minister of the Crown revokes a certificate issued under section 27, 79 or 111, the Minister must notify the Commissioner.

Information provided to the Commissioner

131 Disclosure of information to the Commissioner

(1) No enactment or rule of law prohibiting or restricting the disclosure of information precludes a person from providing the Commissioner with information necessary for the discharge of the Commissioner's functions.

(2) But this section does not authorise the making of a disclosure which is prohibited by any of Parts 1 to 7 or Chapter 1 of Part 9 of the Investigatory Powers Act 2016.

(3) Until the repeal of Part 1 of the Regulation of Investigatory Powers Act 2000 by paragraphs 45 and 54 of Schedule 10 to the Investigatory Powers Act 2016 is fully in force, subsection (2) has effect as if it included a reference to that Part.

132 Confidentiality of information

(1) A person who is or has been the Commissioner, or a member of the Commissioner's staff or an agent of the Commissioner, must not disclose information which—

    (a) has been obtained by, or provided to, the Commissioner in the course of, or for the purposes of, the discharging of the Commissioner's functions,

    (b) relates to an identified or identifiable individual or business, and

    (c) is not available to the public from other sources at the time of the disclosure and has not previously been available to the public from other sources,

unless the disclosure is made with lawful authority.

(2) For the purposes of subsection (1), a disclosure is made with lawful authority only if and to the extent that—

    (a) the disclosure was made with the consent of the individual or of the person for the time being carrying on the business,

    (b) the information was obtained or provided as described in subsection (1)(a) for the purpose of its being made available to the public (in whatever manner),

    (c) the disclosure was made for the purposes of, and is necessary for, the discharge of one or more of the Commissioner's functions,

    (d) the disclosure was made for the purposes of, and is necessary for, the discharge of an EU obligation,

    (e) the disclosure was made for the purposes of criminal or civil proceedings, however arising, or

    (f) having regard to the rights, freedoms and legitimate interests of any person, the disclosure was necessary in the public interest.

(3) It is an offence for a person knowingly or recklessly to disclose information in contravention of subsection (1).

133 Guidance about privileged communications

(1) The Commissioner must produce and publish guidance about—

    (a) how the Commissioner proposes to secure that privileged communications which the Commissioner obtains or has access to in the course of carrying out the Commissioner's functions are used or disclosed only so far as necessary for carrying out those functions, and

    (b)   how the Commissioner proposes to comply with restrictions and prohibitions on obtaining or having access to privileged communications which are imposed by an enactment.

(2)   The Commissioner —
    (a)   may alter or replace the guidance, and
    (b)   must publish any altered or replacement guidance.

(3)   The Commissioner must consult the Secretary of State before publishing guidance under this section (including altered or replacement guidance).

(4)   The Commissioner must arrange for guidance under this section (including altered or replacement guidance) to be laid before Parliament.

(5)   In this section, "privileged communications" means —
    (a)   communications made —
        (i)   between a professional legal adviser and the adviser's client, and
        (ii)   in connection with the giving of legal advice to the client with respect to legal obligations, liabilities or rights, and
    (b)   communications made —
        (i)   between a professional legal adviser and the adviser's client or between such an adviser or client and another person,
        (ii)   in connection with or in contemplation of legal proceedings, and
        (iii)   for the purposes of such proceedings.

(6)   In subsection (5) —
    (a)   references to the client of a professional legal adviser include references to a person acting on behalf of the client, and
    (b)   references to a communication include —
        (i)   a copy or other record of the communication, and
        (ii)   anything enclosed with or referred to in the communication if made as described in subsection (5)(a)(ii) or in subsection (5)(b)(ii) and (iii).

Fees

134   Fees for services

The Commissioner may require a person other than a data subject or a data protection officer to pay a reasonable fee for a service provided to the person, or at the person's request, which the Commissioner is required or authorised to provide under the data protection legislation.

135   Manifestly unfounded or excessive requests by data subjects etc

(1)   Where a request to the Commissioner from a data subject or a data protection officer is manifestly unfounded or excessive, the Commissioner may —
    (a)   charge a reasonable fee for dealing with the request, or
    (b)   refuse to act on the request.

(2) An example of a request that may be excessive is one that merely repeats the substance of previous requests.

(3) In any proceedings where there is an issue as to whether a request described in subsection (1) is manifestly unfounded or excessive, it is for the Commissioner to show that it is.

(4) Subsections (1) and (3) apply only in cases in which the Commissioner does not already have such powers and obligations under Article 57(4) of the GDPR.

136 Guidance about fees

(1) The Commissioner must produce and publish guidance about the fees the Commissioner proposes to charge in accordance with—
   (a) section 134 or 135, or
   (b) Article 57(4) of the GDPR.

(2) Before publishing the guidance, the Commissioner must consult the Secretary of State.

Charges

137 Charges payable to the Commissioner by controllers

(1) The Secretary of State may by regulations require controllers to pay charges of an amount specified in the regulations to the Commissioner.

(2) Regulations under subsection (1) may require a controller to pay a charge regardless of whether the Commissioner has provided, or proposes to provide, a service to the controller.

(3) Regulations under subsection (1) may—
   (a) make provision about the time or times at which, or period or periods within which, a charge must be paid;
   (b) make provision for cases in which a discounted charge is payable;
   (c) make provision for cases in which no charge is payable;
   (d) make provision for cases in which a charge which has been paid is to be refunded.

(4) In making regulations under subsection (1), the Secretary of State must have regard to the desirability of securing that the charges payable to the Commissioner under such regulations are sufficient to offset—
   (a) expenses incurred by the Commissioner in discharging the Commissioner's functions—
      (i) under the data protection legislation,
      (ii) under the Data Protection Act 1998,
      (iii) under or by virtue of sections 108 and 109 of the Digital Economy Act 2017, and
      (iv) under or by virtue of the Privacy and Electronic Communications (EC Directive) Regulations 2003 (S.I. 2003/2426),
   (b) any expenses of the Secretary of State in respect of the Commissioner so far as attributable to those functions,

    (c)   to the extent that the Secretary of State considers appropriate, any deficit previously incurred (whether before or after the passing of this Act) in respect of the expenses mentioned in paragraph (a), and

    (d)   to the extent that the Secretary of State considers appropriate, expenses incurred by the Secretary of State in respect of the inclusion of any officers or staff of the Commissioner in any scheme under section 1 of the Superannuation Act 1972 or section 1 of the Public Service Pensions Act 2013.

  (5)   The Secretary of State may from time to time require the Commissioner to provide information about the expenses referred to in subsection (4)(a).

  (6)   The Secretary of State may by regulations make provision —

    (a)   requiring a controller to provide information to the Commissioner, or

    (b)   enabling the Commissioner to require a controller to provide information to the Commissioner,

for either or both of the purposes mentioned in subsection (7).

  (7)   Those purposes are —

    (a)   determining whether a charge is payable by the controller under regulations under subsection (1);

    (b)   determining the amount of a charge payable by the controller.

  (8)   The provision that may be made under subsection (6)(a) includes provision requiring a controller to notify the Commissioner of a change in the controller's circumstances of a kind specified in the regulations.

138   Regulations under section 137: supplementary

  (1)   Before making regulations under section 137(1) or (6), the Secretary of State must consult such representatives of persons likely to be affected by the regulations as the Secretary of State thinks appropriate (and see also section 182).

  (2)   The Commissioner —

    (a)   must keep under review the working of regulations under section 137(1) or (6), and

    (b)   may from time to time submit proposals to the Secretary of State for amendments to be made to the regulations.

  (3)   The Secretary of State must review the working of regulations under section 137(1) or (6) —

    (a)   at the end of the period of 5 years beginning with the making of the first set of regulations under section 108 of the Digital Economy Act 2017, and

    (b)   at the end of each subsequent 5 year period.

  (4)   Regulations under section 137(1) are subject to the negative resolution procedure if —

    (a)   they only make provision increasing a charge for which provision is made by previous regulations under section 137(1) or section 108(1) of the Digital Economy Act 2017, and

    (b)   they do so to take account of an increase in the retail prices index since the previous regulations were made.

(5) Subject to subsection (4), regulations under section 137(1) or (6) are subject to the affirmative resolution procedure.

(6) In subsection (4), "the retail prices index" means —

    (a) the general index of retail prices (for all items) published by the Statistics Board, or

    (b) where that index is not published for a month, any substitute index or figures published by the Board.

(7) Regulations under section 137(1) or (6) may not apply to —

    (a) Her Majesty in her private capacity,

    (b) Her Majesty in right of the Duchy of Lancaster, or

    (c) the Duke of Cornwall.

Reports etc

139 Reporting to Parliament

(1) The Commissioner must —

    (a) produce a general report on the carrying out of the Commissioner's functions annually,

    (b) arrange for it to be laid before Parliament, and

    (c) publish it.

(2) The report must include the annual report required under Article 59 of the GDPR.

(3) The Commissioner may produce other reports relating to the carrying out of the Commissioner's functions and arrange for them to be laid before Parliament.

140 Publication by the Commissioner

A duty under this Act for the Commissioner to publish a document is a duty for the Commissioner to publish it, or to arrange for it to be published, in such form and manner as the Commissioner considers appropriate.

141 Notices from the Commissioner

(1) This section applies in relation to a notice authorised or required by this Act to be given to a person by the Commissioner.

(2) The notice may be given to an individual —

    (a) by delivering it to the individual,

    (b) by sending it to the individual by post addressed to the individual at his or her usual or last-known place of residence or business, or

    (c) by leaving it for the individual at that place.

(3) The notice may be given to a body corporate or unincorporate —

    (a) by sending it by post to the proper officer of the body at its principal office, or

    (b) by addressing it to the proper officer of the body and leaving it at that office.

(4)   The notice may be given to a partnership in Scotland —
    (a)   by sending it by post to the principal office of the partnership, or
    (b)   by addressing it to that partnership and leaving it at that office.

(5)   The notice may be given to the person by other means, including by electronic means, with the person's consent.

(6)   In this section —
    "principal office", in relation to a registered company, means its registered office;
    "proper officer", in relation to any body, means the secretary or other executive officer charged with the conduct of its general affairs;
    "registered company" means a company registered under the enactments relating to companies for the time being in force in the United Kingdom.

(7)   This section is without prejudice to any other lawful method of giving a notice.

PART 6

ENFORCEMENT

Information notices

142   Information notices

(1)   The Commissioner may, by written notice (an "information notice") —
    (a)   require a controller or processor to provide the Commissioner with information that the Commissioner reasonably requires for the purposes of carrying out the Commissioner's functions under the data protection legislation, or
    (b)   require any person to provide the Commissioner with information that the Commissioner reasonably requires for the purposes of —
        (i)   investigating a suspected failure of a type described in section 149(2) or a suspected offence under this Act, or
        (ii)   determining whether the processing of personal data is carried out by an individual in the course of a purely personal or household activity.

(2)   An information notice must state —
    (a)   whether it is given under subsection (1)(a), (b)(i) or (b)(ii), and
    (b)   why the Commissioner requires the information.

(3)   An information notice —
    (a)   may specify or describe particular information or a category of information;
    (b)   may specify the form in which the information must be provided;
    (c)   may specify the time at which, or the period within which, the information must be provided;
    (d)   may specify the place where the information must be provided;
(but see the restrictions in subsections (5) to (7)).

(4)   An information notice must provide information about —
    (a)   the consequences of failure to comply with it, and

(b)   the rights under sections 162 and 164 (appeals etc).

(5)   An information notice may not require a person to provide information before the end of the period within which an appeal can be brought against the notice.

(6)   If an appeal is brought against an information notice, the information need not be provided pending the determination or withdrawal of the appeal.

(7)   If an information notice —

    (a)   states that, in the Commissioner's opinion, the information is required urgently, and

    (b)   gives the Commissioner's reasons for reaching that opinion,

subsections (5) and (6) do not apply but the notice must not require the information to be provided before the end of the period of 24 hours beginning when the notice is given.

(8)   The Commissioner may cancel an information notice by written notice to the person to whom it was given.

(9)   In subsection (1), in relation to a person who is a controller or processor for the purposes of the GDPR, the reference to a controller or processor includes a representative of a controller or processor designated under Article 27 of the GDPR (representatives of controllers or processors not established in the European Union).

(10)   Section 3(14)(c) does not apply to the reference to the processing of personal data in subsection (1)(b).

143   Information notices: restrictions

(1)   The Commissioner may not give an information notice with respect to the processing of personal data for the special purposes unless —

    (a)   a determination under section 174 with respect to the data or the processing has taken effect, or

    (b)   the Commissioner —

        (i)   has reasonable grounds for suspecting that such a determination could be made, and

        (ii)   the information is required for the purposes of making such a determination.

(2)   An information notice does not require a person to give the Commissioner information to the extent that requiring the person to do so would involve an infringement of the privileges of either House of Parliament.

(3)   An information notice does not require a person to give the Commissioner information in respect of a communication which is made —

    (a)   between a professional legal adviser and the adviser's client, and

    (b)   in connection with the giving of legal advice to the client with respect to obligations, liabilities or rights under the data protection legislation.

(4)   An information notice does not require a person to give the Commissioner information in respect of a communication which is made —

    (a)   between a professional legal adviser and the adviser's client or between such an adviser or client and another person,

    (b)   in connection with or in contemplation of proceedings under or arising out of the data protection legislation, and

    (c)   for the purposes of such proceedings.

(5)   In subsections (3) and (4), references to the client of a professional legal adviser include references to a person acting on behalf of the client.

(6)   An information notice does not require a person to provide the Commissioner with information if doing so would, by revealing evidence of the commission of an offence expose the person to proceedings for that offence.

(7)   The reference to an offence in subsection (6) does not include an offence under —

    (a)   this Act;

    (b)   section 5 of the Perjury Act 1911 (false statements made otherwise than on oath);

    (c)   section 44(2) of the Criminal Law (Consolidation) (Scotland) Act 1995 (false statements made otherwise than on oath);

    (d)   Article 10 of the Perjury (Northern Ireland) Order 1979 (S.I. 1979/1714 (N.I. 19)) (false statutory declarations and other false unsworn statements).

(8)   An oral or written statement provided by a person in response to an information notice may not be used in evidence against that person on a prosecution for an offence under this Act (other than an offence under section 144) unless in the proceedings —

    (a)   in giving evidence the person provides information inconsistent with the statement, and

    (b)   evidence relating to the statement is adduced, or a question relating to it is asked, by that person or on that person's behalf.

(9)   In subsection (6), in relation to an information notice given to a representative of a controller or processor designated under Article 27 of the GDPR, the reference to the person providing the information being exposed to proceedings for an offence includes a reference to the controller or processor being exposed to such proceedings.

144   False statements made in response to information notices

It is an offence for a person, in response to an information notice —

    (a)   to make a statement which the person knows to be false in a material respect, or

    (b)   recklessly to make a statement which is false in a material respect.

145   Information orders

(1)   This section applies if, on an application by the Commissioner, a court is satisfied that a person has failed to comply with a requirement of an information notice.

(2)   The court may make an order requiring the person to provide to the Commissioner some or all of the following —

    (a)   information referred to in the information notice;

    (b)   other information which the court is satisfied the Commissioner requires, having regard to the statement included in the notice in accordance with section 142(2)(b).

    (3)   The order—

        (a)   may specify the form in which the information must be provided,

        (b)   must specify the time at which, or the period within which, the information must be provided, and

        (c)   may specify the place where the information must be provided.

Assessment notices

146   Assessment notices

    (1)   The Commissioner may by written notice (an "assessment notice") require a controller or processor to permit the Commissioner to carry out an assessment of whether the controller or processor has complied or is complying with the data protection legislation.

    (2)   An assessment notice may require the controller or processor to do any of the following—

        (a)   permit the Commissioner to enter specified premises;

        (b)   direct the Commissioner to documents on the premises that are of a specified description;

        (c)   assist the Commissioner to view information of a specified description that is capable of being viewed using equipment on the premises;

        (d)   comply with a request from the Commissioner for a copy (in such form as may be requested) of—

            (i)   the documents to which the Commissioner is directed;

            (ii)   the information which the Commissioner is assisted to view;

        (e)   direct the Commissioner to equipment or other material on the premises which is of a specified description;

        (f)   permit the Commissioner to inspect or examine the documents, information, equipment or material to which the Commissioner is directed or which the Commissioner is assisted to view;

        (g)   provide the Commissioner with an explanation of such documents, information, equipment or material;

        (h)   permit the Commissioner to observe the processing of personal data that takes place on the premises;

        (i)   make available for interview by the Commissioner a specified number of people of a specified description who process personal data on behalf of the controller, not exceeding the number who are willing to be interviewed.

    (3)   In subsection (2), references to the Commissioner include references to the Commissioner's officers and staff.

    (4)   An assessment notice must, in relation to each requirement imposed by the notice, specify the time or times at which, or period or periods within which, the requirement must be complied with (but see the restrictions in subsections (6) to (9)).

    (5)   An assessment notice must provide information about—

        (a)   the consequences of failure to comply with it, and

        (b)   the rights under sections 162 and 164 (appeals etc).

(6)   An assessment notice may not require a person to do anything before the end of the period within which an appeal can be brought against the notice.

(7)   If an appeal is brought against an assessment notice, the controller or processor need not comply with a requirement in the notice pending the determination or withdrawal of the appeal.

(8)   If an assessment notice —
   (a)   states that, in the Commissioner's opinion, it is necessary for the controller or processor to comply with a requirement in the notice urgently,
   (b)   gives the Commissioner's reasons for reaching that opinion, and
   (c)   does not meet the conditions in subsection (9)(a) to (d),
   subsections (6) and (7) do not apply but the notice must not require the controller or processor to comply with the requirement before the end of the period of 7 days beginning when the notice is given.

(9)   If an assessment notice —
   (a)   states that, in the Commissioner's opinion, there are reasonable grounds for suspecting that a controller or processor has failed or is failing as described in section 149(2) or that an offence under this Act has been or is being committed,
   (b)   indicates the nature of the suspected failure or offence,
   (c)   does not specify domestic premises,
   (d)   states that, in the Commissioner's opinion, it is necessary for the controller or processor to comply with a requirement in the notice in less than 7 days, and
   (e)   gives the Commissioner's reasons for reaching that opinion,
   subsections (6) and (7) do not apply.

(10)   The Commissioner may cancel an assessment notice by written notice to the controller or processor to whom it was given.

(11)   Where the Commissioner gives an assessment notice to a processor, the Commissioner must, so far as reasonably practicable, give a copy of the notice to each controller for whom the processor processes personal data.

(12)   In this section —
   "domestic premises" means premises, or a part of premises, used as a dwelling;
   "specified" means specified in an assessment notice.

147   Assessment notices: restrictions

(1)   An assessment notice does not require a person to do something to the extent that requiring the person to do it would involve an infringement of the privileges of either House of Parliament.

(2)   An assessment notice does not have effect so far as compliance would result in the disclosure of a communication which is made —
   (a)   between a professional legal adviser and the adviser's client, and
   (b)   in connection with the giving of legal advice to the client with respect to obligations, liabilities or rights under the data protection legislation.

(3) An assessment notice does not have effect so far as compliance would result in the disclosure of a communication which is made —

    (a) between a professional legal adviser and the adviser's client or between such an adviser or client and another person,

    (b) in connection with or in contemplation of proceedings under or arising out of the data protection legislation, and

    (c) for the purposes of such proceedings.

(4) In subsections (2) and (3) —

    (a) references to the client of a professional legal adviser include references to a person acting on behalf of such a client, and

    (b) references to a communication include —

        (i) a copy or other record of the communication, and

        (ii) anything enclosed with or referred to in the communication if made as described in subsection (2)(b) or in subsection (3)(b) and (c).

(5) The Commissioner may not give a controller or processor an assessment notice with respect to the processing of personal data for the special purposes.

(6) The Commissioner may not give an assessment notice to —

    (a) a body specified in section 23(3) of the Freedom of Information Act 2000 (bodies dealing with security matters), or

    (b) the Office for Standards in Education, Children's Services and Skills in so far as it is a controller or processor in respect of information processed for the purposes of functions exercisable by Her Majesty's Chief Inspector of Education, Children's Services and Skills by virtue of section 5(1)(a) of the Care Standards Act 2000.

Information notices and assessment notices: destruction of documents etc

148 Destroying or falsifying information and documents etc

(1) This section applies where a person —

    (a) has been given an information notice requiring the person to provide the Commissioner with information, or

    (b) has been given an assessment notice requiring the person to direct the Commissioner to a document, equipment or other material or to assist the Commissioner to view information.

(2) It is an offence for the person —

    (a) to destroy or otherwise dispose of, conceal, block or (where relevant) falsify all or part of the information, document, equipment or material, or

    (b) to cause or permit the destruction, disposal, concealment, blocking or (where relevant) falsification of all or part of the information, document, equipment or material,

with the intention of preventing the Commissioner from viewing, or being provided with or directed to, all or part of the information, document, equipment or material.

(3) It is a defence for a person charged with an offence under subsection (2) to prove that the destruction, disposal, concealment, blocking or falsification would have occurred in the absence of the person being given the notice.

Enforcement notices

149 Enforcement notices

(1) Where the Commissioner is satisfied that a person has failed, or is failing, as described in subsection (2), (3), (4) or (5), the Commissioner may give the person a written notice (an "enforcement notice") which requires the person—

    (a) to take steps specified in the notice, or

    (b) to refrain from taking steps specified in the notice,

or both (and see also sections 150 and 151).

(2) The first type of failure is where a controller or processor has failed, or is failing, to comply with any of the following—

    (a) a provision of Chapter II of the GDPR or Chapter 2 of Part 3 or Chapter 2 of Part 4 of this Act (principles of processing);

    (b) a provision of Articles 12 to 22 of the GDPR or Part 3 or 4 of this Act conferring rights on a data subject;

    (c) a provision of Articles 25 to 39 of the GDPR or section 64 or 65 of this Act (obligations of controllers and processors);

    (d) a requirement to communicate a personal data breach to the Commissioner or a data subject under section 67, 68 or 108 of this Act;

    (e) the principles for transfers of personal data to third countries, non-Convention countries and international organisations in Articles 44 to 49 of the GDPR or in sections 73 to 78 or 109 of this Act.

(3) The second type of failure is where a monitoring body has failed, or is failing, to comply with an obligation under Article 41 of the GDPR (monitoring of approved codes of conduct).

(4) The third type of failure is where a person who is a certification provider—

    (a) does not meet the requirements for accreditation,

    (b) has failed, or is failing, to comply with an obligation under Article 42 or 43 of the GDPR (certification of controllers and processors), or

    (c) has failed, or is failing, to comply with any other provision of the GDPR (whether in the person's capacity as a certification provider or otherwise).

(5) The fourth type of failure is where a controller has failed, or is failing, to comply with regulations under section 137.

(6) An enforcement notice given in reliance on subsection (2), (3) or (5) may only impose requirements which the Commissioner considers appropriate for the purpose of remedying the failure.

(7) An enforcement notice given in reliance on subsection (4) may only impose requirements which the Commissioner considers appropriate having regard to the failure (whether or not for the purpose of remedying the failure).

(8) The Secretary of State may by regulations confer power on the Commissioner to give an enforcement notice in respect of other failures to comply with the data protection legislation.

(9) Regulations under this section—

    (a) may make provision about the giving of an enforcement notice in respect of the failure, including by amending this section and sections 150 to 152,

    (b)   may make provision about the giving of an information notice, an assessment notice or a penalty notice, or about powers of entry and inspection, in connection with the failure, including by amending sections 142, 143, 146, 147 and 155 to 157 and Schedules 15 and 16, and

    (c)   are subject to the affirmative resolution procedure.

150   Enforcement notices: supplementary

(1)   An enforcement notice must—

    (a)   state what the person has failed or is failing to do, and

    (b)   give the Commissioner's reasons for reaching that opinion.

(2)   In deciding whether to give an enforcement notice in reliance on section 149(2), the Commissioner must consider whether the failure has caused or is likely to cause any person damage or distress.

(3)   In relation to an enforcement notice given in reliance on section 149(2), the Commissioner's power under section 149(1)(b) to require a person to refrain from taking specified steps includes power—

    (a)   to impose a ban relating to all processing of personal data, or

    (b)   to impose a ban relating only to a specified description of processing of personal data, including by specifying one or more of the following—

        (i)   a description of personal data;

        (ii)   the purpose or manner of the processing;

        (iii)   the time when the processing takes place.

(4)   An enforcement notice may specify the time or times at which, or period or periods within which, a requirement imposed by the notice must be complied with (but see the restrictions in subsections (6) to (8)).

(5)   An enforcement notice must provide information about—

    (a)   the consequences of failure to comply with it, and

    (b)   the rights under sections 162 and 164 (appeals etc).

(6)   An enforcement notice must not specify a time for compliance with a requirement in the notice which falls before the end of the period within which an appeal can be brought against the notice.

(7)   If an appeal is brought against an enforcement notice, a requirement in the notice need not be complied with pending the determination or withdrawal of the appeal.

(8)   If an enforcement notice—

    (a)   states that, in the Commissioner's opinion, it is necessary for a requirement to be complied with urgently, and

    (b)   gives the Commissioner's reasons for reaching that opinion,

subsections (6) and (7) do not apply but the notice must not require the requirement to be complied with before the end of the period of 24 hours beginning when the notice is given.

(9)   In this section, "specified" means specified in an enforcement notice.

151   Enforcement notices: rectification and erasure of personal data etc

(1)   Subsections (2) and (3) apply where an enforcement notice is given in respect of a failure by a controller or processor—

    (a)   to comply with a data protection principle relating to accuracy, or

    (b)   to comply with a data subject's request to exercise rights under Article 16, 17 or 18 of the GDPR (right to rectification, erasure or restriction on processing) or section 46, 47 or 100 of this Act.

(2)   If the enforcement notice requires the controller or processor to rectify or erase inaccurate personal data, it may also require the controller or processor to rectify or erase any other data which—

    (a)   is held by the controller or processor, and

    (b)   contains an expression of opinion which appears to the Commissioner to be based on the inaccurate personal data.

(3)   Where a controller or processor has accurately recorded personal data provided by the data subject or a third party but the data is inaccurate, the enforcement notice may require the controller or processor—

    (a)   to take steps specified in the notice to ensure the accuracy of the data,

    (b)   if relevant, to secure that the data indicates the data subject's view that the data is inaccurate, and

    (c)   to supplement the data with a statement of the true facts relating to the matters dealt with by the data that is approved by the Commissioner,

(as well as imposing requirements under subsection (2)).

(4)   When deciding what steps it is reasonable to specify under subsection (3)(a), the Commissioner must have regard to the purpose for which the data was obtained and further processed.

(5)   Subsections (6) and (7) apply where—

    (a)   an enforcement notice requires a controller or processor to rectify or erase personal data, or

    (b)   the Commissioner is satisfied that the processing of personal data which has been rectified or erased by the controller or processor involved a failure described in subsection (1).

(6)   An enforcement notice may, if reasonably practicable, require the controller or processor to notify third parties to whom the data has been disclosed of the rectification or erasure.

(7)   In determining whether it is reasonably practicable to require such notification, the Commissioner must have regard, in particular, to the number of people who would have to be notified.

(8)   In this section, "data protection principle relating to accuracy" means the principle in—

    (a)   Article 5(1)(d) of the GDPR,

    (b)   section 38(1) of this Act, or

    (c)   section 89 of this Act.

152 Enforcement notices: restrictions

(1) The Commissioner may not give a controller or processor an enforcement notice in reliance on section 149(2) with respect to the processing of personal data for the special purposes unless —

    (a) a determination under section 174 with respect to the data or the processing has taken effect, and

    (b) a court has granted leave for the notice to be given.

(2) A court must not grant leave for the purposes of subsection (1)(b) unless it is satisfied that —

    (a) the Commissioner has reason to suspect a failure described in section 149(2) which is of substantial public importance, and

    (b) the controller or processor has been given notice of the application for leave in accordance with rules of court or the case is urgent.

(3) An enforcement notice does not require a person to do something to the extent that requiring the person to do it would involve an infringement of the privileges of either House of Parliament.

(4) In the case of a joint controller in respect of the processing of personal data to which Part 3 or 4 applies whose responsibilities for compliance with that Part are determined in an arrangement under section 58 or 104, the Commissioner may only give the controller an enforcement notice in reliance on section 149(2) if the controller is responsible for compliance with the provision, requirement or principle in question.

153 Enforcement notices: cancellation and variation

(1) The Commissioner may cancel or vary an enforcement notice by giving written notice to the person to whom it was given.

(2) A person to whom an enforcement notice is given may apply in writing to the Commissioner for the cancellation or variation of the notice.

(3) An application under subsection (2) may be made only —

    (a) after the end of the period within which an appeal can be brought against the notice, and

    (b) on the ground that, by reason of a change of circumstances, one or more of the provisions of that notice need not be complied with in order to remedy the failure identified in the notice.

Powers of entry and inspection

154 Powers of entry and inspection

Schedule 15 makes provision about powers of entry and inspection.

Penalties

155 Penalty notices

(1) If the Commissioner is satisfied that a person —

    (a) has failed or is failing as described in section 149(2), (3), (4) or (5), or

      (b)   has failed to comply with an information notice, an assessment notice or an enforcement notice,

the Commissioner may, by written notice (a "penalty notice"), require the person to pay to the Commissioner an amount in sterling specified in the notice.

(2)   Subject to subsection (4), when deciding whether to give a penalty notice to a person and determining the amount of the penalty, the Commissioner must have regard to the following, so far as relevant —

      (a)   to the extent that the notice concerns a matter to which the GDPR applies, the matters listed in Article 83(1) and (2) of the GDPR;

      (b)   to the extent that the notice concerns another matter, the matters listed in subsection (3).

(3)   Those matters are —

      (a)   the nature, gravity and duration of the failure;

      (b)   the intentional or negligent character of the failure;

      (c)   any action taken by the controller or processor to mitigate the damage or distress suffered by data subjects;

      (d)   the degree of responsibility of the controller or processor, taking into account technical and organisational measures implemented by the controller or processor in accordance with section 57, 66, 103 or 107;

      (e)   any relevant previous failures by the controller or processor;

      (f)   the degree of co-operation with the Commissioner, in order to remedy the failure and mitigate the possible adverse effects of the failure;

      (g)   the categories of personal data affected by the failure;

      (h)   the manner in which the infringement became known to the Commissioner, including whether, and if so to what extent, the controller or processor notified the Commissioner of the failure;

      (i)   the extent to which the controller or processor has complied with previous enforcement notices or penalty notices;

      (j)   adherence to approved codes of conduct or certification mechanisms;

      (k)   any other aggravating or mitigating factor applicable to the case, including financial benefits gained, or losses avoided, as a result of the failure (whether directly or indirectly);

      (l)   whether the penalty would be effective, proportionate and dissuasive.

(4)   Subsections (2) and (3) do not apply in the case of a decision or determination relating to a failure described in section 149(5).

(5)   Schedule 16 makes further provision about penalty notices, including provision requiring the Commissioner to give a notice of intent to impose a penalty and provision about payment, variation, cancellation and enforcement.

(6)   The Secretary of State may by regulations —

      (a)   confer power on the Commissioner to give a penalty notice in respect of other failures to comply with the data protection legislation, and

      (b)   provide for the maximum penalty that may be imposed in relation to such failures to be either the standard maximum amount or the higher maximum amount.

(7)   Regulations under this section —

    (a)   may make provision about the giving of penalty notices in respect of the failure,

    (b)   may amend this section and sections 156 to 158, and

    (c)   are subject to the affirmative resolution procedure.

(8)   In this section, "higher maximum amount" and "standard maximum amount" have the same meaning as in section 157.

156 Penalty notices: restrictions

(1)   The Commissioner may not give a controller or processor a penalty notice in reliance on section 149(2) with respect to the processing of personal data for the special purposes unless —

    (a)   a determination under section 174 with respect to the data or the processing has taken effect, and

    (b)   a court has granted leave for the notice to be given.

(2)   A court must not grant leave for the purposes of subsection (1)(b) unless it is satisfied that —

    (a)   the Commissioner has reason to suspect a failure described in section 149(2) which is of substantial public importance, and

    (b)   the controller or processor has been given notice of the application for leave in accordance with rules of court or the case is urgent.

(3)   The Commissioner may not give a controller or processor a penalty notice with respect to the processing of personal data where the purposes and manner of the processing are determined by or on behalf of either House of Parliament.

(4)   The Commissioner may not give a penalty notice to —

    (a)   the Crown Estate Commissioners, or

    (b)   a person who is a controller by virtue of section 209(4) (controller for the Royal Household etc).

(5)   In the case of a joint controller in respect of the processing of personal data to which Part 3 or 4 applies whose responsibilities for compliance with that Part are determined in an arrangement under section 58 or 104, the Commissioner may only give the controller a penalty notice in reliance on section 149(2) if the controller is responsible for compliance with the provision, requirement or principle in question.

157 Maximum amount of penalty

(1)   In relation to an infringement of a provision of the GDPR, the maximum amount of the penalty that may be imposed by a penalty notice is —

    (a)   the amount specified in Article 83 of the GDPR, or

    (b)   if an amount is not specified there, the standard maximum amount.

(2)   In relation to an infringement of a provision of Part 3 of this Act, the maximum amount of the penalty that may be imposed by a penalty notice is —

    (a)   in relation to a failure to comply with section 35, 36, 37, 38(1), 39(1), 40, 44, 45, 46, 47, 48, 49, 52, 53, 73, 74, 75, 76, 77 or 78, the higher maximum amount, and

    (b)   otherwise, the standard maximum amount.

(3)   In relation to an infringement of a provision of Part 4 of this Act, the maximum amount of the penalty that may be imposed by a penalty notice is—

    (a)   in relation to a failure to comply with section 86, 87, 88, 89, 90, 91, 93, 94, 100 or 109, the higher maximum amount, and

    (b)   otherwise, the standard maximum amount.

(4)   In relation to a failure to comply with an information notice, an assessment notice or an enforcement notice, the maximum amount of the penalty that may be imposed by a penalty notice is the higher maximum amount.

(5)   The "higher maximum amount" is—

    (a)   in the case of an undertaking, 20 million Euros or 4% of the undertaking's total annual worldwide turnover in the preceding financial year, whichever is higher, or

    (b)   in any other case, 20 million Euros.

(6)   The "standard maximum amount" is—

    (a)   in the case of an undertaking, 10 million Euros or 2% of the undertaking's total annual worldwide turnover in the preceding financial year, whichever is higher, or

    (b)   in any other case, 10 million Euros.

(7)   The maximum amount of a penalty in sterling must be determined by applying the spot rate of exchange set by the Bank of England on the day on which the penalty notice is given.

158   Fixed penalties for non-compliance with charges regulations

(1)   The Commissioner must produce and publish a document specifying the amount of the penalty for a failure to comply with regulations made under section 137.

(2)   The Commissioner may specify different amounts for different types of failure.

(3)   The maximum amount that may be specified is 150% of the highest charge payable by a controller in respect of a financial year in accordance with the regulations, disregarding any discount available under the regulations.

(4)   The Commissioner—

    (a)   may alter or replace the document, and

    (b)   must publish any altered or replacement document.

(5)   Before publishing a document under this section (including any altered or replacement document), the Commissioner must consult—

    (a)   the Secretary of State, and

    (b)   such other persons as the Commissioner considers appropriate.

(6)   The Commissioner must arrange for a document published under this section (including any altered or replacement document) to be laid before Parliament.

159   Amount of penalties: supplementary

(1)   For the purposes of Article 83 of the GDPR and section 157, the Secretary of State may by regulations—

    (a)   provide that a person of a description specified in the regulations is or is not an undertaking, and

    (b)   make provision about how an undertaking's turnover is to be determined.

(2)   For the purposes of Article 83 of the GDPR, section 157 and section 158, the Secretary of State may by regulations provide that a period is or is not a financial year.

(3)   Regulations under this section are subject to the affirmative resolution procedure.

Guidance

160   Guidance about regulatory action

(1)   The Commissioner must produce and publish guidance about how the Commissioner proposes to exercise the Commissioner's functions in connection with—
    (a)   information notices,
    (b)   assessment notices,
    (c)   enforcement notices, and
    (d)   penalty notices.

(2)   The Commissioner may produce and publish guidance about how the Commissioner proposes to exercise the Commissioner's other functions under this Part.

(3)   In relation to information notices, the guidance must include—
    (a)   provision specifying factors to be considered in determining the time at which, or the period within which, information is to be required to be provided;
    (b)   provision about the circumstances in which the Commissioner would consider it appropriate to give an information notice to a person in reliance on section 142(7) (urgent cases);
    (c)   provision about how the Commissioner will determine how to proceed if a person does not comply with an information notice.

(4)   In relation to assessment notices, the guidance must include—
    (a)   provision specifying factors to be considered in determining whether to give an assessment notice to a person;
    (b)   provision about the circumstances in which the Commissioner would consider it appropriate to give an assessment notice in reliance on section 146(8) or (9) (urgent cases);
    (c)   provision specifying descriptions of documents or information that—
       (i)   are not to be examined or inspected in accordance with an assessment notice, or
       (ii)   are to be so examined or inspected only by a person of a description specified in the guidance;
    (d)   provision about the nature of inspections and examinations carried out in accordance with an assessment notice;
    (e)   provision about the nature of interviews carried out in accordance with an assessment notice;
    (f)   provision about the preparation, issuing and publication by the Commissioner of assessment reports in respect of controllers and processors that have been given assessment notices;

     (g)   provision about how the Commissioner will determine how to proceed if a person does not comply with an assessment notice.

(5)   The guidance produced in accordance with subsection (4)(c) must include provisions that relate to—

     (a)   documents and information concerning an individual's physical or mental health;

     (b)   documents and information concerning the provision of social care for an individual.

(6)   In relation to enforcement notices, the guidance must include—

     (a)   provision specifying factors to be considered in determining whether to give an enforcement notice to a person;

     (b)   provision about the circumstances in which the Commissioner would consider it appropriate to give an enforcement notice to a person in reliance on section 150(8) (urgent cases);

     (c)   provision about how the Commissioner will determine how to proceed if a person does not comply with an enforcement notice.

(7)   In relation to penalty notices, the guidance must include—

     (a)   provision about the circumstances in which the Commissioner would consider it appropriate to issue a penalty notice;

     (b)   provision about the circumstances in which the Commissioner would consider it appropriate to allow a person to make oral representations about the Commissioner's intention to give the person a penalty notice;

     (c)   provision explaining how the Commissioner will determine the amount of penalties;

     (d)   provision about how the Commissioner will determine how to proceed if a person does not comply with a penalty notice.

(8)   The Commissioner—

     (a)   may alter or replace guidance produced under this section, and

     (b)   must publish any altered or replacement guidance.

(9)   Before producing guidance under this section (including any altered or replacement guidance), the Commissioner must consult—

     (a)   the Secretary of State, and

     (b)   such other persons as the Commissioner considers appropriate.

(10)   Section 161 applies in relation to the first guidance under subsection (1).

(11)   The Commissioner must arrange for other guidance under this section (including any altered or replacement guidance) to be laid before Parliament.

(12)   In this section, "social care" has the same meaning as in Part 1 of the Health and Social Care Act 2008 (see section 9(3) of that Act).

161   Approval of first guidance about regulatory action

(1)   When the first guidance is produced under section 160(1)—

     (a)   the Commissioner must submit the final version to the Secretary of State, and

     (b)   the Secretary of State must lay the guidance before Parliament.

(2) If, within the 40-day period, either House of Parliament resolves not to approve the guidance—

    (a) the Commissioner must not issue the guidance, and

    (b) the Commissioner must produce another version of the guidance (and this section applies to that version).

(3) If, within the 40-day period, no such resolution is made—

    (a) the Commissioner must issue the guidance, and

    (b) the guidance comes into force at the end of the period of 21 days beginning with the day on which it is issued.

(4) Nothing in subsection (2)(a) prevents another version of the guidance being laid before Parliament.

(5) In this section, "the 40-day period" means—

    (a) if the guidance is laid before both Houses of Parliament on the same day, the period of 40 days beginning with that day, or

    (b) if the guidance is laid before the Houses of Parliament on different days, the period of 40 days beginning with the later of those days.

(6) In calculating the 40-day period, no account is to be taken of any period during which Parliament is dissolved or prorogued or during which both Houses of Parliament are adjourned for more than 4 days.

Appeals etc

162 Rights of appeal

(1) A person who is given any of the following notices may appeal to the Tribunal—

    (a) an information notice;

    (b) an assessment notice;

    (c) an enforcement notice;

    (d) a penalty notice;

    (e) a penalty variation notice.

(2) A person who is given an enforcement notice may appeal to the Tribunal against the refusal of an application under section 153 for the cancellation or variation of the notice.

(3) A person who is given a penalty notice or a penalty variation notice may appeal to the Tribunal against the amount of the penalty specified in the notice, whether or not the person appeals against the notice.

(4) Where a determination is made under section 174 in respect of the processing of personal data, the controller or processor may appeal to the Tribunal against the determination.

163 Determination of appeals

(1) Subsections (2) to (4) apply where a person appeals to the Tribunal under section 162(1) or (3).

(2) The Tribunal may review any determination of fact on which the notice or decision against which the appeal is brought was based.

(3)   If the Tribunal considers—
       (a)   that the notice or decision against which the appeal is brought is not in accordance with the law, or
       (b)   to the extent that the notice or decision involved an exercise of discretion by the Commissioner, that the Commissioner ought to have exercised the discretion differently,
       the Tribunal must allow the appeal or substitute another notice or decision which the Commissioner could have given or made.

(4)   Otherwise, the Tribunal must dismiss the appeal.

(5)   On an appeal under section 162(2), if the Tribunal considers that the enforcement notice ought to be cancelled or varied by reason of a change in circumstances, the Tribunal must cancel or vary the notice.

(6)   On an appeal under section 162(4), the Tribunal may cancel the Commissioner's determination.

164   Applications in respect of urgent notices

(1)   This section applies where an information notice, an assessment notice or an enforcement notice given to a person contains an urgency statement.

(2)   The person may apply to the court for either or both of the following—
       (a)   the disapplication of the urgency statement in relation to some or all of the requirements of the notice;
       (b)   a change to the time at which, or the period within which, a requirement of the notice must be complied with.

(3)   On an application under subsection (2), the court may do any of the following—
       (a)   direct that the notice is to have effect as if it did not contain the urgency statement;
       (b)   direct that the inclusion of the urgency statement is not to have effect in relation to a requirement of the notice;
       (c)   vary the notice by changing the time at which, or the period within which, a requirement of the notice must be complied with;
       (d)   vary the notice by making other changes required to give effect to a direction under paragraph (a) or (b) or in consequence of a variation under paragraph (c).

(4)   The decision of the court on an application under this section is final.

(5)   In this section, "urgency statement" means—
       (a)   in relation to an information notice, a statement under section 142(7)(a),
       (b)   in relation to an assessment notice, a statement under section 146(8)(a) or (9)(d), and
       (c)   in relation to an enforcement notice, a statement under section 150(8)(a).

Complaints

165   Complaints by data subjects

(1)   Articles 57(1)(f) and (2) and 77 of the GDPR (data subject's right to lodge a complaint) confer rights on data subjects to complain to the Commissioner if the data subject considers that, in connection with personal data relating to him or her, there is an infringement of the GDPR.

(2)   A data subject may make a complaint to the Commissioner if the data subject considers that, in connection with personal data relating to him or her, there is an infringement of Part 3 or 4 of this Act.

(3)   The Commissioner must facilitate the making of complaints under subsection (2) by taking steps such as providing a complaint form which can be completed electronically and by other means.

(4)   If the Commissioner receives a complaint under subsection (2), the Commissioner must—

    (a)   take appropriate steps to respond to the complaint,

    (b)   inform the complainant of the outcome of the complaint,

    (c)   inform the complainant of the rights under section 166, and

    (d)   if asked to do so by the complainant, provide the complainant with further information about how to pursue the complaint.

(5)   The reference in subsection (4)(a) to taking appropriate steps in response to a complaint includes—

    (a)   investigating the subject matter of the complaint, to the extent appropriate, and

    (b)   informing the complainant about progress on the complaint, including about whether further investigation or co-ordination with another supervisory authority or foreign designated authority is necessary.

(6)   If the Commissioner receives a complaint relating to the infringement of a data subject's rights under provisions adopted by a member State other than the United Kingdom pursuant to the Law Enforcement Directive, the Commissioner must—

    (a)   send the complaint to the relevant supervisory authority for the purposes of that Directive,

    (b)   inform the complainant that the Commissioner has done so, and

    (c)   if asked to do so by the complainant, provide the complainant with further information about how to pursue the complaint.

(7)   In this section—

    "foreign designated authority" means an authority designated for the purposes of Article 13 of the Data Protection Convention by a party, other than the United Kingdom, which is bound by that Convention;

    "supervisory authority" means a supervisory authority for the purposes of Article 51 of the GDPR or Article 41 of the Law Enforcement Directive in a member State other than the United Kingdom.

166   Orders to progress complaints

(1)   This section applies where, after a data subject makes a complaint under section 165 or Article 77 of the GDPR, the Commissioner—

    (a)   fails to take appropriate steps to respond to the complaint,

    (b)   fails to provide the complainant with information about progress on the complaint, or of the outcome of the complaint, before the end of the period of 3 months beginning when the Commissioner received the complaint, or

    (c)   if the Commissioner's consideration of the complaint is not concluded during that period, fails to provide the complainant with such information during a subsequent period of 3 months.

(2)   The Tribunal may, on an application by the data subject, make an order requiring the Commissioner —

    (a)   to take appropriate steps to respond to the complaint, or

    (b)   to inform the complainant of progress on the complaint, or of the outcome of the complaint, within a period specified in the order.

(3)   An order under subsection (2)(a) may require the Commissioner —

    (a)   to take steps specified in the order;

    (b)   to conclude an investigation, or take a specified step, within a period specified in the order.

(4)   Section 165(5) applies for the purposes of subsections (1)(a) and (2)(a) as it applies for the purposes of section 165(4)(a).

Remedies in the court

167   Compliance orders

(1)   This section applies if, on an application by a data subject, a court is satisfied that there has been an infringement of the data subject's rights under the data protection legislation in contravention of that legislation.

(2)   A court may make an order for the purposes of securing compliance with the data protection legislation which requires the controller in respect of the processing, or a processor acting on behalf of that controller —

    (a)   to take steps specified in the order, or

    (b)   to refrain from taking steps specified in the order.

(3)   The order may, in relation to each step, specify the time at which, or the period within which, it must be taken.

(4)   In subsection (1) —

    (a)   the reference to an application by a data subject includes an application made in exercise of the right under Article 79(1) of the GDPR (right to an effective remedy against a controller or processor);

    (b)   the reference to the data protection legislation does not include Part 4 of this Act or regulations made under that Part.

(5)   In relation to a joint controller in respect of the processing of personal data to which Part 3 applies whose responsibilities are determined in an arrangement under section 58, a court may only make an order under this section if the controller is responsible for compliance with the provision of the data protection legislation that is contravened.

168   Compensation for contravention of the GDPR

(1)   In Article 82 of the GDPR (right to compensation for material or non-material damage), "non-material damage" includes distress.

(2)   Subsection (3) applies where —
   (a)   in accordance with rules of court, proceedings under Article 82 of the GDPR are brought by a representative body on behalf of a person, and
   (b)   a court orders the payment of compensation.

(3)   The court may make an order providing for the compensation to be paid on behalf of the person to —
   (a)   the representative body, or
   (b)   such other person as the court thinks fit.

169   Compensation for contravention of other data protection legislation

(1)   A person who suffers damage by reason of a contravention of a requirement of the data protection legislation, other than the GDPR, is entitled to compensation for that damage from the controller or the processor, subject to subsections (2) and (3).

(2)   Under subsection (1) —
   (a)   a controller involved in processing of personal data is liable for any damage caused by the processing, and
   (b)   a processor involved in processing of personal data is liable for damage caused by the processing only if the processor —
      (i)   has not complied with an obligation under the data protection legislation specifically directed at processors, or
      (ii)   has acted outside, or contrary to, the controller's lawful instructions.

(3)   A controller or processor is not liable as described in subsection (2) if the controller or processor proves that the controller or processor is not in any way responsible for the event giving rise to the damage.

(4)   A joint controller in respect of the processing of personal data to which Part 3 or 4 applies whose responsibilities are determined in an arrangement under section 58 or 104 is only liable as described in subsection (2) if the controller is responsible for compliance with the provision of the data protection legislation that is contravened.

(5)   In this section, "damage" includes financial loss and damage not involving financial loss, such as distress.

Offences relating to personal data

170   Unlawful obtaining etc of personal data

(1)   It is an offence for a person knowingly or recklessly —
   (a)   to obtain or disclose personal data without the consent of the controller,
   (b)   to procure the disclosure of personal data to another person without the consent of the controller, or

    (c)   after obtaining personal data, to retain it without the consent of the person who was the controller in relation to the personal data when it was obtained.

(2)   It is a defence for a person charged with an offence under subsection (1) to prove that the obtaining, disclosing, procuring or retaining—

    (a)   was necessary for the purposes of preventing or detecting crime,

    (b)   was required or authorised by an enactment, by a rule of law or by the order of a court or tribunal, or

    (c)   in the particular circumstances, was justified as being in the public interest.

(3)   It is also a defence for a person charged with an offence under subsection (1) to prove that—

    (a)   the person acted in the reasonable belief that the person had a legal right to do the obtaining, disclosing, procuring or retaining,

    (b)   the person acted in the reasonable belief that the person would have had the consent of the controller if the controller had known about the obtaining, disclosing, procuring or retaining and the circumstances of it, or

    (c)   the person acted—

        (i)   for the special purposes,

        (ii)   with a view to the publication by a person of any journalistic, academic, artistic or literary material, and

        (iii)   in the reasonable belief that in the particular circumstances the obtaining, disclosing, procuring or retaining was justified as being in the public interest.

(4)   It is an offence for a person to sell personal data if the person obtained the data in circumstances in which an offence under subsection (1) was committed.

(5)   It is an offence for a person to offer to sell personal data if the person—

    (a)   has obtained the data in circumstances in which an offence under subsection (1) was committed, or

    (b)   subsequently obtains the data in such circumstances.

(6)   For the purposes of subsection (5), an advertisement indicating that personal data is or may be for sale is an offer to sell the data.

(7)   In this section—

    (a)   references to the consent of a controller do not include the consent of a person who is a controller by virtue of Article 28(10) of the GDPR or section 59(8) or 105(3) of this Act (processor to be treated as controller in certain circumstances);

    (b)   where there is more than one controller, such references are references to the consent of one or more of them.

171   Re-identification of de-identified personal data

(1)   It is an offence for a person knowingly or recklessly to re-identify information that is de-identified personal data without the consent of the controller responsible for de-identifying the personal data.

(2)   For the purposes of this section and section 172—

- (a) personal data is "de-identified" if it has been processed in such a manner that it can no longer be attributed, without more, to a specific data subject;
- (b) a person "re-identifies" information if the person takes steps which result in the information no longer being de-identified within the meaning of paragraph (a).

(3) It is a defence for a person charged with an offence under subsection (1) to prove that the re-identification—
- (a) was necessary for the purposes of preventing or detecting crime,
- (b) was required or authorised by an enactment, by a rule of law or by the order of a court or tribunal, or
- (c) in the particular circumstances, was justified as being in the public interest.

(4) It is also a defence for a person charged with an offence under subsection (1) to prove that—
- (a) the person acted in the reasonable belief that the person—
  - (i) is the data subject to whom the information relates,
  - (ii) had the consent of that data subject, or
  - (iii) would have had such consent if the data subject had known about the re-identification and the circumstances of it,
- (b) the person acted in the reasonable belief that the person—
  - (i) is the controller responsible for de-identifying the personal data,
  - (ii) had the consent of that controller, or
  - (iii) would have had such consent if that controller had known about the re-identification and the circumstances of it,
- (c) the person acted—
  - (i) for the special purposes,
  - (ii) with a view to the publication by a person of any journalistic, academic, artistic or literary material, and
  - (iii) in the reasonable belief that in the particular circumstances the re-identification was justified as being in the public interest, or
- (d) the effectiveness testing conditions were met (see section 172).

(5) It is an offence for a person knowingly or recklessly to process personal data that is information that has been re-identified where the person does so—
- (a) without the consent of the controller responsible for de-identifying the personal data, and
- (b) in circumstances in which the re-identification was an offence under subsection (1).

(6) It is a defence for a person charged with an offence under subsection (5) to prove that the processing—
- (a) was necessary for the purposes of preventing or detecting crime,
- (b) was required or authorised by an enactment, by a rule of law or by the order of a court or tribunal, or
- (c) in the particular circumstances, was justified as being in the public interest.

(7) It is also a defence for a person charged with an offence under subsection (5) to prove that—

      (a)   the person acted in the reasonable belief that the processing was lawful,

      (b)   the person acted in the reasonable belief that the person —

          (i)   had the consent of the controller responsible for de-identifying the personal data, or

          (ii)   would have had such consent if that controller had known about the processing and the circumstances of it, or

      (c)   the person acted —

          (i)   for the special purposes,

          (ii)   with a view to the publication by a person of any journalistic, academic, artistic or literary material, and

          (iii)   in the reasonable belief that in the particular circumstances the processing was justified as being in the public interest.

(8)   In this section —

      (a)   references to the consent of a controller do not include the consent of a person who is a controller by virtue of Article 28(10) of the GDPR or section 59(8) or 105(3) of this Act (processor to be treated as controller in certain circumstances);

      (b)   where there is more than one controller, such references are references to the consent of one or more of them.

172   Re-identification: effectiveness testing conditions

(1)   For the purposes of section 171, in relation to a person who re-identifies information that is de-identified personal data, "the effectiveness testing conditions" means the conditions in subsections (2) and (3).

(2)   The first condition is that the person acted —

      (a)   with a view to testing the effectiveness of the de-identification of personal data,

      (b)   without intending to cause, or threaten to cause, damage or distress to a person, and

      (c)   in the reasonable belief that, in the particular circumstances, re-identifying the information was justified as being in the public interest.

(3)   The second condition is that the person notified the Commissioner or the controller responsible for de-identifying the personal data about the re-identification —

      (a)   without undue delay, and

      (b)   where feasible, not later than 72 hours after becoming aware of it.

(4)   Where there is more than one controller responsible for de-identifying personal data, the requirement in subsection (3) is satisfied if one or more of them is notified.

173   Alteration etc of personal data to prevent disclosure to data subject

(1)   Subsection (3) applies where —

      (a)   a request has been made in exercise of a data subject access right, and

      (b)   the person making the request would have been entitled to receive information in response to that request.

(2)   In this section, "data subject access right" means a right under —

      (a)   Article 15 of the GDPR (right of access by the data subject);

(b) Article 20 of the GDPR (right to data portability);

(c) section 45 of this Act (law enforcement processing: right of access by the data subject);

(d) section 94 of this Act (intelligence services processing: right of access by the data subject).

(3) It is an offence for a person listed in subsection (4) to alter, deface, block, erase, destroy or conceal information with the intention of preventing disclosure of all or part of the information that the person making the request would have been entitled to receive.

(4) Those persons are—

(a) the controller, and

(b) a person who is employed by the controller, an officer of the controller or subject to the direction of the controller.

(5) It is a defence for a person charged with an offence under subsection (3) to prove that—

(a) the alteration, defacing, blocking, erasure, destruction or concealment of the information would have occurred in the absence of a request made in exercise of a data subject access right, or

(b) the person acted in the reasonable belief that the person making the request was not entitled to receive the information in response to the request.

The special purposes

174 The special purposes

(1) In this Part, "the special purposes" means one or more of the following—

(a) the purposes of journalism;

(b) academic purposes;

(c) artistic purposes;

(d) literary purposes.

(2) In this Part, "special purposes proceedings" means legal proceedings against a controller or processor which relate, wholly or partly, to personal data processed for the special purposes and which are—

(a) proceedings under section 167 (including proceedings on an application under Article 79 of the GDPR), or

(b) proceedings under Article 82 of the GDPR or section 169.

(3) The Commissioner may make a written determination, in relation to the processing of personal data, that—

(a) the personal data is not being processed only for the special purposes;

(b) the personal data is not being processed with a view to the publication by a person of journalistic, academic, artistic or literary material which has not previously been published by the controller.

(4) The Commissioner must give written notice of the determination to the controller and the processor.

(5) The notice must provide information about the rights of appeal under section 162.

(6) The determination does not take effect until one of the following conditions is satisfied —

    (a) the period for the controller or the processor to appeal against the determination has ended without an appeal having been brought, or

    (b) an appeal has been brought against the determination and —

        (i) the appeal and any further appeal in relation to the determination has been decided or has otherwise ended, and

        (ii) the time for appealing against the result of the appeal or further appeal has ended without another appeal having been brought.

175 Provision of assistance in special purposes proceedings

(1) An individual who is a party, or prospective party, to special purposes proceedings may apply to the Commissioner for assistance in those proceedings.

(2) As soon as reasonably practicable after receiving an application under subsection (1), the Commissioner must decide whether, and to what extent, to grant it.

(3) The Commissioner must not grant the application unless, in the Commissioner's opinion, the case involves a matter of substantial public importance.

(4) If the Commissioner decides not to provide assistance, the Commissioner must, as soon as reasonably practicable, notify the applicant of the decision, giving reasons for the decision.

(5) If the Commissioner decides to provide assistance, the Commissioner must —

    (a) as soon as reasonably practicable, notify the applicant of the decision, stating the extent of the assistance to be provided, and

    (b) secure that the person against whom the proceedings are, or are to be, brought is informed that the Commissioner is providing assistance.

(6) The assistance that may be provided by the Commissioner includes —

    (a) paying costs in connection with the proceedings, and

    (b) indemnifying the applicant in respect of liability to pay costs, expenses or damages in connection with the proceedings.

(7) In England and Wales or Northern Ireland, the recovery of expenses incurred by the Commissioner in providing an applicant with assistance under this section (as taxed or assessed in accordance with rules of court) is to constitute a first charge for the benefit of the Commissioner —

    (a) on any costs which, by virtue of any judgment or order of the court, are payable to the applicant by any other person in respect of the matter in connection with which the assistance is provided, and

    (b) on any sum payable to the applicant under a compromise or settlement arrived at in connection with that matter to avoid, or bring to an end, any proceedings.

(8) In Scotland, the recovery of such expenses (as taxed or assessed in accordance with rules of court) is to be paid to the Commissioner, in priority to other debts —

(a) out of any expenses which, by virtue of any judgment or order of the court, are payable to the applicant by any other person in respect of the matter in connection with which the assistance is provided, and

(b) out of any sum payable to the applicant under a compromise or settlement arrived at in connection with that matter to avoid, or bring to an end, any proceedings.

176 Staying special purposes proceedings

(1) In any special purposes proceedings before a court, if the controller or processor claims, or it appears to the court, that any personal data to which the proceedings relate —

(a) is being processed only for the special purposes,

(b) is being processed with a view to the publication by any person of journalistic, academic, artistic or literary material, and

(c) has not previously been published by the controller,

the court must stay or, in Scotland, sist the proceedings.

(2) In considering, for the purposes of subsection (1)(c), whether material has previously been published, publication in the immediately preceding 24 hours is to be ignored.

(3) Under subsection (1), the court must stay or sist the proceedings until either of the following conditions is met —

(a) a determination of the Commissioner under section 174 with respect to the personal data or the processing takes effect;

(b) where the proceedings were stayed or sisted on the making of a claim, the claim is withdrawn.

177 Guidance about how to seek redress against media organisations

(1) The Commissioner must produce and publish guidance about the steps that may be taken where an individual considers that a media organisation is failing or has failed to comply with the data protection legislation.

(2) In this section, "media organisation" means a body or other organisation whose activities consist of or include journalism.

(3) The guidance must include provision about relevant complaints procedures, including —

(a) who runs them,

(b) what can be complained about, and

(c) how to make a complaint.

(4) For the purposes of subsection (3), relevant complaints procedures include procedures for making complaints to the Commissioner, the Office of Communications, the British Broadcasting Corporation and other persons who produce or enforce codes of practice for media organisations.

(5) The guidance must also include provision about —

(a) the powers available to the Commissioner in relation to a failure to comply with the data protection legislation,

(b) when a claim in respect of such a failure may be made before a court and how to make such a claim,

(c) alternative dispute resolution procedures,

    (d)   the rights of bodies and other organisations to make complaints and claims on behalf of data subjects, and

    (e)   the Commissioner's power to provide assistance in special purpose proceedings.

(6)   The Commissioner —

    (a)   may alter or replace the guidance, and

    (b)   must publish any altered or replacement guidance.

(7)   The Commissioner must produce and publish the first guidance under this section before the end of the period of 1 year beginning when this Act is passed.

178 Review of processing of personal data for the purposes of journalism

(1)   The Commissioner must —

    (a)   review the extent to which, during each review period, the processing of personal data for the purposes of journalism complied with —

        (i)   the data protection legislation, and

        (ii)   good practice in the processing of personal data for the purposes of journalism,

    (b)   prepare a report of the review, and

    (c)   submit the report to the Secretary of State.

(2)   In this section —

    "good practice in the processing of personal data for the purposes of journalism" has the same meaning as in section 124;

    "review period" means —

    (a)   the period of 4 years beginning with the day on which Chapter 2 of Part 2 of this Act comes into force, and

    (b)   each subsequent period of 5 years beginning with the day after the day on which the previous review period ended.

(3)   The Commissioner must start a review under this section, in respect of a review period, within the period of 6 months beginning when the review period ends.

(4)   The Commissioner must submit the report of a review under this section to the Secretary of State —

    (a)   in the case of the first review, before the end of the period of 18 months beginning when the Commissioner started the review, and

    (b)   in the case of each subsequent review, before the end of the period of 12 months beginning when the Commissioner started the review.

(5)   The report must include consideration of the extent of compliance (as described in subsection (1)(a)) in each part of the United Kingdom.

(6)   The Secretary of State must —

    (a)   lay the report before Parliament, and

    (b)   send a copy of the report to —

        (i)   the Scottish Ministers,

        (ii)   the Welsh Ministers, and

        (iii)   the Executive Office in Northern Ireland.

(7)   Schedule 17 makes further provision for the purposes of a review under this section.

179 Effectiveness of the media's dispute resolution procedures

(1) The Secretary of State must, before the end of each review period, lay before Parliament a report produced by the Secretary of State or an appropriate person on —

    (a) the use of relevant alternative dispute resolution procedures, during that period, in cases involving a failure, or alleged failure, by a relevant media organisation to comply with the data protection legislation, and

    (b) the effectiveness of those procedures in such cases.

(2) In this section —

    "appropriate person" means a person who the Secretary of State considers has appropriate experience and skills to produce a report described in subsection (1);

    "relevant alternative dispute resolution procedures" means alternative dispute resolution procedures provided by persons who produce or enforce codes of practice for relevant media organisations;

    "relevant media organisation" means a body or other organisation whose activities consist of or include journalism, other than a broadcaster;

    "review period" means —

        (a) the period of 3 years beginning when this Act is passed, and

        (b) each subsequent period of 3 years.

(3) The Secretary of State must send a copy of the report to —

    (a) the Scottish Ministers,

    (b) the Welsh Ministers, and

    (c) the Executive Office in Northern Ireland.

Jurisdiction of courts

180 Jurisdiction

(1) The jurisdiction conferred on a court by the provisions listed in subsection (2) is exercisable —

    (a) in England and Wales, by the High Court or the county court,

    (b) in Northern Ireland, by the High Court or a county court, and

    (c) in Scotland, by the Court of Session or the sheriff,

subject to subsections (3) and (4).

(2) Those provisions are —

    (a) section 145 (information orders);

    (b) section 152 (enforcement notices and processing for the special purposes);

    (c) section 156 (penalty notices and processing for the special purposes);

    (d) section 167 and Article 79 of the GDPR (compliance orders);

    (e) sections 168 and 169 and Article 82 of the GDPR (compensation).

(3) In relation to the processing of personal data to which Part 4 applies, the jurisdiction conferred by the provisions listed in subsection (2) is exercisable only by the High Court or, in Scotland, the Court of Session.

(4) In relation to an information notice which contains a statement under section 142(7), the jurisdiction conferred on a court by section 145 is exercisable only by the High Court or, in Scotland, the Court of Session.

(5) The jurisdiction conferred on a court by section 164 (applications in respect of urgent notices) is exercisable only by the High Court or, in Scotland, the Court of Session.

Definitions

181 Interpretation of Part 6

In this Part—
 "assessment notice" has the meaning given in section 146;
 "certification provider" has the meaning given in section 17;
 "enforcement notice" has the meaning given in section 149;
 "information notice" has the meaning given in section 142;
 "penalty notice" has the meaning given in section 155;
 "penalty variation notice" has the meaning given in Schedule 16;
 "representative", in relation to a controller or processor, means a person designated by the controller or processor under Article 27 of the GDPR to represent the controller or processor with regard to the controller's or processor's obligations under the GDPR.

PART 7

SUPPLEMENTARY AND FINAL PROVISION

Regulations under this Act

182 Regulations and consultation

(1) Regulations under this Act are to be made by statutory instrument.

(2) Before making regulations under this Act, the Secretary of State must consult—
 (a) the Commissioner, and
 (b) such other persons as the Secretary of State considers appropriate.

(3) Subsection (2) does not apply to regulations made under—
 (a) section 23;
 (b) section 30;
 (c) section 211;
 (d) section 212;
 (e) section 213;
 (f) paragraph 15 of Schedule 2.

(4) Subsection (2) does not apply to regulations made under section 18 where the Secretary of State has made an urgency statement in respect of them.

(5) Regulations under this Act may—
 (a) make different provision for different purposes;
 (b) include consequential, supplementary, incidental, transitional, transitory or saving provision.

(6) Where regulations under this Act are subject to "the negative resolution procedure" the statutory instrument containing the regulations is subject to annulment in pursuance of a resolution of either House of Parliament.

(7) Where regulations under this Act are subject to "the affirmative resolution procedure" the regulations may not be made unless a draft of the statutory instrument containing them has been laid before Parliament and approved by a resolution of each House of Parliament.

(8) Where regulations under this Act are subject to "the made affirmative resolution procedure" —

   (a) the statutory instrument containing the regulations must be laid before Parliament after being made, together with the urgency statement in respect of them, and

   (b) the regulations cease to have effect at the end of the period of 120 days beginning with the day on which the instrument is made, unless within that period the instrument is approved by a resolution of each House of Parliament.

(9) In calculating the period of 120 days, no account is to be taken of any time during which —

   (a) Parliament is dissolved or prorogued, or

   (b) both Houses of Parliament are adjourned for more than 4 days.

(10) Where regulations cease to have effect as a result of subsection (8), that does not —

   (a) affect anything previously done under the regulations, or

   (b) prevent the making of new regulations.

(11) Any provision that may be included in regulations under this Act subject to the negative resolution procedure may be made by regulations subject to the affirmative resolution procedure or the made affirmative resolution procedure.

(12) If a draft of a statutory instrument containing regulations under section 7 would, apart from this subsection, be treated for the purposes of the standing orders of either House of Parliament as a hybrid instrument, it is to proceed in that House as if it were not such an instrument.

(13) A requirement under a provision of this Act to consult may be satisfied by consultation before, as well as by consultation after, the provision comes into force.

(14) In this section, "urgency statement" has the meaning given in section 18(4).

Changes to the Data Protection Convention

183 Power to reflect changes to the Data Protection Convention

(1) The Secretary of State may by regulations make such provision as the Secretary of State considers necessary or appropriate in connection with an amendment of, or an instrument replacing, the Data Protection Convention which has effect, or is expected to have effect, in the United Kingdom.

(2) The power under subsection (1) includes power —

     (a)   to amend or replace the definition of "the Data Protection Convention" in section 3;

     (b)   to amend Chapter 3 of Part 2 of this Act;

     (c)   to amend Part 4 of this Act;

     (d)   to make provision about the functions of the Commissioner, courts or tribunals in connection with processing of personal data to which Chapter 3 of Part 2 or Part 4 of this Act applies, including provision amending Parts 5 to 7 of this Act;

     (e)   to make provision about the functions of the Commissioner in connection with the Data Protection Convention or an instrument replacing that Convention, including provision amending Parts 5 to 7 of this Act;

     (f)   to consequentially amend this Act.

(3)   Regulations under this section are subject to the affirmative resolution procedure.

(4)   Regulations under this section may not be made after the end of the period of 3 years beginning with the day on which this Act is passed.

Rights of the data subject

184   Prohibition of requirement to produce relevant records

(1)   It is an offence for a person ("P1") to require another person to provide P1 with, or give P1 access to, a relevant record in connection with—

     (a)   the recruitment of an employee by P1,

     (b)   the continued employment of a person by P1, or

     (c)   a contract for the provision of services to P1.

(2)   It is an offence for a person ("P2") to require another person to provide P2 with, or give P2 access to, a relevant record if—

     (a)   P2 is involved in the provision of goods, facilities or services to the public or a section of the public, and

     (b)   the requirement is a condition of providing or offering to provide goods, facilities or services to the other person or to a third party.

(3)   It is a defence for a person charged with an offence under subsection (1) or (2) to prove that imposing the requirement—

     (a)   was required or authorised by an enactment, by a rule of law or by the order of a court or tribunal, or

     (b)   in the particular circumstances, was justified as being in the public interest.

(4)   The imposition of the requirement referred to in subsection (1) or (2) is not to be regarded as justified as being in the public interest on the ground that it would assist in the prevention or detection of crime, given Part 5 of the Police Act 1997 (certificates of criminal records etc).

(5)   In subsections (1) and (2), the references to a person who requires another person to provide or give access to a relevant record include a person who asks another person to do so—

     (a)   knowing that, in the circumstances, it would be reasonable for the other person to feel obliged to comply with the request, or

    (b)   being reckless as to whether, in the circumstances, it would be reasonable for the other person to feel obliged to comply with the request,

and the references to a "requirement" in subsections (3) and (4) are to be interpreted accordingly.

(6)   In this section—

        "employment" means any employment, including—

        (a)   work under a contract for services or as an office-holder,

        (b)   work under an apprenticeship,

        (c)   work experience as part of a training course or in the course of training for employment, and

        (d)   voluntary work,

        and "employee" is to be interpreted accordingly;

        "relevant record" has the meaning given in Schedule 18 and references to a relevant record include—

        (a)   a part of such a record, and

        (b)   a copy of, or of part of, such a record.

185   Avoidance of certain contractual terms relating to health records

(1)   A term or condition of a contract is void in so far as it purports to require an individual to supply another person with a record which—

        (a)   consists of the information contained in a health record, and

        (b)   has been or is to be obtained by a data subject in the exercise of a data subject access right.

(2)   A term or condition of a contract is also void in so far as it purports to require an individual to produce such a record to another person.

(3)   The references in subsections (1) and (2) to a record include a part of a record and a copy of all or part of a record.

(4)   In this section, "data subject access right" means a right under—

        (a)   Article 15 of the GDPR (right of access by the data subject);

        (b)   Article 20 of the GDPR (right to data portability);

        (c)   section 45 of this Act (law enforcement processing: right of access by the data subject);

        (d)   section 94 of this Act (intelligence services processing: right of access by the data subject).

186   Data subject's rights and other prohibitions and restrictions

(1)   An enactment or rule of law prohibiting or restricting the disclosure of information, or authorising the withholding of information, does not remove or restrict the obligations and rights provided for in the provisions listed in subsection (2), except as provided by or under the provisions listed in subsection (3).

(2)   The provisions providing obligations and rights are—

        (a)   Chapter III of the GDPR (rights of the data subject),

        (b)   Chapter 3 of Part 3 of this Act (law enforcement processing: rights of the data subject), and

      (c)   Chapter 3 of Part 4 of this Act (intelligence services processing: rights of the data subject).

(3)   The provisions providing exceptions are—

      (a)   in Chapter 2 of Part 2 of this Act, sections 15 and 16 and Schedules 2, 3 and 4,

      (b)   in Chapter 3 of Part 2 of this Act, sections 23, 24, 25 and 26,

      (c)   in Part 3 of this Act, sections 44(4), 45(4) and 48(3), and

      (d)   in Part 4 of this Act, Chapter 6.

Representation of data subjects

187   **Representation of data subjects with their authority**

(1)   In relation to the processing of personal data to which the GDPR applies—

      (a)   Article 80(1) of the GDPR (representation of data subjects) enables a data subject to authorise a body or other organisation which meets the conditions set out in that Article to exercise the data subject's rights under Articles 77, 78 and 79 of the GDPR (rights to lodge complaints and to an effective judicial remedy) on the data subject's behalf, and

      (b)   a data subject may also authorise such a body or organisation to exercise the data subject's rights under Article 82 of the GDPR (right to compensation).

(2)   In relation to the processing of personal data to which the GDPR does not apply, a body or other organisation which meets the conditions in subsections (3) and (4), if authorised to do so by a data subject, may exercise some or all of the following rights of a data subject on the data subject's behalf—

      (a)   rights under section 165(2), (4)(d) and (6)(c) (complaints to the Commissioner);

      (b)   rights under section 166(2) (orders for the Commissioner to progress complaints);

      (c)   rights under section 167(1) (compliance orders);

      (d)   the right to bring judicial review proceedings against the Commissioner.

(3)   The first condition is that the body or organisation, by virtue of its constitution or an enactment—

      (a)   is required (after payment of outgoings) to apply the whole of its income and any capital it expends for charitable or public purposes,

      (b)   is prohibited from directly or indirectly distributing amongst its members any part of its assets (otherwise than for charitable or public purposes), and

      (c)   has objectives which are in the public interest.

(4)   The second condition is that the body or organisation is active in the field of protection of data subjects' rights and freedoms with regard to the protection of their personal data.

(5)   In this Act, references to a "representative body", in relation to a right of a data subject, are to a body or other organisation authorised to exercise the right on the data subject's behalf under Article 80 of the GDPR or this section.

188   Representation of data subjects with their authority: collective proceedings

(1)   The Secretary of State may by regulations make provision for representative bodies to bring proceedings before a court or tribunal in England and Wales or Northern Ireland combining two or more relevant claims.

(2)   In this section, "relevant claim", in relation to a representative body, means a claim in respect of a right of a data subject which the representative body is authorised to exercise on the data subject's behalf under Article 80(1) of the GDPR or section 187.

(3)   The power under subsection (1) includes power −
   (a)   to make provision about the proceedings;
   (b)   to confer functions on a person, including functions involving the exercise of a discretion;
   (c)   to make different provision in relation to England and Wales and in relation to Northern Ireland.

(4)   The provision mentioned in subsection (3)(a) includes provision about −
   (a)   the effect of judgments and orders;
   (b)   agreements to settle claims;
   (c)   the assessment of the amount of compensation;
   (d)   the persons to whom compensation may or must be paid, including compensation not claimed by the data subject;
   (e)   costs.

(5)   Regulations under this section are subject to the negative resolution procedure.

189   Duty to review provision for representation of data subjects

(1)   Before the end of the review period, the Secretary of State must −
   (a)   review the matters listed in subsection (2) in relation to England and Wales and Northern Ireland,
   (b)   prepare a report of the review, and
   (c)   lay a copy of the report before Parliament.

(2)   Those matters are −
   (a)   the operation of Article 80(1) of the GDPR,
   (b)   the operation of section 187,
   (c)   the merits of exercising the power under Article 80(2) of the GDPR (power to enable a body or other organisation which meets the conditions in Article 80(1) of the GDPR to exercise some or all of a data subject's rights under Articles 77, 78 and 79 of the GDPR without being authorised to do so by the data subject),
   (d)   the merits of making equivalent provision in relation to data subjects' rights under Article 82 of the GDPR (right to compensation), and
   (e)   the merits of making provision for a children's rights organisation to exercise some or all of a data subject's rights under Articles 77, 78, 79 and 82 of the GDPR on behalf of a data subject who is a child, with or without being authorised to do so by the data subject.

(3)   "The review period" is the period of 30 months beginning when section 187 comes into force.

(4)   In carrying out the review, the Secretary of State must −

(a) consider the particular needs of children separately from the needs of adults,

(b) have regard to the fact that children have different needs at different stages of development,

(c) carry out an analysis of the particular challenges that children face in authorising, and deciding whether to authorise, other persons to act on their behalf under Article 80(1) of the GDPR or section 187,

(d) consider the support and advice available to children in connection with the exercise of their rights under Articles 77, 78, 79 and 82 of the GDPR by another person on their behalf and the merits of making available other support or advice, and

(e) have regard to the United Kingdom's obligations under the United Nations Convention on the Rights of the Child.

(5) Before preparing the report under subsection (1), the Secretary of State must consult the Commissioner and such other persons as the Secretary of State considers appropriate, including —

(a) persons active in the field of protection of data subjects' rights and freedoms with regard to the protection of their personal data,

(b) children and parents,

(c) children's rights organisations and other persons who appear to the Secretary of State to represent the interests of children,

(d) child development experts, and

(e) trade associations.

(6) In this section —

"children's rights organisation" means a body or other organisation which —

(a) is active in representing the interests of children, and

(b) has objectives which are in the public interest;

"trade association" includes a body representing controllers or processors;

"the United Nations Convention on the Rights of the Child" means the Convention on the Rights of the Child adopted by the General Assembly of the United Nations on 20 November 1989 (including any Protocols to that Convention which are in force in relation to the United Kingdom), subject to any reservations, objections or interpretative declarations by the United Kingdom for the time being in force.

190 Post-review powers to make provision about representation of data subjects

(1) After the report under section 189(1) is laid before Parliament, the Secretary of State may by regulations —

(a) exercise the powers under Article 80(2) of the GDPR in relation to England and Wales and Northern Ireland,

(b) make provision enabling a body or other organisation which meets the conditions in Article 80(1) of the GDPR to exercise a data subject's rights under Article 82 of the GDPR in England and Wales and Northern Ireland without being authorised to do so by the data subject, and

(c) make provision described in section 189(2)(e) in relation to the exercise in England and Wales and Northern Ireland of the rights of a data subject who is a child.

(2) The powers under subsection (1) include power –

    (a) to make provision enabling a data subject to prevent a body or other organisation from exercising, or continuing to exercise, the data subject's rights;

    (b) to make provision about proceedings before a court or tribunal where a body or organisation exercises a data subject's rights;

    (c) to make provision for bodies or other organisations to bring proceedings before a court or tribunal combining two or more claims in respect of a right of a data subject;

    (d) to confer functions on a person, including functions involving the exercise of a discretion;

    (e) to amend sections 166 to 168, 180, 187, 203, 205 and 206;

    (f) to insert new sections and Schedules into Part 6 or 7;

    (g) to make different provision in relation to England and Wales and in relation to Northern Ireland.

(3) The powers under subsection (1)(a) and (b) include power to make provision in relation to data subjects who are children or data subjects who are not children or both.

(4) The provision mentioned in subsection (2)(b) and (c) includes provision about –

    (a) the effect of judgments and orders;

    (b) agreements to settle claims;

    (c) the assessment of the amount of compensation;

    (d) the persons to whom compensation may or must be paid, including compensation not claimed by the data subject;

    (e) costs.

(5) Regulations under this section are subject to the affirmative resolution procedure.

Framework for Data Processing by Government

191 Framework for Data Processing by Government

(1) The Secretary of State may prepare a document, called the Framework for Data Processing by Government, which contains guidance about the processing of personal data in connection with the exercise of functions of –

    (a) the Crown, a Minister of the Crown or a United Kingdom government department, and

    (b) a person with functions of a public nature who is specified or described in regulations made by the Secretary of State.

(2) The document may make provision relating to all of those functions or only to particular functions or persons.

(3) The document may not make provision relating to, or to the functions of, a part of the Scottish Administration, the Welsh Government, a Northern Ireland Minister or a Northern Ireland department.

(4) The Secretary of State may from time to time prepare amendments of the document or a replacement document.

(5)   Before preparing a document or amendments under this section, the Secretary of State must consult—

    (a)   the Commissioner, and

    (b)   any other person the Secretary of State considers it appropriate to consult.

(6)   Regulations under subsection (1)(b) are subject to the negative resolution procedure.

(7)   In this section, "Northern Ireland Minister" includes the First Minister and deputy First Minister in Northern Ireland.

192   Approval of the Framework

(1)   Before issuing a document prepared under section 191, the Secretary of State must lay it before Parliament.

(2)   If, within the 40-day period, either House of Parliament resolves not to approve the document, the Secretary of State must not issue it.

(3)   If no such resolution is made within that period—

    (a)   the Secretary of State must issue the document, and

    (b)   the document comes into force at the end of the period of 21 days beginning with the day on which it is issued.

(4)   Nothing in subsection (2) prevents another version of the document being laid before Parliament.

(5)   In this section, "the 40-day period" means—

    (a)   if the document is laid before both Houses of Parliament on the same day, the period of 40 days beginning with that day, or

    (b)   if the document is laid before the Houses of Parliament on different days, the period of 40 days beginning with the later of those days.

(6)   In calculating the 40-day period, no account is to be taken of any period during which Parliament is dissolved or prorogued or during which both Houses of Parliament are adjourned for more than 4 days.

(7)   This section applies in relation to amendments prepared under section 191 as it applies in relation to a document prepared under that section.

193   Publication and review of the Framework

(1)   The Secretary of State must publish a document issued under section 192(3).

(2)   Where an amendment of a document is issued under section 192(3), the Secretary of State must publish—

    (a)   the amendment, or

    (b)   the document as amended by it.

(3)   The Secretary of State must keep under review the document issued under section 192(3) for the time being in force.

(4)   Where the Secretary of State becomes aware that the terms of such a document could result in a breach of an international obligation of the United Kingdom, the Secretary of State must exercise the power under section 191(4) with a view to remedying the situation.

194 Effect of the Framework

(1) When carrying out processing of personal data which is the subject of a document issued under section 192(3) which is for the time being in force, a person must have regard to the document.

(2) A failure to act in accordance with a provision of such a document does not of itself make a person liable to legal proceedings in a court or tribunal.

(3) A document issued under section 192(3), including an amendment or replacement document, is admissible in evidence in legal proceedings.

(4) In any legal proceedings before a court or tribunal, the court or tribunal must take into account a provision of any document issued under section 192(3) in determining a question arising in the proceedings if—

    (a) the question relates to a time when the provision was in force, and

    (b) the provision appears to the court or tribunal to be relevant to the question.

(5) In determining a question arising in connection with the carrying out of any of the Commissioner's functions, the Commissioner must take into account a provision of a document issued under section 192(3) if—

    (a) the question relates to a time when the provision was in force, and

    (b) the provision appears to the Commissioner to be relevant to the question.

Data-sharing: HMRC and reserve forces

195 Reserve forces: data-sharing by HMRC

(1) The Reserve Forces Act 1996 is amended as follows.

(2) After section 125 insert—

"125A Supply of contact details by HMRC

    (1) This subsection applies to contact details for—

        (a) a member of an ex-regular reserve force, or

        (b) a person to whom section 66 (officers and former servicemen liable to recall) applies,

    which are held by HMRC in connection with a function of HMRC.

    (2) HMRC may supply contact details to which subsection (1) applies to the Secretary of State for the purpose of enabling the Secretary of State—

        (a) to contact a member of an ex-regular reserve force in connection with the person's liability, or potential liability, to be called out for service under Part 6;

        (b) to contact a person to whom section 66 applies in connection with the person's liability, or potential liability, to be recalled for service under Part 7.

    (3) Where a person's contact details are supplied under subsection (2) for a purpose described in that subsection, they may also be used for defence purposes connected with the person's service (whether past, present or future) in the reserve forces or regular services.

(4)   In this section, "HMRC" means Her Majesty's Revenue and Customs.

125B Prohibition on disclosure of contact details supplied under section 125A

(1)   A person who receives information supplied under section 125A may not disclose it except with the consent of the Commissioners for Her Majesty's Revenue and Customs (which may be general or specific).

(2)   A person who contravenes subsection (1) is guilty of an offence.

(3)   It is a defence for a person charged with an offence under this section to prove that the person reasonably believed —
       (a)   that the disclosure was lawful, or
       (b)   that the information had already lawfully been made available to the public.

(4)   Subsections (4) to (7) of section 19 of the Commissioners for Revenue and Customs Act 2005 apply to an offence under this section as they apply to an offence under that section.

(5)   Nothing in section 107 or 108 (institution of proceedings and evidence) applies in relation to an offence under this section.

125C Data protection

(1)   Nothing in section 125A or 125B authorises the making of a disclosure which contravenes the data protection legislation.

(2)   In this section, "the data protection legislation" has the same meaning as in the Data Protection Act 2018 (see section 3 of that Act)."

Offences

196 Penalties for offences

(1)   A person who commits an offence under section 119 or 173 or paragraph 15 of Schedule 15 is liable —
       (a)   on summary conviction in England and Wales, to a fine;
       (b)   on summary conviction in Scotland or Northern Ireland, to a fine not exceeding level 5 on the standard scale.

(2)   A person who commits an offence under section 132, 144, 148, 170, 171 or 184 is liable —
       (a)   on summary conviction in England and Wales, to a fine;
       (b)   on summary conviction in Scotland or Northern Ireland, to a fine not exceeding the statutory maximum;
       (c)   on conviction on indictment, to a fine.

(3)   Subsections (4) and (5) apply where a person is convicted of an offence under section 170 or 184.

(4)   The court by or before which the person is convicted may order a document or other material to be forfeited, destroyed or erased if —
       (a)   it has been used in connection with the processing of personal data, and
       (b)   it appears to the court to be connected with the commission of the offence,

subject to subsection (5).

(5) If a person, other than the offender, who claims to be the owner of the material, or to be otherwise interested in the material, applies to be heard by the court, the court must not make an order under subsection (4) without giving the person an opportunity to show why the order should not be made.

197 Prosecution

(1) In England and Wales, proceedings for an offence under this Act may be instituted only —
   (a) by the Commissioner, or
   (b) by or with the consent of the Director of Public Prosecutions.

(2) In Northern Ireland, proceedings for an offence under this Act may be instituted only —
   (a) by the Commissioner, or
   (b) by or with the consent of the Director of Public Prosecutions for Northern Ireland.

(3) Subject to subsection (4), summary proceedings for an offence under section 173 (alteration etc of personal data to prevent disclosure) may be brought within the period of 6 months beginning with the day on which the prosecutor first knew of evidence that, in the prosecutor's opinion, was sufficient to bring the proceedings.

(4) Such proceedings may not be brought after the end of the period of 3 years beginning with the day on which the offence was committed.

(5) A certificate signed by or on behalf of the prosecutor and stating the day on which the 6 month period described in subsection (3) began is conclusive evidence of that fact.

(6) A certificate purporting to be signed as described in subsection (5) is to be treated as so signed unless the contrary is proved.

(7) In relation to proceedings in Scotland, section 136(3) of the Criminal Procedure (Scotland) Act 1995 (deemed date of commencement of proceedings) applies for the purposes of this section as it applies for the purposes of that section.

198 Liability of directors etc

(1) Subsection (2) applies where —
   (a) an offence under this Act has been committed by a body corporate, and
   (b) it is proved to have been committed with the consent or connivance of or to be attributable to neglect on the part of —
      (i) a director, manager, secretary or similar officer of the body corporate, or
      (ii) a person who was purporting to act in such a capacity.

(2) The director, manager, secretary, officer or person, as well as the body corporate, is guilty of the offence and liable to be proceeded against and punished accordingly.

(3) Where the affairs of a body corporate are managed by its members, subsections (1) and (2) apply in relation to the acts and omissions of a member in

connection with the member's management functions in relation to the body as if the member were a director of the body corporate.

(4) Subsection (5) applies where—

    (a) an offence under this Act has been committed by a Scottish partnership, and

    (b) the contravention in question is proved to have occurred with the consent or connivance of, or to be attributable to any neglect on the part of, a partner.

(5) The partner, as well as the partnership, is guilty of the offence and liable to be proceeded against and punished accordingly.

199 Recordable offences

(1) The National Police Records (Recordable Offences) Regulations 2000 (S.I. 2000/1139) have effect as if the offences under the following provisions were listed in the Schedule to the Regulations—

    (a) section 119;

    (b) section 132;

    (c) section 144;

    (d) section 148;

    (e) section 170;

    (f) section 171;

    (g) section 173;

    (h) section 184;

    (i) paragraph 15 of Schedule 15.

(2) Regulations under section 27(4) of the Police and Criminal Evidence Act 1984 (recordable offences) may repeal subsection (1).

200 Guidance about PACE codes of practice

(1) The Commissioner must produce and publish guidance about how the Commissioner proposes to perform the duty under section 67(9) of the Police and Criminal Evidence Act 1984 (duty to have regard to codes of practice under that Act when investigating offences and charging offenders) in connection with offences under this Act.

(2) The Commissioner—

    (a) may alter or replace the guidance, and

    (b) must publish any altered or replacement guidance.

(3) The Commissioner must consult the Secretary of State before publishing guidance under this section (including any altered or replacement guidance).

(4) The Commissioner must arrange for guidance under this section (including any altered or replacement guidance) to be laid before Parliament.

The Tribunal

201 Disclosure of information to the Tribunal

(1) No enactment or rule of law prohibiting or restricting the disclosure of information precludes a person from providing the First-tier Tribunal or the Upper Tribunal with information necessary for the discharge of—

    (a) its functions under the data protection legislation, or

    (b) its other functions relating to the Commissioner's acts and omissions.

(2) But this section does not authorise the making of a disclosure which is prohibited by any of Parts 1 to 7 or Chapter 1 of Part 9 of the Investigatory Powers Act 2016.

(3) Until the repeal of Part 1 of the Regulation of Investigatory Powers Act 2000 by paragraphs 45 and 54 of Schedule 10 to the Investigatory Powers Act 2016 is fully in force, subsection (2) has effect as if it included a reference to that Part.

202 Proceedings in the First-tier Tribunal: contempt

(1) This section applies where—

    (a) a person does something, or fails to do something, in relation to proceedings before the First-tier Tribunal—

        (i) on an appeal under section 27, 79, 111 or 162, or

        (ii) for an order under section 166, and

    (b) if those proceedings were proceedings before a court having power to commit for contempt, the act or omission would constitute contempt of court.

(2) The First-tier Tribunal may certify the offence to the Upper Tribunal.

(3) Where an offence is certified under subsection (2), the Upper Tribunal may—

    (a) inquire into the matter, and

    (b) deal with the person charged with the offence in any manner in which it could deal with the person if the offence had been committed in relation to the Upper Tribunal.

(4) Before exercising the power under subsection (3)(b), the Upper Tribunal must—

    (a) hear any witness who may be produced against or on behalf of the person charged with the offence, and

    (b) hear any statement that may be offered in defence.

203 Tribunal Procedure Rules

(1) Tribunal Procedure Rules may make provision for regulating—

    (a) the exercise of the rights of appeal conferred by section 27, 79, 111 or 162, and

    (b) the exercise of the rights of data subjects under section 166, including their exercise by a representative body.

(2) In relation to proceedings involving the exercise of those rights, Tribunal Procedure Rules may make provision about—

    (a)   securing the production of material used for the processing of personal data, and

    (b)   the inspection, examination, operation and testing of equipment or material used in connection with the processing of personal data.

Interpretation

204   Meaning of "health professional" and "social work professional"

  (1)   In this Act, "health professional" means any of the following —

    (a)   a registered medical practitioner;

    (b)   a registered nurse or midwife;

    (c)   a registered dentist within the meaning of the Dentists Act 1984 (see section 53 of that Act);

    (d)   a registered dispensing optician or a registered optometrist within the meaning of the Opticians Act 1989 (see section 36 of that Act);

    (e)   a registered osteopath with the meaning of the Osteopaths Act 1993 (see section 41 of that Act);

    (f)   a registered chiropractor within the meaning of the Chiropractors Act 1994 (see section 43 of that Act);

    (g)   a person registered as a member of a profession to which the Health and Social Work Professions Order 2001 (S.I. 2002/254) for the time being extends, other than the social work profession in England;

    (h)   a registered pharmacist or a registered pharmacy technician within the meaning of the Pharmacy Order 2010 (S.I. 2010/231) (see article 3 of that Order);

    (i)   a registered person within the meaning of the Pharmacy (Northern Ireland) Order 1976 (S.I. 1976/1213 (N.I. 22)) (see Article 2 of that Order);

    (j)   a child psychotherapist;

    (k)   a scientist employed by a health service body as head of a department.

  (2)   In this Act, "social work professional" means any of the following —

    (a)   a person registered as a social worker in England in the register maintained under the Health and Social Work Professions Order 2001 (S.I. 2002/254);

    (b)   a person registered as a social worker in the register maintained by Social Care Wales under section 80 of the Regulation and Inspection of Social Care (Wales) Act 2016 (anaw 2);

    (c)   a person registered as a social worker in the register maintained by the Scottish Social Services Council under section 44 of the Regulation of Care (Scotland) Act 2001 (asp 8);

    (d)   a person registered as a social worker in the register maintained by the Northern Ireland Social Care Council under section 3 of the Health and Personal Social Services Act (Northern Ireland) 2001 (c. 3 (N.I.)).

  (3)   In subsection (1)(a) "registered medical practitioner" includes a person who is provisionally registered under section 15 or 21 of the Medical Act 1983 and is engaged in such employment as is mentioned in subsection (3) of that section.

  (4)   In subsection (1)(k) "health service body" means any of the following —

(a)   the Secretary of State in relation to the exercise of functions under section 2A or 2B of, or paragraph 7C, 8 or 12 of Schedule 1 to, the National Health Service Act 2006;

(b)   a local authority in relation to the exercise of functions under section 2B or 111 of, or any of paragraphs 1 to 7B or 13 of Schedule 1 to, the National Health Service Act 2006;

(c)   a National Health Service trust first established under section 25 of the National Health Service Act 2006;

(d)   a Special Health Authority established under section 28 of the National Health Service Act 2006;

(e)   an NHS foundation trust;

(f)   the National Institute for Health and Care Excellence;

(g)   the Health and Social Care Information Centre;

(h)   a National Health Service trust first established under section 5 of the National Health Service and Community Care Act 1990;

(i)   a Local Health Board established under section 11 of the National Health Service (Wales) Act 2006;

(j)   a National Health Service trust first established under section 18 of the National Health Service (Wales) Act 2006;

(k)   a Special Health Authority established under section 22 of the National Health Service (Wales) Act 2006;

(l)   a Health Board within the meaning of the National Health Service (Scotland) Act 1978;

(m)   a Special Health Board within the meaning of the National Health Service (Scotland) Act 1978;

(n)   a National Health Service trust first established under section 12A of the National Health Service (Scotland) Act 1978;

(o)   the managers of a State Hospital provided under section 102 of the National Health Service (Scotland) Act 1978;

(p)   the Regional Health and Social Care Board established under section 7 of the Health and Social Care (Reform) Act (Northern Ireland) 2009 (c. 1 (N.I));

(q)   a special health and social care agency established under the Health and Personal Social Services (Special Agencies) (Northern Ireland) Order 1990 (S.I. 1990/247 (N.I. 3));

(r)   a Health and Social Care trust established under Article 10 of the Health and Personal Social Services (Northern Ireland) Order 1991 (S.I. 1991/194 (N.I. 1)).

205   General interpretation

(1)   In this Act —

"biometric data" means personal data resulting from specific technical processing relating to the physical, physiological or behavioural characteristics of an individual, which allows or confirms the unique identification of that individual, such as facial images or dactyloscopic data;

"data concerning health" means personal data relating to the physical or mental health of an individual, including the provision of health care services, which reveals information about his or her health status;

"enactment" includes —

(a)   an enactment passed or made after this Act,

(b)   an enactment comprised in subordinate legislation,

(c)   an enactment comprised in, or in an instrument made under, a Measure or Act of the National Assembly for Wales,

(d)   an enactment comprised in, or in an instrument made under, an Act of the Scottish Parliament, and

(e)   an enactment comprised in, or in an instrument made under, Northern Ireland legislation;

"genetic data" means personal data relating to the inherited or acquired genetic characteristics of an individual which gives unique information about the physiology or the health of that individual and which results, in particular, from an analysis of a biological sample from the individual in question;

"government department" includes the following (except in the expression "United Kingdom government department") —

(a)   a part of the Scottish Administration;

(b)   a Northern Ireland department;

(c)   the Welsh Government;

(d)   a body or authority exercising statutory functions on behalf of the Crown;

"health record" means a record which —

(a)   consists of data concerning health, and

(b)   has been made by or on behalf of a health professional in connection with the diagnosis, care or treatment of the individual to whom the data relates;

"inaccurate", in relation to personal data, means incorrect or misleading as to any matter of fact;

"international obligation of the United Kingdom" includes —

(a)   an EU obligation, and

(b)   an obligation that arises under an international agreement or arrangement to which the United Kingdom is a party;

"international organisation" means an organisation and its subordinate bodies governed by international law, or any other body which is set up by, or on the basis of, an agreement between two or more countries;

"Minister of the Crown" has the same meaning as in the Ministers of the Crown Act 1975;

"publish" means make available to the public or a section of the public (and related expressions are to be read accordingly);

"subordinate legislation" has the meaning given in the Interpretation Act 1978;

"tribunal" means any tribunal in which legal proceedings may be brought;

"the Tribunal", in relation to an application or appeal under this Act, means —

(a)   the Upper Tribunal, in any case where it is determined by or under Tribunal Procedure Rules that the Upper Tribunal is to hear the application or appeal, or

(b)   the First-tier Tribunal, in any other case.

(2)   References in this Act to a period expressed in hours, days, weeks, months or years are to be interpreted in accordance with Article 3 of Regulation (EEC,

Euratom) No. 1182/71 of the Council of 3 June 1971 determining the rules applicable to periods, dates and time limits, except in —

   (a)   section 125(4), (7) and (8);
   (b)   section 161(3), (5) and (6);
   (c)   section 176(2);
   (d)   section 178(2);
   (e)   section 182(8) and (9);
   (f)   section 183(4);
   (g)   section 192(3), (5) and (6);
   (h)   section 197(3) and (4);
   (i)   paragraph 23(4) and (5) of Schedule 1;
   (j)   paragraphs 5(4) and 6(4) of Schedule 3;
   (k)   Schedule 5;
   (l)   paragraph 11(5) of Schedule 12;
   (m)   Schedule 15;

(and the references in section 5 to terms used in Chapter 2 or 3 of Part 2 do not include references to a period expressed in hours, days, weeks, months or years).

(3)   Section 3(14)(b) (interpretation of references to Chapter 2 of Part 2 in Parts 5 to 7) and the amendments in Schedule 19 which make equivalent provision are not to be treated as implying a contrary intention for the purposes of section 20(2) of the Interpretation Act 1978, or any similar provision in another enactment, as it applies to other references to, or to a provision of, Chapter 2 of Part 2 of this Act.

206 Index of defined expressions

The Table below lists provisions which define or otherwise explain terms defined for this Act, for a Part of this Act or for Chapter 2 or 3 of Part 2 of this Act.

the affirmative resolution procedure	section 182
the applied Chapter 2 (in Chapter 3 of Part 2)	section 22
the applied GDPR	section 3
assessment notice (in Part 6)	section 181
biometric data	section 205
certification provider (in Part 6)	section 181
the Commissioner	section 3
competent authority (in Part 3)	section 30
consent (in Part 4)	section 84
controller	section 3

data concerning health	section 205
the Data Protection Convention	section 3
the data protection legislation	section 3
data subject	section 3
employee (in Parts 3 and 4)	sections 33 and 84
enactment	section 205
enforcement notice (in Part 6)	section 181
filing system	section 3
FOI public authority (in Chapter 3 of Part 2)	section 21
the GDPR	section 3
genetic data	section 205
government department	section 205
health professional	section 204
health record	section 205
identifiable living individual	section 3
inaccurate	section 205
information notice (in Part 6)	section 181
intelligence service (in Part 4)	section 82
international obligation of the United Kingdom	section 205
international organisation	section 205
the Law Enforcement Directive	section 3
the law enforcement purposes (in Part 3)	section 31
the made affirmative resolution procedure	section 182
Minister of the Crown	section 205
the negative resolution procedure	section 182
penalty notice (in Part 6)	section 181
penalty variation notice (in Part 6)	section 181
personal data	section 3

personal data breach (in Parts 3 and 4)	sections 33 and 84
processing	section 3
processor	section 3
profiling (in Part 3)	section 33
public authority (in the GDPR and Part 2)	section 7
public body (in the GDPR and Part 2)	section 7
publish	section 205
recipient (in Parts 3 and 4)	sections 33 and 84
representative (in Part 6)	section 181
representative body (in relation to a right of a data subject)	section 187
restriction of processing (in Parts 3 and 4)	sections 33 and 84
social work professional	section 204
the special purposes (in Part 6)	section 174
special purposes proceedings (in Part 6)	section 174
subordinate legislation	section 205
third country (in Part 3)	section 33
tribunal	section 205
the Tribunal	section 205

Territorial application

207 Territorial application of this Act

(1) This Act applies only to processing of personal data described in subsections (2) and (3).

(2) It applies to the processing of personal data in the context of the activities of an establishment of a controller or processor in the United Kingdom, whether or not the processing takes place in the United Kingdom.

(3) It also applies to the processing of personal data to which Chapter 2 of Part 2 (the GDPR) applies where —

    (a) the processing is carried out in the context of the activities of an establishment of a controller or processor in a country or territory that

            is not a member State, whether or not the processing takes place in such
            a country or territory,

    (b)   the personal data relates to a data subject who is in the United Kingdom
            when the processing takes place, and

    (c)   the processing activities are related to—

        (i)   the offering of goods or services to data subjects in the United
                Kingdom, whether or not for payment, or

        (ii)   the monitoring of data subjects' behaviour in the United
                Kingdom.

(4)   Subsections (1) to (3) have effect subject to any provision in or made under
        section 120 providing for the Commissioner to carry out functions in relation
        to other processing of personal data.

(5)   Section 3(14)(c) does not apply to the reference to the processing of personal
        data in subsection (2).

(6)   The reference in subsection (3) to Chapter 2 of Part 2 (the GDPR) does not
        include that Chapter as applied by Chapter 3 of Part 2 (the applied GDPR).

(7)   In this section, references to a person who has an establishment in the United
        Kingdom include the following—

    (a)   an individual who is ordinarily resident in the United Kingdom,

    (b)   a body incorporated under the law of the United Kingdom or a part of
            the United Kingdom,

    (c)   a partnership or other unincorporated association formed under the
            law of the United Kingdom or a part of the United Kingdom, and

    (d)   a person not within paragraph (a), (b) or (c) who maintains, and carries
            on activities through, an office, branch or agency or other stable
            arrangements in the United Kingdom,

and references to a person who has an establishment in another country or
territory have a corresponding meaning.

General

208   Children in Scotland

(1)   Subsections (2) and (3) apply where a question falls to be determined in
        Scotland as to the legal capacity of a person aged under 16 to—

    (a)   exercise a right conferred by the data protection legislation, or

    (b)   give consent for the purposes of the data protection legislation.

(2)   The person is to be taken to have that capacity where the person has a general
        understanding of what it means to exercise the right or give such consent.

(3)   A person aged 12 or over is to be presumed to be of sufficient age and maturity
        to have such understanding, unless the contrary is shown.

209   Application to the Crown

(1)   This Act binds the Crown.

(2)   For the purposes of the GDPR and this Act, each government department is to
        be treated as a person separate from the other government departments (to the
        extent that is not already the case).

(3) Where government departments are not able to enter into contracts with each other, a provision of the GDPR or this Act that would require relations between them to be governed by a contract (or other binding legal act) in writing is to be treated as satisfied if the relations are the subject of a memorandum of understanding between them.

(4) Where the purposes for which and the manner in which personal data is, or is to be, processed are determined by a person acting on behalf of the Royal Household, the Duchy of Lancaster or the Duchy of Cornwall, the controller in respect of that data for the purposes of the GDPR and this Act is—

    (a) in relation to the Royal Household, the Keeper of the Privy Purse,

    (b) in relation to the Duchy of Lancaster, such person as the Chancellor of the Duchy appoints, and

    (c) in relation to the Duchy of Cornwall, such person as the Duke of Cornwall, or the possessor for the time being of the Duchy of Cornwall, appoints.

(5) Different persons may be appointed under subsection (4)(b) or (c) for different purposes.

(6) As regards criminal liability—

    (a) a government department is not liable to prosecution under this Act;

    (b) nothing in subsection (4) makes a person who is a controller by virtue of that subsection liable to prosecution under this Act;

    (c) a person in the service of the Crown is liable to prosecution under the provisions of this Act listed in subsection (7).

(7) Those provisions are—

    (a) section 119;

    (b) section 170;

    (c) section 171;

    (d) section 173;

    (e) paragraph 15 of Schedule 15.

210 Application to Parliament

(1) Parts 1, 2 and 5 to 7 of this Act apply to the processing of personal data by or on behalf of either House of Parliament.

(2) Where the purposes for which and the manner in which personal data is, or is to be, processed are determined by or on behalf of the House of Commons, the controller in respect of that data for the purposes of the GDPR and this Act is the Corporate Officer of that House.

(3) Where the purposes for which and the manner in which personal data is, or is to be, processed are determined by or on behalf of the House of Lords, the controller in respect of that data for the purposes of the GDPR and this Act is the Corporate Officer of that House.

(4) Subsections (2) and (3) do not apply where the purposes for which and the manner in which the personal data is, or is to be, processed are determined by or on behalf of the Intelligence and Security Committee of Parliament.

(5) As regards criminal liability—

       (a)   nothing in subsection (2) or (3) makes the Corporate Officer of the House of Commons or the Corporate Officer of the House of Lords liable to prosecution under this Act;

       (b)   a person acting on behalf of either House of Parliament is liable to prosecution under the provisions of this Act listed in subsection (6).

(6)   Those provisions are —
       (a)   section 170;
       (b)   section 171;
       (c)   section 173;
       (d)   paragraph 15 of Schedule 15.

211   Minor and consequential provision

(1)   In Schedule 19 —
       (a)   Part 1 contains minor and consequential amendments of primary legislation;
       (b)   Part 2 contains minor and consequential amendments of other legislation;
       (c)   Part 3 contains consequential modifications of legislation;
       (d)   Part 4 contains supplementary provision.

(2)   The Secretary of State may by regulations make provision that is consequential on any provision made by this Act.

(3)   Regulations under subsection (2) —
       (a)   may include transitional, transitory or saving provision;
       (b)   may amend, repeal or revoke an enactment.

(4)   The reference to an enactment in subsection (3)(b) does not include an enactment passed or made after the end of the Session in which this Act is passed.

(5)   Regulations under this section that amend, repeal or revoke primary legislation are subject to the affirmative resolution procedure.

(6)   Any other regulations under this section are subject to the negative resolution procedure.

(7)   In this section, "primary legislation" means —
       (a)   an Act;
       (b)   an Act of the Scottish Parliament;
       (c)   a Measure or Act of the National Assembly for Wales;
       (d)   Northern Ireland legislation.

Final

212   Commencement

(1)   Except as provided by subsections (2) and (3), this Act comes into force on such day as the Secretary of State may by regulations appoint.

(2)   This section and the following provisions come into force on the day on which this Act is passed —

    (a)   sections 1 and 3;

    (b)   section 182;

    (c)   sections 204, 205 and 206;

    (d)   sections 209 and 210;

    (e)   sections 213(2), 214 and 215;

    (f)   any other provision of this Act so far as it confers power to make regulations or Tribunal Procedure Rules or is otherwise necessary for enabling the exercise of such a power on or after the day on which this Act is passed.

(3)   The following provisions come into force at the end of the period of 2 months beginning when this Act is passed —

    (a)   section 124;

    (b)   sections 125, 126 and 127, so far as they relate to a code prepared under section 124;

    (c)   section 177;

    (d)   section 178 and Schedule 17;

    (e)   section 179.

(4)   Regulations under this section may make different provision for different areas.

213   Transitional provision

(1)   Schedule 20 contains transitional, transitory and saving provision.

(2)   The Secretary of State may by regulations make transitional, transitory or saving provision in connection with the coming into force of any provision of this Act or with the GDPR beginning to apply, including provision amending or repealing a provision of Schedule 20.

(3)   Regulations under this section that amend or repeal a provision of Schedule 20 are subject to the negative resolution procedure.

214   Extent

(1)   This Act extends to England and Wales, Scotland and Northern Ireland, subject to —

    (a)   subsections (2) to (5), and

    (b)   paragraph 12 of Schedule 12.

(2)   Section 199 extends to England and Wales only.

(3)   Sections 188, 189 and 190 extend to England and Wales and Northern Ireland only.

(4)   An amendment, repeal or revocation made by this Act has the same extent in the United Kingdom as the enactment amended, repealed or revoked.

(5)   This subsection and the following provisions also extend to the Isle of Man —

    (a)   paragraphs 332 and 434 of Schedule 19;

    (b)   sections 211(1), 212(1) and 213(2), so far as relating to those paragraphs.

(6)   Where there is a power to extend a part of an Act by Order in Council to any of the Channel Islands, the Isle of Man or any of the British overseas territories,

the power may be exercised in relation to an amendment or repeal of that part which is made by or under this Act.

215   Short title

This Act may be cited as the Data Protection Act 2018.

SCHEDULES

SCHEDULE 1   Section 10

SPECIAL CATEGORIES OF PERSONAL DATA AND CRIMINAL CONVICTIONS ETC DATA

PART 1

CONDITIONS RELATING TO EMPLOYMENT, HEALTH AND RESEARCH ETC

Employment, social security and social protection

1   (1) This condition is met if —

      (a) the processing is necessary for the purposes of performing or exercising obligations or rights which are imposed or conferred by law on the controller or the data subject in connection with employment, social security or social protection, and

      (b) when the processing is carried out, the controller has an appropriate policy document in place (see paragraph 39 in Part 4 of this Schedule).

    (2) See also the additional safeguards in Part 4 of this Schedule.

    (3) In this paragraph—

      "social security" includes any of the branches of social security listed in Article 3(1) of Regulation (EC) No. 883/2004 of the European Parliament and of the Council on the co-ordination of social security systems (as amended from time to time);

      "social protection" includes an intervention described in Article 2(b) of Regulation (EC) 458/2007 of the European Parliament and of the Council of 25 April 2007 on the European system of integrated social protection statistics (ESSPROS) (as amended from time to time).

Health or social care purposes

2   (1) This condition is met if the processing is necessary for health or social care purposes.

    (2) In this paragraph "health or social care purposes" means the purposes of —

      (a) preventive or occupational medicine,

      (b) the assessment of the working capacity of an employee,

      (c) medical diagnosis,

      (d) the provision of health care or treatment,

      (e) the provision of social care, or

      (f) the management of health care systems or services or social care systems or services.

132   *Data Protection Act 2018 (c. 12)*
Schedule 1 — Special categories of personal data and criminal convictions etc data
Part 1 — Conditions relating to employment, health and research etc

(3) See also the conditions and safeguards in Article 9(3) of the GDPR (obligations of secrecy) and section 11(1).

Public health

3   This condition is met if the processing —

    (a) is necessary for reasons of public interest in the area of public health, and

    (b) is carried out —

        (i) by or under the responsibility of a health professional, or

        (ii) by another person who in the circumstances owes a duty of confidentiality under an enactment or rule of law.

Research etc

4   This condition is met if the processing —

    (a) is necessary for archiving purposes, scientific or historical research purposes or statistical purposes,

    (b) is carried out in accordance with Article 89(1) of the GDPR (as supplemented by section 19), and

    (c) is in the public interest.

PART 2

SUBSTANTIAL PUBLIC INTEREST CONDITIONS

Requirement for an appropriate policy document when relying on conditions in this Part

5   (1) Except as otherwise provided, a condition in this Part of this Schedule is met only if, when the processing is carried out, the controller has an appropriate policy document in place (see paragraph 39 in Part 4 of this Schedule).

    (2) See also the additional safeguards in Part 4 of this Schedule.

Statutory etc and government purposes

6   (1) This condition is met if the processing —

    (a) is necessary for a purpose listed in sub-paragraph (2), and

    (b) is necessary for reasons of substantial public interest.

    (2) Those purposes are —

    (a) the exercise of a function conferred on a person by an enactment or rule of law;

    (b) the exercise of a function of the Crown, a Minister of the Crown or a government department.

Administration of justice and parliamentary purposes

7   This condition is met if the processing is necessary —

    (a) for the administration of justice, or

    (b) for the exercise of a function of either House of Parliament.

Data Protection Act 2018 (c. 12)
Schedule 1 — Special categories of personal data and criminal convictions etc data
Part 2 — Substantial public interest conditions

133

Equality of opportunity or treatment

8   (1) This condition is met if the processing —

       (a) is of a specified category of personal data, and

       (b) is necessary for the purposes of identifying or keeping under review the existence or absence of equality of opportunity or treatment between groups of people specified in relation to that category with a view to enabling such equality to be promoted or maintained,

      subject to the exceptions in sub-paragraphs (3) to (5).

   (2) In sub-paragraph (1), "specified" means specified in the following table —

Category of personal data	Groups of people (in relation to a category of personal data)
Personal data revealing racial or ethnic origin	People of different racial or ethnic origins
Personal data revealing religious or philosophical beliefs	People holding different religious or philosophical beliefs
Data concerning health	People with different states of physical or mental health
Personal data concerning an individual's sexual orientation	People of different sexual orientation

   (3) Processing does not meet the condition in sub-paragraph (1) if it is carried out for the purposes of measures or decisions with respect to a particular data subject.

   (4) Processing does not meet the condition in sub-paragraph (1) if it is likely to cause substantial damage or substantial distress to an individual.

   (5) Processing does not meet the condition in sub-paragraph (1) if —

       (a) an individual who is the data subject (or one of the data subjects) has given notice in writing to the controller requiring the controller not to process personal data in respect of which the individual is the data subject (and has not given notice in writing withdrawing that requirement),

       (b) the notice gave the controller a reasonable period in which to stop processing such data, and

       (c) that period has ended.

Racial and ethnic diversity at senior levels of organisations

9   (1) This condition is met if the processing —

       (a) is of personal data revealing racial or ethnic origin,

       (b) is carried out as part of a process of identifying suitable individuals to hold senior positions in a particular organisation, a type of organisation or organisations generally,

134   *Data Protection Act 2018 (c. 12)*
Schedule 1 — Special categories of personal data and criminal convictions etc data
Part 2 — Substantial public interest conditions

   (c)   is necessary for the purposes of promoting or maintaining diversity in the racial and ethnic origins of individuals who hold senior positions in the organisation or organisations, and

   (d)   can reasonably be carried out without the consent of the data subject,

subject to the exception in sub-paragraph (3).

(2) For the purposes of sub-paragraph (1)(d), processing can reasonably be carried out without the consent of the data subject only where —

   (a)   the controller cannot reasonably be expected to obtain the consent of the data subject, and

   (b)   the controller is not aware of the data subject withholding consent.

(3) Processing does not meet the condition in sub-paragraph (1) if it is likely to cause substantial damage or substantial distress to an individual.

(4) For the purposes of this paragraph, an individual holds a senior position in an organisation if the individual —

   (a)   holds a position listed in sub-paragraph (5), or

   (b)   does not hold such a position but is a senior manager of the organisation.

(5) Those positions are —

   (a)   a director, secretary or other similar officer of a body corporate;

   (b)   a member of a limited liability partnership;

   (c)   a partner in a partnership within the Partnership Act 1890, a limited partnership registered under the Limited Partnerships Act 1907 or an entity of a similar character formed under the law of a country or territory outside the United Kingdom.

(6) In this paragraph, "senior manager", in relation to an organisation, means a person who plays a significant role in —

   (a)   the making of decisions about how the whole or a substantial part of the organisation's activities are to be managed or organised, or

   (b)   the actual managing or organising of the whole or a substantial part of those activities.

(7) The reference in sub-paragraph (2)(b) to a data subject withholding consent does not include a data subject merely failing to respond to a request for consent.

Preventing or detecting unlawful acts

10   (1) This condition is met if the processing —

   (a)   is necessary for the purposes of the prevention or detection of an unlawful act,

   (b)   must be carried out without the consent of the data subject so as not to prejudice those purposes, and

   (c)   is necessary for reasons of substantial public interest.

(2) If the processing consists of the disclosure of personal data to a competent authority, or is carried out in preparation for such disclosure, the condition in sub-paragraph (1) is met even if, when the processing is carried out, the controller does not have an appropriate policy document in place (see paragraph 5 of this Schedule).

Data Protection Act 2018 (c. 12)
Schedule 1 — Special categories of personal data and criminal convictions etc data
Part 2 — Substantial public interest conditions

135

(3) In this paragraph—
"act" includes a failure to act;
"competent authority" has the same meaning as in Part 3 of this Act (see section 30).

Protecting the public against dishonesty etc

11 (1) This condition is met if the processing—
- (a) is necessary for the exercise of a protective function,
- (b) must be carried out without the consent of the data subject so as not to prejudice the exercise of that function, and
- (c) is necessary for reasons of substantial public interest.

(2) In this paragraph, "protective function" means a function which is intended to protect members of the public against—
- (a) dishonesty, malpractice or other seriously improper conduct,
- (b) unfitness or incompetence,
- (c) mismanagement in the administration of a body or association, or
- (d) failures in services provided by a body or association.

Regulatory requirements relating to unlawful acts and dishonesty etc

12 (1) This condition is met if—
- (a) the processing is necessary for the purposes of complying with, or assisting other persons to comply with, a regulatory requirement which involves a person taking steps to establish whether another person has—
  - (i) committed an unlawful act, or
  - (ii) been involved in dishonesty, malpractice or other seriously improper conduct,
- (b) in the circumstances, the controller cannot reasonably be expected to obtain the consent of the data subject to the processing, and
- (c) the processing is necessary for reasons of substantial public interest.

(2) In this paragraph—
"act" includes a failure to act;
"regulatory requirement" means—
- (a) a requirement imposed by legislation or by a person in exercise of a function conferred by legislation, or
- (b) a requirement forming part of generally accepted principles of good practice relating to a type of body or an activity.

Journalism etc in connection with unlawful acts and dishonesty etc

13 (1) This condition is met if—
- (a) the processing consists of the disclosure of personal data for the special purposes,
- (b) it is carried out in connection with a matter described in sub-paragraph (2),
- (c) it is necessary for reasons of substantial public interest,
- (d) it is carried out with a view to the publication of the personal data by any person, and

136   *Data Protection Act 2018 (c. 12)*
Schedule 1 — Special categories of personal data and criminal convictions etc data
Part 2 — Substantial public interest conditions

     (e)   the controller reasonably believes that publication of the personal data would be in the public interest.

  (2) The matters mentioned in sub-paragraph (1)(b) are any of the following (whether alleged or established) —

     (a)   the commission of an unlawful act by a person;

     (b)   dishonesty, malpractice or other seriously improper conduct of a person;

     (c)   unfitness or incompetence of a person;

     (d)   mismanagement in the administration of a body or association;

     (e)   a failure in services provided by a body or association.

  (3) The condition in sub-paragraph (1) is met even if, when the processing is carried out, the controller does not have an appropriate policy document in place (see paragraph 5 of this Schedule).

  (4) In this paragraph —

     "act" includes a failure to act;

     "the special purposes" means —

        (a)   the purposes of journalism;

        (b)   academic purposes;

        (c)   artistic purposes;

        (d)   literary purposes.

Preventing fraud

14 (1) This condition is met if the processing —

     (a)   is necessary for the purposes of preventing fraud or a particular kind of fraud, and

     (b)   consists of —

        (i)   the disclosure of personal data by a person as a member of an anti-fraud organisation,

        (ii)   the disclosure of personal data in accordance with arrangements made by an anti-fraud organisation, or

        (iii)   the processing of personal data disclosed as described in sub-paragraph (i) or (ii).

  (2) In this paragraph, "anti-fraud organisation" has the same meaning as in section 68 of the Serious Crime Act 2007.

Suspicion of terrorist financing or money laundering

15   This condition is met if the processing is necessary for the purposes of making a disclosure in good faith under either of the following —

     (a)   section 21CA of the Terrorism Act 2000 (disclosures between certain entities within regulated sector in relation to suspicion of commission of terrorist financing offence or for purposes of identifying terrorist property);

     (b)   section 339ZB of the Proceeds of Crime Act 2002 (disclosures within regulated sector in relation to suspicion of money laundering).

Data Protection Act 2018 (c. 12)
Schedule 1 — Special categories of personal data and criminal convictions etc data
Part 2 — Substantial public interest conditions

137

Support for individuals with a particular disability or medical condition

16   (1) This condition is met if the processing —

    (a) is carried out by a not-for-profit body which provides support to individuals with a particular disability or medical condition,

    (b) is of a type of personal data falling within sub-paragraph (2) which relates to an individual falling within sub-paragraph (3),

    (c) is necessary for the purposes of —

        (i)   raising awareness of the disability or medical condition, or

        (ii) providing support to individuals falling within sub-paragraph (3) or enabling such individuals to provide support to each other,

    (d) can reasonably be carried out without the consent of the data subject, and

    (e) is necessary for reasons of substantial public interest.

    (2) The following types of personal data fall within this sub-paragraph —

    (a) personal data revealing racial or ethnic origin;

    (b) genetic data or biometric data;

    (c) data concerning health;

    (d) personal data concerning an individual's sex life or sexual orientation.

    (3) An individual falls within this sub-paragraph if the individual is or has been a member of the body mentioned in sub-paragraph (1)(a) and —

    (a) has the disability or condition mentioned there, has had that disability or condition or has a significant risk of developing that disability or condition, or

    (b) is a relative or carer of an individual who satisfies paragraph (a) of this sub-paragraph.

    (4) For the purposes of sub-paragraph (1)(d), processing can reasonably be carried out without the consent of the data subject only where —

    (a) the controller cannot reasonably be expected to obtain the consent of the data subject, and

    (b) the controller is not aware of the data subject withholding consent.

    (5) In this paragraph —

        "carer" means an individual who provides or intends to provide care for another individual other than —

        (a) under or by virtue of a contract, or

        (b) as voluntary work;

        "disability" has the same meaning as in the Equality Act 2010 (see section 6 of, and Schedule 1 to, that Act).

    (6) The reference in sub-paragraph (4)(b) to a data subject withholding consent does not include a data subject merely failing to respond to a request for consent.

Counselling etc

17   (1) This condition is met if the processing —

138

Data Protection Act 2018 (c. 12)
Schedule 1 — Special categories of personal data and criminal convictions etc data
Part 2 — Substantial public interest conditions

(a)   is necessary for the provision of confidential counselling, advice or support or of another similar service provided confidentially,

(b)   is carried out without the consent of the data subject for one of the reasons listed in sub-paragraph (2), and

(c)   is necessary for reasons of substantial public interest.

(2) The reasons mentioned in sub-paragraph (1)(b) are —

(a)   in the circumstances, consent to the processing cannot be given by the data subject;

(b)   in the circumstances, the controller cannot reasonably be expected to obtain the consent of the data subject to the processing;

(c)   the processing must be carried out without the consent of the data subject because obtaining the consent of the data subject would prejudice the provision of the service mentioned in sub-paragraph (1)(a).

Safeguarding of children and of individuals at risk

18   (1) This condition is met if —

(a)   the processing is necessary for the purposes of —

(i)   protecting an individual from neglect or physical, mental or emotional harm, or

(ii)   protecting the physical, mental or emotional well-being of an individual,

(b)   the individual is —

(i)   aged under 18, or

(ii)   aged 18 or over and at risk,

(c)   the processing is carried out without the consent of the data subject for one of the reasons listed in sub-paragraph (2), and

(d)   the processing is necessary for reasons of substantial public interest.

(2) The reasons mentioned in sub-paragraph (1)(c) are —

(a)   in the circumstances, consent to the processing cannot be given by the data subject;

(b)   in the circumstances, the controller cannot reasonably be expected to obtain the consent of the data subject to the processing;

(c)   the processing must be carried out without the consent of the data subject because obtaining the consent of the data subject would prejudice the provision of the protection mentioned in sub-paragraph (1)(a).

(3) For the purposes of this paragraph, an individual aged 18 or over is "at risk" if the controller has reasonable cause to suspect that the individual —

(a)   has needs for care and support,

(b)   is experiencing, or at risk of, neglect or physical, mental or emotional harm, and

(c)   as a result of those needs is unable to protect himself or herself against the neglect or harm or the risk of it.

(4) In sub-paragraph (1)(a), the reference to the protection of an individual or of the well-being of an individual includes both protection relating to a particular individual and protection relating to a type of individual.

Data Protection Act 2018 (c. 12)
Schedule 1 — Special categories of personal data and criminal convictions etc data
Part 2 — Substantial public interest conditions

139

Safeguarding of economic well-being of certain individuals

19   (1) This condition is met if the processing—

   (a)   is necessary for the purposes of protecting the economic well-being of an individual at economic risk who is aged 18 or over,

   (b)   is of data concerning health,

   (c)   is carried out without the consent of the data subject for one of the reasons listed in sub-paragraph (2), and

   (d)   is necessary for reasons of substantial public interest.

   (2) The reasons mentioned in sub-paragraph (1)(c) are—

   (a)   in the circumstances, consent to the processing cannot be given by the data subject;

   (b)   in the circumstances, the controller cannot reasonably be expected to obtain the consent of the data subject to the processing;

   (c)   the processing must be carried out without the consent of the data subject because obtaining the consent of the data subject would prejudice the provision of the protection mentioned in sub-paragraph (1)(a).

   (3) In this paragraph, "individual at economic risk" means an individual who is less able to protect his or her economic well-being by reason of physical or mental injury, illness or disability.

Insurance

20   (1) This condition is met if the processing—

   (a)   is necessary for an insurance purpose,

   (b)   is of personal data revealing racial or ethnic origin, religious or philosophical beliefs or trade union membership, genetic data or data concerning health, and

   (c)   is necessary for reasons of substantial public interest,

   subject to sub-paragraphs (2) and (3).

   (2) Sub-paragraph (3) applies where—

   (a)   the processing is not carried out for the purposes of measures or decisions with respect to the data subject, and

   (b)   the data subject does not have and is not expected to acquire—

       (i)   rights against, or obligations in relation to, a person who is an insured person under an insurance contract to which the insurance purpose mentioned in sub-paragraph (1)(a) relates, or

       (ii)   other rights or obligations in connection with such a contract.

   (3) Where this sub-paragraph applies, the processing does not meet the condition in sub-paragraph (1) unless, in addition to meeting the requirements in that sub-paragraph, it can reasonably be carried out without the consent of the data subject.

   (4) For the purposes of sub-paragraph (3), processing can reasonably be carried out without the consent of the data subject only where—

   (a)   the controller cannot reasonably be expected to obtain the consent of the data subject, and

   (b)   the controller is not aware of the data subject withholding consent.

140

Data Protection Act 2018 (c. 12)
Schedule 1 — Special categories of personal data and criminal convictions etc data
Part 2 — Substantial public interest conditions

(5) In this paragraph—

"insurance contract" means a contract of general insurance or long-term insurance;

"insurance purpose" means—

    (a)   advising on, arranging, underwriting or administering an insurance contract,

    (b)   administering a claim under an insurance contract, or

    (c)   exercising a right, or complying with an obligation, arising in connection with an insurance contract, including a right or obligation arising under an enactment or rule of law.

(6) The reference in sub-paragraph (4)(b) to a data subject withholding consent does not include a data subject merely failing to respond to a request for consent.

(7) Terms used in the definition of "insurance contract" in sub-paragraph (5) and also in an order made under section 22 of the Financial Services and Markets Act 2000 (regulated activities) have the same meaning in that definition as they have in that order.

Occupational pensions

21 (1) This condition is met if the processing—

    (a)   is necessary for the purpose of making a determination in connection with eligibility for, or benefits payable under, an occupational pension scheme,

    (b)   is of data concerning health which relates to a data subject who is the parent, grandparent, great-grandparent or sibling of a member of the scheme,

    (c)   is not carried out for the purposes of measures or decisions with respect to the data subject, and

    (d)   can reasonably be carried out without the consent of the data subject.

(2) For the purposes of sub-paragraph (1)(d), processing can reasonably be carried out without the consent of the data subject only where—

    (a)   the controller cannot reasonably be expected to obtain the consent of the data subject, and

    (b)   the controller is not aware of the data subject withholding consent.

(3) In this paragraph—

"occupational pension scheme" has the meaning given in section 1 of the Pension Schemes Act 1993;

"member", in relation to a scheme, includes an individual who is seeking to become a member of the scheme.

(4) The reference in sub-paragraph (2)(b) to a data subject withholding consent does not include a data subject merely failing to respond to a request for consent.

Political parties

22 (1) This condition is met if the processing—

    (a)   is of personal data revealing political opinions,

Data Protection Act 2018 (c. 12)   141
Schedule 1 — Special categories of personal data and criminal convictions etc data
Part 2 — Substantial public interest conditions

       (b)   is carried out by a person or organisation included in the register maintained under section 23 of the Political Parties, Elections and Referendums Act 2000, and

       (c)   is necessary for the purposes of the person's or organisation's political activities,

subject to the exceptions in sub-paragraphs (2) and (3).

(2)   Processing does not meet the condition in sub-paragraph (1) if it is likely to cause substantial damage or substantial distress to a person.

(3)   Processing does not meet the condition in sub-paragraph (1) if —

       (a)   an individual who is the data subject (or one of the data subjects) has given notice in writing to the controller requiring the controller not to process personal data in respect of which the individual is the data subject (and has not given notice in writing withdrawing that requirement),

       (b)   the notice gave the controller a reasonable period in which to stop processing such data, and

       (c)   that period has ended.

(4)   In this paragraph, "political activities" include campaigning, fund-raising, political surveys and case-work.

Elected representatives responding to requests

23   (1)   This condition is met if —

       (a)   the processing is carried out —

           (i)   by an elected representative or a person acting with the authority of such a representative,

           (ii)   in connection with the discharge of the elected representative's functions, and

           (iii)   in response to a request by an individual that the elected representative take action on behalf of the individual, and

       (b)   the processing is necessary for the purposes of, or in connection with, the action reasonably taken by the elected representative in response to that request,

subject to sub-paragraph (2).

(2)   Where the request is made by an individual other than the data subject, the condition in sub-paragraph (1) is met only if the processing must be carried out without the consent of the data subject for one of the following reasons —

       (a)   in the circumstances, consent to the processing cannot be given by the data subject;

       (b)   in the circumstances, the elected representative cannot reasonably be expected to obtain the consent of the data subject to the processing;

       (c)   obtaining the consent of the data subject would prejudice the action taken by the elected representative;

       (d)   the processing is necessary in the interests of another individual and the data subject has withheld consent unreasonably.

(3)   In this paragraph, "elected representative" means —

       (a)   a member of the House of Commons;

       (b)   a member of the National Assembly for Wales;

       (c)   a member of the Scottish Parliament;

142

Data Protection Act 2018 (c. 12)
Schedule 1 — Special categories of personal data and criminal convictions etc data
Part 2 — Substantial public interest conditions

    (d)   a member of the Northern Ireland Assembly;

    (e)   a member of the European Parliament elected in the United Kingdom;

    (f)   an elected member of a local authority within the meaning of section 270(1) of the Local Government Act 1972, namely —

        (i)   in England, a county council, a district council, a London borough council or a parish council;

        (ii)   in Wales, a county council, a county borough council or a community council;

    (g)   an elected mayor of a local authority within the meaning of Part 1A or 2 of the Local Government Act 2000;

    (h)   a mayor for the area of a combined authority established under section 103 of the Local Democracy, Economic Development and Construction Act 2009;

    (i)   the Mayor of London or an elected member of the London Assembly;

    (j)   an elected member of —

        (i)   the Common Council of the City of London, or

        (ii)   the Council of the Isles of Scilly;

    (k)   an elected member of a council constituted under section 2 of the Local Government etc (Scotland) Act 1994;

    (l)   an elected member of a district council within the meaning of the Local Government Act (Northern Ireland) 1972 (c. 9 (N.I.));

    (m)   a police and crime commissioner.

  (4) For the purposes of sub-paragraph (3), a person who is —

    (a)   a member of the House of Commons immediately before Parliament is dissolved,

    (b)   a member of the National Assembly for Wales immediately before that Assembly is dissolved,

    (c)   a member of the Scottish Parliament immediately before that Parliament is dissolved, or

    (d)   a member of the Northern Ireland Assembly immediately before that Assembly is dissolved,

is to be treated as if the person were such a member until the end of the fourth day after the day on which the subsequent general election in relation to that Parliament or Assembly is held.

  (5) For the purposes of sub-paragraph (3), a person who is an elected member of the Common Council of the City of London and whose term of office comes to an end at the end of the day preceding the annual Wardmotes is to be treated as if he or she were such a member until the end of the fourth day after the day on which those Wardmotes are held.

Disclosure to elected representatives

24 (1) This condition is met if —

    (a)   the processing consists of the disclosure of personal data —

        (i)   to an elected representative or a person acting with the authority of such a representative, and

        (ii)   in response to a communication to the controller from that representative or person which was made in response to a request from an individual,

Data Protection Act 2018 (c. 12)
Schedule 1 — Special categories of personal data and criminal convictions etc data
Part 2 — Substantial public interest conditions

143

      (b)   the personal data is relevant to the subject matter of that communication, and

      (c)   the disclosure is necessary for the purpose of responding to that communication,

subject to sub-paragraph (2).

(2)   Where the request to the elected representative came from an individual other than the data subject, the condition in sub-paragraph (1) is met only if the disclosure must be made without the consent of the data subject for one of the following reasons —

      (a)   in the circumstances, consent to the processing cannot be given by the data subject;

      (b)   in the circumstances, the elected representative cannot reasonably be expected to obtain the consent of the data subject to the processing;

      (c)   obtaining the consent of the data subject would prejudice the action taken by the elected representative;

      (d)   the processing is necessary in the interests of another individual and the data subject has withheld consent unreasonably.

(3)   In this paragraph, "elected representative" has the same meaning as in paragraph 23.

Informing elected representatives about prisoners

25   (1)   This condition is met if —

      (a)   the processing consists of the processing of personal data about a prisoner for the purpose of informing a member of the House of Commons, a member of the National Assembly for Wales or a member of the Scottish Parliament about the prisoner, and

      (b)   the member is under an obligation not to further disclose the personal data.

(2)   The references in sub-paragraph (1) to personal data about, and to informing someone about, a prisoner include personal data about, and informing someone about, arrangements for the prisoner's release.

(3)   In this paragraph —

      "prison" includes a young offender institution, a remand centre, a secure training centre or a secure college;

      "prisoner" means a person detained in a prison.

Publication of legal judgments

26   This condition is met if the processing —

      (a)   consists of the publication of a judgment or other decision of a court or tribunal, or

      (b)   is necessary for the purposes of publishing such a judgment or decision.

Anti-doping in sport

27   (1)   This condition is met if the processing is necessary —

      (a)   for the purposes of measures designed to eliminate doping which are undertaken by or under the responsibility of a body or association

144

Data Protection Act 2018 (c. 12)
Schedule 1 — Special categories of personal data and criminal convictions etc data
Part 2 — Substantial public interest conditions

that is responsible for eliminating doping in a sport, at a sporting event or in sport generally, or

    (b)   for the purposes of providing information about doping, or suspected doping, to such a body or association.

(2) The reference in sub-paragraph (1)(a) to measures designed to eliminate doping includes measures designed to identify or prevent doping.

(3) If the processing consists of the disclosure of personal data to a body or association described in sub-paragraph (1)(a), or is carried out in preparation for such disclosure, the condition in sub-paragraph (1) is met even if, when the processing is carried out, the controller does not have an appropriate policy document in place (see paragraph 5 of this Schedule).

Standards of behaviour in sport

28   (1) This condition is met if the processing—

    (a)   is necessary for the purposes of measures designed to protect the integrity of a sport or a sporting event,

    (b)   must be carried out without the consent of the data subject so as not to prejudice those purposes, and

    (c)   is necessary for reasons of substantial public interest.

(2) In sub-paragraph (1)(a), the reference to measures designed to protect the integrity of a sport or a sporting event is a reference to measures designed to protect a sport or a sporting event against—

    (a)   dishonesty, malpractice or other seriously improper conduct, or

    (b)   failure by a person participating in the sport or event in any capacity to comply with standards of behaviour set by a body or association with responsibility for the sport or event.

PART 3

ADDITIONAL CONDITIONS RELATING TO CRIMINAL CONVICTIONS ETC

Consent

29   This condition is met if the data subject has given consent to the processing.

Protecting individual's vital interests

30   This condition is met if—

    (a)   the processing is necessary to protect the vital interests of an individual, and

    (b)   the data subject is physically or legally incapable of giving consent.

Processing by not-for-profit bodies

31   This condition is met if the processing is carried out—

    (a)   in the course of its legitimate activities with appropriate safeguards by a foundation, association or other not-for-profit body with a political, philosophical, religious or trade union aim, and

    (b)   on condition that—

Data Protection Act 2018 (c. 12)
Schedule 1 — Special categories of personal data and criminal convictions etc data
Part 3 — Additional conditions relating to criminal convictions etc

145

        (i)   the processing relates solely to the members or to former members of the body or to persons who have regular contact with it in connection with its purposes, and

       (ii)   the personal data is not disclosed outside that body without the consent of the data subjects.

Personal data in the public domain

32   This condition is met if the processing relates to personal data which is manifestly made public by the data subject.

Legal claims

33   This condition is met if the processing —

    (a)   is necessary for the purpose of, or in connection with, any legal proceedings (including prospective legal proceedings),

    (b)   is necessary for the purpose of obtaining legal advice, or

    (c)   is otherwise necessary for the purposes of establishing, exercising or defending legal rights.

Judicial acts

34   This condition is met if the processing is necessary when a court or tribunal is acting in its judicial capacity.

Administration of accounts used in commission of indecency offences involving children

35   (1) This condition is met if —

    (a)   the processing is of personal data about a conviction or caution for an offence listed in sub-paragraph (2),

    (b)   the processing is necessary for the purpose of administering an account relating to the payment card used in the commission of the offence or cancelling that payment card, and

    (c)   when the processing is carried out, the controller has an appropriate policy document in place (see paragraph 39 in Part 4 of this Schedule).

   (2) Those offences are an offence under —

    (a)   section 1 of the Protection of Children Act 1978 (indecent photographs of children),

    (b)   Article 3 of the Protection of Children (Northern Ireland) Order 1978 (S.I. 1978/1047 (N.I. 17)) (indecent photographs of children),

    (c)   section 52 of the Civic Government (Scotland) Act 1982 (indecent photographs etc of children),

    (d)   section 160 of the Criminal Justice Act 1988 (possession of indecent photograph of child),

    (e)   Article 15 of the Criminal Justice (Evidence etc) (Northern Ireland) Order 1988 (S.I. 1988/1847 (N.I. 17)) (possession of indecent photograph of child), or

    (f)   section 62 of the Coroners and Justice Act 2009 (possession of prohibited images of children),

or incitement to commit an offence under any of those provisions.

146   *Data Protection Act 2018 (c. 12)*
Schedule 1 — Special categories of personal data and criminal convictions etc data
Part 3 — Additional conditions relating to criminal convictions etc

(3) See also the additional safeguards in Part 4 of this Schedule.

(4) In this paragraph—

"caution" means a caution given to a person in England and Wales or Northern Ireland in respect of an offence which, at the time when the caution is given, is admitted;

"conviction" has the same meaning as in the Rehabilitation of Offenders Act 1974 or the Rehabilitation of Offenders (Northern Ireland) Order 1978 (S.I. 1978/1908 (N.I. 27));

"payment card" includes a credit card, a charge card and a debit card.

Extension of conditions in Part 2 of this Schedule referring to substantial public interest

36   This condition is met if the processing would meet a condition in Part 2 of this Schedule but for an express requirement for the processing to be necessary for reasons of substantial public interest.

Extension of insurance conditions

37   This condition is met if the processing—

(a) would meet the condition in paragraph 20 in Part 2 of this Schedule (the "insurance condition"), or

(b) would meet the condition in paragraph 36 by virtue of the insurance condition,

but for the requirement for the processing to be processing of a category of personal data specified in paragraph 20(1)(b).

PART 4

APPROPRIATE POLICY DOCUMENT AND ADDITIONAL SAFEGUARDS

Application of this Part of this Schedule

38   This Part of this Schedule makes provision about the processing of personal data carried out in reliance on a condition in Part 1, 2 or 3 of this Schedule which requires the controller to have an appropriate policy document in place when the processing is carried out.

Requirement to have an appropriate policy document in place

39   The controller has an appropriate policy document in place in relation to the processing of personal data in reliance on a condition described in paragraph 38 if the controller has produced a document which—

(a) explains the controller's procedures for securing compliance with the principles in Article 5 of the GDPR (principles relating to processing of personal data) in connection with the processing of personal data in reliance on the condition in question, and

(b) explains the controller's policies as regards the retention and erasure of personal data processed in reliance on the condition, giving an indication of how long such personal data is likely to be retained.

Data Protection Act 2018 (c. 12)
Schedule 1 — Special categories of personal data and criminal convictions etc data
Part 4 — Appropriate policy document and additional safeguards

147

Additional safeguard: retention of appropriate policy document

40   (1)   Where personal data is processed in reliance on a condition described in paragraph 38, the controller must during the relevant period —

      (a)   retain the appropriate policy document,

      (b)   review and (if appropriate) update it from time to time, and

      (c)   make it available to the Commissioner, on request, without charge.

    (2)   "Relevant period", in relation to the processing of personal data in reliance on a condition described in paragraph 38, means a period which —

      (a)   begins when the controller starts to carry out processing of personal data in reliance on that condition, and

      (b)   ends at the end of the period of 6 months beginning when the controller ceases to carry out such processing.

Additional safeguard: record of processing

41   A record maintained by the controller, or the controller's representative, under Article 30 of the GDPR in respect of the processing of personal data in reliance on a condition described in paragraph 38 must include the following information —

      (a)   which condition is relied on,

      (b)   how the processing satisfies Article 6 of the GDPR (lawfulness of processing), and

      (c)   whether the personal data is retained and erased in accordance with the policies described in paragraph 39(b) and, if it is not, the reasons for not following those policies.

SCHEDULE 2   Section 15

EXEMPTIONS ETC FROM THE GDPR

PART 1

ADAPTATIONS AND RESTRICTIONS BASED ON ARTICLES 6(3) AND 23(1)

GDPR provisions to be adapted or restricted: "the listed GDPR provisions"

1   In this Part of this Schedule, "the listed GDPR provisions" means —

      (a)   the following provisions of the GDPR (the rights and obligations in which may be restricted by virtue of Article 23(1) of the GDPR) —

          (i)   Article 13(1) to (3) (personal data collected from data subject: information to be provided);

         (ii)   Article 14(1) to (4) (personal data collected other than from data subject: information to be provided);

        (iii)   Article 15(1) to (3) (confirmation of processing, access to data and safeguards for third country transfers);

        (iv)   Article 16 (right to rectification);

         (v)   Article 17(1) and (2) (right to erasure);

        (vi)   Article 18(1) (restriction of processing);

148

Data Protection Act 2018 (c. 12)
Schedule 2 — Exemptions etc from the GDPR
Part 1 — Adaptations and restrictions based on Articles 6(3) and 23(1)

      (vii)   Article 19 (notification obligation regarding rectification or erasure of personal data or restriction of processing);

      (viii)   Article 20(1) and (2) (right to data portability);

      (ix)   Article 21(1) (objections to processing);

      (x)   Article 5 (general principles) so far as its provisions correspond to the rights and obligations provided for in the provisions mentioned in sub-paragraphs (i) to (ix); and

    (b)   the following provisions of the GDPR (the application of which may be adapted by virtue of Article 6(3) of the GDPR) —

      (i)   Article 5(1)(a) (lawful, fair and transparent processing), other than the lawfulness requirements set out in Article 6;

      (ii)   Article 5(1)(b) (purpose limitation).

Crime and taxation: general

2   (1)   The listed GDPR provisions and Article 34(1) and (4) of the GDPR (communication of personal data breach to the data subject) do not apply to personal data processed for any of the following purposes —

    (a)   the prevention or detection of crime,

    (b)   the apprehension or prosecution of offenders, or

    (c)   the assessment or collection of a tax or duty or an imposition of a similar nature,

to the extent that the application of those provisions would be likely to prejudice any of the matters mentioned in paragraphs (a) to (c).

    (2)   Sub-paragraph (3) applies where —

    (a)   personal data is processed by a person ("Controller 1") for any of the purposes mentioned in sub-paragraph (1)(a) to (c), and

    (b)   another person ("Controller 2") obtains the data from Controller 1 for the purpose of discharging statutory functions and processes it for the purpose of discharging statutory functions.

    (3)   Controller 2 is exempt from the obligations in the following provisions of the GDPR —

    (a)   Article 13(1) to (3) (personal data collected from data subject: information to be provided),

    (b)   Article 14(1) to (4) (personal data collected other than from data subject: information to be provided),

    (c)   Article 15(1) to (3) (confirmation of processing, access to data and safeguards for third country transfers), and

    (d)   Article 5 (general principles) so far as its provisions correspond to the rights and obligations provided for in the provisions mentioned in paragraphs (a) to (c),

to the same extent that Controller 1 is exempt from those obligations by virtue of sub-paragraph (1).

Crime and taxation: risk assessment systems

3   (1)   The GDPR provisions listed in sub-paragraph (3) do not apply to personal data which consists of a classification applied to the data subject as part of a risk assessment system falling within sub-paragraph (2) to the extent that the application of those provisions would prevent the system from operating effectively.

Data Protection Act 2018 (c. 12)
Schedule 2 — Exemptions etc from the GDPR
Part 1 — Adaptations and restrictions based on Articles 6(3) and 23(1)

149

(2) A risk assessment system falls within this sub-paragraph if —

    (a) it is operated by a government department, a local authority or another authority administering housing benefit, and

    (b) it is operated for the purposes of —

        (i) the assessment or collection of a tax or duty or an imposition of a similar nature, or

        (ii) the prevention or detection of crime or apprehension or prosecution of offenders, where the offence concerned involves the unlawful use of public money or an unlawful claim for payment out of public money.

(3) The GDPR provisions referred to in sub-paragraph (1) are the following provisions of the GDPR (the rights and obligations in which may be restricted by virtue of Article 23(1) of the GDPR) —

    (a) Article 13(1) to (3) (personal data collected from data subject: information to be provided);

    (b) Article 14(1) to (4) (personal data collected other than from data subject: information to be provided);

    (c) Article 15(1) to (3) (confirmation of processing, access to data and safeguards for third country transfers);

    (d) Article 5 (general principles) so far as its provisions correspond to the rights and obligations provided for in the provisions mentioned in paragraphs (a) to (c).

Immigration

4 (1) The GDPR provisions listed in sub-paragraph (2) do not apply to personal data processed for any of the following purposes —

    (a) the maintenance of effective immigration control, or

    (b) the investigation or detection of activities that would undermine the maintenance of effective immigration control,

to the extent that the application of those provisions would be likely to prejudice any of the matters mentioned in paragraphs (a) and (b).

(2) The GDPR provisions referred to in sub-paragraph (1) are the following provisions of the GDPR (the rights and obligations in which may be restricted by virtue of Article 23(1) of the GDPR) —

    (a) Article 13(1) to (3) (personal data collected from data subject: information to be provided);

    (b) Article 14(1) to (4) (personal data collected other than from data subject: information to be provided);

    (c) Article 15(1) to (3) (confirmation of processing, access to data and safeguards for third country transfers);

    (d) Article 17(1) and (2) (right to erasure);

    (e) Article 18(1) (restriction of processing);

    (f) Article 21(1) (objections to processing);

    (g) Article 5 (general principles) so far as its provisions correspond to the rights and obligations provided for in the provisions mentioned in sub-paragraphs (a) to (f).

(That is, the listed GDPR provisions other than Article 16 (right to rectification), Article 19 (notification obligation regarding rectification or erasure of personal data or restriction of processing) and Article 20(1) and (2)

150

Data Protection Act 2018 (c. 12)
Schedule 2 — Exemptions etc from the GDPR
Part 1 — Adaptations and restrictions based on Articles 6(3) and 23(1)

(right to data portability) and, subject to sub-paragraph (2)(g) of this paragraph, the provisions of Article 5 listed in paragraph 1(b).)

   (3) Sub-paragraph (4) applies where—

     (a) personal data is processed by a person ("Controller 1"), and

     (b) another person ("Controller 2") obtains the data from Controller 1 for any of the purposes mentioned in sub-paragraph (1)(a) and (b) and processes it for any of those purposes.

   (4) Controller 1 is exempt from the obligations in the following provisions of the GDPR—

     (a) Article 13(1) to (3) (personal data collected from data subject: information to be provided),

     (b) Article 14(1) to (4) (personal data collected other than from data subject: information to be provided),

     (c) Article 15(1) to (3) (confirmation of processing, access to data and safeguards for third country transfers), and

     (d) Article 5 (general principles) so far as its provisions correspond to the rights and obligations provided for in the provisions mentioned in paragraphs (a) to (c),

to the same extent that Controller 2 is exempt from those obligations by virtue of sub-paragraph (1).

Information required to be disclosed by law etc or in connection with legal proceedings

5   (1) The listed GDPR provisions do not apply to personal data consisting of information that the controller is obliged by an enactment to make available to the public, to the extent that the application of those provisions would prevent the controller from complying with that obligation.

   (2) The listed GDPR provisions do not apply to personal data where disclosure of the data is required by an enactment, a rule of law or an order of a court or tribunal, to the extent that the application of those provisions would prevent the controller from making the disclosure.

   (3) The listed GDPR provisions do not apply to personal data where disclosure of the data—

     (a) is necessary for the purpose of, or in connection with, legal proceedings (including prospective legal proceedings),

     (b) is necessary for the purpose of obtaining legal advice, or

     (c) is otherwise necessary for the purposes of establishing, exercising or defending legal rights,

to the extent that the application of those provisions would prevent the controller from making the disclosure.

PART 2

RESTRICTIONS BASED ON ARTICLE 23(1): RESTRICTIONS OF RULES IN ARTICLES 13 TO 21 AND 34

GDPR provisions to be restricted: "the listed GDPR provisions"

6   In this Part of this Schedule, "the listed GDPR provisions" means the following provisions of the GDPR (the rights and obligations in which may be restricted by virtue of Article 23(1) of the GDPR)—

Data Protection Act 2018 (c. 12)
Schedule 2 — Exemptions etc from the GDPR
Part 2 — Restrictions based on Article 23(1): restrictions of rules in Articles 13 to 21 and 34

151

(a)   Article 13(1) to (3) (personal data collected from data subject: information to be provided);

(b)   Article 14(1) to (4) (personal data collected other than from data subject: information to be provided);

(c)   Article 15(1) to (3) (confirmation of processing, access to data and safeguards for third country transfers);

(d)   Article 16 (right to rectification);

(e)   Article 17(1) and (2) (right to erasure);

(f)   Article 18(1) (restriction of processing);

(g)   Article 19 (notification obligation regarding rectification or erasure of personal data or restriction of processing);

(h)   Article 20(1) and (2) (right to data portability);

(i)   Article 21(1) (objections to processing);

(j)   Article 5 (general principles) so far as its provisions correspond to the rights and obligations provided for in the provisions mentioned in sub-paragraphs (a) to (i).

Functions designed to protect the public etc

7   The listed GDPR provisions do not apply to personal data processed for the purposes of discharging a function that—

(a)   is designed as described in column 1 of the Table, and

(b)   meets the condition relating to the function specified in column 2 of the Table,

to the extent that the application of those provisions would be likely to prejudice the proper discharge of the function.

TABLE

Description of function design	*Condition*
1. The function is designed to protect members of the public against— (a) financial loss due to dishonesty, malpractice or other seriously improper conduct by, or the unfitness or incompetence of, persons concerned in the provision of banking, insurance, investment or other financial services or in the management of bodies corporate, or (b) financial loss due to the conduct of discharged or undischarged bankrupts.	The function is— (a) conferred on a person by an enactment, (b) a function of the Crown, a Minister of the Crown or a government department, or (c) of a public nature, and is exercised in the public interest.

152

Data Protection Act 2018 (c. 12)
Schedule 2 — Exemptions etc from the GDPR
Part 2 — Restrictions based on Article 23(1): restrictions of rules in Articles 13 to 21 and 34

Description of function design	*Condition*
2. The function is designed to protect members of the public against— (a) dishonesty, malpractice or other seriously improper conduct, or (b) unfitness or incompetence.	The function is— (a) conferred on a person by an enactment, (b) a function of the Crown, a Minister of the Crown or a government department, or (c) of a public nature, and is exercised in the public interest.
3. The function is designed— (a) to protect charities or community interest companies against misconduct or mismanagement (whether by trustees, directors or other persons) in their administration, (b) to protect the property of charities or community interest companies from loss or misapplication, or (c) to recover the property of charities or community interest companies.	The function is— (a) conferred on a person by an enactment, (b) a function of the Crown, a Minister of the Crown or a government department, or (c) of a public nature, and is exercised in the public interest.
4. The function is designed— (a) to secure the health, safety and welfare of persons at work, or (b) to protect persons other than those at work against risk to health or safety arising out of or in connection with the action of persons at work.	The function is— (a) conferred on a person by an enactment, (b) a function of the Crown, a Minister of the Crown or a government department, or (c) of a public nature, and is exercised in the public interest.
5. The function is designed to protect members of the public against— (a) maladministration by public bodies, (b) failures in services provided by public bodies, or (c) a failure of a public body to provide a service which it is a function of the body to provide.	The function is conferred by any enactment on— (a) the Parliamentary Commissioner for Administration, (b) the Commissioner for Local Administration in England, (c) the Health Service Commissioner for England, (d) the Public Services Ombudsman for Wales, (e) the Northern Ireland Public Services Ombudsman, (f) the Prison Ombudsman for Northern Ireland, or (g) the Scottish Public Services Ombudsman.

Data Protection Act 2018 (c. 12) 153
Schedule 2 — Exemptions etc from the GDPR
Part 2 — Restrictions based on Article 23(1): restrictions of rules in Articles 13 to 21 and 34

Description of function design	*Condition*

6. The function is designed—
  (a) to protect members of the public against conduct which may adversely affect their interests by persons carrying on a business,
  (b) to regulate agreements or conduct which have as their object or effect the prevention, restriction or distortion of competition in connection with any commercial activity, or
  (c) to regulate conduct on the part of one or more undertakings which amounts to the abuse of a dominant position in a market.
	The function is conferred on the Competition and Markets Authority by an enactment.

Audit functions

8   (1) The listed GDPR provisions do not apply to personal data processed for the purposes of discharging a function listed in sub-paragraph (2) to the extent that the application of those provisions would be likely to prejudice the proper discharge of the function.

      (2) The functions are any function that is conferred by an enactment on—
          (a) the Comptroller and Auditor General;
          (b) the Auditor General for Scotland;
          (c) the Auditor General for Wales;
          (d) the Comptroller and Auditor General for Northern Ireland.

Functions of the Bank of England

9   (1) The listed GDPR provisions do not apply to personal data processed for the purposes of discharging a relevant function of the Bank of England to the extent that the application of those provisions would be likely to prejudice the proper discharge of the function.

      (2) "Relevant function of the Bank of England" means—
          (a) a function discharged by the Bank acting in its capacity as a monetary authority (as defined in section 244(2)(c) and (2A) of the Banking Act 2009);
          (b) a public function of the Bank within the meaning of section 349 of the Financial Services and Markets Act 2000;
          (c) a function conferred on the Prudential Regulation Authority by or under the Financial Services and Markets Act 2000 or by another enactment.

Regulatory functions relating to legal services, the health service and children's services

10   (1) The listed GDPR provisions do not apply to personal data processed for the purposes of discharging a function listed in sub-paragraph (2) to the extent

154

Data Protection Act 2018 (c. 12)
Schedule 2 — Exemptions etc from the GDPR
Part 2 — Restrictions based on Article 23(1): restrictions of rules in Articles 13 to 21 and 34

that the application of those provisions would be likely to prejudice the proper discharge of the function.

(2) The functions are—

   (a) a function of the Legal Services Board;

   (b) the function of considering a complaint under the scheme established under Part 6 of the Legal Services Act 2007 (legal complaints);

   (c) the function of considering a complaint under—

      (i) section 14 of the NHS Redress Act 2006,

      (ii) section 113(1) or (2) or section 114(1) or (3) of the Health and Social Care (Community Health and Standards) Act 2003,

      (iii) section 24D or 26 of the Children Act 1989, or

      (iv) Part 2A of the Public Services Ombudsman (Wales) Act 2005;

   (d) the function of considering a complaint or representations under Chapter 1 of Part 10 of the Social Services and Well-being (Wales) Act 2014 (anaw 4).

Regulatory functions of certain other persons

11   The listed GDPR provisions do not apply to personal data processed for the purposes of discharging a function that—

   (a) is a function of a person described in column 1 of the Table, and

   (b) is conferred on that person as described in column 2 of the Table,

to the extent that the application of those provisions would be likely to prejudice the proper discharge of the function.

Data Protection Act 2018 (c. 12)
Schedule 2 — Exemptions etc from the GDPR
Part 2 — Restrictions based on Article 23(1): restrictions of rules in Articles 13 to 21 and 34

155

TABLE

Person on whom function is conferred	How function is conferred
1. The Commissioner.	By or under— (a) the data protection legislation; (b) the Freedom of Information Act 2000; (c) section 244 of the Investigatory Powers Act 2016; (d) the Privacy and Electronic Communications (EC Directive) Regulations 2003 (S.I. 2003/2426); (e) the Environmental Information Regulations 2004 (S.I. 2004/3391); (f) the INSPIRE Regulations 2009 (S.I. 2009/3157); (g) Regulation (EU) No 910/2014 of the European Parliament and of the Council of 23 July 2014 on electronic identification and trust services for electronic transactions in the internal market and repealing Directive 1999/93/EC; (h) the Re-use of Public Sector Information Regulations 2015 (S.I. 2015/1415); (i) the Electronic Identification and Trust Services for Electronic Transactions Regulations 2016 (S.I. 2016/696).

156

Data Protection Act 2018 (c. 12)
Schedule 2 — Exemptions etc from the GDPR
Part 2 — Restrictions based on Article 23(1): restrictions of rules in Articles 13 to 21 and 34

Person on whom function is conferred	*How function is conferred*
2. The Scottish Information Commissioner.	By or under— (a) the Freedom of Information (Scotland) Act 2002 (asp 13); (b) the Environmental Information (Scotland) Regulations 2004 (S.S.I. 2004/520); (c) the INSPIRE (Scotland) Regulations 2009 (S.S.I. 2009/440).
3. The Pensions Ombudsman.	By or under Part 10 of the Pension Schemes Act 1993 or any corresponding legislation having equivalent effect in Northern Ireland.
4. The Board of the Pension Protection Fund.	By or under sections 206 to 208 of the Pensions Act 2004 or any corresponding legislation having equivalent effect in Northern Ireland.
5. The Ombudsman for the Board of the Pension Protection Fund.	By or under any of sections 209 to 218 or 286(1) of the Pensions Act 2004 or any corresponding legislation having equivalent effect in Northern Ireland.
6. The Pensions Regulator.	By an enactment.
7. The Financial Conduct Authority.	By or under the Financial Services and Markets Act 2000 or by another enactment.
8. The Financial Ombudsman.	By or under Part 16 of the Financial Services and Markets Act 2000.
9. The investigator of complaints against the financial regulators.	By or under Part 6 of the Financial Services Act 2012.
10. A consumer protection enforcer, other than the Competition and Markets Authority.	By or under the CPC Regulation.
11. The monitoring officer of a relevant authority.	By or under the Local Government and Housing Act 1989.
12. The monitoring officer of a relevant Welsh authority.	By or under the Local Government Act 2000.

Data Protection Act 2018 (c. 12)
Schedule 2 — Exemptions etc from the GDPR
Part 2 — Restrictions based on Article 23(1): restrictions of rules in Articles 13 to 21 and 34

157

Person on whom function is conferred	How function is conferred
13. The Public Services Ombudsman for Wales.	By or under the Local Government Act 2000.
14. The Charity Commission.	By or under— (a) the Charities Act 1992; (b) the Charities Act 2006; (c) the Charities Act 2011.

12   In the Table in paragraph 11—

"consumer protection enforcer" has the same meaning as "CPC enforcer" in section 213(5A) of the Enterprise Act 2002;

the "CPC Regulation" has the meaning given in section 235A of the Enterprise Act 2002;

the "Financial Ombudsman" means the scheme operator within the meaning of Part 16 of the Financial Services and Markets Act 2000 (see section 225 of that Act);

the "investigator of complaints against the financial regulators" means the person appointed under section 84(1)(b) of the Financial Services Act 2012;

"relevant authority" has the same meaning as in section 5 of the Local Government and Housing Act 1989, and "monitoring officer", in relation to such an authority, means a person designated as such under that section;

"relevant Welsh authority" has the same meaning as "relevant authority" in section 49(6) of the Local Government Act 2000, and "monitoring officer", in relation to such an authority, has the same meaning as in Part 3 of that Act.

Parliamentary privilege

13   The listed GDPR provisions and Article 34(1) and (4) of the GDPR (communication of personal data breach to the data subject) do not apply to personal data where this is required for the purpose of avoiding an infringement of the privileges of either House of Parliament.

Judicial appointments, judicial independence and judicial proceedings

14   (1) The listed GDPR provisions do not apply to personal data processed for the purposes of assessing a person's suitability for judicial office or the office of Queen's Counsel.

(2) The listed GDPR provisions do not apply to personal data processed by—
   (a) an individual acting in a judicial capacity, or
   (b) a court or tribunal acting in its judicial capacity.

(3) As regards personal data not falling within sub-paragraph (1) or (2), the listed GDPR provisions do not apply to the extent that the application of those provisions would be likely to prejudice judicial independence or judicial proceedings.

158   *Data Protection Act 2018 (c. 12)*
                                    Schedule 2 — Exemptions etc from the GDPR
              Part 2 — Restrictions based on Article 23(1): restrictions of rules in Articles 13 to 21 and 34

Crown honours, dignities and appointments

15   (1) The listed GDPR provisions do not apply to personal data processed for the purposes of the conferring by the Crown of any honour or dignity.

     (2) The listed GDPR provisions do not apply to personal data processed for the purposes of assessing a person's suitability for any of the following offices —
          (a) archbishops and diocesan and suffragan bishops in the Church of England;
          (b) deans of cathedrals of the Church of England;
          (c) deans and canons of the two Royal Peculiars;
          (d) the First and Second Church Estates Commissioners;
          (e) lord-lieutenants;
          (f) Masters of Trinity College and Churchill College, Cambridge;
          (g) the Provost of Eton;
          (h) the Poet Laureate;
          (i) the Astronomer Royal.

     (3) The Secretary of State may by regulations amend the list in sub-paragraph (2) to —
          (a) remove an office, or
          (b) add an office to which appointments are made by Her Majesty.

     (4) Regulations under sub-paragraph (3) are subject to the affirmative resolution procedure.

PART 3

RESTRICTION BASED ON ARTICLE 23(1): PROTECTION OF RIGHTS OF OTHERS

Protection of the rights of others: general

16   (1) Article 15(1) to (3) of the GDPR (confirmation of processing, access to data and safeguards for third country transfers), and Article 5 of the GDPR so far as its provisions correspond to the rights and obligations provided for in Article 15(1) to (3), do not oblige a controller to disclose information to the data subject to the extent that doing so would involve disclosing information relating to another individual who can be identified from the information.

     (2) Sub-paragraph (1) does not remove the controller's obligation where —
          (a) the other individual has consented to the disclosure of the information to the data subject, or
          (b) it is reasonable to disclose the information to the data subject without the consent of the other individual.

     (3) In determining whether it is reasonable to disclose the information without consent, the controller must have regard to all the relevant circumstances, including —
          (a) the type of information that would be disclosed,
          (b) any duty of confidentiality owed to the other individual,
          (c) any steps taken by the controller with a view to seeking the consent of the other individual,
          (d) whether the other individual is capable of giving consent, and
          (e) any express refusal of consent by the other individual.

Data Protection Act 2018 (c. 12)   159
Schedule 2 — Exemptions etc from the GDPR
Part 3 — Restriction based on Article 23(1): protection of rights of others

(4) For the purposes of this paragraph—

    (a) "information relating to another individual" includes information identifying the other individual as the source of information;

    (b) an individual can be identified from information to be provided to a data subject by a controller if the individual can be identified from—

        (i) that information, or

        (ii) that information and any other information that the controller reasonably believes the data subject is likely to possess or obtain.

Assumption of reasonableness for health workers, social workers and education workers

17 (1) For the purposes of paragraph 16(2)(b), it is to be considered reasonable for a controller to disclose information to a data subject without the consent of the other individual where—

    (a) the health data test is met,

    (b) the social work data test is met, or

    (c) the education data test is met.

(2) The health data test is met if—

    (a) the information in question is contained in a health record, and

    (b) the other individual is a health professional who has compiled or contributed to the health record or who, in his or her capacity as a health professional, has been involved in the diagnosis, care or treatment of the data subject.

(3) The social work data test is met if—

    (a) the other individual is—

        (i) a children's court officer,

        (ii) a person who is or has been employed by a person or body referred to in paragraph 8 of Schedule 3 in connection with functions exercised in relation to the information, or

        (iii) a person who has provided for reward a service that is similar to a service provided in the exercise of any relevant social services functions, and

    (b) the information relates to the other individual in an official capacity or the other individual supplied the information—

        (i) in an official capacity, or

        (ii) in a case within paragraph (a)(iii), in connection with providing the service mentioned in paragraph (a)(iii).

(4) The education data test is met if—

    (a) the other individual is an education-related worker, or

    (b) the other individual is employed by an education authority (within the meaning of the Education (Scotland) Act 1980) in pursuance of its functions relating to education and—

        (i) the information relates to the other individual in his or her capacity as such an employee, or

        (ii) the other individual supplied the information in his or her capacity as such an employee.

(5) In this paragraph—

160

Data Protection Act 2018 (c. 12)
Schedule 2 — Exemptions etc from the GDPR
Part 3 — Restriction based on Article 23(1): protection of rights of others

"children's court officer" means a person referred to in paragraph 8(1)(q), (r), (s), (t) or (u) of Schedule 3;

"education-related worker" means a person referred to in paragraph 14(4)(a) or (b) or 16(4)(a), (b) or (c) of Schedule 3 (educational records);

"relevant social services functions" means functions specified in paragraph 8(1)(a), (b), (c) or (d) of Schedule 3.

PART 4

RESTRICTIONS BASED ON ARTICLE 23(1): RESTRICTIONS OF RULES IN ARTICLES 13 TO 15

GDPR provisions to be restricted: "the listed GDPR provisions"

18   In this Part of this Schedule, "the listed GDPR provisions" means the following provisions of the GDPR (the rights and obligations in which may be restricted by virtue of Article 23(1) of the GDPR) —

   (a)   Article 13(1) to (3) (personal data collected from data subject: information to be provided);

   (b)   Article 14(1) to (4) (personal data collected other than from data subject: information to be provided);

   (c)   Article 15(1) to (3) (confirmation of processing, access to data and safeguards for third country transfers);

   (d)   Article 5 (general principles) so far as its provisions correspond to the rights and obligations provided for in the provisions mentioned in sub-paragraphs (a) to (c).

Legal professional privilege

19   The listed GDPR provisions do not apply to personal data that consists of —

   (a)   information in respect of which a claim to legal professional privilege or, in Scotland, confidentiality of communications, could be maintained in legal proceedings, or

   (b)   information in respect of which a duty of confidentiality is owed by a professional legal adviser to a client of the adviser.

Self incrimination

20   (1)   A person need not comply with the listed GDPR provisions to the extent that compliance would, by revealing evidence of the commission of an offence, expose the person to proceedings for that offence.

     (2)   The reference to an offence in sub-paragraph (1) does not include an offence under —

        (a)   this Act,

        (b)   section 5 of the Perjury Act 1911 (false statements made otherwise than on oath),

        (c)   section 44(2) of the Criminal Law (Consolidation) (Scotland) Act 1995 (false statements made otherwise than on oath), or

        (d)   Article 10 of the Perjury (Northern Ireland) Order 1979 (S.I. 1979/1714 (N.I. 19)) (false statutory declarations and other false unsworn statements).

Data Protection Act 2018 (c. 12) 161
Schedule 2 — Exemptions etc from the GDPR
Part 4 — Restrictions based on Article 23(1): restrictions of rules in Articles 13 to 15

    (3) Information disclosed by any person in compliance with Article 15 of the GDPR is not admissible against the person in proceedings for an offence under this Act.

Corporate finance

21 (1) The listed GDPR provisions do not apply to personal data processed for the purposes of or in connection with a corporate finance service provided by a relevant person to the extent that either Condition A or Condition B is met.

    (2) Condition A is that the application of the listed GDPR provisions would be likely to affect the price of an instrument.

    (3) Condition B is that —

      (a) the relevant person reasonably believes that the application of the listed GDPR provisions to the personal data in question could affect a decision of a person —

        (i) whether to deal in, subscribe for or issue an instrument, or

        (ii) whether to act in a way likely to have an effect on a business activity (such as an effect on the industrial strategy of a person, the capital structure of an undertaking or the legal or beneficial ownership of a business or asset), and

      (b) the application of the listed GDPR provisions to that personal data would have a prejudicial effect on the orderly functioning of financial markets or the efficient allocation of capital within the economy.

    (4) In this paragraph —

      "corporate finance service" means a service consisting in —

        (a) underwriting in respect of issues of, or the placing of issues of, any instrument,

        (b) services relating to such underwriting, or

        (c) advice to undertakings on capital structure, industrial strategy and related matters and advice and service relating to mergers and the purchase of undertakings;

      "instrument" means an instrument listed in section C of Annex 1 to Directive 2004/39/EC of the European Parliament and of the Council of 21 April 2004 on markets in financial instruments, and references to an instrument include an instrument not yet in existence but which is to be or may be created;

      "price" includes value;

      "relevant person" means —

        (a) a person who, by reason of a permission under Part 4A of the Financial Services and Markets Act 2000, is able to carry on a corporate finance service without contravening the general prohibition;

        (b) an EEA firm of the kind mentioned in paragraph 5(a) or (b) of Schedule 3 to that Act which has qualified for authorisation under paragraph 12 of that Schedule, and may lawfully carry on a corporate finance service;

        (c) a person who is exempt from the general prohibition in respect of any corporate finance service —

          (i) as a result of an exemption order made under section 38(1) of that Act, or

162

Data Protection Act 2018 (c. 12)
Schedule 2 — Exemptions etc from the GDPR
Part 4 — Restrictions based on Article 23(1): restrictions of rules in Articles 13 to 15

          (ii)   by reason of section 39(1) of that Act (appointed representatives);

    (d)   a person, not falling within paragraph (a), (b) or (c), who may lawfully carry on a corporate finance service without contravening the general prohibition;

    (e)   a person who, in the course of employment, provides to their employer a service falling within paragraph (b) or (c) of the definition of "corporate finance service";

    (f)   a partner who provides to other partners in the partnership a service falling within either of those paragraphs.

(5)   In the definition of "relevant person" in sub-paragraph (4), references to "the general prohibition" are to the general prohibition within the meaning of section 19 of the Financial Services and Markets Act 2000.

Management forecasts

22   The listed GDPR provisions do not apply to personal data processed for the purposes of management forecasting or management planning in relation to a business or other activity to the extent that the application of those provisions would be likely to prejudice the conduct of the business or activity concerned.

Negotiations

23   The listed GDPR provisions do not apply to personal data that consists of records of the intentions of the controller in relation to any negotiations with the data subject to the extent that the application of those provisions would be likely to prejudice those negotiations.

Confidential references

24   The listed GDPR provisions do not apply to personal data consisting of a reference given (or to be given) in confidence for the purposes of —

    (a)   the education, training or employment (or prospective education, training or employment) of the data subject,

    (b)   the placement (or prospective placement) of the data subject as a volunteer,

    (c)   the appointment (or prospective appointment) of the data subject to any office, or

    (d)   the provision (or prospective provision) by the data subject of any service.

Exam scripts and exam marks

25   (1)   The listed GDPR provisions do not apply to personal data consisting of information recorded by candidates during an exam.

    (2)   Where personal data consists of marks or other information processed by a controller —

    (a)   for the purposes of determining the results of an exam, or

    (b)   in consequence of the determination of the results of an exam,

the duty in Article 12(3) or (4) of the GDPR for the controller to provide information requested by the data subject within a certain time period, as it

Data Protection Act 2018 (c. 12)
Schedule 2 — Exemptions etc from the GDPR
Part 4 — Restrictions based on Article 23(1): restrictions of rules in Articles 13 to 15

163

applies to Article 15 of the GDPR (confirmation of processing, access to data and safeguards for third country transfers), is modified as set out in sub-paragraph (3).

(3) Where a question arises as to whether the controller is obliged by Article 15 of the GDPR to disclose personal data, and the question arises before the day on which the exam results are announced, the controller must provide the information mentioned in Article 12(3) or (4) —

    (a) before the end of the period of 5 months beginning when the question arises, or

    (b) if earlier, before the end of the period of 40 days beginning with the announcement of the results.

(4) In this paragraph, "exam" means an academic, professional or other examination used for determining the knowledge, intelligence, skill or ability of a candidate and may include an exam consisting of an assessment of the candidate's performance while undertaking work or any other activity.

(5) For the purposes of this paragraph, the results of an exam are treated as announced when they are first published or, if not published, first communicated to the candidate.

PART 5

EXEMPTIONS ETC BASED ON ARTICLE 85(2) FOR REASONS OF FREEDOM OF EXPRESSION AND INFORMATION

Journalistic, academic, artistic and literary purposes

26 (1) In this paragraph, "the special purposes" means one or more of the following —

    (a) the purposes of journalism;

    (b) academic purposes;

    (c) artistic purposes;

    (d) literary purposes.

(2) Sub-paragraph (3) applies to the processing of personal data carried out for the special purposes if —

    (a) the processing is being carried out with a view to the publication by a person of journalistic, academic, artistic or literary material, and

    (b) the controller reasonably believes that the publication of the material would be in the public interest.

(3) The listed GDPR provisions do not apply to the extent that the controller reasonably believes that the application of those provisions would be incompatible with the special purposes.

(4) In determining whether publication would be in the public interest the controller must take into account the special importance of the public interest in the freedom of expression and information.

(5) In determining whether it is reasonable to believe that publication would be in the public interest, the controller must have regard to any of the codes of practice or guidelines listed in sub-paragraph (6) that is relevant to the publication in question.

164

Data Protection Act 2018 (c. 12)
Schedule 2 — Exemptions etc from the GDPR
Part 5 — Exemptions etc based on Article 85(2) for reasons of freedom of expression and information

(6) The codes of practice and guidelines are—

    (a)   BBC Editorial Guidelines;

    (b)   Ofcom Broadcasting Code;

    (c)   Editors' Code of Practice.

(7) The Secretary of State may by regulations amend the list in sub-paragraph (6).

(8) Regulations under sub-paragraph (7) are subject to the affirmative resolution procedure.

(9) For the purposes of this paragraph, the listed GDPR provisions are the following provisions of the GDPR (which may be exempted or derogated from by virtue of Article 85(2) of the GDPR)—

    (a)   in Chapter II of the GDPR (principles)—

        (i)   Article 5(1)(a) to (e) (principles relating to processing);

        (ii)   Article 6 (lawfulness);

        (iii)   Article 7 (conditions for consent);

        (iv)   Article 8(1) and (2) (child's consent);

        (v)   Article 9 (processing of special categories of data);

        (vi)   Article 10 (data relating to criminal convictions etc);

        (vii)   Article 11(2) (processing not requiring identification);

    (b)   in Chapter III of the GDPR (rights of the data subject)—

        (i)   Article 13(1) to (3) (personal data collected from data subject: information to be provided);

        (ii)   Article 14(1) to (4) (personal data collected other than from data subject: information to be provided);

        (iii)   Article 15(1) to (3) (confirmation of processing, access to data and safeguards for third country transfers);

        (iv)   Article 16 (right to rectification);

        (v)   Article 17(1) and (2) (right to erasure);

        (vi)   Article 18(1)(a), (b) and (d) (restriction of processing);

        (vii)   Article 19 (notification obligation regarding rectification or erasure of personal data or restriction of processing);

        (viii)   Article 20(1) and (2) (right to data portability);

        (ix)   Article 21(1) (objections to processing);

    (c)   in Chapter IV of the GDPR (controller and processor)—

        (i)   Article 34(1) and (4) (communication of personal data breach to the data subject);

        (ii)   Article 36 (requirement for controller to consult Commissioner prior to high risk processing);

    (d)   in Chapter V of the GDPR (transfers of data to third countries etc), Article 44 (general principles for transfers);

    (e)   in Chapter VII of the GDPR (co-operation and consistency)—

        (i)   Articles 60 to 62 (co-operation);

        (ii)   Articles 63 to 67 (consistency).

Data Protection Act 2018 (c. 12)
Schedule 2 — Exemptions etc from the GDPR
Part 6 — Derogations etc based on Article 89 for research, statistics and archiving

165

PART 6

DEROGATIONS ETC BASED ON ARTICLE 89 FOR RESEARCH, STATISTICS AND ARCHIVING

Research and statistics

27 (1) The listed GDPR provisions do not apply to personal data processed for —
    (a) scientific or historical research purposes, or
    (b) statistical purposes,
to the extent that the application of those provisions would prevent or seriously impair the achievement of the purposes in question.
This is subject to sub-paragraph (3).

    (2) For the purposes of this paragraph, the listed GDPR provisions are the following provisions of the GDPR (the rights in which may be derogated from by virtue of Article 89(2) of the GDPR) —
    (a) Article 15(1) to (3) (confirmation of processing, access to data and safeguards for third country transfers);
    (b) Article 16 (right to rectification);
    (c) Article 18(1) (restriction of processing);
    (d) Article 21(1) (objections to processing).

    (3) The exemption in sub-paragraph (1) is available only where —
    (a) the personal data is processed in accordance with Article 89(1) of the GDPR (as supplemented by section 19), and
    (b) as regards the disapplication of Article 15(1) to (3), the results of the research or any resulting statistics are not made available in a form which identifies a data subject.

Archiving in the public interest

28 (1) The listed GDPR provisions do not apply to personal data processed for archiving purposes in the public interest to the extent that the application of those provisions would prevent or seriously impair the achievement of those purposes.
This is subject to sub-paragraph (3).

    (2) For the purposes of this paragraph, the listed GDPR provisions are the following provisions of the GDPR (the rights in which may be derogated from by virtue of Article 89(3) of the GDPR) —
    (a) Article 15(1) to (3) (confirmation of processing, access to data and safeguards for third country transfers);
    (b) Article 16 (right to rectification);
    (c) Article 18(1) (restriction of processing);
    (d) Article 19 (notification obligation regarding rectification or erasure of personal data or restriction of processing);
    (e) Article 20(1) (right to data portability);
    (f) Article 21(1) (objections to processing).

    (3) The exemption in sub-paragraph (1) is available only where the personal data is processed in accordance with Article 89(1) of the GDPR (as supplemented by section 19).

166   *Data Protection Act 2018 (c. 12)*
Schedule 3 — Exemptions etc from the GDPR: health, social work, education and child abuse data
Part 1 — GDPR provisions to be restricted

SCHEDULE 3   Section 15

EXEMPTIONS ETC FROM THE GDPR: HEALTH, SOCIAL WORK, EDUCATION AND CHILD ABUSE
DATA

PART 1

GDPR PROVISIONS TO BE RESTRICTED

1   In this Schedule "the listed GDPR provisions" means the following
         provisions of the GDPR (the rights and obligations in which may be
         restricted by virtue of Article 23(1) of the GDPR) —
         (a)   Article 13(1) to (3) (personal data collected from data subject:
                information to be provided);
         (b)   Article 14(1) to (4) (personal data collected other than from data
                subject: information to be provided);
         (c)   Article 15(1) to (3) (confirmation of processing, access to data and
                safeguards for third country transfers);
         (d)   Article 16 (right to rectification);
         (e)   Article 17(1) and (2) (right to erasure);
         (f)   Article 18(1) (restriction of processing);
         (g)   Article 20(1) and (2) (right to data portability);
         (h)   Article 21(1) (objections to processing);
         (i)   Article 5 (general principles) so far as its provisions correspond to the
                rights and obligations provided for in the provisions mentioned in
                sub-paragraphs (a) to (h).

PART 2

HEALTH DATA

Definitions

2   (1) In this Part of this Schedule —
               "the appropriate health professional", in relation to a question as to
               whether the serious harm test is met with respect to data concerning
               health, means —
               (a)   the health professional who is currently or was most recently
                      responsible for the diagnosis, care or treatment of the data
                      subject in connection with the matters to which the data
                      relates,
               (b)   where there is more than one such health professional, the
                      health professional who is the most suitable to provide an
                      opinion on the question, or
               (c)   a health professional who has the necessary experience and
                      qualifications to provide an opinion on the question, where —
                      (i)   there is no health professional available falling within
                             paragraph (a) or (b), or
                      (ii)   the controller is the Secretary of State and data is
                             processed in connection with the exercise of the
                             functions conferred on the Secretary of State by or
                             under the Child Support Act 1991 and the Child

Support Act 1995, or the Secretary of State's functions in relation to social security or war pensions, or

(iii) the controller is the Department for Communities in Northern Ireland and data is processed in connection with the exercise of the functions conferred on the Department by or under the Child Support (Northern Ireland) Order 1991 (S.I. 1991/2628 (N.I. 23)) and the Child Support (Northern Ireland) Order 1995 (S.I. 1995/2702 (N.I. 13));

"war pension" has the same meaning as in section 25 of the Social Security Act 1989 (establishment and functions of war pensions committees).

(2) For the purposes of this Part of this Schedule, the "serious harm test" is met with respect to data concerning health if the application of Article 15 of the GDPR to the data would be likely to cause serious harm to the physical or mental health of the data subject or another individual.

Exemption from the listed GDPR provisions: data processed by a court

3 (1) The listed GDPR provisions do not apply to data concerning health if—

(a) it is processed by a court,

(b) it consists of information supplied in a report or other evidence given to the court in the course of proceedings to which rules listed in sub-paragraph (2) apply, and

(c) in accordance with those rules, the data may be withheld by the court in whole or in part from the data subject.

(2) Those rules are—

(a) the Magistrates' Courts (Children and Young Persons) Rules (Northern Ireland) 1969 (S.R. (N.I.) 1969 No. 221);

(b) the Magistrates' Courts (Children and Young Persons) Rules 1992 (S.I. 1992/2071 (L. 17));

(c) the Family Proceedings Rules (Northern Ireland) 1996 (S.R. (N.I.) 1996 No. 322);

(d) the Magistrates' Courts (Children (Northern Ireland) Order 1995) Rules (Northern Ireland) 1996 (S.R. (N. I.) 1996 No. 323);

(e) the Act of Sederunt (Child Care and Maintenance Rules) 1997 (S.I. 1997/291 (S. 19));

(f) the Sheriff Court Adoption Rules 2009;

(g) the Family Procedure Rules 2010 (S.I. 2010/2955 (L. 17));

(h) the Children's Hearings (Scotland) Act 2011 (Rules of Procedure in Children's Hearings) Rules 2013 (S.S.I. 2013/194).

Exemption from the listed GDPR provisions: data subject's expectations and wishes

4 (1) This paragraph applies where a request for data concerning health is made in exercise of a power conferred by an enactment or rule of law and—

(a) in relation to England and Wales or Northern Ireland, the data subject is an individual aged under 18 and the person making the request has parental responsibility for the data subject,

168

Data Protection Act 2018 (c. 12)
Schedule 3 — Exemptions etc from the GDPR: health, social work, education and child abuse data
Part 2 — Health data

      (b)   in relation to Scotland, the data subject is an individual aged under 16 and the person making the request has parental responsibilities for the data subject, or

      (c)   the data subject is incapable of managing his or her own affairs and the person making the request has been appointed by a court to manage those affairs.

  (2) The listed GDPR provisions do not apply to data concerning health to the extent that complying with the request would disclose information —

      (a)   which was provided by the data subject in the expectation that it would not be disclosed to the person making the request,

      (b)   which was obtained as a result of any examination or investigation to which the data subject consented in the expectation that the information would not be so disclosed, or

      (c)   which the data subject has expressly indicated should not be so disclosed.

  (3) The exemptions under sub-paragraph (2)(a) and (b) do not apply if the data subject has expressly indicated that he or she no longer has the expectation mentioned there.

Exemption from Article 15 of the GDPR: serious harm

5   (1) Article 15(1) to (3) of the GDPR (confirmation of processing, access to data and safeguards for third country transfers) do not apply to data concerning health to the extent that the serious harm test is met with respect to the data.

  (2) A controller who is not a health professional may not rely on sub-paragraph (1) to withhold data concerning health unless the controller has obtained an opinion from the person who appears to the controller to be the appropriate health professional to the effect that the serious harm test is met with respect to the data.

  (3) An opinion does not count for the purposes of sub-paragraph (2) if —

      (a)   it was obtained before the beginning of the relevant period, or

      (b)   it was obtained during that period but it is reasonable in all the circumstances to re-consult the appropriate health professional.

  (4) In this paragraph, "the relevant period" means the period of 6 months ending with the day on which the opinion would be relied on.

Restriction of Article 15 of the GDPR: prior opinion of appropriate health professional

6   (1) Article 15(1) to (3) of the GDPR (confirmation of processing, access to data and safeguards for third country transfers) do not permit the disclosure of data concerning health by a controller who is not a health professional unless the controller has obtained an opinion from the person who appears to the controller to be the appropriate health professional to the effect that the serious harm test is not met with respect to the data.

  (2) Sub-paragraph (1) does not apply to the extent that the controller is satisfied that the data concerning health has already been seen by, or is within the knowledge of, the data subject.

  (3) An opinion does not count for the purposes of sub-paragraph (1) if —

      (a)   it was obtained before the beginning of the relevant period, or

(b) it was obtained during that period but it is reasonable in all the circumstances to re-consult the appropriate health professional.

(4) In this paragraph, "the relevant period" means the period of 6 months ending with the day on which the opinion would be relied on.

PART 3

SOCIAL WORK DATA

Definitions

7 (1) In this Part of this Schedule—

"education data" has the meaning given by paragraph 17 of this Schedule;

"Health and Social Care trust" means a Health and Social Care trust established under the Health and Personal Social Services (Northern Ireland) Order 1991 (S.I. 1991/194 (N.I. 1));

"Principal Reporter" means the Principal Reporter appointed under the Children's Hearings (Scotland) Act 2011 (asp 1), or an officer of the Scottish Children's Reporter Administration to whom there is delegated under paragraph 10(1) of Schedule 3 to that Act any function of the Principal Reporter;

"social work data" means personal data which—

(a) is data to which paragraph 8 applies, but

(b) is not education data or data concerning health.

(2) For the purposes of this Part of this Schedule, the "serious harm test" is met with respect to social work data if the application of Article 15 of the GDPR to the data would be likely to prejudice carrying out social work, because it would be likely to cause serious harm to the physical or mental health of the data subject or another individual.

(3) In sub-paragraph (2), "carrying out social work" is to be taken to include doing any of the following—

(a) the exercise of any functions mentioned in paragraph 8(1)(a), (d), (f) to (j), (m), (p), (s), (t), (u), (v) or (w);

(b) the provision of any service mentioned in paragraph 8(1)(b), (c) or (k);

(c) the exercise of the functions of a body mentioned in paragraph 8(1)(e) or a person mentioned in paragraph 8(1)(q) or (r).

(4) In this Part of this Schedule, a reference to a local authority, in relation to data processed or formerly processed by it, includes a reference to the Council of the Isles of Scilly, in relation to data processed or formerly processed by the Council in connection with any functions mentioned in paragraph 8(1)(a)(ii) which are or have been conferred on the Council by an enactment.

8 (1) This paragraph applies to personal data falling within any of the following descriptions—

(a) data processed by a local authority—

(i) in connection with its social services functions (within the meaning of the Local Authority Social Services Act 1970 or the Social Services and Well-being (Wales) Act 2014 (anaw 4))

170

Data Protection Act 2018 (c. 12)
Schedule 3 — Exemptions etc from the GDPR: health, social work, education and child abuse data
Part 3 — Social work data

or any functions exercised by local authorities under the Social Work (Scotland) Act 1968 or referred to in section 5(1B) of that Act, or

    (ii)   in the exercise of other functions but obtained or consisting of information obtained in connection with any of the functions mentioned in sub-paragraph (i);

(b)   data processed by the Regional Health and Social Care Board —

    (i)   in connection with the provision of social care within the meaning of section 2(5) of the Health and Social Care (Reform) Act (Northern Ireland) 2009 (c. 1 (N.I.)), or

    (ii)   in the exercise of other functions but obtained or consisting of information obtained in connection with the provision of that care;

(c)   data processed by a Health and Social Care trust —

    (i)   in connection with the provision of social care within the meaning of section 2(5) of the Health and Social Care (Reform) Act (Northern Ireland) 2009 (c. 1 (N.I.)) on behalf of the Regional Health and Social Care Board by virtue of an authorisation made under Article 3(1) of the Health and Personal Social Services (Northern Ireland) Order 1994 (S.I. 1994/429 (N.I. 2)), or

    (ii)   in the exercise of other functions but obtained or consisting of information obtained in connection with the provision of that care;

(d)   data processed by a council in the exercise of its functions under Part 2 of Schedule 9 to the Health and Social Services and Social Security Adjudications Act 1983;

(e)   data processed by —

    (i)   a probation trust established under section 5 of the Offender Management Act 2007, or

    (ii)   the Probation Board for Northern Ireland established by the Probation Board (Northern Ireland) Order 1982 (S.I. 1982/713 (N.I. 10));

(f)   data processed by a local authority in the exercise of its functions under section 36 of the Children Act 1989 or Chapter 2 of Part 6 of the Education Act 1996, so far as those functions relate to ensuring that children of compulsory school age (within the meaning of section 8 of the Education Act 1996) receive suitable education whether by attendance at school or otherwise;

(g)   data processed by the Education Authority in the exercise of its functions under Article 55 of the Children (Northern Ireland) Order 1995 (S.I. 1995/755 (N.I. 2)) or Article 45 of, and Schedule 13 to, the Education and Libraries (Northern Ireland) Order 1986 (S.I. 1986/594 (N.I. 3)), so far as those functions relate to ensuring that children of compulsory school age (within the meaning of Article 46 of the Education and Libraries (Northern Ireland) Order 1986) receive efficient full-time education suitable to their age, ability and aptitude and to any special educational needs they may have, either by regular attendance at school or otherwise;

(h)   data processed by an education authority in the exercise of its functions under sections 35 to 42 of the Education (Scotland) Act 1980 so far as those functions relate to ensuring that children of school age (within the meaning of section 31 of the Education

(Scotland) Act 1980) receive efficient education suitable to their age, ability and aptitude, whether by attendance at school or otherwise;

(i) data relating to persons detained in a hospital at which high security psychiatric services are provided under section 4 of the National Health Service Act 2006 and processed by a Special Health Authority established under section 28 of that Act in the exercise of any functions similar to any social services functions of a local authority;

(j) data relating to persons detained in special accommodation provided under Article 110 of the Mental Health (Northern Ireland) Order 1986 (S.I. 1986/595 (N.I. 4)) and processed by a Health and Social Care trust in the exercise of any functions similar to any social services functions of a local authority;

(k) data which—

    (i) is processed by the National Society for the Prevention of Cruelty to Children, or by any other voluntary organisation or other body designated under this paragraph by the Secretary of State or the Department of Health in Northern Ireland, and

    (ii) appears to the Secretary of State or the Department, as the case may be, to be processed for the purposes of the provision of any service similar to a service provided in the exercise of any functions specified in paragraph (a), (b), (c) or (d);

(l) data processed by a body mentioned in sub-paragraph (2)—

    (i) which was obtained, or consists of information which was obtained, from an authority or body mentioned in any of paragraphs (a) to (k) or from a government department, and

    (ii) in the case of data obtained, or consisting of information obtained, from an authority or body mentioned in any of paragraphs (a) to (k), fell within any of those paragraphs while processed by the authority or body;

(m) data processed by a National Health Service trust first established under section 25 of the National Health Service Act 2006, section 18 of the National Health Service (Wales) Act 2006 or section 5 of the National Health Service and Community Care Act 1990 in the exercise of any functions similar to any social services functions of a local authority;

(n) data processed by an NHS foundation trust in the exercise of any functions similar to any social services functions of a local authority;

(o) data processed by a government department—

    (i) which was obtained, or consists of information which was obtained, from an authority or body mentioned in any of paragraphs (a) to (n), and

    (ii) which fell within any of those paragraphs while processed by that authority or body;

(p) data processed for the purposes of the functions of the Secretary of State pursuant to section 82(5) of the Children Act 1989;

(q) data processed by—

    (i) a children's guardian appointed under Part 16 of the Family Procedure Rules 2010 (S.I. 2010/2955 (L. 17)),

    (ii) a guardian ad litem appointed under Article 60 of the Children (Northern Ireland) Order 1995 (S.I. 1995/755

             (N.I. 2)) or Article 66 of the Adoption (Northern Ireland) Order 1987 (S.I. 1987/2203 (N.I. 22)), or

      (iii)   a safeguarder appointed under section 30(2) or 31(3) of the Children's Hearings (Scotland) Act 2011 (asp 1);

    (r)   data processed by the Principal Reporter;

    (s)   data processed by an officer of the Children and Family Court Advisory and Support Service for the purpose of the officer's functions under section 7 of the Children Act 1989 or Part 16 of the Family Procedure Rules 2010 (S.I. 2010/2955 (L. 17));

    (t)   data processed by the Welsh family proceedings officer for the purposes of the functions under section 7 of the Children Act 1989 or Part 16 of the Family Procedure Rules 2010;

    (u)   data processed by an officer of the service appointed as guardian ad litem under Part 16 of the Family Procedure Rules 2010;

    (v)   data processed by the Children and Family Court Advisory and Support Service for the purpose of its functions under section 12(1) and (2) and section 13(1), (2) and (4) of the Criminal Justice and Court Services Act 2000;

    (w)   data processed by the Welsh Ministers for the purposes of their functions under section 35(1) and (2) and section 36(1), (2), (4), (5) and (6) of the Children Act 2004;

    (x)   data processed for the purposes of the functions of the appropriate Minister pursuant to section 12 of the Adoption and Children Act 2002 (independent review of determinations).

  (2) The bodies referred to in sub-paragraph (1)(l) are —

    (a)   a National Health Service trust first established under section 25 of the National Health Service Act 2006 or section 18 of the National Health Service (Wales) Act 2006;

    (b)   a National Health Service trust first established under section 5 of the National Health Service and Community Care Act 1990;

    (c)   an NHS foundation trust;

    (d)   a clinical commissioning group established under section 14D of the National Health Service Act 2006;

    (e)   the National Health Service Commissioning Board;

    (f)   a Local Health Board established under section 11 of the National Health Service (Wales) Act 2006;

    (g)   a Health Board established under section 2 of the National Health Service (Scotland) Act 1978.

Exemption from the listed GDPR provisions: data processed by a court

9   (1) The listed GDPR provisions do not apply to data that is not education data or data concerning health if —

    (a)   it is processed by a court,

    (b)   it consists of information supplied in a report or other evidence given to the court in the course of proceedings to which rules listed in sub-paragraph (2) apply, and

    (c)   in accordance with any of those rules, the data may be withheld by the court in whole or in part from the data subject.

  (2) Those rules are —

Data Protection Act 2018 (c. 12)   173
Schedule 3 — Exemptions etc from the GDPR: health, social work, education and child abuse data
Part 3 — Social work data

    (a)   the Magistrates' Courts (Children and Young Persons) Rules (Northern Ireland) 1969 (S.R. (N.I.) 1969 No. 221);

    (b)   the Magistrates' Courts (Children and Young Persons) Rules 1992 (S.I. 1992/2071 (L. 17));

    (c)   the Family Proceedings Rules (Northern Ireland) 1996 (S.R. (N.I.) 1996 No. 322);

    (d)   the Magistrates' Courts (Children (Northern Ireland) Order 1995) Rules (Northern Ireland) 1996 (S.R. (N. I.) 1996 No. 323);

    (e)   the Act of Sederunt (Child Care and Maintenance Rules) 1997 (S.I. 1997/291 (S. 19));

    (f)   the Sheriff Court Adoption Rules 2009;

    (g)   the Family Procedure Rules 2010 (S.I. 2010/2955 (L. 17));

    (h)   the Children's Hearings (Scotland) Act 2011 (Rules of Procedure in Children's Hearings) Rules 2013 (S.S.I. 2013/194).

Exemption from the listed GDPR provisions: data subject's expectations and wishes

10   (1)   This paragraph applies where a request for social work data is made in exercise of a power conferred by an enactment or rule of law and —

    (a)   in relation to England and Wales or Northern Ireland, the data subject is an individual aged under 18 and the person making the request has parental responsibility for the data subject,

    (b)   in relation to Scotland, the data subject is an individual aged under 16 and the person making the request has parental responsibilities for the data subject, or

    (c)   the data subject is incapable of managing his or her own affairs and the person making the request has been appointed by a court to manage those affairs.

    (2)   The listed GDPR provisions do not apply to social work data to the extent that complying with the request would disclose information —

    (a)   which was provided by the data subject in the expectation that it would not be disclosed to the person making the request,

    (b)   which was obtained as a result of any examination or investigation to which the data subject consented in the expectation that the information would not be so disclosed, or

    (c)   which the data subject has expressly indicated should not be so disclosed.

    (3)   The exemptions under sub-paragraph (2)(a) and (b) do not apply if the data subject has expressly indicated that he or she no longer has the expectation mentioned there.

Exemption from Article 15 of the GDPR: serious harm

11   Article 15(1) to (3) of the GDPR (confirmation of processing, access to data and safeguards for third country transfers) do not apply to social work data to the extent that the serious harm test is met with respect to the data.

Restriction of Article 15 of the GDPR: prior opinion of Principal Reporter

12   (1)   This paragraph applies where —

174

Data Protection Act 2018 (c. 12)
Schedule 3 — Exemptions etc from the GDPR: health, social work, education and child abuse data
Part 3 — Social work data

    (a) a question arises as to whether a controller who is a social work authority is obliged by Article 15(1) to (3) of the GDPR (confirmation of processing, access to data and safeguards for third country transfers) to disclose social work data, and

    (b) the data —

        (i) originated from or was supplied by the Principal Reporter acting in pursuance of the Principal Reporter's statutory duties, and

        (ii) is not data which the data subject is entitled to receive from the Principal Reporter.

(2) The controller must inform the Principal Reporter of the fact that the question has arisen before the end of the period of 14 days beginning when the question arises.

(3) Article 15(1) to (3) of the GDPR (confirmation of processing, access to data and safeguards for third country transfers) do not permit the controller to disclose the data to the data subject unless the Principal Reporter has informed the controller that, in the opinion of the Principal Reporter, the serious harm test is not met with respect to the data.

(4) In this paragraph "social work authority" means a local authority for the purposes of the Social Work (Scotland) Act 1968.

PART 4

EDUCATION DATA

Educational records

13   In this Part of this Schedule "educational record" means a record to which paragraph 14, 15 or 16 applies.

14 (1) This paragraph applies to a record of information which —

    (a) is processed by or on behalf of the proprietor of, or a teacher at, a school in England and Wales specified in sub-paragraph (3),

    (b) relates to an individual who is or has been a pupil at the school, and

    (c) originated from, or was supplied by or on behalf of, any of the persons specified in sub-paragraph (4).

(2) But this paragraph does not apply to information which is processed by a teacher solely for the teacher's own use.

(3) The schools referred to in sub-paragraph (1)(a) are —

    (a) a school maintained by a local authority;

    (b) an Academy school;

    (c) an alternative provision Academy;

    (d) an independent school that is not an Academy school or an alternative provision Academy;

    (e) a non-maintained special school.

(4) The persons referred to in sub-paragraph (1)(c) are —

    (a) an employee of the local authority which maintains the school;

    (b) in the case of —

(i) a voluntary aided, foundation or foundation special school (within the meaning of the School Standards and Framework Act 1998),

(ii) an Academy school,

(iii) an alternative provision Academy,

(iv) an independent school that is not an Academy school or an alternative provision Academy, or

(v) a non-maintained special school,

a teacher or other employee at the school (including an educational psychologist engaged by the proprietor under a contract for services);

(c) the pupil to whom the record relates;

(d) a parent, as defined by section 576(1) of the Education Act 1996, of that pupil.

(5) In this paragraph—

"independent school" has the meaning given by section 463 of the Education Act 1996;

"local authority" has the same meaning as in that Act (see sections 579(1) and 581 of that Act);

"non-maintained special school" has the meaning given by section 337A of that Act;

"proprietor" has the meaning given by section 579(1) of that Act.

15 (1) This paragraph applies to a record of information which is processed—

(a) by an education authority in Scotland, and

(b) for the purpose of the relevant function of the authority.

(2) But this paragraph does not apply to information which is processed by a teacher solely for the teacher's own use.

(3) For the purposes of this paragraph, information processed by an education authority is processed for the purpose of the relevant function of the authority if the processing relates to the discharge of that function in respect of a person—

(a) who is or has been a pupil in a school provided by the authority, or

(b) who receives, or has received, further education provided by the authority.

(4) In this paragraph "the relevant function" means, in relation to each education authority, its function under section 1 of the Education (Scotland) Act 1980 and section 7(1) of the Self-Governing Schools etc. (Scotland) Act 1989.

16 (1) This paragraph applies to a record of information which—

(a) is processed by or on behalf of the Board of Governors, proprietor or trustees of, or a teacher at, a school in Northern Ireland specified in sub-paragraph (3),

(b) relates to an individual who is or has been a pupil at the school, and

(c) originated from, or was supplied by or on behalf of, any of the persons specified in sub-paragraph (4).

(2) But this paragraph does not apply to information which is processed by a teacher solely for the teacher's own use.

(3) The schools referred to in sub-paragraph (1)(a) are —

    (a)   a grant-aided school;

    (b)   an independent school.

(4) The persons referred to in sub-paragraph (1)(c) are —

    (a)   a teacher at the school;

    (b)   an employee of the Education Authority, other than a teacher at the school;

    (c)   an employee of the Council for Catholic Maintained Schools, other than a teacher at the school;

    (d)   the pupil to whom the record relates;

    (e)   a parent, as defined by Article 2(2) of the Education and Libraries (Northern Ireland) Order 1986 (S.I. 1986/594 (N.I. 3)).

(5) In this paragraph, "grant-aided school", "independent school", "proprietor" and "trustees" have the same meaning as in the Education and Libraries (Northern Ireland) Order 1986 (S.I. 1986/594 (N.I. 3)).

Other definitions

17   (1)   In this Part of this Schedule —

    "education authority" and "further education" have the same meaning as in the Education (Scotland) Act 1980;

    "education data" means personal data consisting of information which —

        (a)   constitutes an educational record, but

        (b)   is not data concerning health;

    "Principal Reporter" means the Principal Reporter appointed under the Children's Hearings (Scotland) Act 2011 (asp 1), or an officer of the Scottish Children's Reporter Administration to whom there is delegated under paragraph 10(1) of Schedule 3 to that Act any function of the Principal Reporter;

    "pupil" means —

        (a)   in relation to a school in England and Wales, a registered pupil within the meaning of the Education Act 1996,

        (b)   in relation to a school in Scotland, a pupil within the meaning of the Education (Scotland) Act 1980, and

        (c)   in relation to a school in Northern Ireland, a registered pupil within the meaning of the Education and Libraries (Northern Ireland) Order 1986 (S.I. 1986/594 (N.I. 3));

    "school" —

        (a)   in relation to England and Wales, has the same meaning as in the Education Act 1996,

        (b)   in relation to Scotland, has the same meaning as in the Education (Scotland) Act 1980, and

        (c)   in relation to Northern Ireland, has the same meaning as in the Education and Libraries (Northern Ireland) Order 1986;

    "teacher" includes —

        (a)   in Great Britain, head teacher, and

        (b)   in Northern Ireland, the principal of a school.

(2) For the purposes of this Part of this Schedule, the "serious harm test" is met with respect to education data if the application of Article 15 of the GDPR to the data would be likely to cause serious harm to the physical or mental health of the data subject or another individual.

Exemption from the listed GDPR provisions: data processed by a court

18 (1) The listed GDPR provisions do not apply to education data if—

    (a) it is processed by a court,

    (b) it consists of information supplied in a report or other evidence given to the court in the course of proceedings to which rules listed in sub-paragraph (2) apply, and

    (c) in accordance with those rules, the data may be withheld by the court in whole or in part from the data subject.

(2) Those rules are—

    (a) the Magistrates' Courts (Children and Young Persons) Rules (Northern Ireland) 1969 (S.R. (N.I.) 1969 No. 221);

    (b) the Magistrates' Courts (Children and Young Persons) Rules 1992 (S.I. 1992/2071 (L. 17));

    (c) the Family Proceedings Rules (Northern Ireland) 1996 (S.R. (N.I.) 1996 No. 322);

    (d) the Magistrates' Courts (Children (Northern Ireland) Order 1995) Rules (Northern Ireland) 1996 (S.R. (N. I.) 1996 No. 323);

    (e) the Act of Sederunt (Child Care and Maintenance Rules) 1997 (S.I. 1997/291 (S. 19));

    (f) the Sheriff Court Adoption Rules 2009;

    (g) the Family Procedure Rules 2010 (S.I. 2010/2955 (L. 17));

    (h) the Children's Hearings (Scotland) Act 2011 (Rules of Procedure in Children's Hearings) Rules 2013 (S.S.I. 2013/194).

Exemption from Article 15 of the GDPR: serious harm

19 Article 15(1) to (3) of the GDPR (confirmation of processing, access to data and safeguards for third country transfers) do not apply to education data to the extent that the serious harm test is met with respect to the data.

Restriction of Article 15 of the GDPR: prior opinion of Principal Reporter

20 (1) This paragraph applies where—

    (a) a question arises as to whether a controller who is an education authority is obliged by Article 15(1) to (3) of the GDPR (confirmation of processing, access to data and safeguards for third country transfers) to disclose education data, and

    (b) the controller believes that the data—

        (i) originated from or was supplied by or on behalf of the Principal Reporter acting in pursuance of the Principal Reporter's statutory duties, and

        (ii) is not data which the data subject is entitled to receive from the Principal Reporter.

178

Data Protection Act 2018 (c. 12)
Schedule 3 — Exemptions etc from the GDPR: health, social work, education and child abuse data
Part 4 — Education data

(2) The controller must inform the Principal Reporter of the fact that the question has arisen before the end of the period of 14 days beginning when the question arises.

(3) Article 15(1) to (3) of the GDPR (confirmation of processing, access to data and safeguards for third country transfers) do not permit the controller to disclose the data to the data subject unless the Principal Reporter has informed the controller that, in the opinion of the Principal Reporter, the serious harm test is not met with respect to the data.

PART 5

CHILD ABUSE DATA

Exemption from Article 15 of the GDPR: child abuse data

21 (1) This paragraph applies where a request for child abuse data is made in exercise of a power conferred by an enactment or rule of law and —

   (a) the data subject is an individual aged under 18 and the person making the request has parental responsibility for the data subject, or

   (b) the data subject is incapable of managing his or her own affairs and the person making the request has been appointed by a court to manage those affairs.

   (2) Article 15(1) to (3) of the GDPR (confirmation of processing, access to data and safeguards for third country transfers) do not apply to child abuse data to the extent that the application of that provision would not be in the best interests of the data subject.

   (3) "Child abuse data" is personal data consisting of information as to whether the data subject is or has been the subject of, or may be at risk of, child abuse.

   (4) For this purpose, "child abuse" includes physical injury (other than accidental injury) to, and physical and emotional neglect, ill-treatment and sexual abuse of, an individual aged under 18.

   (5) This paragraph does not apply in relation to Scotland.

SCHEDULE 4   Section 15

EXEMPTIONS ETC FROM THE GDPR: DISCLOSURE PROHIBITED OR RESTRICTED BY AN ENACTMENT

GDPR provisions to be restricted: "the listed GDPR provisions"

1   In this Schedule "the listed GDPR provisions" means the following provisions of the GDPR (the rights and obligations in which may be restricted by virtue of Article 23(1) of the GDPR) —

   (a) Article 15(1) to (3) (confirmation of processing, access to data and safeguards for third country transfers);

   (b) Article 5 (general principles) so far as its provisions correspond to the rights and obligations provided for in Article 15(1) to (3).

Human fertilisation and embryology information

2   The listed GDPR provisions do not apply to personal data consisting of information the disclosure of which is prohibited or restricted by any of sections 31, 31ZA to 31ZE and 33A to 33D of the Human Fertilisation and Embryology Act 1990.

Adoption records and reports

3   (1) The listed GDPR provisions do not apply to personal data consisting of information the disclosure of which is prohibited or restricted by an enactment listed in sub-paragraph (2), (3) or (4).

    (2) The enactments extending to England and Wales are —
        (a) regulation 14 of the Adoption Agencies Regulations 1983 (S.I. 1983/1964);
        (b) regulation 41 of the Adoption Agencies Regulations 2005 (S.I. 2005/389);
        (c) regulation 42 of the Adoption Agencies (Wales) Regulations 2005 (S.I. 2005/1313 (W. 95));
        (d) rules 5, 6, 9, 17, 18, 21, 22 and 53 of the Adoption Rules 1984 (S.I. 1984/265);
        (e) rules 24, 29, 30, 65, 72, 73, 77, 78 and 83 of the Family Procedure (Adoption) Rules 2005 (S.I. 2005/2795 (L. 22));
        (f) in the Family Procedure Rules 2010 (S.I. 2010/2955 (L. 17)), rules 14.6, 14.11, 14.12, 14.13, 14.14, 14.24, 16.20 (so far as it applies to a children's guardian appointed in proceedings to which Part 14 of those Rules applies), 16.32 and 16.33 (so far as it applies to a children and family reporter in proceedings to which Part 14 of those Rules applies).

    (3) The enactments extending to Scotland are —
        (a) regulation 23 of the Adoption Agencies (Scotland) Regulations 1996 (S.I. 1996/3266 (S. 254));
        (b) rule 67.3 of the Act of Sederunt (Rules of the Court of Session 1994) 1994 (S.I. 1994/1443 (S. 69));
        (c) rules 10.3, 17.2, 21, 25, 39, 43.3, 46.2 and 47 of the Act of Sederunt (Sheriff Court Rules Amendment) (Adoption and Children (Scotland) Act 2007) 2009 (S.S.I. 2009/284);
        (d) sections 53 and 55 of the Adoption and Children (Scotland) Act 2007 (asp 4);
        (e) regulation 28 of the Adoption Agencies (Scotland) Regulations 2009 (S.S.I. 2009/154);
        (f) regulation 3 of the Adoption (Disclosure of Information and Medical Information about Natural Parents) (Scotland) Regulations 2009 (S.S.I. 2009/268).

    (4) The enactments extending to Northern Ireland are —
        (a) Articles 50 and 54 of the Adoption (Northern Ireland) Order 1987 (S.I. 1987/2203 (N.I. 22));
        (b) rule 53 of Order 84 of the Rules of the Court of Judicature (Northern Ireland) 1980 (S.R. (N.I.) 1980 No. 346);

(c)   rules 4A.4(5), 4A.5(1), 4A.6(6), 4A.22(5) and 4C.7 of Part IVA of the Family Proceedings Rules (Northern Ireland) 1996 (S.R. (N.I.) 1996 No. 322).

Statements of special educational needs

4   (1)   The listed GDPR provisions do not apply to personal data consisting of information the disclosure of which is prohibited or restricted by an enactment listed in sub-paragraph (2).

(2)   The enactments are —

(a)   regulation 17 of the Special Educational Needs and Disability Regulations 2014 (S.I. 2014/1530);

(b)   regulation 10 of the Additional Support for Learning (Co-ordinated Support Plan) (Scotland) Amendment Regulations 2005 (S.S.I. 2005/518);

(c)   regulation 22 of the Education (Special Educational Needs) Regulations (Northern Ireland) 2005 (S.R. (N.I.) 2005 No. 384).

Parental order records and reports

5   (1)   The listed GDPR provisions do not apply to personal data consisting of information the disclosure of which is prohibited or restricted by an enactment listed in sub-paragraph (2), (3) or (4).

(2)   The enactments extending to England and Wales are —

(a)   sections 60, 77, 78 and 79 of the Adoption and Children Act 2002, as applied with modifications by regulation 2 of and Schedule 1 to the Human Fertilisation and Embryology (Parental Orders) Regulations 2010 (S.I. 2010/985) in relation to parental orders made under —

(i)   section 30 of the Human Fertilisation and Embryology Act 1990, or

(ii)   section 54 of the Human Fertilisation and Embryology Act 2008;

(b)   rules made under section 144 of the Magistrates' Courts Act 1980 by virtue of section 141(1) of the Adoption and Children Act 2002, as applied with modifications by regulation 2 of and Schedule 1 to the Human Fertilisation and Embryology (Parental Orders) Regulations 2010, so far as the rules relate to —

(i)   the appointment and duties of the parental order reporter, and

(ii)   the keeping of registers and the custody, inspection and disclosure of documents and information relating to parental order proceedings or related proceedings;

(c)   rules made under section 75 of the Courts Act 2003 by virtue of section 141(1) of the Adoption and Children Act 2002, as applied with modifications by regulation 2 of Schedule 1 to the Human Fertilisation and Embryology (Parental Orders) Regulations 2010 (S.I. 2010/985), so far as the rules relate to —

(i)   the appointment and duties of the parental order reporter, and

(ii)   the keeping of registers and the custody, inspection and disclosure of documents and information relating to parental order proceedings or related proceedings.

(3) The enactments extending to Scotland are —

    (a) sections 53 and 55 of the Adoption and Children (Scotland) Act 2007 (asp 4), as applied with modifications by regulation 4 of and Schedule 3 to the Human Fertilisation and Embryology (Parental Orders) Regulations 2010 (S.I. 2010/985) in relation to parental orders made under —

        (i) section 30 of the Human Fertilisation and Embryology Act 1990, or

        (ii) section 54 of the Human Fertilisation and Embryology Act 2008;

    (b) rules 2.47 and 2.59 of the Act of Sederunt (Child Care and Maintenance Rules) 1997 (S.I. 1997/291 (S. 19));

    (c) rules 21 and 25 of the Sheriff Court Adoption Rules 2009.

(4) The enactments extending to Northern Ireland are —

    (a) Articles 50 and 54 of the Adoption (Northern Ireland) Order 1987 (S.I. 1987/2203 (N.I. 22)), as applied with modifications by regulation 3 of and Schedule 2 to the Human Fertilisation and Embryology (Parental Orders) Regulations 2010 in respect of parental orders made under —

        (i) section 30 of the Human Fertilisation and Embryology Act 1990, or

        (ii) section 54 of the Human Fertilisation and Embryology Act 2008;

    (b) rules 4, 5 and 16 of Order 84A of the Rules of the Court of Judicature (Northern Ireland) 1980 (S.R. (N.I.) 1980 No. 346);

    (c) rules 3, 4 and 15 of Order 50A of the County Court Rules (Northern Ireland) 1981 (S.R. (N.I.) 1981 No. 225).

Information provided by Principal Reporter for children's hearing

6   The listed GDPR provisions do not apply to personal data consisting of information the disclosure of which is prohibited or restricted by any of the following enactments —

    (a) section 178 of the Children's Hearings (Scotland) Act 2011 (asp 1);

    (b) the Children's Hearings (Scotland) Act 2011 (Rules of Procedure in Children's Hearings) Rules 2013 (S.S.I. 2013/194).

SCHEDULE 5

Section 17

ACCREDITATION OF CERTIFICATION PROVIDERS: REVIEWS AND APPEALS

Introduction

1   (1) This Schedule applies where —

    (a) a person ("the applicant") applies to an accreditation authority for accreditation as a certification provider, and

    (b) is dissatisfied with the decision on that application.

(2) In this Schedule —

    "accreditation authority" means —

        (a)   the Commissioner, or

        (b)   the national accreditation body;

"certification provider" and "national accreditation body" have the same meaning as in section 17.

Review

2   (1) The applicant may ask the accreditation authority to review the decision.

     (2) The request must be made in writing before the end of the period of 28 days beginning with the day on which the person receives written notice of the accreditation authority's decision.

     (3) The request must specify —

        (a)   the decision to be reviewed, and

        (b)   the reasons for asking for the review.

     (4) The request may be accompanied by additional documents which the applicant wants the accreditation authority to take into account for the purposes of the review.

     (5) If the applicant makes a request in accordance with sub-paragraphs (1) to (4), the accreditation authority must —

        (a)   review the decision, and

        (b)   inform the applicant of the outcome of the review in writing before the end of the period of 28 days beginning with the day on which the request for a review is received.

Right to appeal

3   (1) If the applicant is dissatisfied with the decision on the review under paragraph 2, the applicant may ask the accreditation authority to refer the decision to an appeal panel constituted in accordance with paragraph 4.

     (2) The request must be made in writing before the end of the period of 3 months beginning with the day on which the person receives written notice of the decision on the review.

     (3) A request must specify —

        (a)   the decision to be referred to the appeal panel, and

        (b)   the reasons for asking for it to be referred.

     (4) The request may be accompanied by additional documents which the applicant wants the appeal panel to take into account.

     (5) The applicant may discontinue an appeal at any time by giving notice in writing to the accreditation authority.

Appeal panel

4   (1) If the applicant makes a request in accordance with paragraph 3, an appeal panel must be established in accordance with this paragraph.

     (2) An appeal panel must consist of a chair and at least two other members.

     (3) Where the request relates to a decision of the Commissioner —

   (a) the Secretary of State may appoint one person to be a member of the appeal panel other than the chair, and

   (b) subject to paragraph (a), the Commissioner must appoint the members of the appeal panel.

(4) Where the request relates to a decision of the national accreditation body—

   (a) the Secretary of State—

     (i) may appoint one person to be a member of the appeal panel other than the chair, or

     (ii) may direct the Commissioner to appoint one person to be a member of the appeal panel other than the chair, and

   (b) subject to paragraph (a), the chair of the national accreditation body must appoint the members of the appeal panel.

(5) A person may not be a member of an appeal panel if the person—

   (a) has a commercial interest in the decision referred to the panel,

   (b) has had any prior involvement in any matters relating to the decision, or

   (c) is an employee or officer of the accreditation authority.

(6) The Commissioner may not be a member of an appeal panel to which a decision of the Commissioner is referred.

(7) The applicant may object to all or any of the members of the appeal panel appointed under sub-paragraph (3) or (4).

(8) If the applicant objects to a member of the appeal panel under sub-paragraph (7), the person who appointed that member must appoint a replacement.

(9) The applicant may not object to a member of the appeal panel appointed under sub-paragraph (8).

Hearing

5 (1) If the appeal panel considers it necessary, a hearing must be held at which both the applicant and the accreditation authority may be represented.

  (2) Any additional documents which the applicant or the accreditation authority want the appeal panel to take into account must be submitted to the chair of the appeal panel at least 5 working days before the hearing.

  (3) The appeal panel may allow experts and witnesses to give evidence at a hearing.

Decision following referral to appeal panel

6 (1) The appeal panel must, before the end of the period of 28 days beginning with the day on which the appeal panel is established in accordance with paragraph 4—

   (a) make a reasoned recommendation in writing to the accreditation authority, and

   (b) give a copy of the recommendation to the applicant.

  (2) For the purposes of sub-paragraph (1), where there is an objection under paragraph 4(7), an appeal panel is not to be taken to be established in

accordance with paragraph 4 until the replacement member is appointed (or, if there is more than one objection, until the last replacement member is appointed).

(3)   The accreditation authority must, before the end of the period of 3 working days beginning with the day on which the authority receives the recommendation —

    (a)   make a reasoned final decision in writing, and

    (b)   give a copy of the decision to the applicant.

(4)   Where the accreditation authority is the national accreditation body, the recommendation must be given to, and the final decision must be made by, the chief executive of that body.

Meaning of "working day"

7   In this Schedule, "working day" means any day other than —

    (a)   Saturday or Sunday,

    (b)   Christmas Day or Good Friday, or

    (c)   a day which is a bank holiday under the Banking and Financial Dealings Act 1971 in any part of the United Kingdom.

SCHEDULE 6   Section 22

THE APPLIED GDPR AND THE APPLIED CHAPTER 2

PART 1

MODIFICATIONS TO THE GDPR

Introductory

1   In its application by virtue of section 22(1), the GDPR has effect as if it were modified as follows.

References to the GDPR and its provisions

2   (1)   References to "this Regulation" and to provisions of the GDPR have effect as references to the applied GDPR and to the provisions of the applied GDPR.

(2)   But sub-paragraph (1) does not have effect —

    (a)   in the case of the references which are modified or inserted by paragraphs 9(f)(ii), 15(b), 16(a)(ii), 35, 36(a) and (e)(ii) and 38(a)(i);

    (b)   in relation to the references in points (a) and (b) of paragraph 2 of Article 61, as inserted by paragraph 49.

References to Union law and Member State law

3   (1)   References to "Union law", "Member State law", "the law of a Member State" and "Union or Member State law" have effect as references to domestic law.

(2)   Sub-paragraph (1) is subject to the specific modifications made in this Part of this Schedule.

Data Protection Act 2018 (c. 12)   185
Schedule 6 — The applied GDPR and the applied Chapter 2
Part 1 — Modifications to the GDPR

(3) In this paragraph, "domestic law" means the law of the United Kingdom, or of a part of the United Kingdom, and includes law in the form of an enactment, an instrument made under Her Majesty's prerogative or a rule of law.

References to the Union and to Member States

4   (1) References to "the Union", "a Member State" and "Member States" have effect as references to the United Kingdom.

     (2) Sub-paragraph (1) is subject to the specific modifications made in this Part of this Schedule (including paragraph 3(1)).

References to supervisory authorities

5   (1) References to a "supervisory authority", a "competent supervisory authority" or "supervisory authorities", however expressed, have effect as references to the Commissioner.

     (2) Sub-paragraph (1) does not apply to the references in—
       (a) Article 4(21) as modified by paragraph 9(f);
       (b) Article 57(1)(h);
       (c) Article 61(1) inserted by paragraph 49.

     (3) Sub-paragraph (1) is also subject to the specific modifications made in this Part of this Schedule.

References to the national parliament

6   References to "the national parliament" have effect as references to both Houses of Parliament.

Chapter I of the GDPR (general provisions)

7   For Article 2 (material scope) substitute—

     "2   This Regulation applies to the processing of personal data to which Chapter 3 of Part 2 of the 2018 Act applies (see section 21 of that Act)."

8   For Article 3 substitute—

"Article 3

Territorial application

Subsections (1), (2) and (7) of section 207 of the 2018 Act have effect for the purposes of this Regulation as they have effect for the purposes of that Act but as if the following were omitted—
     (a) in subsection (1), the reference to subsection (3), and
     (b) in subsection (7), the words following paragraph (d)."

9   In Article 4 (definitions)—
     (a) in paragraph (7) (meaning of "controller"), for "; where the purposes and means of such processing are determined by Union or Member State law, the controller or the specific criteria for its nomination may

186   *Data Protection Act 2018 (c. 12)*
Schedule 6 — The applied GDPR and the applied Chapter 2
Part 1 — Modifications to the GDPR

be provided for by Union or Member State law" substitute ", subject to section 6 of the 2018 Act (meaning of "controller")";

(b)   after paragraph (7) insert—

"(7A)   "the 2018 Act" means the Data Protection Act 2018 as applied by section 22 of that Act and further modified by section 3 of that Act.";

(c)   omit paragraph (16) (meaning of "main establishment");

(d)   omit paragraph (17) (meaning of "representative");

(e)   in paragraph (20) (meaning of "binding corporate rules"), for "on the territory of a Member State" substitute "in the United Kingdom";

(f)   in paragraph (21) (meaning of "supervisory authority")—

(i)   after "a Member State" insert "(other than the United Kingdom)";

(ii)   for "Article 51" substitute "Article 51 of the GDPR";

(g)   after paragraph (21) insert—

"(21A)   "the Commissioner" means the Information Commissioner (see section 114 of the 2018 Act);";

(h)   omit paragraph (22) (meaning of "supervisory authority concerned");

(i)   omit paragraph (23) (meaning of "cross-border processing");

(j)   omit paragraph (24) (meaning of "relevant and reasoned objection");

(k)   after paragraph (26) insert—

"(27)   "the GDPR" has the meaning given in section 3(10) of the 2018 Act.

(28)   "domestic law" has the meaning given in paragraph 3(3) of Schedule 6 to the 2018 Act."

Chapter II of the GDPR (principles)

10   In Article 6 (lawfulness of processing)—

(a)   omit paragraph 2;

(b)   in paragraph 3, for the first subparagraph substitute—

"In addition to the provision made in section 15 of and Part 1 of Schedule 2 to the 2018 Act, a legal basis for the processing referred to in point (c) and (e) of paragraph 1 may be laid down by the Secretary of State in regulations (see section 16 of the 2018 Act).";

(c)   in paragraph 3, in the second subparagraph, for "The Union or the Member State law shall" substitute "The regulations must".

11   In Article 8 (conditions applicable to child's consent in relation to information society services)—

(a)   in paragraph 1, for the second subparagraph substitute—

"This paragraph is subject to section 9 of the 2018 Act.";

(b)   in paragraph 3, for "the general contract law of Member States" substitute "the general law of contract as it operates in domestic law".

12   In Article 9 (processing of special categories of personal data)—

Data Protection Act 2018 (c. 12) 187
Schedule 6 — The applied GDPR and the applied Chapter 2
Part 1 — Modifications to the GDPR

>   (a)   in paragraph 2(a), omit ", except where Union or Member State law provide that the prohibition referred to in paragraph 1 may not be lifted by the data subject";
>
>   (b)   in paragraph 2(b), for "Union or Member State law" substitute "domestic law (see section 10 of the 2018 Act)";
>
>   (c)   in paragraph 2, for point (g) substitute—
>
> > "(g)   processing is necessary for reasons of substantial public interest and is authorised by domestic law (see section 10 of the 2018 Act);";
>
>   (d)   in paragraph 2(h), for "Union or Member State law" substitute "domestic law (see section 10 of the 2018 Act)";
>
>   (e)   in paragraph 2(i), for "Union or Member State law" insert "domestic law (see section 10 of the 2018 Act);";
>
>   (f)   in paragraph 2, for point (j) substitute—
>
> > "(j)   processing is necessary for archiving purposes in the public interest, scientific or historical research purposes or statistical purposes in accordance with Article 89(1) (as supplemented by section 19 of the 2018 Act) and is authorised by domestic law (see section 10 of that Act).";
>
>   (g)   in paragraph 3, for "national competent bodies", in both places, substitute "a national competent body of the United Kingdom";
>
>   (h)   omit paragraph 4.

13   In Article 10 (processing of personal data relating to criminal convictions and offences), in the first sentence, for "Union or Member State law providing for appropriate safeguards for the rights and freedoms of data subjects" substitute "domestic law (see section 10 of the 2018 Act)".

Section 1 of Chapter III of the GDPR (rights of the data subject: transparency and modalities)

14   In Article 12 (transparent information etc for the exercise of the rights of the data subject), omit paragraph 8.

Section 2 of Chapter III of the GDPR (rights of the data subject: information and access to personal data)

15   In Article 13 (personal data collected from data subject: information to be provided), in paragraph 1—

>   (a)   in point (a), omit "and, where applicable, of the controller's representative";
>
>   (b)   in point (f), after "the Commission" insert "pursuant to Article 45(3) of the GDPR".

16   In Article 14 (personal data collected other than from data subject: information to be provided)—

>   (a)   in paragraph 1—
>
> >   (i)   in point (a), omit "and, where applicable, of the controller's representative";
> >
> >   (ii)   in point (f), after "the Commission" insert "pursuant to Article 45(3) of the GDPR";
>
>   (b)   in paragraph 5(c), for "Union or Member State law to which the controller is subject" substitute "a rule of domestic law".

188
Data Protection Act 2018 (c. 12)
Schedule 6 — The applied GDPR and the applied Chapter 2
Part 1 — Modifications to the GDPR

Section 3 of Chapter III of the GDPR (rights of the data subject: rectification and erasure)

17   In Article 17 (right to erasure ('right to be forgotten')) —

    (a)   in paragraph 1(e), for "in Union or Member State law to which the controller is subject" substitute "under domestic law";

    (b)   in paragraph 3(b), for "by Union or Member State law to which the controller is subject" substitute "under domestic law".

18   In Article 18 (right to restriction of processing), in paragraph 2, for "of the Union or of a Member State" substitute "of the United Kingdom".

Section 4 of Chapter III of the GDPR (rights of the data subject: right to object and automated individual decision-making)

19   In Article 21 (right to object), in paragraph 5, omit ", and notwithstanding Directive 2002/58/EC,".

20   In Article 22 (automated individual decision-making, including profiling), for paragraph 2(b) substitute —

    "(b)   is a qualifying significant decision for the purposes of section 14 of the 2018 Act; or".

Section 5 of Chapter III of the GDPR (rights of the data subject: restrictions)

21   In Article 23 (restrictions), in paragraph 1 —

    (a)   for "Union or Member State law to which the data controller or processor is subject" substitute "In addition to the provision made by section 15 of and Schedules 2, 3 and 4 to the 2018 Act, the Secretary of State";

    (b)   in point (e), for "of the Union or of a Member State", in both places, substitute "of the United Kingdom";

    (c)   after point (j) insert —

    "See section 16 of the 2018 Act."

Section 1 of Chapter IV of the GDPR (controller and processor: general obligations)

22   In Article 26 (joint controllers), in paragraph 1, for "Union or Member State law to which the controllers are subject" substitute "domestic law".

23   Omit Article 27 (representatives of controllers or processors not established in the Union).

24   In Article 28 (processor) —

    (a)   in paragraph 3, in point (a), for "Union or Member State law to which the processor is subject" substitute "domestic law";

    (b)   in paragraph 3, in the second subparagraph, for "other Union or Member State data protection provisions" substitute "any other rule of domestic law relating to data protection";

    (c)   in paragraph 6, for "paragraphs 7 and 8" substitute "paragraph 8";

    (d)   omit paragraph 7;

    (e)   in paragraph 8, omit "and in accordance with the consistency mechanism referred to in Article 63".

25   In Article 30 (records of processing activities) —

Data Protection Act 2018 (c. 12)
Schedule 6 — The applied GDPR and the applied Chapter 2
Part 1 — Modifications to the GDPR

189

(a) in paragraph 1, in the first sentence, omit "and, where applicable, the controller's representative,";

(b) in paragraph 1, in point (a), omit ", the controller's representative";

(c) in paragraph 1, in point (g), after "32(1)" insert "or section 28(3) of the 2018 Act";

(d) in paragraph 2, in the first sentence, omit "and, where applicable, the processor's representative";

(e) in paragraph 2, in point (a), omit "the controller's or the processor's representative, and";

(f) in paragraph 2, in point (d), after "32(1)" insert "or section 28(3) of the 2018 Act";

(g) in paragraph 4, omit "and, where applicable, the controller's or the processor's representative,".

26   In Article 31 (co-operation with the supervisory authority), omit "and, where applicable, their representatives,".

Section 3 of Chapter IV of the GDPR (controller and processor: data protection impact assessment and prior consultation)

27   In Article 35 (data protection impact assessment), omit paragraphs 4, 5, 6 and 10.

28   In Article 36 (prior consultation) —

(a) for paragraph 4 substitute —

"4   The Secretary of State must consult the Commissioner during the preparation of any proposal for a legislative measure which relates to processing.";

(b) omit paragraph 5.

Section 4 of Chapter IV of the GDPR (controller and processor: data protection officer)

29   In Article 37 (designation of data protection officers), omit paragraph 4.

30   In Article 39 (tasks of the data protection officer), in paragraph 1(a) and (b), for "other Union or Member State data protection provisions" substitute "other rules of domestic law relating to data protection".

Section 5 of Chapter IV of the GDPR (controller and processor: codes of conduct and certification)

31   In Article 40 (codes of conduct) —

(a) in paragraph 1, for "The Member States, the supervisory authorities, the Board and the Commission shall" substitute "The Commissioner must";

(b) omit paragraph 3;

(c) in paragraph 6, omit ", and where the code of conduct concerned does not relate to processing activities in several Member States";

(d) omit paragraphs 7 to 11.

32   In Article 41 (monitoring of approved codes of conduct), omit paragraph 3.

33   In Article 42 (certification) —

(a) in paragraph 1 —

190

Data Protection Act 2018 (c. 12)
Schedule 6 — The applied GDPR and the applied Chapter 2
Part 1 — Modifications to the GDPR

          (i)   for "The Member States, the supervisory authorities, the Board and the Commission" substitute "The Commissioner";

          (ii)   omit ", in particular at Union level,";

   (b)   omit paragraph 2;

   (c)   in paragraph 5, omit "or by the Board pursuant to Article 63. Where the criteria are approved by the Board, this may result in a common certification, the European Data Protection Seal";

   (d)   omit paragraph 8.

34   In Article 43 (certification bodies) —

   (a)   in paragraph 1, in the second sentence, for "Member States shall ensure that those certification bodies are" substitute "Those certification bodies must be";

   (b)   in paragraph 2, in point (b), omit "or by the Board pursuant to Article 63";

   (c)   in paragraph 3, omit "or by the Board pursuant to Article 63";

   (d)   in paragraph 6, omit the second and third sentences;

   (e)   omit paragraphs 8 and 9.

Chapter V of the GDPR (transfers of data to third countries or international organisations)

35   In Article 45 (transfers on the basis of an adequacy decision) —

   (a)   in paragraph 1, after "decided" insert "in accordance with Article 45 of the GDPR";

   (b)   after paragraph 1 insert —

       "1A   But a transfer of personal data to a third country or international organisation must not take place under paragraph 1, if the Commission's decision in relation to the third country (including a territory or sector within it) or the international organisation —

          (a)   is suspended,

          (b)   has been amended, or

          (c)   has been repealed,

       by the Commission under Article 45(5) of the GDPR.";

   (c)   omit paragraphs 2 to 8;

   (d)   in paragraph 9, for "of this Article" substitute "of Article 45 of the GDPR".

36   In Article 46 (transfers subject to appropriate safeguards) —

   (a)   in paragraph 1, for "Article 45(3)" substitute "Article 45(3) of the GDPR";

   (b)   in paragraph 2, omit point (c);

   (c)   in paragraph 2, in point (d), omit "and approved by the Commission pursuant to the examination procedure referred to in Article 93(2)";

   (d)   omit paragraph 4;

   (e)   in paragraph 5 —

          (i)   in the first sentence, for "a Member State or supervisory authority" substitute "the Commissioner";

          (ii)   in the second sentence, for "this Article" substitute "Article 46 of the GDPR".

Data Protection Act 2018 (c. 12)
Schedule 6 — The applied GDPR and the applied Chapter 2
Part 1 — Modifications to the GDPR

191

37   In Article 47 (binding corporate rules) —
    (a) in paragraph 1, in the first sentence, omit "in accordance with the consistency mechanism set out in Article 63";
    (b) in paragraph 2, in point (e), for "the competent courts of the Member States" substitute "a court";
    (c) in paragraph 2, in point (f), for "on the territory of a Member State" substitute "in the United Kingdom";
    (d) omit paragraph 3.

38   In Article 49 (derogations for specific situations) —
    (a) in paragraph 1, in the first sentence —
       (i) for "Article 45(3)" substitute "Article 45(3) of the GDPR";
       (ii) for "Article 46" substitute "Article 46 of this Regulation";
    (b) in paragraph 4, for "Union law or in the law of the Member State to which the controller is subject" substitute "domestic law (see section 18 of the 2018 Act which makes certain provision about the public interest)";
    (c) for paragraph 5 substitute —

      "5   Paragraph 1 is subject to any regulations made under section 18(2) of the 2018 Act."

39   In Article 50 (international co-operation for the protection of personal data), omit "the Commission and".

Section 1 of Chapter VI of the GDPR (independent supervisory authorities: independent status)

40   In Article 51 (supervisory authority) —
    (a) in paragraph 1 —
       (i) for "Each Member State shall provide for one or more independent public authorities to be" substitute "The Commissioner is";
       (ii) omit "and to facilitate the free flow of personal data within the Union ('supervisory authority')";
    (b) omit paragraphs 2 to 4.

41   In Article 52 (independence) —
    (a) in paragraph 2 —
       (i) for "The member or members of each supervisory authority" substitute "The Commissioner";
       (ii) for "their", in both places, substitute "the Commissioner's";
    (b) in paragraph 3 —
       (i) for "Member or members of each supervisory authority" substitute "The Commissioner";
       (ii) for "their", in both places, substitute "the Commissioner's";
    (c) omit paragraphs 4 to 6.

42   Omit Article 53 (general conditions for the members of the supervisory authority).

43   Omit Article 54 (rules on the establishment of the supervisory authority).

192   *Data Protection Act 2018 (c. 12)*
Schedule 6 — The applied GDPR and the applied Chapter 2
Part 1 — Modifications to the GDPR

Section 2 of Chapter VI of the GDPR (independent supervisory authorities: competence, tasks and powers)

44   In Article 55 (competence) —
        (a)   in paragraph 1, omit "on the territory of its own Member State";
        (b)   omit paragraph 2.

45   Omit Article 56 (competence of the lead supervisory authority).

46   In Article 57 (tasks) —
        (a)   in paragraph 1, in the first sentence, for "each supervisory authority shall on its territory" substitute "the Commissioner is to";
        (b)   in paragraph 1, in point (e), omit "and, if appropriate, cooperate with the supervisory authorities in other Member States to that end";
        (c)   in paragraph 1, in point (f), omit "or coordination with another supervisory authority";
        (d)   in paragraph 1, omit points (g), (k) and (t);
        (e)   after paragraph 1 insert —

              "1A   In this Article and Article 58, references to "this Regulation" have effect as references to this Regulation and section 28(3) of the 2018 Act."

47   In Article 58 (powers) —
        (a)   in paragraph 1, in point (a), omit ", and, where applicable, the controller's or the processor's representative";
        (b)   in paragraph 1, in point (f), for "Union or Member State procedural law" substitute "domestic law";
        (c)   in paragraph 3, in point (b), for "the Member State government" substitute "the Secretary of State";
        (d)   in paragraph 3, omit point (c);
        (e)   omit paragraphs 4 to 6.

48   In Article 59 (activity reports) —
        (a)   for ", the government and other authorities as designated by Member State law" substitute "and the Secretary of State";
        (b)   omit ", to the Commission and to the Board".

Chapter VII of the GDPR (co-operation and consistency)

49   For Articles 60 to 76 substitute —

                        "Article 61

            Co-operation with other supervisory authorities etc

        1   The Commissioner may, in connection with carrying out the Commissioner's functions under this Regulation —
                (a)   co-operate with, provide assistance to and seek assistance from other supervisory authorities;
                (b)   conduct joint operations with other supervisory authorities, including joint investigations and joint enforcement measures.

Data Protection Act 2018 (c. 12)
Schedule 6 — The applied GDPR and the applied Chapter 2
Part 1 — Modifications to the GDPR

193

2   The Commissioner must, in carrying out the Commissioner's functions under this Regulation, have regard to —

    (a)   decisions, advice, guidelines, recommendations and best practices issued by the European Data Protection Board established under Article 68 of the GDPR;

    (b)   any implementing acts adopted by the Commission under Article 67 of the GDPR (exchange of information)."

Chapter VIII of the GDPR (remedies, liability and penalties)

50   In Article 77 (right to lodge a complaint with a supervisory authority) —

    (a)   in paragraph 1, omit "in particular in the Member State of his or her habitual residence, place of work or place of the alleged infringement";

    (b)   in paragraph 2, for "The supervisory authority with which the complaint has been lodged" substitute "The Commissioner".

51   In Article 78 (right to an effective judicial remedy against a supervisory authority) —

    (a)   omit paragraph 2;

    (b)   for paragraph 3 substitute —

       "3   Proceedings against the Commissioner are to be brought before a court in the United Kingdom.";

    (c)   omit paragraph 4.

52   In Article 79 (right to an effective judicial remedy against a controller or processor), for paragraph 2 substitute —

       "2   Proceedings against a controller or a processor are to be brought before a court (see section 180 of the 2018 Act)."

53   In Article 80 (representation of data subjects) —

    (a)   in paragraph 1, omit "where provided for by Member State law";

    (b)   in paragraph 2, for "Member States" substitute "The Secretary of State";

    (c)   after that paragraph insert —

       "3   The power under paragraph 2 may only be exercised by making regulations under section 190 of the 2018 Act."

54   Omit Article 81 (suspension of proceedings).

55   In Article 82 (right to compensation and liability), for paragraph 6 substitute —

       "6   Proceedings for exercising the right to receive compensation are to be brought before a court (see section 180 of the 2018 Act)."

56   In Article 83 (general conditions for imposing administrative fines) —

    (a)   in paragraph 5, in point (d), for "pursuant to Member State law adopted under Chapter IX" substitute "under Part 5 or 6 of Schedule 2 to the 2018 Act or under regulations made under section 16 of that Act";

    (b)   in paragraph 7 —

       (i)   for "each Member State" substitute "the Secretary of State";

194

Data Protection Act 2018 (c. 12)
Schedule 6 — The applied GDPR and the applied Chapter 2
Part 1 — Modifications to the GDPR

   (ii) for "that Member State" substitute "the United Kingdom";

  (c) for paragraph 8 substitute—

    "8 Section 115(9) of the 2018 Act makes provision about the exercise of the Commissioner's powers under this Article. Part 6 of the 2018 Act (enforcement) makes further provision in connection with administrative penalties (including provision about appeals).";

  (d) omit paragraph 9.

57 In Article 84 (penalties)—

  (a) for paragraph 1 substitute—

    "1 The rules on other penalties applicable to infringements of this Regulation are set out in the 2018 Act (see in particular Part 6 (enforcement)).";

  (b) omit paragraph 2.

Chapter IX of the GDPR (provisions relating to specific processing situations)

58 In Article 85 (processing and freedom of expression and information)—

  (a) omit paragraph 1;

  (b) in paragraph 2, for "Member States shall" substitute "the Secretary of State, in addition to the relevant provisions, may by way of regulations (see section 16 of the 2018 Act),";

  (c) in paragraph 2, at the end insert—

    "In this paragraph, "the relevant provisions" means section 15 of and Part 5 of Schedule 2 to the 2018 Act.";

  (d) omit paragraph 3.

59 In Article 86 (processing and public access to official documents), for "Union or Member State law to which the public authority or body is subject" substitute "domestic law".

60 Omit Article 87 (processing of national identification number).

61 Omit Article 88 (processing in the context of employment).

62 In Article 89 (safeguards and derogations relating to processing for archiving purposes etc)—

  (a) in paragraph 2, for "Union or Member State law may" substitute "the Secretary of State, in addition to the relevant provisions, may in regulations (see section 16 of the 2018 Act)";

  (b) in paragraph 3, for "Union or Member State law may" substitute "the Secretary of State, in addition to the relevant provisions, may in regulations (see section 16 of the 2018 Act)";

  (c) after paragraph 3 insert—

    "3A In this Article "the relevant provisions" means section 15 of and Part 6 of Schedule 2 to the 2018 Act."

63 Omit Article 90 (obligations of secrecy).

64 Omit Article 91 (existing data protection rules of churches and religious associations).

Data Protection Act 2018 (c. 12)
Schedule 6 — The applied GDPR and the applied Chapter 2
Part 1 — Modifications to the GDPR

195

Chapter X of the GDPR (delegated acts and implementing acts)

65   Omit Article 92 (exercise of the delegation).

66   Omit Article 93 (committee procedure).

Chapter XI of the GDPR (final provisions)

67   Omit Article 94 (repeal of Directive 95/46/EC).

68   Omit Article 95 (relationship with Directive 2002/58/EC).

69   In Article 96 (relationship with previously concluded Agreements), for "by Member States" substitute "by the United Kingdom or the Commissioner".

70   Omit Article 97 (Commission reports).

71   Omit Article 98 (Commission reviews).

72   Omit Article 99 (entry into force and application).

PART 2

MODIFICATIONS TO CHAPTER 2 OF PART 2

Introductory

73   In its application by virtue of section 22(2), Chapter 2 of Part 2 has effect as if it were modified as follows.

General modifications

74   (1) References to Chapter 2 of Part 2 and the provisions of that Chapter have effect as references to the applied Chapter 2 and the provisions of the applied Chapter 2.

     (2) References to the GDPR and to the provisions of the GDPR have effect as references to the applied GDPR and to the provisions of the applied GDPR, except in section 18(2)(a).

     (3) References to the processing of personal data to which Chapter 2 applies have effect as references to the processing of personal data to which Chapter 3 applies.

Exemptions

75   In section 16 (power to make further exemptions etc by regulations), in subsection (1)(a), for "Member State law" substitute "the Secretary of State".

SCHEDULE 7   Section 30

COMPETENT AUTHORITIES

1   Any United Kingdom government department other than a non-ministerial government department.

2   The Scottish Ministers.

3   Any Northern Ireland department.

4   The Welsh Ministers.

Chief officers of police and other policing bodies

5   The chief constable of a police force maintained under section 2 of the Police
         Act 1996.

6   The Commissioner of Police of the Metropolis.

7   The Commissioner of Police for the City of London.

8   The Chief Constable of the Police Service of Northern Ireland.

9   The chief constable of the Police Service of Scotland.

10   The chief constable of the British Transport Police.

11   The chief constable of the Civil Nuclear Constabulary.

12   The chief constable of the Ministry of Defence Police.

13   The Provost Marshal of the Royal Navy Police.

14   The Provost Marshal of the Royal Military Police.

15   The Provost Marshal of the Royal Air Force Police.

16   The chief officer of —
         (a)   a body of constables appointed under provision incorporating
               section 79 of the Harbours, Docks, and Piers Clauses Act 1847;
         (b)   a body of constables appointed under an order made under section
               14 of the Harbours Act 1964;
         (c)   the body of constables appointed under section 154 of the Port of
               London Act 1968 (c.xxxii).

17   A body established in accordance with a collaboration agreement under
         section 22A of the Police Act 1996.

18   The Director General of the Independent Office for Police Conduct.

19   The Police Investigations and Review Commissioner.

20   The Police Ombudsman for Northern Ireland.

Other authorities with investigatory functions

21   The Commissioners for Her Majesty's Revenue and Customs.

22   The Welsh Revenue Authority.

23   Revenue Scotland.

24   The Director General of the National Crime Agency.

25   The Director of the Serious Fraud Office.

26   The Director of Border Revenue.

27   The Financial Conduct Authority.

28   The Health and Safety Executive.

29   The Competition and Markets Authority.

30   The Gas and Electricity Markets Authority.

31   The Food Standards Agency.

32   Food Standards Scotland.

33   Her Majesty's Land Registry.

34   The Criminal Cases Review Commission.

35   The Scottish Criminal Cases Review Commission.

Authorities with functions relating to offender management

36   A provider of probation services (other than the Secretary of State), acting in pursuance of arrangements made under section 3(2) of the Offender Management Act 2007.

37   The Youth Justice Board for England and Wales.

38   The Parole Board for England and Wales.

39   The Parole Board for Scotland.

40   The Parole Commissioners for Northern Ireland.

41   The Probation Board for Northern Ireland.

42   The Prisoner Ombudsman for Northern Ireland.

43   A person who has entered into a contract for the running of, or part of —
      (a)   a prison or young offender institution under section 84 of the Criminal Justice Act 1991, or
      (b)   a secure training centre under section 7 of the Criminal Justice and Public Order Act 1994.

44   A person who has entered into a contract with the Secretary of State —
      (a)   under section 80 of the Criminal Justice Act 1991 for the purposes of prisoner escort arrangements, or
      (b)   under paragraph 1 of Schedule 1 to the Criminal Justice and Public Order Act 1994 for the purposes of escort arrangements.

45   A person who is, under or by virtue of any enactment, responsible for securing the electronic monitoring of an individual.

46   A youth offending team established under section 39 of the Crime and Disorder Act 1998.

Other authorities

47   The Director of Public Prosecutions.

48   The Director of Public Prosecutions for Northern Ireland.

49   The Lord Advocate.

50   A Procurator Fiscal.

51   The Director of Service Prosecutions.

52   The Information Commissioner.

53   The Scottish Information Commissioner.

54   The Scottish Courts and Tribunal Service.

55   The Crown agent.

56   A court or tribunal.

SCHEDULE 8   Section 35(5)

CONDITIONS FOR SENSITIVE PROCESSING UNDER PART 3

Statutory etc purposes

1   This condition is met if the processing —
        (a)   is necessary for the exercise of a function conferred on a person by an
              enactment or rule of law, and
        (b)   is necessary for reasons of substantial public interest.

Administration of justice

2   This condition is met if the processing is necessary for the administration of
        justice.

Protecting individual's vital interests

3   This condition is met if the processing is necessary to protect the vital
        interests of the data subject or of another individual.

Safeguarding of children and of individuals at risk

4   (1) This condition is met if —
        (a)   the processing is necessary for the purposes of —
              (i)   protecting an individual from neglect or physical, mental or
                     emotional harm, or
              (ii)   protecting the physical, mental or emotional well-being of an
                     individual,
        (b)   the individual is —
              (i)   aged under 18, or
              (ii)   aged 18 or over and at risk,
        (c)   the processing is carried out without the consent of the data subject
              for one of the reasons listed in sub-paragraph (2), and
        (d)   the processing is necessary for reasons of substantial public interest.

     (2) The reasons mentioned in sub-paragraph (1)(c) are —
        (a)   in the circumstances, consent to the processing cannot be given by
              the data subject;

    (b)   in the circumstances, the controller cannot reasonably be expected to obtain the consent of the data subject to the processing;

    (c)   the processing must be carried out without the consent of the data subject because obtaining the consent of the data subject would prejudice the provision of the protection mentioned in sub-paragraph (1)(a).

(3)   For the purposes of this paragraph, an individual aged 18 or over is "at risk" if the controller has reasonable cause to suspect that the individual—

    (a)   has needs for care and support,

    (b)   is experiencing, or at risk of, neglect or physical, mental or emotional harm, and

    (c)   as a result of those needs is unable to protect himself or herself against the neglect or harm or the risk of it.

(4)   In sub-paragraph (1)(a), the reference to the protection of an individual or of the well-being of an individual includes both protection relating to a particular individual and protection relating to a type of individual.

Personal data already in the public domain

5   This condition is met if the processing relates to personal data which is manifestly made public by the data subject.

Legal claims

6   This condition is met if the processing—

    (a)   is necessary for the purpose of, or in connection with, any legal proceedings (including prospective legal proceedings),

    (b)   is necessary for the purpose of obtaining legal advice, or

    (c)   is otherwise necessary for the purposes of establishing, exercising or defending legal rights.

Judicial acts

7   This condition is met if the processing is necessary when a court or other judicial authority is acting in its judicial capacity.

Preventing fraud

8   (1)   This condition is met if the processing—

    (a)   is necessary for the purposes of preventing fraud or a particular kind of fraud, and

    (b)   consists of—

        (i)   the disclosure of personal data by a competent authority as a member of an anti-fraud organisation,

        (ii)   the disclosure of personal data by a competent authority in accordance with arrangements made by an anti-fraud organisation, or

        (iii)   the processing of personal data disclosed as described in sub-paragraph (i) or (ii).

(2)   In this paragraph, "anti-fraud organisation" has the same meaning as in section 68 of the Serious Crime Act 2007.

Archiving etc

9   This condition is met if the processing is necessary —
       (a)   for archiving purposes in the public interest,
       (b)   for scientific or historical research purposes, or
       (c)   for statistical purposes.

SCHEDULE 9   Section 86

CONDITIONS FOR PROCESSING UNDER PART 4

1   The data subject has given consent to the processing.

2   The processing is necessary —
       (a)   for the performance of a contract to which the data subject is a party,
              or
       (b)   in order to take steps at the request of the data subject prior to
              entering into a contract.

3   The processing is necessary for compliance with a legal obligation to which
       the controller is subject, other than an obligation imposed by contract.

4   The processing is necessary in order to protect the vital interests of the data
       subject or of another individual.

5   The processing is necessary —
       (a)   for the administration of justice,
       (b)   for the exercise of any functions of either House of Parliament,
       (c)   for the exercise of any functions conferred on a person by an
              enactment or rule of law,
       (d)   for the exercise of any functions of the Crown, a Minister of the
              Crown or a government department, or
       (e)   for the exercise of any other functions of a public nature exercised in
              the public interest by a person.

6 (1) The processing is necessary for the purposes of legitimate interests pursued
        by —
        (a)   the controller, or
        (b)   the third party or parties to whom the data is disclosed.

   (2) Sub-paragraph (1) does not apply where the processing is unwarranted in
        any particular case because of prejudice to the rights and freedoms or
        legitimate interests of the data subject.

   (3) In this paragraph, "third party", in relation to personal data, means a person
        other than the data subject, the controller or a processor or other person
        authorised to process personal data for the controller or processor.

SCHEDULE 10

CONDITIONS FOR SENSITIVE PROCESSING UNDER PART 4

Consent to particular processing

1   The data subject has given consent to the processing.

Right or obligation relating to employment

2   The processing is necessary for the purposes of exercising or performing any right or obligation which is conferred or imposed by an enactment or rule of law on the controller in connection with employment.

Vital interests of a person

3   The processing is necessary —

    (a)   in order to protect the vital interests of the data subject or of another person, in a case where —

        (i)   consent cannot be given by or on behalf of the data subject, or

        (ii)   the controller cannot reasonably be expected to obtain the consent of the data subject, or

    (b)   in order to protect the vital interests of another person, in a case where consent by or on behalf of the data subject has been unreasonably withheld.

Safeguarding of children and of individuals at risk

4   (1) This condition is met if —

    (a)   the processing is necessary for the purposes of —

        (i)   protecting an individual from neglect or physical, mental or emotional harm, or

        (ii)   protecting the physical, mental or emotional well-being of an individual,

    (b)   the individual is —

        (i)   aged under 18, or

        (ii)   aged 18 or over and at risk,

    (c)   the processing is carried out without the consent of the data subject for one of the reasons listed in sub-paragraph (2), and

    (d)   the processing is necessary for reasons of substantial public interest.

    (2) The reasons mentioned in sub-paragraph (1)(c) are —

    (a)   in the circumstances, consent to the processing cannot be given by the data subject;

    (b)   in the circumstances, the controller cannot reasonably be expected to obtain the consent of the data subject to the processing;

    (c)   the processing must be carried out without the consent of the data subject because obtaining the consent of the data subject would prejudice the provision of the protection mentioned in sub-paragraph (1)(a).

    (3) For the purposes of this paragraph, an individual aged 18 or over is "at risk" if the controller has reasonable cause to suspect that the individual —

        (a)   has needs for care and support,

        (b)   is experiencing, or at risk of, neglect or physical, mental or emotional harm, and

        (c)   as a result of those needs is unable to protect himself or herself against the neglect or harm or the risk of it.

(4)   In sub-paragraph (1)(a), the reference to the protection of an individual or of the well-being of an individual includes both protection relating to a particular individual and protection relating to a type of individual.

Data already published by data subject

5   The information contained in the personal data has been made public as a result of steps deliberately taken by the data subject.

Legal proceedings etc

6   The processing —

        (a)   is necessary for the purpose of, or in connection with, any legal proceedings (including prospective legal proceedings),

        (b)   is necessary for the purpose of obtaining legal advice, or

        (c)   is otherwise necessary for the purposes of establishing, exercising or defending legal rights.

Administration of justice, parliamentary, statutory etc and government purposes

7   The processing is necessary —

        (a)   for the administration of justice,

        (b)   for the exercise of any functions of either House of Parliament,

        (c)   for the exercise of any functions conferred on any person by an enactment or rule of law, or

        (d)   for the exercise of any functions of the Crown, a Minister of the Crown or a government department.

Medical purposes

8   (1)   The processing is necessary for medical purposes and is undertaken by —

        (a)   a health professional, or

        (b)   a person who in the circumstances owes a duty of confidentiality which is equivalent to that which would arise if that person were a health professional.

(2)   In this paragraph, "medical purposes" includes the purposes of preventative medicine, medical diagnosis, medical research, the provision of care and treatment and the management of healthcare services.

Equality

9   (1)   The processing —

        (a)   is of sensitive personal data consisting of information as to racial or ethnic origin,

        (b)   is necessary for the purpose of identifying or keeping under review the existence or absence of equality of opportunity or treatment between persons of different racial or ethnic origins, with a view to enabling such equality to be promoted or maintained, and

(c) is carried out with appropriate safeguards for the rights and freedoms of data subjects.

(2) In this paragraph, "sensitive personal data" means personal data the processing of which constitutes sensitive processing (see section 86(7)).

SCHEDULE 11

Section 112

OTHER EXEMPTIONS UNDER PART 4

Preliminary

1   In this Schedule, "the listed provisions" means —
         (a) Chapter 2 of Part 4 (the data protection principles), except section 86(1)(a) and (2) and Schedules 9 and 10;
         (b) Chapter 3 of Part 4 (rights of data subjects);
         (c) in Chapter 4 of Part 4, section 108 (communication of personal data breach to the Commissioner).

Crime

2   The listed provisions do not apply to personal data processed for any of the following purposes —
         (a) the prevention and detection of crime, or
         (b) the apprehension and prosecution of offenders,
         to the extent that the application of the listed provisions would be likely to prejudice any of the matters mentioned in paragraph (a) or (b).

Information required to be disclosed by law etc or in connection with legal proceedings

3   (1) The listed provisions do not apply to personal data consisting of information that the controller is obliged by an enactment to make available to the public, to the extent that the application of the listed provisions would prevent the controller from complying with that obligation.

     (2) The listed provisions do not apply to personal data where disclosure of the data is required by an enactment, a rule of law or the order of a court, to the extent that the application of the listed provisions would prevent the controller from making the disclosure.

     (3) The listed provisions do not apply to personal data where disclosure of the data —
         (a) is necessary for the purpose of, or in connection with, legal proceedings (including prospective legal proceedings),
         (b) is necessary for the purpose of obtaining legal advice, or
         (c) is otherwise necessary for the purposes of establishing, exercising or defending legal rights,
         to the extent that the application of the listed provisions would prevent the controller from making the disclosure.

Parliamentary privilege

4   The listed provisions do not apply to personal data where this is required for
         the purpose of avoiding an infringement of the privileges of either House of
         Parliament.

Judicial proceedings

5   The listed provisions do not apply to personal data to the extent that the
         application of the listed provisions would be likely to prejudice judicial
         proceedings.

Crown honours and dignities

6   The listed provisions do not apply to personal data processed for the
         purposes of the conferring by the Crown of any honour or dignity.

Armed forces

7   The listed provisions do not apply to personal data to the extent that the
         application of the listed provisions would be likely to prejudice the combat
         effectiveness of any of the armed forces of the Crown.

Economic well-being

8   The listed provisions do not apply to personal data to the extent that the
         application of the listed provisions would be likely to prejudice the
         economic well-being of the United Kingdom.

Legal professional privilege

9   The listed provisions do not apply to personal data that consists of —
         (a)   information in respect of which a claim to legal professional
               privilege or, in Scotland, confidentiality of communications, could be
               maintained in legal proceedings, or
         (b)   information in respect of which a duty of confidentiality is owed by
               a professional legal adviser to a client of the adviser.

Negotiations

10   The listed provisions do not apply to personal data that consists of records
         of the intentions of the controller in relation to any negotiations with the data
         subject to the extent that the application of the listed provisions would be
         likely to prejudice the negotiations.

Confidential references given by the controller

11   The listed provisions do not apply to personal data consisting of a reference
         given (or to be given) in confidence by the controller for the purposes of —
         (a)   the education, training or employment (or prospective education,
               training or employment) of the data subject,
         (b)   the appointment (or prospective appointment) of the data subject to
               any office, or

        (c)   the provision (or prospective provision) by the data subject of any service.

Exam scripts and marks

12   (1) The listed provisions do not apply to personal data consisting of information recorded by candidates during an exam.

     (2) Where personal data consists of marks or other information processed by a controller —

        (a)   for the purposes of determining the results of an exam, or

        (b)   in consequence of the determination of the results of an exam,

     section 94 has effect subject to sub-paragraph (3).

     (3) Where the relevant time falls before the results of the exam are announced, the period mentioned in section 94(10)(b) is extended until the earlier of —

        (a)   the end of the period of 5 months beginning with the relevant time, and

        (b)   the end of the period of 40 days beginning with the announcement of the results.

     (4) In this paragraph —

        "exam" means an academic, professional or other examination used for determining the knowledge, intelligence, skill or ability of a candidate and may include an exam consisting of an assessment of the candidate's performance while undertaking work or any other activity;

        "the relevant time" has the same meaning as in section 94.

     (5) For the purposes of this paragraph, the results of an exam are treated as announced when they are first published or, if not published, first communicated to the candidate.

Research and statistics

13   (1) The listed provisions do not apply to personal data processed for —

        (a)   scientific or historical research purposes, or

        (b)   statistical purposes,

     to the extent that the application of those provisions would prevent or seriously impair the achievement of the purposes in question.

     (2) The exemption in sub-paragraph (1) is available only where —

        (a)   the personal data is processed subject to appropriate safeguards for the rights and freedoms of data subjects, and

        (b)   the results of the research or any resulting statistics are not made available in a form which identifies a data subject.

Archiving in the public interest

14   (1) The listed provisions do not apply to personal data processed for archiving purposes in the public interest to the extent that the application of those provisions would prevent or seriously impair the achievement of those purposes.

(2) The exemption in sub-paragraph (1) is available only where the personal data is processed subject to appropriate safeguards for the rights and freedoms of data subjects.

SCHEDULE 12   Section 114

THE INFORMATION COMMISSIONER

Status and capacity

1   (1) The Commissioner is to continue to be a corporation sole.

   (2) The Commissioner and the Commissioner's officers and staff are not to be regarded as servants or agents of the Crown.

Appointment

2   (1) The Commissioner is to be appointed by Her Majesty by Letters Patent.

   (2) No recommendation may be made to Her Majesty for the appointment of a person as the Commissioner unless the person concerned has been selected on merit on the basis of fair and open competition.

   (3) The Commissioner is to hold office for such term not exceeding 7 years as may be determined at the time of the Commissioner's appointment, subject to paragraph 3.

   (4) A person cannot be appointed as the Commissioner more than once.

Resignation and removal

3   (1) The Commissioner may be relieved of office by Her Majesty at the Commissioner's own request.

   (2) The Commissioner may be removed from office by Her Majesty on an Address from both Houses of Parliament.

   (3) No motion is to be made in either House of Parliament for such an Address unless a Minister of the Crown has presented a report to that House stating that the Minister is satisfied that one or both of the following grounds is made out—
   (a) the Commissioner is guilty of serious misconduct;
   (b) the Commissioner no longer fulfils the conditions required for the performance of the Commissioner's functions.

Salary etc

4   (1) The Commissioner is to be paid such salary as may be specified by a resolution of the House of Commons.

   (2) There is to be paid in respect of the Commissioner such pension as may be specified by a resolution of the House of Commons.

   (3) A resolution for the purposes of this paragraph may—
   (a) specify the salary or pension,

(b) specify the salary or pension and provide for it to be increased by reference to such variables as may be specified in the resolution, or

(c) provide that the salary or pension is to be the same as, or calculated on the same basis as, that payable to, or in respect of, a person employed in a specified office under, or in a specified capacity in the service of, the Crown.

(4) A resolution for the purposes of this paragraph may take effect from—

(a) the date on which it is passed, or

(b) from an earlier date or later date specified in the resolution.

(5) A resolution for the purposes of this paragraph may make different provision in relation to the pension payable to, or in respect of, different holders of the office of Commissioner.

(6) A salary or pension payable under this paragraph is to be charged on and issued out of the Consolidated Fund.

(7) In this paragraph, "pension" includes an allowance or gratuity and a reference to the payment of a pension includes a reference to the making of payments towards the provision of a pension.

Officers and staff

5 (1) The Commissioner—

(a) must appoint one or more deputy commissioners, and

(b) may appoint other officers and staff.

(2) The Commissioner is to determine the remuneration and other conditions of service of people appointed under this paragraph.

(3) The Commissioner may pay pensions, allowances or gratuities to, or in respect of, people appointed under this paragraph, including pensions, allowances or gratuities paid by way of compensation in respect of loss of office or employment.

(4) The references in sub-paragraph (3) to paying pensions, allowances or gratuities includes making payments towards the provision of pensions, allowances or gratuities.

(5) In making appointments under this paragraph, the Commissioner must have regard to the principle of selection on merit on the basis of fair and open competition.

(6) The Employers' Liability (Compulsory Insurance) Act 1969 does not require insurance to be effected by the Commissioner.

Carrying out of the Commissioner's functions by officers and staff

6 (1) The functions of the Commissioner are to be carried out by the deputy commissioner or deputy commissioners if—

(a) there is a vacancy in the office of the Commissioner, or

(b) the Commissioner is for any reason unable to act.

(2) When the Commissioner appoints a second or subsequent deputy commissioner, the Commissioner must specify which deputy commissioner is to carry out which of the Commissioner's functions in the circumstances

referred to in sub-paragraph (1).

(3) A function of the Commissioner may, to the extent authorised by the Commissioner, be carried out by any of the Commissioner's officers or staff.

Authentication of the seal of the Commissioner

7   The application of the seal of the Commissioner is to be authenticated by —
        (a) the Commissioner's signature, or
        (b) the signature of another person authorised for the purpose.

Presumption of authenticity of documents issued by the Commissioner

8   A document purporting to be an instrument issued by the Commissioner and to be —
        (a) duly executed under the Commissioner's seal, or
        (b) signed by or on behalf of the Commissioner,
        is to be received in evidence and is to be deemed to be such an instrument unless the contrary is shown.

Money

9   The Secretary of State may make payments to the Commissioner out of money provided by Parliament.

Fees etc and other sums

10   (1) All fees, charges, penalties and other sums received by the Commissioner in carrying out the Commissioner's functions are to be paid by the Commissioner to the Secretary of State.

     (2) Sub-paragraph (1) does not apply where the Secretary of State, with the consent of the Treasury, otherwise directs.

     (3) Any sums received by the Secretary of State under sub-paragraph (1) are to be paid into the Consolidated Fund.

Accounts

11   (1) The Commissioner must —
        (a) keep proper accounts and other records in relation to the accounts, and
        (b) prepare in respect of each financial year a statement of account in such form as the Secretary of State may direct.

     (2) The Commissioner must send a copy of the statement to the Comptroller and Auditor General —
        (a) on or before 31 August next following the end of the year to which the statement relates, or
        (b) on or before such earlier date after the end of that year as the Treasury may direct.

     (3) The Comptroller and Auditor General must examine, certify and report on the statement.

(4) The Commissioner must arrange for copies of the statement and the Comptroller and Auditor General's report to be laid before Parliament.

(5) In this paragraph, "financial year" means a period of 12 months beginning with 1 April.

Scotland

12   Paragraphs 1(1), 7 and 8 do not extend to Scotland.

SCHEDULE 13

Section 116

OTHER GENERAL FUNCTIONS OF THE COMMISSIONER

General tasks

1   (1) The Commissioner must—

  (a) monitor and enforce Parts 3 and 4 of this Act;

  (b) promote public awareness and understanding of the risks, rules, safeguards and rights in relation to processing of personal data to which those Parts apply;

  (c) advise Parliament, the government and other institutions and bodies on legislative and administrative measures relating to the protection of individuals' rights and freedoms with regard to processing of personal data to which those Parts apply;

  (d) promote the awareness of controllers and processors of their obligations under Parts 3 and 4 of this Act;

  (e) on request, provide information to a data subject concerning the exercise of the data subject's rights under Parts 3 and 4 of this Act and, if appropriate, co-operate with LED supervisory authorities and foreign designated authorities to provide such information;

  (f) co-operate with LED supervisory authorities and foreign designated authorities with a view to ensuring the consistency of application and enforcement of the Law Enforcement Directive and the Data Protection Convention, including by sharing information and providing mutual assistance;

  (g) conduct investigations on the application of Parts 3 and 4 of this Act, including on the basis of information received from an LED supervisory authority, a foreign designated authority or another public authority;

  (h) monitor relevant developments to the extent that they have an impact on the protection of personal data, including the development of information and communication technologies;

  (i) contribute to the activities of the European Data Protection Board established by the GDPR in connection with the processing of personal data to which the Law Enforcement Directive applies.

(2) Section 3(14)(c) does not apply to the reference to personal data in sub-paragraph (1)(h).

General powers

2   The Commissioner has the following investigative, corrective, authorisation and advisory powers in relation to processing of personal data to which Part 3 or 4 of this Act applies —

   (a)   to notify the controller or the processor of an alleged infringement of Part 3 or 4 of this Act;

   (b)   to issue warnings to a controller or processor that intended processing operations are likely to infringe provisions of Part 3 or 4 of this Act;

   (c)   to issue reprimands to a controller or processor where processing operations have infringed provisions of Part 3 or 4 of this Act;

   (d)   to issue, on the Commissioner's own initiative or on request, opinions to Parliament, the government or other institutions and bodies as well as to the public on any issue related to the protection of personal data.

Definitions

3   In this Schedule —

      "foreign designated authority" means an authority designated for the purposes of Article 13 of the Data Protection Convention by a party, other than the United Kingdom, which is bound by that Convention;

      "LED supervisory authority" means a supervisory authority for the purposes of Article 41 of the Law Enforcement Directive in a member State other than the United Kingdom.

SCHEDULE 14   Section 118

CO-OPERATION AND MUTUAL ASSISTANCE

PART 1

LAW ENFORCEMENT DIRECTIVE

Co-operation

1   (1)   The Commissioner may provide information or assistance to an LED supervisory authority to the extent that, in the opinion of the Commissioner, providing that information or assistance is necessary for the performance of the recipient's data protection functions.

     (2)   The Commissioner may ask an LED supervisory authority to provide information or assistance which the Commissioner requires for the performance of the Commissioner's data protection functions.

     (3)   In this paragraph, "data protection functions" means functions relating to the protection of individuals with respect to the processing of personal data.

Requests for information and assistance from LED supervisory authorities

2   (1)   This paragraph applies where the Commissioner receives a request from an LED supervisory authority for information or assistance referred to in Article 41 of the Law Enforcement Directive and the request —

        (a)   explains the purpose of and reasons for the request, and

        (b)   contains all other information necessary to enable the Commissioner to respond.

    (2)   The Commissioner must —

        (a)   take all appropriate measures required to reply to the request without undue delay and, in any event, before the end of the period of 1 month beginning with receipt of the request, and

        (b)   inform the LED supervisory authority of the results or, as the case may be, of the progress of the measures taken in order to respond to the request.

    (3)   The Commissioner must not refuse to comply with the request unless —

        (a)   the Commissioner does not have power to do what is requested, or

        (b)   complying with the request would infringe the Law Enforcement Directive, EU legislation or the law of the United Kingdom or a part of the United Kingdom.

    (4)   If the Commissioner refuses to comply with a request from an LED supervisory authority, the Commissioner must inform the authority of the reasons for the refusal.

    (5)   As a general rule, the Commissioner must provide information requested by LED supervisory authorities by electronic means using a standardised format.

Fees

3   (1)   Subject to sub-paragraph (2), any information or assistance that is required to be provided by this Part of this Schedule must be provided free of charge.

    (2)   The Commissioner may enter into agreements with other LED supervisory authorities for the Commissioner and other authorities to indemnify each other for expenditure arising from the provision of assistance in exceptional circumstances.

Restrictions on use of information

4   Where the Commissioner receives information from an LED supervisory authority as a result of a request under paragraph 1(2), the Commissioner may use the information only for the purposes specified in the request.

LED supervisory authority

5   In this Part of this Schedule, "LED supervisory authority" means a supervisory authority for the purposes of Article 41 of the Law Enforcement Directive in a member State other than the United Kingdom.

212

Data Protection Act 2018 (c. 12)
Schedule 14 — Co-operation and mutual assistance
Part 2 — Data Protection Convention

PART 2

DATA PROTECTION CONVENTION

Co-operation between the Commissioner and foreign designated authorities

6   (1) The Commissioner must, at the request of a foreign designated authority—

    (a) provide that authority with such information referred to in Article 13(3)(a) of the Data Protection Convention (information on law and administrative practice in the field of data protection) as is the subject of the request, and

    (b) take appropriate measures in accordance with Article 13(3)(b) of the Data Protection Convention for providing that authority with information relating to the processing of personal data in the United Kingdom.

    (2) The Commissioner may ask a foreign designated authority—

    (a) to provide the Commissioner with information referred to in Article 13(3) of the Data Protection Convention, or

    (b) to take appropriate measures to provide such information.

Assisting persons resident outside the UK with requests under Article 14 of the Convention

7   (1) This paragraph applies where a request for assistance in exercising any of the rights referred to in Article 8 of the Data Protection Convention in the United Kingdom is made by a person resident outside the United Kingdom, including where the request is forwarded to the Commissioner through the Secretary of State or a foreign designated authority.

    (2) The Commissioner must take appropriate measures to assist the person to exercise those rights.

Assisting UK residents with requests under Article 8 of the Convention

8   (1) This paragraph applies where a request for assistance in exercising any of the rights referred to in Article 8 of the Data Protection Convention in a country or territory (other than the United Kingdom) specified in the request is—

    (a) made by a person resident in the United Kingdom, and

    (b) submitted through the Commissioner under Article 14(2) of the Convention.

    (2) If the Commissioner is satisfied that the request contains all necessary particulars referred to in Article 14(3) of the Data Protection Convention, the Commissioner must send the request to the foreign designated authority in the specified country or territory.

    (3) Otherwise, the Commissioner must, where practicable, notify the person making the request of the reasons why the Commissioner is not required to assist.

Restrictions on use of information

9   Where the Commissioner receives information from a foreign designated authority as a result of—

(a)   a request made by the Commissioner under paragraph 6(2), or

(b)   a request received by the Commissioner under paragraph 6(1) or 7,

the Commissioner may use the information only for the purposes specified in the request.

Foreign designated authority

10   In this Part of this Schedule, "foreign designated authority" means an authority designated for the purposes of Article 13 of the Data Protection Convention by a party, other than the United Kingdom, which is bound by that Data Protection Convention.

SCHEDULE 15   Section 154

POWERS OF ENTRY AND INSPECTION

Issue of warrants in connection with non-compliance and offences

1   (1) This paragraph applies if a judge of the High Court, a circuit judge or a District Judge (Magistrates' Courts) is satisfied by information on oath supplied by the Commissioner that—

(a)   there are reasonable grounds for suspecting that—

(i)   a controller or processor has failed or is failing as described in section 149(2), or

(ii)   an offence under this Act has been or is being committed, and

(b)   there are reasonable grounds for suspecting that evidence of the failure or of the commission of the offence is to be found on premises specified in the information or is capable of being viewed using equipment on such premises.

(2) The judge may grant a warrant to the Commissioner.

Issue of warrants in connection with assessment notices

2   (1) This paragraph applies if a judge of the High Court, a circuit judge or a District Judge (Magistrates' Courts) is satisfied by information on oath supplied by the Commissioner that a controller or processor has failed to comply with a requirement imposed by an assessment notice.

(2) The judge may, for the purpose of enabling the Commissioner to determine whether the controller or processor has complied or is complying with the data protection legislation, grant a warrant to the Commissioner in relation to premises that were specified in the assessment notice.

Restrictions on issuing warrants: processing for the special purposes

3   A judge must not issue a warrant under this Schedule in respect of personal data processed for the special purposes unless a determination under section 174 with respect to the data or the processing has taken effect.

Restrictions on issuing warrants: procedural requirements

4   (1) A judge must not issue a warrant under this Schedule unless satisfied that—

     (a)   the conditions in sub-paragraphs (2) to (4) are met,

     (b)   compliance with those conditions would defeat the object of entry to the premises in question, or

     (c)   the Commissioner requires access to the premises in question urgently.

(2)   The first condition is that the Commissioner has given 7 days' notice in writing to the occupier of the premises in question demanding access to the premises.

(3)   The second condition is that—

     (a)   access to the premises was demanded at a reasonable hour and was unreasonably refused, or

     (b)   entry to the premises was granted but the occupier unreasonably refused to comply with a request by the Commissioner or the Commissioner's officers or staff to be allowed to do any of the things referred to in paragraph 5.

(4)   The third condition is that, since the refusal, the occupier of the premises—

     (a)   has been notified by the Commissioner of the application for the warrant, and

     (b)   has had an opportunity to be heard by the judge on the question of whether or not the warrant should be issued.

(5)   In determining whether the first condition is met, an assessment notice given to the occupier is to be disregarded.

Content of warrants

5   (1)   A warrant issued under this Schedule must authorise the Commissioner or any of the Commissioner's officers or staff—

     (a)   to enter the premises,

     (b)   to search the premises, and

     (c)   to inspect, examine, operate and test any equipment found on the premises which is used or intended to be used for the processing of personal data.

(2)   A warrant issued under paragraph 1 must authorise the Commissioner or any of the Commissioner's officers or staff—

     (a)   to inspect and seize any documents or other material found on the premises which may be evidence of the failure or offence mentioned in that paragraph,

     (b)   to require any person on the premises to provide, in an appropriate form, a copy of information capable of being viewed using equipment on the premises which may be evidence of that failure or offence,

     (c)   to require any person on the premises to provide an explanation of any document or other material found on the premises and of any information capable of being viewed using equipment on the premises, and

     (d)   to require any person on the premises to provide such other information as may reasonably be required for the purpose of determining whether the controller or processor has failed or is failing as described in section 149(2).

(3) A warrant issued under paragraph 2 must authorise the Commissioner or any of the Commissioner's officers or staff —

   (a) to inspect and seize any documents or other material found on the premises which may enable the Commissioner to determine whether the controller or processor has complied or is complying with the data protection legislation,

   (b) to require any person on the premises to provide, in an appropriate form, a copy of information capable of being viewed using equipment on the premises which may enable the Commissioner to make such a determination,

   (c) to require any person on the premises to provide an explanation of any document or other material found on the premises and of any information capable of being viewed using equipment on the premises, and

   (d) to require any person on the premises to provide such other information as may reasonably be required for the purpose of determining whether the controller or processor has complied or is complying with the data protection legislation.

(4) A warrant issued under this Schedule must authorise the Commissioner or any of the Commissioner's officers or staff to do the things described in sub-paragraphs (1) to (3) at any time in the period of 7 days beginning with the day on which the warrant is issued.

(5) For the purposes of this paragraph, a copy of information is in an "appropriate form" if —

   (a) it can be taken away, and

   (b) it is visible and legible or it can readily be made visible and legible.

Copies of warrants

6   A judge who issues a warrant under this Schedule must—

   (a) issue two copies of it, and

   (b) certify them clearly as copies.

Execution of warrants: reasonable force

7   A person executing a warrant issued under this Schedule may use such reasonable force as may be necessary.

Execution of warrants: time when executed

8   A warrant issued under this Schedule may be executed only at a reasonable hour, unless it appears to the person executing it that there are grounds for suspecting that exercising it at a reasonable hour would defeat the object of the warrant.

Execution of warrants: occupier of premises

9   (1) If an occupier of the premises in respect of which a warrant is issued under this Schedule is present when the warrant is executed, the person executing the warrant must—

   (a) show the occupier the warrant, and

   (b) give the occupier a copy of it.

(2) Otherwise, a copy of the warrant must be left in a prominent place on the premises.

Execution of warrants: seizure of documents etc

10 (1) This paragraph applies where a person executing a warrant under this Schedule seizes something.

(2) The person must, on request —
   (a) give a receipt for it, and
   (b) give an occupier of the premises a copy of it.

(3) Sub-paragraph (2)(b) does not apply if the person executing the warrant considers that providing a copy would result in undue delay.

(4) Anything seized may be retained for so long as is necessary in all the circumstances.

Matters exempt from inspection and seizure: privileged communications

11 (1) The powers of inspection and seizure conferred by a warrant issued under this Schedule are not exercisable in respect of a communication which is made —
   (a) between a professional legal adviser and the adviser's client, and
   (b) in connection with the giving of legal advice to the client with respect to obligations, liabilities or rights under the data protection legislation.

(2) The powers of inspection and seizure conferred by a warrant issued under this Schedule are not exercisable in respect of a communication which is made —
   (a) between a professional legal adviser and the adviser's client or between such an adviser or client and another person,
   (b) in connection with or in contemplation of proceedings under or arising out of the data protection legislation, and
   (c) for the purposes of such proceedings.

(3) Sub-paragraphs (1) and (2) do not prevent the exercise of powers conferred by a warrant issued under this Schedule in respect of —
   (a) anything in the possession of a person other than the professional legal adviser or the adviser's client, or
   (b) anything held with the intention of furthering a criminal purpose.

(4) The references to a communication in sub-paragraphs (1) and (2) include —
   (a) a copy or other record of the communication, and
   (b) anything enclosed with or referred to in the communication if made as described in sub-paragraph (1)(b) or in sub-paragraph (2)(b) and (c).

(5) In sub-paragraphs (1) to (3), the references to the client of a professional legal adviser include a person acting on behalf of such a client.

Matters exempt from inspection and seizure: Parliamentary privilege

12   The powers of inspection and seizure conferred by a warrant issued under
         this Schedule are not exercisable where their exercise would involve an
         infringement of the privileges of either House of Parliament.

Partially exempt material

13 (1) This paragraph applies if a person in occupation of premises in respect of
         which a warrant is issued under this Schedule objects to the inspection or
         seizure of any material under the warrant on the grounds that it consists
         partly of matters in respect of which those powers are not exercisable.

    (2) The person must, if the person executing the warrant so requests, provide
         that person with a copy of so much of the material as is not exempt from
         those powers.

Return of warrants

14 (1) Where a warrant issued under this Schedule is executed —
         (a)   it must be returned to the court from which it was issued after being
               executed, and
         (b)   the person by whom it is executed must write on the warrant a
               statement of the powers that have been exercised under the warrant.

    (2) Where a warrant issued under this Schedule is not executed, it must be
         returned to the court from which it was issued within the time authorised
         for its execution.

Offences

15 (1) It is an offence for a person —
         (a)   intentionally to obstruct a person in the execution of a warrant issued
               under this Schedule, or
         (b)   to fail without reasonable excuse to give a person executing such a
               warrant such assistance as the person may reasonably require for the
               execution of the warrant.

    (2) It is an offence for a person —
         (a)   to make a statement in response to a requirement under paragraph
               5(2)(c) or (d) or (3)(c) or (d) which the person knows to be false in a
               material respect, or
         (b)   recklessly to make a statement in response to such a requirement
               which is false in a material respect.

Self-incrimination

16 (1) An explanation given, or information provided, by a person in response to a
         requirement under paragraph 5(2)(c) or (d) or (3)(c) or (d) may only be used
         in evidence against that person —
         (a)   on a prosecution for an offence under a provision listed in sub-
               paragraph (2), or
         (b)   on a prosecution for any other offence where —
               (i)   in giving evidence that person makes a statement
                     inconsistent with that explanation or information, and

         (ii)   evidence relating to that explanation or information is adduced, or a question relating to it is asked, by that person or on that person's behalf.

  (2)   Those provisions are —

     (a)   paragraph 15,

     (b)   section 5 of the Perjury Act 1911 (false statements made otherwise than on oath),

     (c)   section 44(2) of the Criminal Law (Consolidation) (Scotland) Act 1995 (false statements made otherwise than on oath), or

     (d)   Article 10 of the Perjury (Northern Ireland) Order 1979 (S.I. 1979/1714 (N.I. 19)) (false statutory declarations and other false unsworn statements).

Vessels, vehicles etc

17   In this Schedule —

     (a)   "premises" includes a vehicle, vessel or other means of transport, and

     (b)   references to the occupier of premises include the person in charge of a vehicle, vessel or other means of transport.

Scotland

18   In the application of this Schedule to Scotland —

     (a)   references to a judge of the High Court have effect as if they were references to a judge of the Court of Session,

     (b)   references to a circuit judge have effect as if they were references to the sheriff or the summary sheriff,

     (c)   references to information on oath have effect as if they were references to evidence on oath, and

     (d)   references to the court from which the warrant was issued have effect as if they were references to the sheriff clerk.

Northern Ireland

19   In the application of this Schedule to Northern Ireland —

     (a)   references to a circuit judge have effect as if they were references to a county court judge, and

     (b)   references to information on oath have effect as if they were references to a complaint on oath.

SCHEDULE 16   Section 155

PENALTIES

Meaning of "penalty"

1   In this Schedule, "penalty" means a penalty imposed by a penalty notice.

Notice of intent to impose penalty

2   (1)   Before giving a person a penalty notice, the Commissioner must, by written notice (a "notice of intent") inform the person that the Commissioner intends to give a penalty notice.

    (2)   The Commissioner may not give a penalty notice to a person in reliance on a notice of intent after the end of the period of 6 months beginning when the notice of intent is given, subject to sub-paragraph (3).

    (3)   The period for giving a penalty notice to a person may be extended by agreement between the Commissioner and the person.

Contents of notice of intent

3   (1)   A notice of intent must contain the following information —
      (a)   the name and address of the person to whom the Commissioner proposes to give a penalty notice;
      (b)   the reasons why the Commissioner proposes to give a penalty notice (see sub-paragraph (2));
      (c)   an indication of the amount of the penalty the Commissioner proposes to impose, including any aggravating or mitigating factors that the Commissioner proposes to take into account.

    (2)   The information required under sub-paragraph (1)(b) includes —
      (a)   a description of the circumstances of the failure, and
      (b)   where the notice is given in respect of a failure described in section 149(2), the nature of the personal data involved in the failure.

    (3)   A notice of intent must also —
      (a)   state that the person may make written representations about the Commissioner's intention to give a penalty notice, and
      (b)   specify the period within which such representations may be made.

    (4)   The period specified for making written representations must be a period of not less than 21 days beginning when the notice of intent is given.

    (5)   If the Commissioner considers that it is appropriate for the person to have an opportunity to make oral representations about the Commissioner's intention to give a penalty notice, the notice of intent must also —
      (a)   state that the person may make such representations, and
      (b)   specify the arrangements for making such representations and the time at which, or the period within which, they may be made.

Giving a penalty notice

4   (1)   The Commissioner may not give a penalty notice before a time, or before the end of a period, specified in the notice of intent for making oral or written representations.

    (2)   When deciding whether to give a penalty notice to a person and determining the amount of the penalty, the Commissioner must consider any oral or written representations made by the person in accordance with the notice of intent.

Contents of penalty notice

5 (1) A penalty notice must contain the following information—
   (a) the name and address of the person to whom it is addressed;
   (b) details of the notice of intent given to the person;
   (c) whether the Commissioner received oral or written representations in accordance with the notice of intent;
   (d) the reasons why the Commissioner proposes to impose the penalty (see sub-paragraph (2));
   (e) the reasons for the amount of the penalty, including any aggravating or mitigating factors that the Commissioner has taken into account;
   (f) details of how the penalty is to be paid;
   (g) details of the rights of appeal under section 162;
   (h) details of the Commissioner's enforcement powers under this Schedule.

   (2) The information required under sub-paragraph (1)(d) includes—
   (a) a description of the circumstances of the failure, and
   (b) where the notice is given in respect of a failure described in section 149(2), the nature of the personal data involved in the failure.

Period for payment of penalty

6 (1) A penalty must be paid to the Commissioner within the period specified in the penalty notice.

   (2) The period specified must be a period of not less than 28 days beginning when the penalty notice is given.

Variation of penalty

7 (1) The Commissioner may vary a penalty notice by giving written notice (a "penalty variation notice") to the person to whom it was given.

   (2) A penalty variation notice must specify—
   (a) the penalty notice concerned, and
   (b) how it is varied.

   (3) A penalty variation notice may not—
   (a) reduce the period for payment of the penalty;
   (b) increase the amount of the penalty;
   (c) otherwise vary the penalty notice to the detriment of the person to whom it was given.

   (4) If—
   (a) a penalty variation notice reduces the amount of the penalty, and
   (b) when that notice is given, an amount has already been paid that exceeds the amount of the reduced penalty,
   the Commissioner must repay the excess.

Cancellation of penalty

8 (1) The Commissioner may cancel a penalty notice by giving written notice to the person to whom it was given.

(2) If a penalty notice is cancelled, the Commissioner—

    (a) may not take any further action under section 155 or this Schedule in relation to the failure to which that notice relates, and

    (b) must repay any amount that has been paid in accordance with that notice.

Enforcement of payment

9   (1) The Commissioner must not take action to recover a penalty unless—

    (a) the period specified in accordance with paragraph 6 has ended,

    (b) any appeals against the penalty notice have been decided or otherwise ended,

    (c) if the penalty notice has been varied, any appeals against the penalty variation notice have been decided or otherwise ended, and

    (d) the period for the person to whom the penalty notice was given to appeal against the penalty, and any variation of it, has ended.

(2) In England and Wales, a penalty is recoverable—

    (a) if the county court so orders, as if it were payable under an order of that court;

    (b) if the High Court so orders, as if it were payable under an order of that court.

(3) In Scotland, a penalty may be enforced in the same manner as an extract registered decree arbitral bearing a warrant for execution issued by the sheriff court of any sheriffdom in Scotland.

(4) In Northern Ireland, a penalty is recoverable—

    (a) if a county court so orders, as if it were payable under an order of that court;

    (b) if the High Court so orders, as if it were payable under an order of that court.

SCHEDULE 17

Section 178

REVIEW OF PROCESSING OF PERSONAL DATA FOR THE PURPOSES OF JOURNALISM

Interpretation

1   In this Schedule—

    "relevant period" means—

        (a) the period of 18 months beginning when the Commissioner starts the first review under section 178, and

        (b) the period of 12 months beginning when the Commissioner starts a subsequent review under that section;

    "the relevant review", in relation to a relevant period, means the review under section 178 which the Commissioner must produce a report about by the end of that period.

Information notices

2   (1) This paragraph applies where the Commissioner gives an information notice during a relevant period.

       (2) If the information notice —

          (a) states that, in the Commissioner's opinion, the information is required for the purposes of the relevant review, and

          (b) gives the Commissioner's reasons for reaching that opinion,

       subsections (5) and (6) of section 142 do not apply but the notice must not require the information to be provided before the end of the period of 24 hours beginning when the notice is given.

Assessment notices

3   (1) Sub-paragraph (2) applies where the Commissioner gives an assessment notice to a person during a relevant period.

       (2) If the assessment notice —

          (a) states that, in the Commissioner's opinion, it is necessary for the controller or processor to comply with a requirement in the notice for the purposes of the relevant review, and

          (b) gives the Commissioner's reasons for reaching that opinion,

       subsections (6) and (7) of section 146 do not apply but the notice must not require the controller or processor to comply with the requirement before the end of the period of 7 days beginning when the notice is given.

       (3) During a relevant period, section 147 has effect as if for subsection (5) there were substituted —

          "(5) The Commissioner may not give a controller or processor an assessment notice with respect to the processing of personal data for the special purposes unless a determination under section 174 with respect to the data or the processing has taken effect."

Applications in respect of urgent notices

4   Section 164 applies where an information notice or assessment notice contains a statement under paragraph 2(2)(a) or 3(2)(a) as it applies where such a notice contains a statement under section 142(7)(a) or 146(8)(a).

SCHEDULE 18   Section 184

RELEVANT RECORDS

Relevant records

1   (1) In section 184, "relevant record" means —

          (a) a relevant health record (see paragraph 2),

          (b) a relevant record relating to a conviction or caution (see paragraph 3), or

          (c) a relevant record relating to statutory functions (see paragraph 4).

(2) A record is not a "relevant record" to the extent that it relates, or is to relate, only to personal data which falls within section 21(2) (manual unstructured personal data held by FOI public authorities).

Relevant health records

2   "Relevant health record" means a health record which has been or is to be obtained by a data subject in the exercise of a data subject access right.

Relevant records relating to a conviction or caution

3   (1) "Relevant record relating to a conviction or caution" means a record which—

    (a)   has been or is to be obtained by a data subject in the exercise of a data subject access right from a person listed in sub-paragraph (2), and

    (b)   contains information relating to a conviction or caution.

    (2) Those persons are—

    (a)   the chief constable of a police force maintained under section 2 of the Police Act 1996;

    (b)   the Commissioner of Police of the Metropolis;

    (c)   the Commissioner of Police for the City of London;

    (d)   the Chief Constable of the Police Service of Northern Ireland;

    (e)   the chief constable of the Police Service of Scotland;

    (f)   the Director General of the National Crime Agency;

    (g)   the Secretary of State.

    (3) In this paragraph—

    "caution" means a caution given to a person in England and Wales or Northern Ireland in respect of an offence which, at the time when the caution is given, is admitted;

    "conviction" has the same meaning as in the Rehabilitation of Offenders Act 1974 or the Rehabilitation of Offenders (Northern Ireland) Order 1978 (S.I. 1978/1908 (N.I. 27)).

Relevant records relating to statutory functions

4   (1) "Relevant record relating to statutory functions" means a record which—

    (a)   has been or is to be obtained by a data subject in the exercise of a data subject access right from a person listed in sub-paragraph (2), and

    (b)   contains information relating to a relevant function in relation to that person.

    (2) Those persons are—

    (a)   the Secretary of State;

    (b)   the Department for Communities in Northern Ireland;

    (c)   the Department of Justice in Northern Ireland;

    (d)   the Scottish Ministers;

    (e)   the Disclosure and Barring Service.

    (3) In relation to the Secretary of State, the "relevant functions" are—

    (a)   the Secretary of State's functions in relation to a person sentenced to detention under—

(i)   section 92 of the Powers of Criminal Courts (Sentencing) Act 2000,

(ii)   section 205(2) or 208 of the Criminal Procedure (Scotland) Act 1995, or

(iii)   Article 45 of the Criminal Justice (Children) (Northern Ireland) Order 1998 (S.I. 1998/1504 (N.I. 9));

(b)   the Secretary of State's functions in relation to a person imprisoned or detained under —

(i)   the Prison Act 1952,

(ii)   the Prisons (Scotland) Act 1989, or

(iii)   the Prison Act (Northern Ireland) 1953 (c. 18 (N.I.));

(c)   the Secretary of State's functions under —

(i)   the Social Security Contributions and Benefits Act 1992,

(ii)   the Social Security Administration Act 1992,

(iii)   the Jobseekers Act 1995,

(iv)   Part 5 of the Police Act 1997,

(v)   Part 1 of the Welfare Reform Act 2007, or

(vi)   Part 1 of the Welfare Reform Act 2012.

(4)   In relation to the Department for Communities in Northern Ireland, the "relevant functions" are its functions under —

(a)   the Social Security Contributions and Benefits (Northern Ireland) Act 1992,

(b)   the Social Security Administration (Northern Ireland) Act 1992,

(c)   the Jobseekers (Northern Ireland) Order 1995 (S.I. 1995/2705 (N.I. 15)), or

(d)   Part 1 of the Welfare Reform Act (Northern Ireland) 2007 (c. 2 (N.I.)).

(5)   In relation to the Department of Justice in Northern Ireland, the "relevant functions" are its functions under Part 5 of the Police Act 1997.

(6)   In relation to the Scottish Ministers, the "relevant functions" are their functions under

(a)   Part 5 of the Police Act 1997, or

(b)   Parts 1 and 2 of the Protection of Vulnerable Groups (Scotland) Act 2007 (asp 14).

(7)   In relation to the Disclosure and Barring Service, the "relevant functions" are its functions under —

(a)   Part 5 of the Police Act 1997,

(b)   the Safeguarding Vulnerable Groups Act 2006, or

(c)   the Safeguarding Vulnerable Groups (Northern Ireland) Order 2007 (S.I. 2007/1351 (N.I. 11)).

Data subject access right

5   In this Schedule, "data subject access right" means a right under —

(a)   Article 15 of the GDPR (right of access by the data subject);

(b)   Article 20 of the GDPR (right to data portability);

(c)   section 45 of this Act (law enforcement processing: right of access by the data subject);

(d) section 94 of this Act (intelligence services processing: right of access by the data subject).

Records stating that personal data is not processed

6 For the purposes of this Schedule, a record which states that a controller is not processing personal data relating to a particular matter is to be taken to be a record containing information relating to that matter.

Power to amend

7 (1) The Secretary of State may by regulations amend this Schedule.

(2) Regulations under this paragraph are subject to the affirmative resolution procedure.

SCHEDULE 19   Section 211

MINOR AND CONSEQUENTIAL AMENDMENTS

PART 1

AMENDMENTS OF PRIMARY LEGISLATION

Registration Service Act 1953 (c. 37)

1 (1) Section 19AC of the Registration Service Act 1953 (codes of practice) is amended as follows.

(2) In subsection (2), for "issued under section 52B (data-sharing code) of the Data Protection Act 1998" substitute "prepared under section 121 of the Data Protection Act 2018 (data-sharing code) and issued under section 125(4) of that Act".

(3) In subsection (11), for "section 51(3) of the Data Protection Act 1998" substitute "section 128 of the Data Protection Act 2018".

Veterinary Surgeons Act 1966 (c. 36)

2 (1) Section 1A of the Veterinary Surgeons Act 1966 (functions of the Royal College of Veterinary Surgeons as competent authority) is amended as follows.

(2) In subsection (8) —
    (a) omit "personal data protection legislation in the United Kingdom that implements",
    (b) for paragraph (a) substitute —
        "(a) the GDPR; and", and
    (c) in paragraph (b), at the beginning insert "legislation in the United Kingdom that implements".

(3) In subsection (9), after "section" insert " —
        "the GDPR" means Regulation (EU) 2016/679 of the European Parliament and of the Council of 27 April 2016 on the protection of

226

Data Protection Act 2018 (c. 12)
Schedule 19 — Minor and consequential amendments
Part 1 — Amendments of primary legislation

natural persons with regard to the processing of personal data and on the free movement of such data (General Data Protection Regulation), read with Chapter 2 of Part 2 of the Data Protection Act 2018;".

Parliamentary Commissioner Act 1967 (c. 13)

3   In section 11AA(1) of the Parliamentary Commissioner Act 1967 (disclosure of information by Parliamentary Commissioner to Information Commissioner) —

(a)   in paragraph (a), for sub-paragraph (i) substitute —

"(i)   sections 142 to 154, 160 to 164 or 174 to 176 of, or Schedule 15 to, the Data Protection Act 2018 (certain provisions relating to enforcement),", and

(b)   for paragraph (b) substitute —

"(b)   the commission of an offence under —

(i)   a provision of the Data Protection Act 2018 other than paragraph 15 of Schedule 15 (obstruction of execution of warrant etc), or

(ii)   section 77 of the Freedom of Information Act 2000 (offence of altering etc records with intent to prevent disclosure)."

Local Government Act 1974 (c. 7)

4   The Local Government Act 1974 is amended as follows.

5   In section 33A(1) (disclosure of information by Local Commissioner to Information Commissioner) —

(a)   in paragraph (a), for sub-paragraph (i) substitute —

"(i)   sections 142 to 154, 160 to 164 or 174 to 176 of, or Schedule 15 to, the Data Protection Act 2018 (certain provisions relating to enforcement),", and

(b)   for paragraph (b) substitute —

"(b)   the commission of an offence under —

(i)   a provision of the Data Protection Act 2018 other than paragraph 15 of Schedule 15 (obstruction of execution of warrant etc), or

(ii)   section 77 of the Freedom of Information Act 2000 (offence of altering etc records with intent to prevent disclosure)."

6   In section 34O(1) (disclosure of information by Local Commissioner to Information Commissioner) —

(a)   in paragraph (a), for sub-paragraph (i) substitute —

"(i)   sections 142 to 154, 160 to 164 or 174 to 176 of, or Schedule 15 to, the Data Protection Act 2018 (certain provisions relating to enforcement),", and

(b)   for paragraph (b) substitute —

"(b)   the commission of an offence under —

> > > (i)   a provision of the Data Protection Act 2018 other than paragraph 15 of Schedule 15 (obstruction of execution of warrant etc), or
> > >
> > > (ii) section 77 of the Freedom of Information Act 2000 (offence of altering etc records with intent to prevent disclosure)."

Consumer Credit Act 1974 (c. 39)

7   The Consumer Credit Act 1974 is amended as follows.

8   In section 157(2A) (duty to disclose name etc of agency) —

> (a)   in paragraph (a), for "the Data Protection Act 1998" substitute "the GDPR", and
>
> (b)   in paragraph (b), after "any" insert "other".

9   In section 159(1)(a) (correction of wrong information) for "section 7 of the Data Protection Act 1998" substitute "Article 15(1) to (3) of the GDPR (confirmation of processing, access to data and safeguards for third country transfers)".

10   In section 189(1) (definitions), at the appropriate place insert —

> ""the GDPR" has the same meaning as in Parts 5 to 7 of the Data Protection Act 2018 (see section 3(10), (11) and (14) of that Act);".

Pharmacy (Northern Ireland) Order 1976 (S.I. 1976/1213 (N.I. 22))

11   The Pharmacy (Northern Ireland) Order 1976 is amended as follows.

12   In article 2(2) (interpretation), omit the definition of "Directive 95/46/EC".

13   In article 8D (European professional card), after paragraph (3) insert —

> "(4)   In Schedule 2C, "the GDPR" means Regulation (EU) 2016/679 of the European Parliament and of the Council of 27 April 2016 on the protection of natural persons with regard to the processing of personal data and on the free movement of such data (General Data Protection Regulation), read with Chapter 2 of Part 2 of the Data Protection Act 2018."

14   In article 22A(6) (Directive 2005/36/EC: functions of competent authority etc.), before sub-paragraph (a) insert —

> "(za)   "the GDPR" means Regulation (EU) 2016/679 of the European Parliament and of the Council of 27 April 2016 on the protection of natural persons with regard to the processing of personal data and on the free movement of such data (General Data Protection Regulation), read with Chapter 2 of Part 2 of the Data Protection Act 2018;".

15   (1) Schedule 2C (Directive 2005/36/EC: European professional card) is amended as follows.

     (2) In paragraph 8(1) (access to data), for "Directive 95/46/EC" substitute "the GDPR".

     (3) In paragraph 9 (processing data), omit sub-paragraph (2) (deeming the Society to be the controller for the purposes of Directive 95/46/EC).

228   *Data Protection Act 2018 (c. 12)*
                                                        Schedule 19 — Minor and consequential amendments
                                                               Part 1 — Amendments of primary legislation

16   (1)   The table in Schedule 2D (functions of the Society under Directive 2005/36/EC) is amended as follows.

      (2)   In the entry for Article 56(2), in the second column, for "Directive 95/46/EC" substitute "the GDPR".

      (3)   In the entry for Article 56a(4), in the second column, for "Directive 95/46/EC" substitute "the GDPR".

17   (1)   Paragraph 2 of Schedule 3 (fitness to practice: disclosure of information) is amended as follows.

      (2)   In sub-paragraph (2)(a), after "provision" insert "or the GDPR".

      (3)   For sub-paragraph (3) substitute—

             "(3)   In determining for the purposes of sub-paragraph (2)(a) whether a disclosure is prohibited, it is to be assumed for the purposes of paragraph 5(2) of Schedule 2 to the Data Protection Act 2018 and paragraph 3(2) of Schedule 11 to that Act (exemptions from certain provisions of the data protection legislation: disclosures required by law) that the disclosure is required by this paragraph."

      (4)   After sub-paragraph (4) insert—

             "(5)   In this paragraph, "the GDPR" and references to Schedule 2 to the Data Protection Act 2018 have the same meaning as in Parts 5 to 7 of that Act (see section 3(10), (11) and (14) of that Act)."

Representation of the People Act 1983 (c. 2)

18   (1)   Schedule 2 to the Representation of the People Act 1983 (provisions which may be contained in regulations as to registration etc) is amended as follows.

      (2)   In paragraph 1A(5), for "the Data Protection Act 1998" substitute "Parts 5 to 7 of the Data Protection Act 2018 (see section 3(4) and (14) of that Act)".

      (3)   In paragraph 8C(2), for "the Data Protection Act 1998" substitute "Parts 5 to 7 of the Data Protection Act 2018 (see section 3(4) and (14) of that Act)".

      (4)   In paragraph 11A—
             (a)   in sub-paragraph (1) for "who are data users to supply data, or documents containing information extracted from data and" substitute "to supply information", and
             (b)   omit sub-paragraph (2).

Medical Act 1983 (c. 54)

19   The Medical Act 1983 is amended as follows.

20   (1)   Section 29E (evidence) is amended as follows.

      (2)   In subsection (5), after "enactment" insert "or the GDPR".

      (3)   For subsection (7) substitute—

             "(7)   In determining for the purposes of subsection (5) whether a disclosure is prohibited, it is to be assumed for the purposes of paragraph 5(2) of Schedule 2 to the Data Protection Act 2018 and paragraph 3(2) of Schedule 11 to that Act (exemptions from certain

Data Protection Act 2018 (c. 12)
Schedule 19 — Minor and consequential amendments
Part 1 — Amendments of primary legislation

229

provisions of the data protection legislation: disclosures required by law) that the disclosure is required by this section."

(4) In subsection (9), at the end insert—

""the GDPR" and references to Schedule 2 to the Data Protection Act 2018 have the same meaning as in Parts 5 to 7 of that Act (see section 3(10), (11) and (14) of that Act)."

21 (1) Section 35A (General Medical Council's power to require disclosure of information) is amended as follows.

(2) In subsection (4), after "enactment" insert "or the GDPR".

(3) For subsection (5A) substitute—

"(5A) In determining for the purposes of subsection (4) whether a disclosure is prohibited, it is to be assumed for the purposes of paragraph 5(2) of Schedule 2 to the Data Protection Act 2018 and paragraph 3(2) of Schedule 11 to that Act (exemptions from certain provisions of the data protection legislation: disclosures required by law) that the disclosure is required by this section."

(4) In subsection (7), at the end insert—

""the GDPR" and references to Schedule 2 to the Data Protection Act 2018 have the same meaning as in Parts 5 to 7 of that Act (see section 3(10), (11) and (14) of that Act)."

22 In section 49B(7) (Directive 2005/36: designation of competent authority etc.), after "Schedule 4A" insert "—

"the GDPR" means Regulation (EU) 2016/679 of the European Parliament and of the Council of 27 April 2016 on the protection of natural persons with regard to the processing of personal data and on the free movement of such data (General Data Protection Regulation), read with Chapter 2 of Part 2 of the Data Protection Act 2018;"".

23 In section 55(1) (interpretation), omit the definition of "Directive 95/46/EC".

24 (1) Paragraph 9B of Schedule 1 (incidental powers of the General Medical Council) is amended as follows.

(2) In sub-paragraph (2)(a), after "enactment" insert "or the GPDR".

(3) After sub-paragraph (3) insert—

"(4) In this paragraph, "the GDPR" has the same meaning as in Parts 5 to 7 of the Data Protection Act 2018 (see section 3(10), (11) and (14) of that Act)."

25 (1) Paragraph 5A of Schedule 4 (professional performance assessments and health assessments) is amended as follows.

(2) In sub-paragraph (8), after "enactment" insert "or the GDPR".

(3) For sub-paragraph (8A) substitute—

"(8A) In determining for the purposes of sub-paragraph (8) whether a disclosure is prohibited, it is to be assumed for the purposes of paragraph 5(2) of Schedule 2 to the Data Protection Act 2018 and paragraph 3(2) of Schedule 11 to that Act (exemptions from certain

230   *Data Protection Act 2018 (c. 12)*
                                           Schedule 19 − Minor and consequential amendments
                                              Part 1 − Amendments of primary legislation

provisions of the data protection legislation: disclosures required by law) that the disclosure is required by this paragraph."

(4) After sub-paragraph (13) insert −

"(14) In this paragraph, "the GDPR" and references to Schedule 2 to the Data Protection Act 2018 have the same meaning as in Parts 5 to 7 of that Act (see section 3(10), (11) and (14) of that Act)."

26 (1) The table in Schedule 4A (functions of the General Medical Council as competent authority under Directive 2005/36) is amended as follows.

(2) In the entry for Article 56(2), in the second column, for "Directive 95/46/EC" substitute "the GDPR".

(3) In the entry for Article 56a(4), in the second column, for "Directive 95/46/ EC" substitute "the GDPR".

Dentists Act 1984 (c. 24)

27   The Dentists Act 1984 is amended as follows.

28 (1) Section 33B (the General Dental Council's power to require disclosure of information: the dental profession) is amended as follows.

(2) In subsection (3), after "enactment" insert "or relevant provision of the GDPR".

(3) For subsection (4) substitute −

"(4)   For the purposes of subsection (3) −
               "relevant enactment" means any enactment other than −
                    (a)   this Act, or
                    (b)   the listed provisions in paragraph 1 of Schedule 11 to the Data Protection Act 2018 (exemptions to Part 4: disclosures required by law);
               "relevant provision of the GDPR" means any provision of the GDPR apart from the listed GDPR provisions in paragraph 1 of Schedule 2 to the Data Protection Act 2018 (GDPR provisions to be adapted or restricted: disclosures required by law)."

(4) After subsection (10) insert −

"(11)   In this section, "the GDPR" and references to Schedule 2 to the Data Protection Act 2018 have the same meaning as in Parts 5 to 7 of that Act (see section 3(10), (11) and (14) of that Act)."

29   In section 36ZA(6) (Directive 2005/36: designation of competent authority etc), after "Schedule 4ZA −" insert −
               ""the GDPR" means Regulation (EU) 2016/679 of the European Parliament and of the Council of 27 April 2016 on the protection of natural persons with regard to the processing of personal data and on the free movement of such data (General Data Protection Regulation), read with Chapter 2 of Part 2 of the Data Protection Act 2018;"."

Data Protection Act 2018 (c. 12)
Schedule 19 – Minor and consequential amendments
Part 1 – Amendments of primary legislation

231

30 (1) Section 36Y (the General Dental Council's power to require disclosure of information: professions complementary to dentistry) is amended as follows.

    (2) In subsection (3), after "enactment" insert "or relevant provision of the GDPR".

    (3) For subsection (4) substitute—

        "(4) For the purposes of subsection (3)—

            "relevant enactment" means any enactment other than—

                (a) this Act, or

                (b) the listed provisions in paragraph 1 of Schedule 11 to the Data Protection Act 2018 (exemptions to Part 4: disclosures required by law);

            "relevant provision of the GDPR" means any provision of the GDPR apart from the listed GDPR provisions in paragraph 1 of Schedule 2 to the Data Protection Act 2018 (GDPR provisions to be adapted or restricted: disclosures required by law)."

    (4) After subsection (10) insert—

        "(11) In this section, "the GDPR" and references to Schedule 2 to the Data Protection Act 2018 have the same meaning as in Parts 5 to 7 of that Act (see section 3(10), (11) and (14) of that Act)."

31 In section 53(1) (interpretation), omit the definition of "Directive 95/46/EC".

32 (1) The table in Schedule 4ZA (Directive 2005/36: functions of the General Dental Council under section 36ZA(3)) is amended as follows.

    (2) In the entry for Article 56(2), in the second column, for "Directive 95/46/EC" substitute "the GDPR".

    (3) In the entry for Article 56a(4), in the second column, for "Directive 95/46/EC" substitute "the GDPR".

Companies Act 1985 (c. 6)

33 In section 449(11) of the Companies Act 1985 (provision for security of information obtained), for "the Data Protection Act 1998" substitute "the data protection legislation".

Access to Medical Reports Act 1988 (c. 28)

34 In section 2(1) of the Access to Medical Reports Act 1988 (interpretation), for the definition of "health professional" substitute—

        ""health professional" has the same meaning as in the Data Protection Act 2018 (see section 204 of that Act);".

Opticians Act 1989 (c. 44)

35 (1) Section 13B of the Opticians Act 1989 (the Council's power to require disclosure of information) is amended as follows.

    (2) In subsection (3), after "enactment" insert "or the GDPR".

232   *Data Protection Act 2018 (c. 12)*
Schedule 19 — Minor and consequential amendments
Part 1 — Amendments of primary legislation

(3) For subsection (4) substitute —

 "(4) In determining for the purposes of subsection (3) whether a disclosure is prohibited, it is to be assumed for the purposes of paragraph 5(2) of Schedule 2 to the Data Protection Act 2018 and paragraph 3(2) of Schedule 11 to that Act (exemptions from certain provisions of the data protection legislation: disclosures required by law) that the disclosure is required by this section."

(4) After subsection (9) insert —

 "(10) In this section, "the GDPR" and references to Schedule 2 to the Data Protection Act 2018 have the same meaning as in Parts 5 to 7 of that Act (see section 3(10), (11) and (14) of that Act)."

Access to Health Records Act 1990 (c. 23)

36 The Access to Health Records Act 1990 is amended as follows.

37 For section 2 substitute —

 "2 Health professionals

  In this Act, "health professional" has the same meaning as in the Data Protection Act 2018 (see section 204 of that Act)."

38 (1) Section 3 (right of access to health records) is amended as follows.

 (2) In subsection (2), omit "Subject to subsection (4) below,".

 (3) In subsection (4), omit from "other than the following" to the end.

Human Fertilisation and Embryology Act 1990 (c. 37)

39 (1) Section 33D of the Human Fertilisation and Embryology Act 1990 (disclosure for the purposes of medical or other research) is amended as follows.

 (2) In subsection (6), for "the Data Protection Act 1998" substitute "the data protection legislation".

 (3) In subsection (9), at the appropriate place insert —
    ""the data protection legislation" has the same meaning as in the Data Protection Act 2018 (see section 3 of that Act)."

Trade Union and Labour Relations (Consolidation) Act 1992 (c. 52)

40 (1) Section 251B of the Trade Union and Labour Relations (Consolidation) Act 1992 (prohibition on disclosure of information) is amended as follows.

 (2) In subsection (3), for "the Data Protection Act 1998" substitute "the data protection legislation".

 (3) After subsection (6) insert —

  "(7) In this section, "the data protection legislation" has the same meaning as in the Data Protection Act 2018 (see section 3 of that Act)."

Data Protection Act 2018 (c. 12)
Schedule 19 – Minor and consequential amendments
Part 1 – Amendments of primary legislation

233

Tribunals and Inquiries Act 1992 (c. 53)

41   In the table in Part 1 of Schedule 1 to the Tribunals and Inquiries Act 1992 (tribunals to which the Act applies), in the second column, in paragraph 14(a), for "section 6 of the Data Protection Act 1998" substitute "section 114 of the Data Protection Act 2018".

Industrial Relations (Northern Ireland) Order 1992 (S.I. 1992/807 (N.I. 5))

42   (1) Article 90B of the Industrial Relations (Northern Ireland) Order 1992 (prohibition on disclosure of information held by the Labour Relations Agency) is amended as follows.

      (2) In paragraph (3), for "the Data Protection Act 1998" substitute "the data protection legislation".

      (3) After paragraph (6) insert —

            "(7)   In this Article, "the data protection legislation" has the same meaning as in the Data Protection Act 2018 (see section 3 of that Act)."

Health Service Commissioners Act 1993 (c. 46)

43   In section 18A(1) of the Health Service Commissioners Act 1993 (power to disclose information) —
      (a)   in paragraph (a), for sub-paragraph (i) substitute —
                  "(i)   sections 142 to 154, 160 to 164 or 174 to 176 of, or Schedule 15 to, the Data Protection Act 2018 (certain provisions relating to enforcement),", and
      (b)   for paragraph (b) substitute —
                  "(b)   the commission of an offence under —
                        (i)   a provision of the Data Protection Act 2018 other than paragraph 15 of Schedule 15 (obstruction of execution of warrant etc), or
                        (ii)   section 77 of the Freedom of Information Act 2000 (offence of altering etc records with intent to prevent disclosure)."

Data Protection Act 1998 (c. 29)

44   The Data Protection Act 1998 is repealed, with the exception of section 62 and paragraphs 13, 15, 16, 18 and 19 of Schedule 15 (which amend other enactments).

Crime and Disorder Act 1998 (c. 37)

45   In section 17A(4) of the Crime and Disorder Act 1998 (sharing of information), for "(within the meaning of the Data Protection Act 1998)" substitute "(within the meaning of Parts 5 to 7 of the Data Protection Act 2018 (see section 3(2) and (14) of that Act))".

234

Data Protection Act 2018 (c. 12)
Schedule 19 — Minor and consequential amendments
Part 1 — Amendments of primary legislation

Food Standards Act 1999 (c. 28)

46 (1) Section 19 of the Food Standards Act 1999 (publication etc by the Food Standards Agency of advice and information) is amended as follows.

    (2) In subsection (2), for "the Data Protection Act 1998" substitute "the data protection legislation".

    (3) In subsection (8), after "section" insert "—

        "the data protection legislation" has the same meaning as in the Data Protection Act 2018 (see section 3 of that Act);".

Immigration and Asylum Act 1999 (c. 33)

47 (1) Section 13 of the Immigration and Asylum Act 1999 (proof of identity of persons to be removed or deported) is amended as follows.

    (2) For subsection (4) substitute—

      "(4)   For the purposes of Article 49(1)(d) of the GDPR, the provision under this section of identification data is a transfer of personal data which is necessary for important reasons of public interest."

    (3) After subsection (4) insert—

      "(4A)   "The GDPR" has the same meaning as in Parts 5 to 7 of the Data Protection Act 2018 (see section 3(10), (11) and (14) of that Act)."

Financial Services and Markets Act 2000 (c. 8)

48 The Financial Services and Markets Act 2000 is amended as follows.

49 In section 86(9) (exempt offers to the public), for "the Data Protection Act 1998 or any directly applicable EU legislation relating to data protection" substitute "—

      (a)   the data protection legislation, or

      (b)   any directly applicable EU legislation which is not part of the data protection legislation but which relates to data protection".

50 In section 391A(6)(b) (publication: special provisions relating to the capital requirements directive), for "the Data Protection Act 1998" substitute "the data protection legislation".

51 In section 391C(7)(a) (publication: special provisions relating to the UCITS directive), for "the Data Protection Act 1998" substitute "the data protection legislation".

52 In section 391D(9)(a) (publication: special provisions relating to the markets in financial instruments directive), for "the Data Protection Act 1998" substitute "the data protection legislation".

53 In section 417 (definitions), at the appropriate place insert—

      ""the data protection legislation" has the same meaning as in the Data Protection Act 2018 (see section 3 of that Act);".

Data Protection Act 2018 (c. 12)   235
Schedule 19 – Minor and consequential amendments
Part 1 – Amendments of primary legislation

Terrorism Act 2000 (c. 11)

54   In section 21F(2)(d) of the Terrorism Act 2000 (other permitted disclosures between institutions etc) for "(within the meaning of section 1 of the Data Protection Act 1998)" substitute "(within the meaning of Parts 5 to 7 of the Data Protection Act 2018 (see section 3(2) and (14) of that Act))".

Freedom of Information Act 2000 (c. 36)

55   The Freedom of Information Act 2000 is amended as follows.

56   In section 2(3) (absolute exemptions), for paragraph (f) substitute—
        "(f)   section 40(1),
        (fa)   section 40(2) so far as relating to cases where the first condition referred to in that subsection is satisfied,".

57   In section 18 (the Information Commissioner), omit subsection (1).

58 (1) Section 40 (personal information) is amended as follows.

    (2) In subsection (2)—
        (a)   in paragraph (a), for "do" substitute "does", and
        (b)   in paragraph (b), for "either the first or the second" substitute "the first, second or third".

    (3) For subsection (3) substitute—

        "(3A)   The first condition is that the disclosure of the information to a member of the public otherwise than under this Act—
            (a)   would contravene any of the data protection principles, or
            (b)   would do so if the exemptions in section 24(1) of the Data Protection Act 2018 (manual unstructured data held by public authorities) were disregarded.

        (3B)   The second condition is that the disclosure of the information to a member of the public otherwise than under this Act would contravene Article 21 of the GDPR (general processing: right to object to processing)."

    (4) For subsection (4) substitute—

        "(4A)   The third condition is that—
            (a)   on a request under Article 15(1) of the GDPR (general processing: right of access by the data subject) for access to personal data, the information would be withheld in reliance on provision made by or under section 15, 16 or 26 of, or Schedule 2, 3 or 4 to, the Data Protection Act 2018, or
            (b)   on a request under section 45(1)(b) of that Act (law enforcement processing: right of access by the data subject), the information would be withheld in reliance on subsection (4) of that section."

    (5) For subsection (5) substitute—

        "(5A)   The duty to confirm or deny does not arise in relation to information which is (or if it were held by the public authority would be) exempt information by virtue of subsection (1).

236   *Data Protection Act 2018 (c. 12)*
                        Schedule 19 — Minor and consequential amendments
                                Part 1 — Amendments of primary legislation

(5B)   The duty to confirm or deny does not arise in relation to other information if or to the extent that any of the following applies —

   (a)   giving a member of the public the confirmation or denial that would have to be given to comply with section 1(1)(a) —

      (i)   would (apart from this Act) contravene any of the data protection principles, or

      (ii)   would do so if the exemptions in section 24(1) of the Data Protection Act 2018 (manual unstructured data held by public authorities) were disregarded;

   (b)   giving a member of the public the confirmation or denial that would have to be given to comply with section 1(1)(a) would (apart from this Act) contravene Article 21 of the GDPR (general processing: right to object to processing);

   (c)   on a request under Article 15(1) of the GDPR (general processing: right of access by the data subject) for confirmation of whether personal data is being processed, the information would be withheld in reliance on a provision listed in subsection (4A)(a);

   (d)   on a request under section 45(1)(a) of the Data Protection Act 2018 (law enforcement processing: right of access by the data subject), the information would be withheld in reliance on subsection (4) of that section."

(6)   Omit subsection (6).

(7)   For subsection (7) substitute —

   "(7)   In this section —

      "the data protection principles" means the principles set out in —

         (a)   Article 5(1) of the GDPR, and

         (b)   section 34(1) of the Data Protection Act 2018;

      "data subject" has the same meaning as in the Data Protection Act 2018 (see section 3 of that Act);

      "the GDPR", "personal data", "processing" and references to a provision of Chapter 2 of Part 2 of the Data Protection Act 2018 have the same meaning as in Parts 5 to 7 of that Act (see section 3(2), (4), (10), (11) and (14) of that Act).

(8)   In determining for the purposes of this section whether the lawfulness principle in Article 5(1)(a) of the GDPR would be contravened by the disclosure of information, Article 6(1) of the GDPR (lawfulness) is to be read as if the second sub-paragraph (disapplying the legitimate interests gateway in relation to public authorities) were omitted."

59   Omit section 49 (reports to be laid before Parliament).

60   For section 61 (appeal proceedings) substitute —

   "61   Appeal proceedings

   (1)   Tribunal Procedure Rules may make provision for regulating the exercise of rights of appeal conferred by sections 57(1) and (2) and 60(1) and (4).

Data Protection Act 2018 (c. 12) 237
Schedule 19 — Minor and consequential amendments
Part 1 — Amendments of primary legislation

(2) In relation to appeals under those provisions, Tribunal Procedure Rules may make provision about—

    (a) securing the production of material used for the processing of personal data, and

    (b) the inspection, examination, operation and testing of equipment or material used in connection with the processing of personal data.

(3) Subsection (4) applies where—

    (a) a person does something, or fails to do something, in relation to proceedings before the First-tier Tribunal on an appeal under those provisions, and

    (b) if those proceedings were proceedings before a court having power to commit for contempt, the act or omission would constitute contempt of court.

(4) The First-tier Tribunal may certify the offence to the Upper Tribunal.

(5) Where an offence is certified under subsection (4), the Upper Tribunal may—

    (a) inquire into the matter, and

    (b) deal with the person charged with the offence in any manner in which it could deal with the person if the offence had been committed in relation to the Upper Tribunal.

(6) Before exercising the power under subsection (5)(b), the Upper Tribunal must—

    (a) hear any witness who may be produced against or on behalf of the person charged with the offence, and

    (b) hear any statement that may be offered in defence.

(7) In this section, "personal data" and "processing" have the same meaning as in Parts 5 to 7 of the Data Protection Act 2018 (see section 3(2), (4) and (14) of that Act)."

61 In section 76(1) (disclosure of information between Commissioner and ombudsmen), for "the Data Protection Act 1998" substitute "the data protection legislation".

62 After section 76A insert—

"76B Disclosure of information to Tribunal

(1) No enactment or rule of law prohibiting or restricting the disclosure of information precludes a person from providing the First-tier Tribunal or the Upper Tribunal with information necessary for the discharge of their functions in connection with appeals under section 60 of this Act.

(2) But this section does not authorise the making of a disclosure which is prohibited by any of Parts 1 to 7 or Chapter 1 of Part 9 of the Investigatory Powers Act 2016.

(3) Until the repeal of Part 1 of the Regulation of Investigatory Powers Act 2000 by paragraphs 45 and 54 of Schedule 10 to the Investigatory Powers Act 2016 is fully in force, subsection (2) has effect as if it included a reference to that Part."

238   *Data Protection Act 2018 (c. 12)*
Schedule 19 — Minor and consequential amendments
Part 1 — Amendments of primary legislation

63   In section 77(1)(b) (offence of altering etc records with intent to prevent disclosure), omit "or section 7 of the Data Protection Act 1998,".

64   In section 84 (interpretation), at the appropriate place insert —

> ""the data protection legislation" has the same meaning as in the Data Protection Act 2018 (see section 3 of that Act);".

Political Parties, Elections and Referendums Act 2000 (c. 41)

65   (1) Paragraph 28 of Schedule 19C to the Political Parties, Elections and Referendums Act 2000 (civil sanctions: disclosure of information) is amended as follows.

      (2) In sub-paragraph (4)(a), for "the Data Protection Act 1998" substitute "the data protection legislation".

      (3) After sub-paragraph (5) insert —

> "(6) In this paragraph, "the data protection legislation" has the same meaning as in the Data Protection Act 2018 (see section 3 of that Act)."

Public Finance and Accountability (Scotland) Act 2000 (asp 1)

66   The Public Finance and Accountability (Scotland) Act 2000 is amended as follows.

67   In section 26B(3)(a) (voluntary disclosure of data to Audit Scotland), for "the Data Protection Act 1998 (c. 29)" substitute "the data protection legislation".

68   In section 26C(3)(a) (power to require disclosure of data), for "the Data Protection Act 1998 (c. 29)" substitute "the data protection legislation".

69   In section 29(1) (interpretation), at the appropriate place insert —

> ""the data protection legislation" has the same meaning as in the Data Protection Act 2018 (see section 3 of that Act);".

Criminal Justice and Police Act 2001 (c. 16)

70   The Criminal Justice and Police Act 2001 is amended as follows.

71   In section 57(1) (retention of seized items) —
          (a) omit paragraph (m), and
          (b) after paragraph (s) insert —

> "(t) paragraph 10 of Schedule 15 to the Data Protection Act 2018;".

72   In section 65(7) (meaning of "legal privilege") —
          (a) for "paragraph 1 of Schedule 9 to the Data Protection Act 1998 (c. 29)" substitute "paragraphs 1 and 2 of Schedule 15 to the Data Protection Act 2018", and
          (b) for "paragraph 9" substitute "paragraph 11 (matters exempt from inspection and seizure: privileged communications)".

73   In Schedule 1 (powers of seizure) —
          (a) omit paragraph 65, and

Data Protection Act 2018 (c. 12) 239
Schedule 19 — Minor and consequential amendments
Part 1 — Amendments of primary legislation

(b) after paragraph 73R insert —

"Data Protection Act 2018

> 73S The power of seizure conferred by paragraphs 1 and 2 of Schedule 15 to the Data Protection Act 2018 (powers of entry and inspection)."

Anti-terrorism, Crime and Security Act 2001 (c.24)

74 The Anti-terrorism, Crime and Security Act 2001 is amended as follows.

75 (1) Section 19 (disclosure of information held by revenue departments) is amended as follows.

(2) In subsection (7), for "the Data Protection Act 1998 (c. 29)" substitute "the data protection legislation".

(3) In subsection (9), after "section" insert " —
> "the data protection legislation" has the same meaning as in the Data Protection Act 2018 (see section 3 of that Act);".

76 (1) Part 1 of Schedule 4 (extension of existing disclosure powers) is amended as follows.

(2) Omit paragraph 42.

(3) After paragraph 53F insert —

> "53G Section 132(3) of the Data Protection Act 2018."

Health and Personal Social Services Act (Northern Ireland) 2001 (c. 3 (N.I.))

77 (1) Section 7A of the Health and Personal Social Services Act (Northern Ireland) 2001 (power to obtain information etc) is amended as follows.

(2) In subsection (3), after "provision" insert "or the GDPR".

(3) For subsection (5) substitute —

> "(5) In determining for the purposes of subsection (3) whether a disclosure is prohibited, it is to be assumed for the purposes of paragraph 5(2) of Schedule 2 to the Data Protection Act 2018 and paragraph 3(2) of Schedule 11 to that Act (exemptions from certain provisions of the data protection legislation: disclosures required by law) that the disclosure is required by this section."

(4) After subsection (7) insert —

> "(8) In this section, "the GDPR" and references to Schedule 2 to the Data Protection Act 2018 have the same meaning as in Parts 5 to 7 of that Act (see section 3(10), (11) and (14) of that Act)."

Justice (Northern Ireland) Act 2002 (c. 26)

78 (1) Section 5A of the Justice (Northern Ireland) Act 2002 (disclosure of information to the Commission) is amended as follows.

240

Data Protection Act 2018 (c. 12)
Schedule 19 — Minor and consequential amendments
Part 1 — Amendments of primary legislation

(2) In subsection (3)(a), for "the Data Protection Act 1998" substitute "the data protection legislation".

(3) After subsection (9) insert—

"(10) In this section, "the data protection legislation" has the same meaning as in the Data Protection Act 2018 (see section 3 of that Act)."

Proceeds of Crime Act 2002 (c. 29)

79 The Proceeds of Crime Act 2002 is amended as follows.

80 In section 333C(2)(d) (other permitted disclosures between institutions etc), for "(within the meaning of section 1 of the Data Protection Act 1998)" substitute "(within the meaning of Parts 5 to 7 of the Data Protection Act 2018 (see section 3(2) and (14) of that Act))".

81 In section 436(3)(a) (disclosure of information to certain Directors), for "the Data Protection Act 1998 (c. 29)" substitute "the data protection legislation".

82 In section 438(8)(a) (disclosure of information by certain Directors), for "the Data Protection Act 1998 (c. 29)" substitute "the data protection legislation".

83 In section 439(3)(a) (disclosure of information to Lord Advocate and to Scottish Ministers), for "the Data Protection Act 1998 (c. 29)" substitute "the data protection legislation".

84 In section 441(7)(a) (disclosure of information by Lord Advocate and Scottish Ministers), for "the Data Protection Act 1998 (c. 29)" substitute "the data protection legislation".

85 After section 442 insert—

"442A Data protection legislation

In this Part, "the data protection legislation" has the same meaning as in the Data Protection Act 2018 (see section 3 of that Act)."

Enterprise Act 2002 (c. 40)

86 (1) Section 237 of the Enterprise Act 2002 (general restriction on disclosure) is amended as follows.

(2) In subsection (4), for "the Data Protection Act 1998 (c. 29)" substitute "the data protection legislation".

(3) After subsection (6) insert—

"(7) In this section, "the data protection legislation" has the same meaning as in the Data Protection Act 2018 (see section 3 of that Act)."

Scottish Public Services Ombudsman Act 2002 (asp 11)

87 (1) In Schedule 5 to the Scottish Public Services Ombudsman Act 2002 (disclosure of information by the Ombudsman), the entry for the Information Commissioner is amended as follows.

Data Protection Act 2018 (c. 12) 241
Schedule 19 — Minor and consequential amendments
Part 1 — Amendments of primary legislation

(2) In paragraph 1, for sub-paragraph (a) substitute —
"(a) sections 142 to 154, 160 to 164 or 174 to 176 of, or Schedule 15 to, the Data Protection Act 2018 (certain provisions relating to enforcement),".

(3) For paragraph 2 substitute —
"2 The commission of an offence under —
(a) a provision of the Data Protection Act 2018 other than paragraph 15 of Schedule 15 (obstruction of execution of warrant etc), or
(b) section 77 of the Freedom of Information Act 2000 (offence of altering etc records with intent to prevent disclosure)."

Freedom of Information (Scotland) Act 2002 (asp 13)

88 The Freedom of Information (Scotland) Act 2002 is amended as follows.

89 In section 2(2)(e)(ii) (absolute exemptions), omit "by virtue of subsection (2)(a)(i) or (b) of that section".

90 (1) Section 38 (personal information) is amended as follows.

(2) In subsection (1), for paragraph (b) substitute —
"(b) personal data and the first, second or third condition is satisfied (see subsections (2A) to (3A));".

(3) For subsection (2) substitute —
"(2A) The first condition is that the disclosure of the information to a member of the public otherwise than under this Act —
(a) would contravene any of the data protection principles, or
(b) would do so if the exemptions in section 24(1) of the Data Protection Act 2018 (manual unstructured data held by public authorities) were disregarded.

(2B) The second condition is that the disclosure of the information to a member of the public otherwise than under this Act would contravene Article 21 of the GDPR (general processing: right to object to processing)."

(4) For subsection (3) substitute —
"(3A) The third condition is that —
(a) on a request under Article 15(1) of the GDPR (general processing: right of access by the data subject) for access to personal data, the information would be withheld in reliance on provision made by or under section 15, 16 or 26 of, or Schedule 2, 3 or 4 to, the Data Protection Act 2018, or
(b) on a request under section 45(1)(b) of that Act (law enforcement processing: right of access by the data subject), the information would be withheld in reliance on subsection (4) of that section."

(5) Omit subsection (4).

(6) In subsection (5), for the definitions of "the data protection principles" and

242

Data Protection Act 2018 (c. 12)
Schedule 19 — Minor and consequential amendments
Part 1 — Amendments of primary legislation

of "data subject" and "personal data" substitute—

> ""the data protection principles" means the principles set out in—
>> (a) Article 5(1) of the GDPR, and
>> (b) section 34(1) of the Data Protection Act 2018;
>
> "data subject" has the same meaning as in the Data Protection Act 2018 (see section 3 of that Act);
>
> "the GDPR", "personal data", "processing" and references to a provision of Chapter 2 of Part 2 of the Data Protection Act 2018 have the same meaning as in Parts 5 to 7 of that Act (see section 3(2), (4), (10), (11) and (14) of that Act);".

(7) After that subsection insert—

> "(5A) In determining for the purposes of this section whether the lawfulness principle in Article 5(1)(a) of the GDPR would be contravened by the disclosure of information, Article 6(1) of the GDPR (lawfulness) is to be read as if the second sub-paragraph (disapplying the legitimate interests gateway in relation to public authorities) were omitted."

Courts Act 2003 (c. 39)

91   Schedule 5 to the Courts Act 2003 (collection of fines) is amended as follows.

92   (1) Paragraph 9C (disclosure of information in connection with making of attachment of earnings orders or applications for benefit deductions: supplementary) is amended as follows.

(2) In sub-paragraph (5), for "the Data Protection Act 1998" substitute "the data protection legislation".

(3) After sub-paragraph (5) insert—

> "(6) In this paragraph, "the data protection legislation" has the same meaning as in the Data Protection Act 2018 (see section 3 of that Act)."

93   (1) Paragraph 10A (attachment of earnings orders (Justice Act (Northern Ireland) 2016): disclosure of information) is amended as follows.

(2) In sub-paragraph (7), for "the Data Protection Act 1998" substitute "the data protection legislation".

(3) In sub-paragraph (8), at the appropriate place insert—

> ""the data protection legislation" has the same meaning as in the Data Protection Act 2018 (see section 3 of that Act);".

Sexual Offences Act 2003 (c. 42)

94   (1) Section 94 of the Sexual Offences Act 2003 (Part 2: supply of information to the Secretary of State etc for verification) is amended as follows.

(2) In subsection (6), for "the Data Protection Act 1998 (c. 29)" substitute "the data protection legislation".

Data Protection Act 2018 (c. 12)
Schedule 19 — Minor and consequential amendments
Part 1 — Amendments of primary legislation

243

    (3) In subsection (8), at the appropriate place insert—

             ""the data protection legislation" has the same meaning as in the Data Protection Act 2018 (see section 3 of that Act);".

Criminal Justice Act 2003 (c. 44)

95   The Criminal Justice Act 2003 is amended as follows.

96   In section 327A(9) (disclosure of information about convictions etc of child sex offenders to members of the public), for "the Data Protection Act 1998" substitute "the data protection legislation".

97   In section 327B (disclosure of information about convictions etc of child sex offenders to members of the public: interpretation), after subsection (4) insert—

    "(4A) "The data protection legislation" has the same meaning as in the Data Protection Act 2018 (see section 3 of that Act)."

Mental Health (Care and Treatment) (Scotland) Act 2003 (asp 13)

98 (1) Section 279 of the Mental Health (Care and Treatment) (Scotland) Act 2003 (information for research) is amended as follows.

    (2) In subsection (2), for "research purposes within the meaning given by section 33 of the Data Protection Act 1998 (c. 29) (research, history and statistics)" substitute "purposes mentioned in Article 89(1) of the GDPR (archiving in the public interest, scientific or historical research and statistics)".

    (3) After subsection (9) insert—

    "(10) In this section, "the GDPR" means Regulation (EU) 2016/679 of the European Parliament and of the Council of 27 April 2016 on the protection of natural persons with regard to the processing of personal data and on the free movement of such data (General Data Protection Regulation)."

Public Audit (Wales) Act 2004 (c. 23)

99 (1) Section 64C of the Public Audit (Wales) Act 2004 (voluntary provision of data) is amended as follows.

    (2) In subsection (3)(a), for "the Data Protection Act 1998 (c. 29)" substitute "the data protection legislation".

    (3) In subsection (5), at the beginning insert "In this section—

         "the data protection legislation" has the same meaning as in the Data Protection Act 2018 (see section 3 of that Act);".

Companies (Audit, Investigations and Community Enterprise) Act 2004 (c. 27)

100   The Companies (Audit, Investigations and Community Enterprise) Act 2004 is amended as follows.

101 (1) Section 15A (disclosure of information by tax authorities) is amended as follows.

244

Data Protection Act 2018 (c. 12)
Schedule 19 — Minor and consequential amendments
Part 1 — Amendments of primary legislation

(2) In subsection (2) —

    (a) omit "within the meaning of the Data Protection Act 1998", and

    (b) for "that Act" substitute "the data protection legislation".

(3) After subsection (7) insert —

> "(8) In this section —
>
> > "the data protection legislation" has the same meaning as in the Data Protection Act 2018 (see section 3 of that Act);
> >
> > "personal data" has the same meaning as in Parts 5 to 7 of that Act (see section 3(2) and (14) of that Act)."

102 (1) Section 15D (permitted disclosure of information obtained under compulsory powers) is amended as follows.

(2) In subsection (7), for "the Data Protection Act 1998" substitute "the data protection legislation".

(3) After subsection (7) insert —

> "(8) In this section, "the data protection legislation" has the same meaning as in the Data Protection Act 2018 (see section 3 of that Act)."

Domestic Violence, Crime and Victims Act 2004 (c. 28)

103 (1) Section 54 of the Domestic Violence, Crime and Victims Act 2004 (disclosure of information) is amended as follows.

(2) In subsection (7), for "the Data Protection Act 1998 (c. 29)" substitute "the data protection legislation".

(3) After subsection (8) insert —

> "(9) In this section, "the data protection legislation" has the same meaning as in the Data Protection Act 2018 (see section 3 of that Act)."

Children Act 2004 (c. 31)

104 The Children Act 2004 is amended as follows.

105 (1) Section 12 (information databases) is amended as follows.

(2) In subsection (13)(e) for "the Data Protection Act 1998 (c. 29)" substitute "the data protection legislation".

(3) After subsection (13) insert —

> "(14) In this section, "the data protection legislation" has the same meaning as in the Data Protection Act 2018 (see section 3 of that Act)."

106 (1) Section 29 (information databases: Wales) is amended as follows.

(2) In subsection (14)(e) for "the Data Protection Act 1998 (c. 29)" substitute "the data protection legislation".

Data Protection Act 2018 (c. 12) 245
Schedule 19 – Minor and consequential amendments
Part 1 – Amendments of primary legislation

(3) After subsection (14) insert—

"(15) In this section, "the data protection legislation" has the same meaning as in the Data Protection Act 2018 (see section 3 of that Act)."

Constitutional Reform Act 2005 (c. 4)

107 (1) Section 107 of the Constitutional Reform Act 2005 (disclosure of information to the Commission) is amended as follows.

(2) In subsection (3)(a), for "the Data Protection Act 1998 (c. 29)" substitute "the data protection legislation".

(3) After subsection (9) insert—

"(10) In this section, "the data protection legislation" has the same meaning as in the Data Protection Act 2018 (see section 3 of that Act)."

Mental Capacity Act 2005 (c. 9)

108 In section 64 of the Mental Capacity Act 2005 (interpretation), for the definition of "health record" substitute—
""health record" has the same meaning as in the Data Protection Act 2018 (see section 205 of that Act);".

Public Services Ombudsman (Wales) Act 2005 (c. 10)

109 (1) Section 34X of the Public Services Ombudsman (Wales) Act 2005 (disclosure of information) is amended as follows.

(2) In subsection (4), for paragraph (a) substitute—
"(a) sections 142 to 154, 160 to 164 or 174 to 176 of, or Schedule 15 to, the Data Protection Act 2018 (certain provisions relating to enforcement);".

(3) For subsection (5) substitute—

"(5) The offences are those under—
(a) a provision of the Data Protection Act 2018 other than paragraph 15 of Schedule 15 (obstruction of execution of warrant etc);
(b) section 77 of the Freedom of Information Act 2000 (offence of altering etc records with intent to prevent disclosure)."

Commissioners for Revenue and Customs Act 2005 (c. 11)

110 (1) Section 22 of the Commissioners for Revenue and Customs Act 2005 (data protection, etc) is amended as follows.

(2) The existing text becomes subsection (1).

(3) In that subsection, in paragraph (a), for "the Data Protection Act 1998 (c. 29)" substitute "the data protection legislation".

246   *Data Protection Act 2018 (c. 12)*
Schedule 19 — Minor and consequential amendments
Part 1 — Amendments of primary legislation

(4) After that subsection insert—

  "(2) In this section, "the data protection legislation" has the same meaning as in the Data Protection Act 2018 (see section 3 of that Act)."

Gambling Act 2005 (c. 19)

111 (1) Section 352 of the Gambling Act 2005 (data protection) is amended as follows.

  (2) The existing text becomes subsection (1).

  (3) In that subsection, for "the Data Protection Act 1998 (c. 29)" substitute "the data protection legislation".

  (4) After that subsection insert—

   "(2) In this section, "the data protection legislation" has the same meaning as in the Data Protection Act 2018 (see section 3 of that Act)."

Commissioner for Older People (Wales) Act 2006 (c. 30)

112 (1) Section 18 of the Commissioner for Older People (Wales) Act 2006 (power to disclose information) is amended as follows.

  (2) In subsection (7), for paragraph (a) substitute—

   "(a) sections 142 to 154, 160 to 164 or 174 to 176 of, or Schedule 15 to, the Data Protection Act 2018 (certain provisions relating to enforcement);".

  (3) For subsection (8) substitute—

   "(8) The offences are those under—

    (a) a provision of the Data Protection Act 2018 other than paragraph 15 of Schedule 15 (obstruction of execution of warrant etc); or

    (b) section 77 of the Freedom of Information Act 2000 (offence of altering etc records with intent to prevent disclosure)."

National Health Service Act 2006 (c. 41)

113 The National Health Service Act 2006 is amended as follows.

114 (1) Section 251 (control of patient information) is amended as follows.

  (2) In subsection (7), for "made by or under the Data Protection Act 1998 (c 29)" substitute "of the data protection legislation".

  (3) In subsection (13), at the appropriate place insert—

     ""the data protection legislation" has the same meaning as in the Data Protection Act 2018 (see section 3 of that Act);".

115 (1) Section 264C (provision and disclosure of information about health service products: supplementary) is amended as follows.

  (2) In subsection (2), for "the Data Protection Act 1998" substitute "the data protection legislation".

Data Protection Act 2018 (c. 12) 247
Schedule 19 — Minor and consequential amendments
Part 1 — Amendments of primary legislation

(3) After subsection (3) insert —

"(4) In this section, "the data protection legislation" has the same meaning as in the Data Protection Act 2018 (see section 3 of that Act)."

116 In paragraph 7B(3) of Schedule 1 (further provision about the Secretary of State and services under the Act), for "has the same meaning as in the Data Protection Act 1998" substitute "has the same meaning as in Parts 5 to 7 of the Data Protection Act 2018 (see section 3(4) and (14) of that Act)".

National Health Service (Wales) Act 2006 (c. 42)

117 The National Health Service (Wales) Act 2006 is amended as follows.

118 (1) Section 201C (provision of information about medical supplies: supplementary) is amended as follows.

(2) In subsection (2), for "the Data Protection Act 1998" substitute "the data protection legislation".

(3) After subsection (3) insert —

"(4) In this section, "the data protection legislation" has the same meaning as in the Data Protection Act 2018 (see section 3 of that Act)."

119 In paragraph 7B(3) of Schedule 1 (further provision about the Welsh Ministers and services under the Act), for "has the same meaning as in the Data Protection Act 1998" substitute "has the same meaning as in Parts 5 to 7 of the Data Protection Act 2018 (see section 3(4) and (14) of that Act)".

Companies Act 2006 (c. 46)

120 The Companies Act 2006 is amended as follows.

121 In section 458(2) (disclosure of information by tax authorities) —
   (a) for "within the meaning of the Data Protection Act 1998 (c. 29)" substitute "within the meaning of Parts 5 to 7 of the Data Protection Act 2018 (see section 3(2) and (14) of that Act)", and
   (b) for "that Act" substitute "the data protection legislation".

122 In section 461(7) (permitted disclosure of information obtained under compulsory powers), for "the Data Protection Act 1998 (c. 29)" substitute "the data protection legislation".

123 In section 948(9) (restrictions on disclosure) for "the Data Protection Act 1998 (c. 29)" substitute "the data protection legislation".

124 In section 1173(1) (minor definitions: general), at the appropriate place insert —

""the data protection legislation" has the same meaning as in the Data Protection Act 2018 (see section 3 of that Act);".

125 In section 1224A(7) (restrictions on disclosure), for "the Data Protection Act 1998" substitute "the data protection legislation".

248   *Data Protection Act 2018 (c. 12)*
                            Schedule 19 — Minor and consequential amendments
                                    Part 1 — Amendments of primary legislation

126   In section 1253D(3) (restriction on transfer of audit working papers to third countries), for "the Data Protection Act 1998" substitute "the data protection legislation".

127   In section 1261(1) (minor definitions: Part 42), at the appropriate place insert—

> ""the data protection legislation" has the same meaning as in the Data Protection Act 2018 (see section 3 of that Act);".

128   In section 1262 (index of defined expressions: Part 42), at the appropriate place insert—

"the data protection legislation	section 1261(1)".

129   In Schedule 8 (index of defined expressions: general), at the appropriate place insert—

"the data protection legislation	section 1173(1)".

Tribunals, Courts and Enforcement Act 2007 (c. 15)

130   The Tribunals, Courts and Enforcement Act 2007 is amended as follows.

131   In section 11(5)(b) (right to appeal to Upper Tribunal), for "section 28(4) or (6) of the Data Protection Act 1998 (c. 29)" substitute "section 27(3) or (5), 79(5) or (7) or 111(3) or (5) of the Data Protection Act 2018".

132   In section 13(8)(a) (right to appeal to the Court of Appeal), for "section 28(4) or (6) of the Data Protection Act 1998 (c. 29)" substitute "section 27(3) or (5), 79(5) or (7) or 111(3) or (5) of the Data Protection Act 2018".

Statistics and Registration Service Act 2007 (c. 18)

133   The Statistics and Registration Service Act 2007 is amended as follows.

134 (1) Section 45 (information held by HMRC) is amended as follows.

   (2) In subsection (4A), for "section 51(3) of the Data Protection Act 1998" substitute "section 128 of the Data Protection Act 2018".

   (3) In subsection (4B), for "the Data Protection Act 1998" substitute "the Data Protection Act 2018".

135 (1) Section 45A (information held by other public authorities) is amended as follows.

   (2) In subsection (8), for "section 51(3) of the Data Protection Act 1998" substitute "section 128 of the Data Protection Act 2018".

   (3) In subsection (9), for "the Data Protection Act 1998" substitute "the data protection legislation".

   (4) In subsection (12)(a), for "the Data Protection Act 1998" substitute "the data protection legislation".

Data Protection Act 2018 (c. 12) 249
Schedule 19 — Minor and consequential amendments
Part 1 — Amendments of primary legislation

(5) In subsection 12(c), after the first "legislation" insert "(which is not part of the data protection legislation)".

136 (1) Section 45B(3) (access to information held by Crown bodies etc) is amended as follows.

(2) In paragraph (a), for "the Data Protection Act 1998" substitute "the data protection legislation".

(3) In paragraph (c), after the first "legislation" insert "(which is not part of the data protection legislation)".

137 (1) Section 45C(13) (power to require disclosures by other public authorities) is amended as follows.

(2) In paragraph (b), for "the Data Protection Act 1998" substitute "the data protection legislation".

(3) In paragraph (d), after the first "legislation" insert "(which is not part of the data protection legislation)".

138 In section 45D(9)(b) (power to require disclosure by undertakings), for "the Data Protection Act 1998" substitute "the data protection legislation".

139 (1) Section 45E (further provision about powers in sections 45B, 45C and 45D) is amended as follows.

(2) In subsection (6), for "issued under section 52B (data-sharing code) of the Data Protection Act 1998" substitute "prepared under section 121 of the Data Protection Act 2018 (data-sharing code) and issued under section 125(4) of that Act".

(3) In subsection (16), for "section 51(3) of the Data Protection Act 1998" substitute "section 128 of the Data Protection Act 2018".

(4) In subsection (17), for "the Data Protection Act 1998" substitute "the data protection legislation".

140 (1) Section 53A (disclosure by the Statistics Board to devolved administrations) is amended as follows.

(2) In subsection (9), for "section 51(3) of the Data Protection Act 1998" substitute "section 128 of the Data Protection Act 2018".

(3) In subsection (10), for "the Data Protection Act 1998" substitute "the data protection legislation".

(4) In subsection (12)(b), for "the Data Protection Act 1998" substitute "the data protection legislation".

141 (1) Section 54 (Data Protection Act 1998 and Human Rights Act 1998) is amended as follows.

(2) In the heading, omit "Data Protection Act 1998 and".

(3) Omit paragraph (a) (together with the final "or").

142 In section 67 (general interpretation: Part 1), at the appropriate place insert—
""the data protection legislation" has the same meaning as in the Data Protection Act 2018 (see section 3 of that Act);".

250

Data Protection Act 2018 (c. 12)
Schedule 19 — Minor and consequential amendments
Part 1 — Amendments of primary legislation

Serious Crime Act 2007 (c. 27)

143   The Serious Crime Act 2007 is amended as follows.

144 (1) Section 5A (verification and disclosure of information) is amended as follows.

   (2) In subsection (6) —
      (a) for "the Data Protection Act 1998" substitute "the data protection legislation", and
      (b) for "are" substitute "is".

   (3) After subsection (6) insert —

      "(7) In this section, "the data protection legislation" has the same meaning as in the Data Protection Act 2018 (see section 3 of that Act)."

145 (1) Section 68 (disclosure of information to prevent fraud) is amended as follows.

   (2) In subsection (4)(a), for "the Data Protection Act 1998 (c. 29)" substitute "the data protection legislation".

   (3) In subsection (8), at the appropriate place insert —
         ""the data protection legislation" has the same meaning as in the Data Protection Act 2018 (see section 3 of that Act)."

146 (1) Section 85 (disclosure of information by Revenue and Customs) is amended as follows.

   (2) In subsection (8)(a), for "the Data Protection Act 1998 (c. 29)" substitute "the data protection legislation".

   (3) In subsection (9), at the appropriate place insert —
         ""the data protection legislation" has the same meaning as in the Data Protection Act 2018 (see section 3 of that Act)."

Legal Services Act 2007 (c. 29)

147 (1) Section 169 of the Legal Services Act 2007 (disclosure of information to the Legal Services Board) is amended as follows.

   (2) In subsection (3)(a), for "the Data Protection Act 1998 (c. 29)" substitute "the data protection legislation".

   (3) After subsection (8) insert —

      "(9) In this section, "the data protection legislation" has the same meaning as in the Data Protection Act 2018 (see section 3 of that Act)."

Adoption and Children (Scotland) Act 2007 (asp 4)

148   In section 74 of the Adoption and Children (Scotland) Act 2007 (disclosure

Data Protection Act 2018 (c. 12)
Schedule 19 — Minor and consequential amendments
Part 1 — Amendments of primary legislation

251

of medical information about parents), for subsection (5) substitute—

    "(5)   In subsection (4)(e), "processing" has the same meaning as in Parts 5 to 7 of the Data Protection Act 2018 (see section 3(4) and (14) of that Act)."

Criminal Justice and Immigration Act 2008 (c. 4)

149   The Criminal Justice and Immigration Act 2008 is amended as follows.

150   Omit—

    (a)   section 77 (power to alter penalty for unlawfully obtaining etc personal data), and

    (b)   section 78 (new defence for obtaining etc for journalism and other special purposes).

151 (1) Section 114 (supply of information to Secretary of State etc) is amended as follows.

    (2) In subsection (5), for "the Data Protection Act 1998 (c. 29)" substitute "the data protection legislation".

    (3) After subsection (6) insert—

      "(6A)   In this section, "the data protection legislation" has the same meaning as in the Data Protection Act 2018 (see section 3 of that Act)."

Regulatory Enforcement and Sanctions Act 2008 (c. 13)

152 (1) Section 70 of the Regulatory Enforcement and Sanctions Act 2008 (disclosure of information) is amended as follows.

    (2) In subsection (4)(a), for "the Data Protection Act 1998 (c. 29)" substitute "the data protection legislation".

    (3) After subsection (5) insert—

      "(6)   In this section, "the data protection legislation" has the same meaning as in the Data Protection Act 2018 (see section 3 of that Act)."

Health and Social Care Act 2008 (c. 14)

153   In section 20A(5) of the Health and Social Care Act 2008 (functions relating to processing of information by registered persons), in the definition of "processing", for "the Data Protection Act 1998" substitute "Parts 5 to 7 of the Data Protection Act 2018 (see section 3(4) and (14) of that Act);".

Counter-Terrorism Act 2008 (c. 28)

154 (1) Section 20 of the Counter-Terrorism Act 2008 (disclosure and the intelligence services: supplementary provisions) is amended as follows.

    (2) In subsection (2)(a), for "the Data Protection Act 1998 (c. 29)" substitute "the data protection legislation".

252   *Data Protection Act 2018 (c. 12)*
Schedule 19 — Minor and consequential amendments
Part 1 — Amendments of primary legislation

  (3) After subsection (4) insert —

    "(5) In this section, "the data protection legislation" has the same meaning as in the Data Protection Act 2018 (see section 3 of that Act)."

Public Health etc. (Scotland) Act 2008 (asp 5)

155 (1) Section 117 of the Public Health etc. (Scotland) Act 2008 (disclosure of information) is amended as follows.

  (2) In subsection (6), for "the Data Protection Act 1998 (c. 29)" substitute "the data protection legislation".

  (3) After subsection (7) insert —

    "(7A) In this section, "the data protection legislation" has the same meaning as in the Data Protection Act 2018 (see section 3 of that Act)."

Banking Act 2009 (c. 1)

156 (1) Section 83ZY of the Banking Act 2009 (special resolution regime: publication of notices etc) is amended as follows.

  (2) In subsection (10), for "the Data Protection Act 1998" substitute "the data protection legislation".

  (3) In subsection (11), after "section" insert " —
     "the data protection legislation" has the same meaning as in the Data Protection Act 2018 (see section 3 of that Act);".

Borders, Citizenship and Immigration Act 2009 (c. 11)

157 (1) Section 19 of the Borders, Citizenship and Immigration Act 2009 (use and disclosure of customs information: application of statutory provisions) is amended as follows.

  (2) In subsection (1)(a), for "the Data Protection Act 1998 (c. 29)" substitute "the data protection legislation".

  (3) After subsection (4) insert —

    "(5) In this section, "the data protection legislation" has the same meaning as in the Data Protection Act 2018 (see section 3 of that Act)."

Marine and Coastal Access Act 2009 (c. 23)

158 The Marine and Coastal Access Act 2009 is amended as follows.

159 (1) Paragraph 13 of Schedule 7 (further provision about civil sanctions under Part 4: disclosure of information) is amended as follows.

  (2) In sub-paragraph (5)(a), for "the Data Protection Act 1998 (c. 29)" substitute "the data protection legislation".

Data Protection Act 2018 (c. 12)
Schedule 19 — Minor and consequential amendments
Part 1 — Amendments of primary legislation

253

(3) After sub-paragraph (6) insert—

"(7) In this paragraph, "the data protection legislation" has the same meaning as in the Data Protection Act 2018 (see section 3 of that Act)."

160 (1) Paragraph 9 of Schedule 10 (further provision about fixed monetary penalties: disclosure of information) is amended as follows.

(2) In sub-paragraph (5)(a), for "the Data Protection Act 1998 (c. 29)" substitute "the data protection legislation".

(3) After sub-paragraph (6) insert—

"(7) In this paragraph, "the data protection legislation" has the same meaning as in the Data Protection Act 2018 (see section 3 of that Act)."

Coroners and Justice Act 2009 (c. 25)

161 In Schedule 21 to the Coroners and Justice Act 2009 (minor and consequential amendments), omit paragraph 29(3).

Broads Authority Act 2009 (c. i)

162 (1) Section 38 of the Broads Authority Act 2009 (provision of information) is amended as follows.

(2) In subsection (3), for "the Data Protection Act 1998 (c. 29)" substitute "the data protection legislation".

(3) In subsection (6), after "section" insert "—
"the data protection legislation" has the same meaning as in the Data Protection Act 2018 (see section 3 of that Act);".

Health and Social Care (Reform) Act (Northern Ireland) 2009 (c. 1 (N.I.))

163 (1) Section 13 of the Health and Social Care (Reform) Act (Northern Ireland) 2009 (functions of the Regional Agency) is amended as follows.

(2) In subsection (8), for "the Data Protection Act 1998 (c. 29)" substitute "the data protection legislation".

(3) After subsection (8) insert—

"(9) In this section, "the data protection legislation" has the same meaning as in the Data Protection Act 2018 (see section 3 of that Act)."

Terrorist Asset-Freezing etc. Act 2010 (c. 38)

164 (1) Section 25 of the Terrorist Asset-Freezing etc. Act 2010 (application of provisions) is amended as follows.

(2) In subsection (2)(a), for "the Data Protection Act 1998" substitute "the data protection legislation".

254 *Data Protection Act 2018 (c. 12)*
Schedule 19 − Minor and consequential amendments
Part 1 − Amendments of primary legislation

(3) In subsection (6), at the appropriate place insert—

""the data protection legislation" has the same meaning as in the Data Protection Act 2018 (see section 3 of that Act);".

Marine (Scotland) Act 2010 (asp 5)

165 (1) Paragraph 12 of Schedule 2 to the Marine (Scotland) Act 2010 (further provision about civil sanctions under Part 4: disclosure of information) is amended as follows.

(2) In sub-paragraph (5)(a), for "the Data Protection Act 1998 (c. 29)" substitute "the data protection legislation".

(3) After sub-paragraph (6) insert—

"(7) In this paragraph, "the data protection legislation" has the same meaning as in the Data Protection Act 2018 (see section 3 of that Act)."

Charities Act 2011 (c. 25)

166 (1) Section 59 of the Charities Act 2011 (disclosure: supplementary) is amended as follows.

(2) The existing text becomes subsection (1).

(3) In that subsection, in paragraph (a), for "the Data Protection Act 1998" substitute "the data protection legislation".

(4) After that subsection insert—

"(2) In this section, "the data protection legislation" has the same meaning as in the Data Protection Act 2018 (see section 3 of that Act)."

Welsh Language (Wales) Measure 2011 (nawm 1)

167 The Welsh Language (Wales) Measure 2011 is amended as follows.

168 (1) Section 22 (power to disclose information) is amended as follows.

(2) In subsection (4)—
   (a) in the English language text, for paragraph (a) substitute—
       "(a) sections 142 to 154, 160 to 164 or 174 to 176 of, or Schedule 15 to, the Data Protection Act 2018 (certain provisions relating to enforcement);", and
   (b) in the Welsh language text, for paragraph (a) substitute—
       "(a) adrannau 142 i 154, 160 i 164, neu 174 i 176 o Ddeddf Diogelu Data 2018 neu Atodlen 15 i'r Ddeddf honno (darpariaethau penodol yn ymwneud â gorfodi);".

(3) For subsection (5)—
   (a) in the English language text substitute—

       "(5) The offences referred to under subsection (3)(b) are those under—

Data Protection Act 2018 (c. 12) 255
Schedule 19 – Minor and consequential amendments
Part 1 – Amendments of primary legislation

(a)   a provision of the Data Protection Act 2018 other than paragraph 15 of Schedule 15 (obstruction of exercise of warrant etc); or

(b)   section 77 of the Freedom of Information Act 2000 (offence of altering etc records with intent to prevent disclosure).", and

(b)   in the Welsh language text substitute—

"(5)   Y tramgwyddau y cyfeirir atynt yn is-adran (3)(b) yw'r rhai—

(a)   o dan ddarpariaeth yn Neddf Diogelu Data 2018 ac eithrio paragraff 15 o Atodlen 15 (rhwystro gweithredu gwarant etc); neu

(b)   o dan adran 77 o Ddeddf Rhyddid Gwybodaeth 2000 (trosedd o altro etc cofnodion gyda'r bwriad o atal datgelu)."

(4) In subsection (8)—

(a)   in the English language text, for "the Data Protection Act 1998" substitute "the data protection legislation", and

(b)   in the Welsh language text, for "gymhwyso Deddf Diogelu Data 1998" substitute "gymhwyso'r ddeddfwriaeth diogelu data".

(5) In subsection (9)—

(a)   at the appropriate place in the English language text insert—

""the data protection legislation" ("*y ddeddfwriaeth diogelu data*") has the same meaning as in the Data Protection Act 2018 (see section 3 of that Act);", and

(b)   at the appropriate place in the Welsh language text insert—

"mae i "y ddeddfwriaeth diogelu data" yr un ystyr ag a roddir i "the data protection legislation" yn Neddf Diogelu Data 2018 (gweler adran 3 o'r Ddeddf honno);".

169 (1) Paragraph 8 of Schedule 2 (inquiries by the Commissioner: reports) is amended as follows.

(2) In sub-paragraph (7)—

(a)   in the English language text, for "the Data Protection Act 1998" substitute "the data protection legislation", and

(b)   in the Welsh language text, for "gymhwyso Deddf Diogelu Data 1998" substitute "gymhwyso'r ddeddfwriaeth diogelu data".

(3) In sub-paragraph (8)—

(a)   in the English language text, after "this paragraph" insert "—

"the data protection legislation" ("*y ddeddfwriaeth diogelu data*") has the same meaning as in the Data Protection Act 2018 (see section 3 of that Act);", and

(b)   in the Welsh language text, after "hwn" insert—

"mae i "y ddeddfwriaeth diogelu data" yr un ystyr ag a roddir i "the data protection legislation" yn Neddf Diogelu Data 2018 (gweler adran 3 o'r Ddeddf honno);".

256

Data Protection Act 2018 (c. 12)
Schedule 19 — Minor and consequential amendments
Part 1 — Amendments of primary legislation

Safeguarding Board Act (Northern Ireland) 2011 (c. 7 (N.I))

170 (1) Section 10 of the Safeguarding Board Act (Northern Ireland) 2011 (duty to co-operate) is amended as follows.

(2) In subsection (3), for "the Data Protection Act 1998 (c. 29)" substitute "the data protection legislation".

(3) After subsection (3) insert—

"(4) In this section, "the data protection legislation" has the same meaning as in the Data Protection Act 2018 (see section 3 of that Act)."

Health and Social Care Act 2012 (c. 7)

171 The Health and Social Care Act 2012 is amended as follows.

172 In section 250(7) (power to publish information standards), for the definition of "processing" substitute—

""processing" has the same meaning as in Parts 5 to 7 of the Data Protection Act 2018 (see section 3(4) and (14) of that Act);".

173 (1) Section 251A (consistent identifiers) is amended as follows.

(2) In subsection (7)(a), for "made by or under the Data Protection Act 1998" substitute "of the data protection legislation".

(3) After subsection (8) insert—

"(9) In this section, "the data protection legislation" has the same meaning as in the Data Protection Act 2018 (see section 3 of that Act)."

174 (1) Section 251B (duty to share information) is amended as follows.

(2) In subsection (5)(a), for "made by or under the Data Protection Act 1998" substitute "of the data protection legislation".

(3) After subsection (6) insert—

"(7) In this section, "the data protection legislation" has the same meaning as in the Data Protection Act 2018 (see section 3 of that Act)."

Protection of Freedoms Act 2012 (c. 9)

175 The Protection of Freedoms Act 2012 is amended as follows.

176 (1) Section 27 (exceptions and further provision about consent and notification) is amended as follows.

(2) In subsection (5), for "the Data Protection Act 1998" substitute "the data protection legislation".

(3) After subsection (5) insert—

"(6) In this section, "the data protection legislation" has the same meaning as in the Data Protection Act 2018 (see section 3 of that Act)."

Data Protection Act 2018 (c. 12) 257
Schedule 19 — Minor and consequential amendments
Part 1 — Amendments of primary legislation

177   In section 28(1) (interpretation: Chapter 2), for the definition of "processing" substitute—

>   ""processing" has the same meaning as in Parts 5 to 7 of the Data Protection Act 2018 (see section 3(4) and (14) of that Act);".

178   In section 29(7) (code of practice for surveillance camera systems), for the definition of "processing" substitute—

>   ""processing" has the same meaning as in Parts 5 to 7 of the Data Protection Act 2018 (see section 3(4) and (14) of that Act);".

HGV Road User Levy Act 2013 (c. 7)

179 (1) Section 14A of the HGV Road User Levy Act 2013 (disclosure of information by Revenue and Customs) is amended as follows.

    (2) In subsection (5), for "the Data Protection Act 1998" substitute "the data protection legislation".

    (3) After subsection (5) insert—

>   "(6) In this section, "the data protection legislation" has the same meaning as in the Data Protection Act 2018 (see section 3 of that Act)."

Crime and Courts Act 2013 (c. 22)

180   The Crime and Courts Act 2013 is amended as follows.

181 (1) Section 42 (other interpretive provisions) is amended as follows.

    (2) In subsection (5)(a), for "section 13 of the Data Protection Act 1998 (damage or distress suffered as a result of a contravention of a requirement of that Act)" substitute "Article 82 of the GDPR or section 168 or 169 of the Data Protection Act 2018 (compensation for contravention of the data protection legislation)".

    (3) After subsection (5) insert—

>   "(5A) In subsection (5)(a), "the GDPR" has the same meaning as in Parts 5 to 7 of the Data Protection Act 2018 (see section 3(10), (11) and (14) of that Act)."

182 (1) Paragraph 1 of Schedule 7 (statutory restrictions on disclosure) is amended as follows.

    (2) The existing text becomes sub-paragraph (1).

    (3) In that sub-paragraph, in paragraph (a)—
        (a)   for "the Data Protection Act 1998" substitute "the data protection legislation", and
        (b)   for "are" substitute "is".

    (4) After that sub-paragraph, insert—

>   "(2) In this paragraph, "the data protection legislation" has the same meaning as in the Data Protection Act 2018 (see section 3 of that Act)."

258

Data Protection Act 2018 (c. 12)
Schedule 19 — Minor and consequential amendments
Part 1 — Amendments of primary legislation

Marine Act (Northern Ireland) 2013 (c. 10 (N.I.))

183 (1) Paragraph 8 of Schedule 2 to the Marine Act (Northern Ireland) 2013 (further provision about fixed monetary penalties under section 35: disclosure of information) is amended as follows.

(2) In sub-paragraph (5)(a), for "the Data Protection Act 1998" substitute "the data protection legislation".

(3) After sub-paragraph (6) insert—

"(7) In this paragraph, "the data protection legislation" has the same meaning as in the Data Protection Act 2018 (see section 3 of that Act)."

Local Audit and Accountability Act 2014 (c. 2)

184 (1) Paragraph 3 of Schedule 9 to the Local Audit and Accountability Act 2014 (data matching: voluntary provision of data) is amended as follows.

(2) In sub-paragraph (3)(a), for "the Data Protection Act 1998" substitute "the data protection legislation".

(3) After sub-paragraph (3) insert—

"(3A) "The data protection legislation" has the same meaning as in the Data Protection Act 2018 (see section 3 of that Act)."

(4) In sub-paragraph (4), for "comprise or include" substitute "comprises or includes".

Anti-social Behaviour, Crime and Policing Act 2014 (c. 12)

185 (1) Paragraph 7 of Schedule 4 to the Anti-social Behaviour, Crime and Policing Act 2014 (anti-social behaviour case reviews: information) is amended as follows.

(2) In sub-paragraph (4)—
   (a) for "the Data Protection Act 1998" substitute "the data protection legislation", and
   (b) for "are" substitute "is".

(3) After sub-paragraph (5) insert—

"(6) In this paragraph, "the data protection legislation" has the same meaning as in the Data Protection Act 2018 (see section 3 of that Act)."

Immigration Act 2014 (c. 22)

186 (1) Paragraph 6 of Schedule 6 to the Immigration Act 2014 (information: limitation on powers) is amended as follows.

(2) The existing text becomes sub-paragraph (1).

(3) In that sub-paragraph, in paragraph (a)—
   (a) for "the Data Protection Act 1998" substitute "the data protection legislation", and

Data Protection Act 2018 (c. 12)
Schedule 19 − Minor and consequential amendments
Part 1 − Amendments of primary legislation

259

      (b)   for "are" substitute "is".

   (4) After that sub-paragraph insert −

       "(2) In this paragraph, "the data protection legislation" has the same meaning as in the Data Protection Act 2018 (see section 3 of that Act)."

Care Act 2014 (c. 23)

187   In section 67(9) of the Care Act 2014 (involvement in assessment, plans etc), for paragraph (a) substitute −

       "(a)   a health record (within the meaning given in section 205 of the Data Protection Act 2018),".

Social Services and Well-being (Wales) Act 2014 (anaw 4)

188   In section 18(10)(b) of the Social Services and Well-being (Wales) Act 2014 (registers of sight-impaired, hearing-impaired and other disabled people) −

      (a)   in the English language text, for "(within the meaning of the Data Protection Act 1998)" substitute "(within the meaning of Parts 5 to 7 of the Data Protection Act 2018 (see section 3(2) and (14) of that Act))", and

      (b)   in the Welsh language text, for "(o fewn ystyr "personal data" yn Neddf Diogelu Data 1998)" substitute "(o fewn ystyr "personal data" yn Rhan 5 i 7 o Ddeddf Diogelu Data 2018 (gweler adran 3(2) a (14) o'r Ddeddf honno))".

Counter-Terrorism and Security Act 2015 (c. 6)

189 (1) Section 38 of the Counter-Terrorism and Security Act 2015 (support etc for people vulnerable to being drawn into terrorism: co-operation) is amended as follows.

   (2) In subsection (4)(a), for "the Data Protection Act 1998" substitute "the data protection legislation".

   (3) After subsection (4) insert −

    "(4A) "The data protection legislation" has the same meaning as in the Data Protection Act 2018 (see section 3 of that Act)."

Small Business, Enterprise and Employment Act 2015 (c. 26)

190 (1) Section 6 of the Small Business, Enterprise and Employment Act 2015 (application of listed provisions to designated credit reference agencies) is amended as follows.

   (2) In subsection (7) −

      (a)   for paragraph (b) substitute −

         "(b)   Article 15(1) to (3) of the GDPR (confirmation of processing, access to data and safeguards for third country transfers);", and

      (b)   omit paragraph (c).

260   *Data Protection Act 2018 (c. 12)*
                                    Schedule 19 — Minor and consequential amendments
                                    Part 1 — Amendments of primary legislation

(3) After subsection (7) insert—

"(7A) In subsection (7) "the GDPR" has the same meaning as in Parts 5 to 7 of the Data Protection Act 2018 (see section 3(10), (11) and (14) of that Act)."

Modern Slavery Act 2015 (c. 30)

191 (1) Section 54A of the Modern Slavery Act 2015 (Gangmasters and Labour Abuse Authority: information gateways) is amended as follows.

(2) In subsection (5)(a), for "the Data Protection Act 1998" substitute "the data protection legislation".

(3) In subsection (9), after "section" insert "—
            "the data protection legislation" has the same meaning as in the Data Protection Act 2018 (see section 3 of that Act);".

Human Trafficking and Exploitation (Criminal Justice and Support for Victims) Act (Northern Ireland) 2015 (c. 2 (N.I.))

192   The Human Trafficking and Exploitation (Criminal Justice and Support for Victims) Act (Northern Ireland) 2015 is amended as follows.

193   In section 13(5) (duty to notify National Crime Agency about suspected victims of certain offences) for "the Data Protection Act 1998" substitute "the data protection legislation".

194   In section 25(1) (interpretation of this Act), at the appropriate place insert—
            ""the data protection legislation" has the same meaning as in the Data Protection Act 2018 (see section 3 of that Act);".

195   In paragraph 18(5) of Schedule 3 (supply of information to relevant Northern Ireland departments, Secretary of State, etc) for "the Data Protection Act 1998" substitute "the data protection legislation".

Justice Act (Northern Ireland) 2015 (c. 9 (N.I.))

196 (1) Section 72 of the Justice Act (Northern Ireland) 2015 (supply of information to relevant Northern Ireland departments or Secretary of State) is amended as follows.

(2) In subsection (5), for "the Data Protection Act 1998" substitute "the data protection legislation".

(3) In subsection (7), at the appropriate place insert—
            ""the data protection legislation" has the same meaning as in the Data Protection Act 2018 (see section 3 of that Act);".

Immigration Act 2016 (c. 19)

197 (1) Section 7 of the Immigration Act 2016 (information gateways: supplementary) is amended as follows.

(2) In subsection (2)(a), for "the Data Protection Act 1998" substitute "the data protection legislation".

Data Protection Act 2018 (c. 12) 261
Schedule 19 — Minor and consequential amendments
Part 1 — Amendments of primary legislation

(3) In subsection (11), at the appropriate place insert—

> ""the data protection legislation" has the same meaning as in the Data Protection Act 2018 (see section 3 of that Act);".

Investigatory Powers Act 2016 (c. 25)

198   The Investigatory Powers Act 2016 is amended as follows.

199   In section 1(5)(b), for sub-paragraph (ii) substitute—

> "(ii)   in section 170 of the Data Protection Act 2018 (unlawful obtaining etc of personal data),".

200   In section 199 (bulk personal datasets: interpretation), for subsection (2) substitute—

> "(2)   In this Part, "personal data" means—
>
> (a)   personal data within the meaning of section 3(2) of the Data Protection Act 2018 which is subject to processing described in section 82(1) of that Act, and
>
> (b)   data relating to a deceased individual where the data would fall within paragraph (a) if it related to a living individual."

201   In section 202(4) (restriction on use of class BPD warrants), in the definition of "sensitive personal data", for "which is of a kind mentioned in section 2(a) to (f) of the Data Protection Act 1998" substitute "the processing of which would be sensitive processing for the purposes of section 86(7) of the Data Protection Act 2018".

202   In section 206 (additional safeguards for health records), for subsection (7) substitute—

> "(7)   In subsection (6)—
>
> "health professional" has the same meaning as in the Data Protection Act 2018 (see section 204(1) of that Act);
>
> "health service body" has meaning given by section 204(4) of that Act."

203 (1) Section 237 (information gateway) is amended as follows.

(2) In subsection (2), for "the Data Protection Act 1998" substitute "the data protection legislation".

(3) After subsection (2) insert—

> "(3)   In this section, "the data protection legislation" has the same meaning as in the Data Protection Act 2018 (see section 3 of that Act)."

Public Services Ombudsman Act (Northern Ireland) 2016 (c. 4 (N.I.))

204 (1) Section 49 of the Police Services Ombudsman Act (Northern Ireland) 2016 (disclosure of information) is amended as follows.

(2) In subsection (4), for paragraph (a) substitute—

> "(a)   sections 142 to 154, 160 to 164 and 174 to 176 of, or Schedule 15 to, the Data Protection Act 2018 (certain provisions relating to enforcement),".

262   *Data Protection Act 2018 (c. 12)*
                                 Schedule 19 — Minor and consequential amendments
                                     Part 1 — Amendments of primary legislation

(3) For subsection (5) substitute —

   "(5) The offences are those under —

      (a) any provision of the Data Protection Act 2018 other than paragraph 15 of Schedule 15 (powers of entry and inspection: offences),

      (b) section 77 of the Freedom of Information Act 2000 (offence of altering etc records with intent to prevent disclosure)."

(4) After subsection (6) insert —

   "(7) In this section, "the data protection legislation" has the same meaning as in the Data Protection Act 2018 (see section 3 of that Act)."

Health and Social Care (Control of Data Processing) Act (Northern Ireland) 2016 (c. 12 (N.I.))

205 (1) Section 1 of the Health and Social Care (Control of Data Processing) Act (Northern Ireland) 2016 (control of information of a relevant person) is amended as follows.

  (2) In subsection (8), for "made by or under the Data Protection Act 1998" substitute "of the data protection legislation".

  (3) After subsection (12) insert —

   "(12A) In this section, "the data protection legislation" has the same meaning as in the Data Protection Act 2018 (see section 3 of that Act)."

Mental Capacity Act (Northern Ireland) 2016 (c. 18 (N.I.))

206   In section 306(1) of the Mental Capacity Act (Northern Ireland) 2016 (definitions for purposes of Act), for the definition of "health record" substitute —

         ""health record" has the meaning given by section 205 of the Data Protection Act 2018;".

Justice Act (Northern Ireland) 2016 (c. 21 (N.I.))

207   The Justice Act (Northern Ireland) 2016 is amended as follows.

208 (1) Section 17 (disclosure of information) is amended as follows.

  (2) In subsection (7), for "the Data Protection Act 1998" substitute "the data protection legislation".

  (3) In subsection (8), after "section" insert " —

         "the data protection legislation" has the same meaning as in the Data Protection Act 2018 (see section 3 of that Act);".

209   In section 44(3) (disclosure of information) —

      (a) in paragraph (a), for "Part 5 of the Data Protection Act 1998" substitute "sections 142 to 154, 160 to 164 or 174 to 176 of, or Schedule 15 to, the Data Protection Act 2018", and

      (b) for paragraph (b) substitute —

            "(b) the commission of an offence under —

Data Protection Act 2018 (c. 12)
Schedule 19 – Minor and consequential amendments
Part 1 – Amendments of primary legislation

263

(i) a provision of the Data Protection Act 2018 other than paragraph 15 of Schedule 15 (obstruction of execution of warrant etc); or

(ii) section 77 of the Freedom of Information Act 2000 (offence of altering etc records with intent to prevent disclosure)."

Policing and Crime Act 2017 (c. 3)

210 (1) Section 50 of the Policing and Crime Act 2017 (Freedom of Information Act etc: Police Federation for England and Wales) is amended as follows.

(2) The existing text becomes subsection (1).

(3) In that subsection, in paragraph (b), for "the Data Protection Act 1998" substitute "the data protection legislation".

(4) After that subsection, insert—

"(2) In this section, "the data protection legislation" has the same meaning as in the Data Protection Act 2018 (see section 3 of that Act)."

Children and Social Work Act 2017 (c. 12)

211 In Schedule 5 to the Children and Social Work Act 2017—
(a) in Part 1 (general amendments to do with social workers etc in England), omit paragraph 6, and
(b) in Part 2 (renaming of Health and Social Work Professions Order 2001), omit paragraph 47(g).

Higher Education and Research Act 2017 (c. 29)

212 The Higher Education and Research Act 2017 is amended as follows.

213 (1) Section 63 (cooperation and information sharing by the Office for Students) is amended as follows.

(2) In subsection (6), for "the Data Protection Act 1998" substitute "the data protection legislation".

(3) In subsection (7), at the appropriate place insert—
        ""the data protection legislation" has the same meaning as in the Data Protection Act 2018 (see section 3 of that Act);".

214 (1) Section 112 (cooperation and information sharing between the Office for Students and UKRI) is amended as follows.

(2) In subsection (6), for "the Data Protection Act 1998" substitute "the data protection legislation".

(3) After subsection (6) insert —

"(7) In this section, "the data protection legislation" has the same meaning as in the Data Protection Act 2018 (see section 3 of that Act)."

264   *Data Protection Act 2018 (c. 12)*
                                   Schedule 19 — Minor and consequential amendments
                                        Part 1 — Amendments of primary legislation

Digital Economy Act 2017 (c. 30)

215   The Digital Economy Act 2017 is amended as follows.

216   (1) Section 40 (further provisions about disclosures under sections 35 to 39) is
          amended as follows.

      (2) In subsection (8)(a), for "the Data Protection Act 1998" substitute "the data
          protection legislation".

      (3) After subsection (10) insert—

          "(11)   In this section, "the data protection legislation" has the same
                  meaning as in the Data Protection Act 2018 (see section 3 of that
                  Act)."

217   (1) Section 43 (codes of practice) is amended as follows.

      (2) In subsection (2), for "issued under section 52B (data-sharing code) of the
          Data Protection Act 1998" substitute "prepared under section 121 of the Data
          Protection Act 2018 (data-sharing code) and issued under section 125(4) of
          that Act".

      (3) In subsection (13), for "section 51(3) of the Data Protection Act 1998"
          substitute "section 128 of the Data Protection Act 2018".

218   (1) Section 49 (further provision about disclosures under section 48) is amended
          as follows.

      (2) In subsection (8)(a), for "the Data Protection Act 1998" substitute "the data
          protection legislation".

      (3) After subsection (10) insert—

          "(11)   In this section, "the data protection legislation" has the same
                  meaning as in the Data Protection Act 2018 (see section 3 of that
                  Act)."

219   (1) Section 52 (code of practice) is amended as follows.

      (2) In subsection (2), for "issued under section 52B (data-sharing code) of the
          Data Protection Act 1998" substitute "prepared under section 121 of the Data
          Protection Act 2018 (data-sharing code) and issued under section 125(4) of
          that Act".

      (3) In subsection (13), for "section 51(3) of the Data Protection Act 1998"
          substitute "section 128 of the Data Protection Act 2018 (other codes of
          practice)".

220   (1) Section 57 (further provision about disclosures under section 56) is amended
          as follows.

      (2) In subsection (8)(a), for "the Data Protection Act 1998" substitute "the data
          protection legislation".

      (3) After subsection (10) insert—

          "(11)   In this section, "the data protection legislation" has the same
                  meaning as in the Data Protection Act 2018 (see section 3 of that
                  Act)."

Data Protection Act 2018 (c. 12) 265
Schedule 19 — Minor and consequential amendments
Part 1 — Amendments of primary legislation

221 (1) Section 60 (code of practice) is amended as follows.

    (2) In subsection (2), for "issued under section 52B (data-sharing code) of the Data Protection Act 1998" substitute "prepared under section 121 of the Data Protection Act 2018 (data-sharing code) and issued under section 125(4) of that Act".

    (3) In subsection (13), for "section 51(3) of the Data Protection Act 1998" substitute "section 128 of the Data Protection Act 2018 (other codes of practice)".

222 (1) Section 65 (supplementary provision about disclosures under section 64) is amended as follows.

    (2) In subsection (2)(a), for "the Data Protection Act 1998" substitute "the data protection legislation".

    (3) After subsection (8) insert—

       "(9) In this section, "the data protection legislation" has the same meaning as in the Data Protection Act 2018 (see section 3 of that Act)."

223 (1) Section 70 (code of practice) is amended as follows.

    (2) In subsection (2), for "issued under section 52B (data-sharing code) of the Data Protection Act 1998" substitute "prepared under section 121 of the Data Protection Act 2018 (data-sharing code) and issued under section 125(4) of that Act".

    (3) In subsection (15), for "section 51(3) of the Data Protection Act 1998" substitute "section 128 of the Data Protection Act 2018 (other codes of practice)".

224 Omit sections 108 to 110 (charges payable to the Information Commissioner).

Landfill Disposals Tax (Wales) Act 2017 (anaw 3)

225 (1) Section 60 of the Landfill Disposals Tax (Wales) Act 2017 (disclosure of information to the Welsh Revenue Authority) is amended as follows.

    (2) In subsection (4)(a)—
      (a) in the English language text, for "the Data Protection Act 1998 (c. 29)" substitute "the data protection legislation", and
      (b) in the Welsh language text, for "torri Deddf Diogelu Data 1998 (p. 29)" substitute "torri'r ddeddfwriaeth diogelu data".

    (3) After subsection (7)—
      (a) in the English language text insert—

        "(8) In this section, "the data protection legislation" has the same meaning as in the Data Protection Act 2018 (see section 3 of that Act).", and
      (b) in the Welsh language text insert—

        "(8) Yn yr adran hon, mae i "y ddeddfwriaeth diogelu data" yr un ystyr ag a roddir i "the data protection legislation" yn Neddf Diogelu Data 2018 (gweler adran 3 o'r Ddeddf honno)."

266   *Data Protection Act 2018 (c. 12)*
Schedule 19 — Minor and consequential amendments
Part 1 — Amendments of primary legislation

Additional Learning Needs and Educational Tribunal (Wales) Act 2018 (anaw 2)

226 (1) Section 4 of the Additional Learning Needs and Educational Tribunal (Wales) Act 2018 (additional learning needs code) is amended as follows.

(2) In the English language text—
   (a) in subsection (9), omit from "and in this subsection" to the end, and
   (b) after subsection (9) insert—

   "(9A) In subsection (9)—
      "data subject" ("*testun y data*") has the meaning given by section 3(5) of the Data Protection Act 2018;
      "personal data" ("*data personol*") has the same meaning as in Parts 5 to 7 of that Act (see section 3(2) and (14) of that Act)."

(3) In the Welsh language text—
   (a) in subsection (9), omit from "ac yn yr is-adran hon" to the end, and
   (b) after subsection (9) insert—

   "(9A) Yn is-adran (9)—
      mae i "data personol" yr un ystyr ag a roddir i "personal data" yn Rhannau 5 i 7 o Ddeddf Diogelu Data 2018 (gweler adran 3(2) a (14) o'r Ddeddf honno);
      mae i "testun y data" yr ystyr a roddir i "data subject" gan adran 3(5) o'r Ddeddf honno."

This Act

227 (1) Section 204 of this Act (meaning of "health professional" and "social work professional") is amended as follows (to reflect the arrangements for the registration of social workers in England under Part 2 of the Children and Social Work Act 2017).

(2) In subsection (1)(g)—
   (a) omit "and Social Work", and
   (b) omit ", other than the social work profession in England".

(3) In subsection (2), for paragraph (a) substitute—
   "(a) a person registered as a social worker in the register maintained by Social Work England under section 39(1) of the Children and Social Work Act 2017;".

PART 2

AMENDMENTS OF OTHER LEGISLATION

Estate Agents (Specified Offences) (No. 2) Order 1991 (S.I. 1991/1091)

228   In the table in the Schedule to the Estate Agents (Specified Offences) (No. 2)

Order 1991 (specified offences), at the end insert—

"Data Protection Act 2018	Section 144	False statements made in response to an information notice
	Section 148	Destroying or falsifying information and documents etc"

Channel Tunnel (International Arrangements) Order 1993 (S.I. 1993/1813)

229 (1) Article 4 of the Channel Tunnel (International Arrangements) Order 1993 (application of enactments) is amended as follows.

(2) In paragraph (2)—

(a) for "section 5 of the Data Protection Act 1998 ("the 1998 Act"), data which are" substitute "section 207 of the Data Protection Act 2018 ("the 2018 Act"), data which is",

(b) for "data controller" substitute "controller",

(c) after "in the context of" insert "the activities of", and

(d) for "and the 1998 Act" substitute "and the 2018 Act".

(3) In paragraph (3)—

(a) for "section 5 of the 1998 Act, data which are" substitute "section 207 of the 2018 Act, data which is",

(b) for "data controller" substitute "controller",

(c) after "in the context of" insert "the activities of", and

(d) for "and the 1998 Act" substitute "and the 2018 Act".

Access to Health Records (Northern Ireland) Order 1993 (S.I. 1993/1250 (N.I. 4))

230 The Access to Health Records (Northern Ireland) Order 1993 is amended as follows.

231 In Article 4 (health professionals), for paragraph (1) substitute—

"(1) In this Order, "health professional" has the same meaning as in the Data Protection Act 2018 (see section 204 of that Act)."

232 In Article 5(4)(a) (fees for access to health records), for "under section 7 of the Data Protection Act 1998" substitute "made by the Department".

Channel Tunnel (Miscellaneous Provisions) Order 1994 (S.I. 1994/1405)

233 In article 4 of the Channel Tunnel (Miscellaneous Provisions) Order 1994 (application of enactments), for paragraphs (2) and (3) substitute—

"(2) For the purposes of section 207 of the Data Protection Act 2018 ("the 2018 Act"), data which is processed in a control zone in Belgium, in connection with the carrying out of frontier controls, by an officer belonging to the United Kingdom is to be treated as processed by a controller established in the United Kingdom in the context of the

268   *Data Protection Act 2018 (c. 12)*
                                    Schedule 19 — Minor and consequential amendments
                                    Part 2 — Amendments of other legislation

activities of that establishment (and accordingly the 2018 Act applies in respect of such data).

(3)   For the purposes of section 207 of the 2018 Act, data which is processed in a control zone in Belgium, in connection with the carrying out of frontier controls, by an officer belonging to the Kingdom of Belgium is to be treated as processed by a controller established in the Kingdom of Belgium in the context of the activities of that establishment (and accordingly the 2018 Act does not apply in respect of such data)."

European Primary and Specialist Dental Qualifications Regulations 1998 (S.I. 1998/811)

234   The European Primary and Specialist Dental Qualifications Regulations 1998 are amended as follows.

235   (1)   Regulation 2(1) (interpretation) is amended as follows.

(2)   Omit the definition of "Directive 95/46/EC".

(3)   At the appropriate place insert—

""the GDPR" means Regulation (EU) 2016/679 of the European Parliament and of the Council of 27 April 2016 on the protection of natural persons with regard to the processing of personal data and on the free movement of such data (General Data Protection Regulation), read with Chapter 2 of Part 2 of the Data Protection Act 2018;".

236   (1)   The table in Schedule A1 (functions of the GDC under Directive 2005/36) is amended as follows.

(2)   In the entry for Article 56(2), in the second column, for "Directive 95/46/EC" substitute "the GDPR".

(3)   In the entry for Article 56a(4), in the second column, for "Directive 95/46/EC" substitute "the GDPR".

Scottish Parliamentary Corporate Body (Crown Status) Order 1999 (S.I. 1999/677)

237   For article 7 of the Scottish Parliamentary Corporate Body (Crown Status) Order 1999 substitute—

"7   **Data Protection Act 2018**

(1)   The Parliamentary corporation is to be treated as a Crown body for the purposes of the Data Protection Act 2018 to the extent specified in this article.

(2)   The Parliamentary corporation is to be treated as a government department for the purposes of the following provisions—
   (a)   section 8(d) (lawfulness of processing under the GDPR: public interest etc),
   (b)   section 209 (application to the Crown),
   (c)   paragraph 6 of Schedule 1 (statutory etc and government purposes),
   (d)   paragraph 7 of Schedule 2 (exemptions from the GDPR: functions designed to protect the public etc), and

Data Protection Act 2018 (c. 12) 269
Schedule 19 — Minor and consequential amendments
Part 2 — Amendments of other legislation

       (e)   paragraph 8(1)(o) of Schedule 3 (exemptions from the GDPR: health data).

  (3)   In the provisions mentioned in paragraph (4)—

       (a)   references to employment by or under the Crown are to be treated as including employment as a member of staff of the Parliamentary corporation, and

       (b)   references to a person in the service of the Crown are to be treated as including a person so employed.

  (4)   The provisions are—

       (a)   section 24(3) (exemption for certain data relating to employment under the Crown), and

       (b)   section 209(6) (application of certain provisions to a person in the service of the Crown).

  (5)   In this article, references to a provision of Chapter 2 of Part 2 of the Data Protection Act 2018 have the same meaning as in Parts 5 to 7 of that Act (see section 3(14) of that Act)."

Northern Ireland Assembly Commission (Crown Status) Order 1999 (S.I. 1999/3145)

238   For article 9 of the Northern Ireland Assembly Commission (Crown Status) Order 1999 substitute—

"9   Data Protection Act 2018

  (1)   The Commission is to be treated as a Crown body for the purposes of the Data Protection Act 2018 to the extent specified in this article.

  (2)   The Commission is to be treated as a government department for the purposes of the following provisions—

       (a)   section 8(d) (lawfulness of processing under the GDPR: public interest etc),

       (b)   section 209 (application to the Crown),

       (c)   paragraph 6 of Schedule 1 (statutory etc and government purposes),

       (d)   paragraph 7 of Schedule 2 (exemptions from the GDPR: functions designed to protect the public etc), and

       (e)   paragraph 8(1)(o) of Schedule 3 (exemptions from the GDPR: health data).

  (3)   In the provisions mentioned in paragraph (4)—

       (a)   references to employment by or under the Crown are to be treated as including employment as a member of staff of the Commission, and

       (b)   references to a person in the service of the Crown are to be treated as including a person so employed.

  (4)   The provisions are—

       (a)   section 24(3) (exemption for certain data relating to employment under the Crown), and

       (b)   section 209(6) (application of certain provisions to a person in the service of the Crown).

270   *Data Protection Act 2018 (c. 12)*
Schedule 19 — Minor and consequential amendments
Part 2 — Amendments of other legislation

(5)   In this article, references to a provision of Chapter 2 of Part 2 of the Data Protection Act 2018 have the same meaning as in Parts 5 to 7 of that Act (see section 3(14) of that Act)."

Data Protection (Corporate Finance Exemption) Order 2000 (S.I. 2000/184)

239   The Data Protection (Corporate Finance Exemption) Order 2000 is revoked.

Data Protection (Conditions under Paragraph 3 of Part II of Schedule 1) Order 2000 (S.I. 2000/185)

240   The Data Protection (Conditions under Paragraph 3 of Part II of Schedule 1) Order 2000 is revoked.

Data Protection (Functions of Designated Authority) Order 2000 (S.I. 2000/186)

241   The Data Protection (Functions of Designated Authority) Order 2000 is revoked.

Data Protection (International Co-operation) Order 2000 (S.I. 2000/190)

242   The Data Protection (International Co-operation) Order 2000 is revoked.

Data Protection (Subject Access) (Fees and Miscellaneous Provisions) Regulations 2000 (S.I. 2000/191)

243   The Data Protection (Subject Access) (Fees and Miscellaneous Provisions) Regulations 2000 are revoked.

Consumer Credit (Credit Reference Agency) Regulations 2000 (S.I. 2000/290)

244   In the Consumer Credit (Credit Reference Agency) Regulations 2000, regulation 4(1) and Schedule 1 (statement of rights under section 9(3) of the Data Protection Act 1998) are revoked.

Data Protection (Subject Access Modification) (Health) Order 2000 (S.I. 2000/413)

245   The Data Protection (Subject Access Modification) (Health) Order 2000 is revoked.

Data Protection (Subject Access Modification) (Education) Order 2000 (S.I. 2000/414)

246   The Data Protection (Subject Access Modification) (Education) Order 2000 is revoked.

Data Protection (Subject Access Modification) (Social Work) Order 2000 (S.I. 2000/415)

247   The Data Protection (Subject Access Modification) (Social Work) Order 2000 is revoked.

Data Protection (Crown Appointments) Order 2000 (S.I. 2000/416)

248   The Data Protection (Crown Appointments) Order 2000 is revoked.

Data Protection Act 2018 (c. 12)
Schedule 19 — Minor and consequential amendments
Part 2 — Amendments of other legislation

271

Data Protection (Processing of Sensitive Personal Data) Order 2000 (S.I. 2000/417)

249   The Data Protection (Processing of Sensitive Personal Data) Order 2000 is revoked.

Data Protection (Miscellaneous Subject Access Exemptions) Order 2000 (S.I. 2000/419)

250   The Data Protection (Miscellaneous Subject Access Exemptions) Order 2000 is revoked.

Data Protection (Designated Codes of Practice) (No. 2) Order 2000 (S.I. 2000/1864)

251   The Data Protection (Designated Codes of Practice) (No. 2) Order 2000 is revoked.

Representation of the People (England and Wales) Regulations 2001 (S.I. 2001/341)

252   The Representation of the People (England and Wales) Regulations 2001 are amended as follows.

253   In regulation 3(1) (interpretation), at the appropriate places insert —
    ""Article 89 GDPR purposes" means the purposes mentioned in Article 89(1) of the GDPR (archiving in the public interest, scientific or historical research and statistics);";
    ""the data protection legislation" has the same meaning as in the Data Protection Act 2018 (see section 3 of that Act);";
    ""the GDPR" means Regulation (EU) 2016/679 of the European Parliament and of the Council of 27 April 2016 on the protection of natural persons with regard to the processing of personal data and on the free movement of such data (General Data Protection Regulation);".

254   In regulation 26(3)(a) (applications for registration), for "the Data Protection Act 1998" substitute "the data protection legislation".

255   In regulation 26A(2)(a) (application for alteration of register in respect of name under section 10ZD), for "the Data Protection Act 1998" substitute "the data protection legislation".

256   In regulation 32ZA(3)(f) (annual canvass), for "the Data Protection Act 1998" substitute "the data protection legislation".

257   In regulation 61A (conditions on the use, supply and inspection of absent voter records or lists), for paragraph (a) (but not the final "or") substitute —
    "(a)   Article 89 GDPR purposes;".

258 (1) Regulation 92(2) (interpretation and application of Part VI etc) is amended as follows.

    (2) After sub-paragraph (b) insert —
        "(ba)   "relevant requirement" means the requirement under Article 89 of the GDPR, read with section 19 of the Data Protection Act 2018, that personal data processed for Article 89 GDPR purposes must be subject to appropriate safeguards."

    (3) Omit sub-paragraphs (c) and (d).

272

Data Protection Act 2018 (c. 12)
Schedule 19 — Minor and consequential amendments
Part 2 — Amendments of other legislation

259   In regulation 96(2A)(b)(i) (restriction on use of the full register), for "section 11(3) of the Data Protection Act 1998" substitute "section 122(5) of the Data Protection Act 2018".

260   In regulation 97(5) and (6) (supply of free copy of full register to the British Library and restrictions on use), for "research purposes in compliance with the relevant conditions" substitute "Article 89 GDPR purposes in accordance with the relevant requirement".

261   In regulation 97A(7) and (8) (supply of free copy of full register to the National Library of Wales and restrictions on use), for "research purposes in compliance with the relevant conditions" substitute "Article 89 GDPR purposes in accordance with the relevant requirement".

262   In regulation 99(6) and (7) (supply of free copy of full register etc to Statistics Board and restrictions on use), for "research purposes in compliance with the relevant conditions" substitute "Article 89 GDPR purposes in accordance with the relevant requirement".

263   In regulation 109A(9) and (10) (supply of free copy of full register to public libraries and local authority archives services and restrictions on use), for "research purposes in compliance with the relevant conditions" substitute "Article 89 GDPR purposes in accordance with the relevant requirement".

264   In regulation 119(2) (conditions on the use, supply and disclosure of documents open to public inspection), for sub-paragraph (i) (but not the final "or") substitute—
          "(i)   Article 89 GDPR purposes;".

Representation of the People (Scotland) Regulations 2001 (S.I. 2001/497)

265   The Representation of the People (Scotland) Regulations 2001 are amended as follows.

266   In regulation 3(1) (interpretation), at the appropriate places, insert—
          ""Article 89 GDPR purposes" means the purposes mentioned in Article 89(1) of the GDPR (archiving in the public interest, scientific or historical research and statistics);";
          ""the data protection legislation" has the same meaning as in the Data Protection Act 2018 (see section 3 of that Act);";
          ""the GDPR" means Regulation (EU) 2016/679 of the European Parliament and of the Council of 27 April 2016 on the protection of natural persons with regard to the processing of personal data and on the free movement of such data (General Data Protection Regulation);".

267   In regulation 26(3)(a) (applications for registration), for "the Data Protection Act 1998" substitute "the data protection legislation".

268   In regulation 26A(2)(a) (application for alteration of register in respect of name under section 10ZD), for "the Data Protection Act 1998" substitute "the data protection legislation".

269   In regulation 32ZA(3)(f) (annual canvass), for "the Data Protection Act 1998" substitute "the data protection legislation".

270   In regulation 61(3) (records and lists kept under Schedule 4), for paragraph

Data Protection Act 2018 (c. 12)
Schedule 19 — Minor and consequential amendments
Part 2 — Amendments of other legislation

273

(a) (but not the final "or") substitute—

> "(a)   Article 89 GDPR purposes;".

271   In regulation 61A (conditions on the use, supply and inspection of absent voter records or lists), for paragraph (a) (but not the final "or") substitute—

> "(a)   Article 89 GDPR purposes;".

272 (1) Regulation 92(2) (interpretation of Part VI etc) is amended as follows.

(2) After sub-paragraph (b) insert—

> "(ba)   "relevant requirement" means the requirement under Article 89 of the GDPR, read with section 19 of the Data Protection Act 2018, that personal data processed for Article 89 GDPR purposes must be subject to appropriate safeguards."

(3) Omit sub-paragraphs (c) and (d).

273   In regulation 95(3)(b)(i) (restriction on use of the full register), for "section 11(3) of the Data Protection Act 1998" substitute "section 122(5) of the Data Protection Act 2018".

274   In regulation 96(5) and (6) (supply of free copy of full register to the National Library of Scotland and the British Library and restrictions on use), for "research purposes in compliance with the relevant conditions" substitute "Article 89 GDPR purposes in accordance with the relevant requirement".

275   In regulation 98(6) and (7) (supply of free copy of full register etc to Statistics Board and restrictions on use), for "research purposes in compliance with the relevant conditions" substitute "Article 89 GDPR purposes in accordance with the relevant requirement".

276   In regulation 108A(9) and (10) (supply of full register to statutory library authorities and local authority archives services and restrictions on use), for "research purposes in compliance with the relevant conditions" substitute "Article 89 GDPR purposes in accordance with the relevant requirement".

277   In regulation 119(2) (conditions on the use, supply and disclosure of documents open to public inspection), for sub-paragraph (i) (but not the final "or") substitute—

> "(i)   Article 89 GDPR purposes;".

Financial Services and Markets Act 2000 (Disclosure of Confidential Information) Regulations 2001 (S.I. 2001/2188)

278 (1) Article 9 of the Financial Services and Markets 2000 (Disclosure of Confidential Information) Regulations 2001 (disclosure by regulators or regulator workers to certain other persons) is amended as follows.

(2) In paragraph (2B), for sub-paragraph (a) substitute—

> "(a)   the disclosure is made in accordance with Chapter V of the GDPR;".

(3) After paragraph (5) insert—

> "(6)   In this article, "the GDPR" has the same meaning as in Parts 5 to 7 of the Data Protection Act 2018 (see section 3(10), (11) and (14) of that Act)."

274

Data Protection Act 2018 (c. 12)
Schedule 19 — Minor and consequential amendments
Part 2 — Amendments of other legislation

Nursing and Midwifery Order 2001 (S.I. 2002/253)

279   The Nursing and Midwifery Order 2001 is amended as follows.

280 (1) Article 3 (the Nursing and Midwifery Council and its Committees) is amended as follows.

(2) In paragraph (18), after "enactment" insert "or the GDPR".

(3) After paragraph (18) insert—

"(19)   In this paragraph, "the GDPR" has the same meaning as in Parts 5 to 7 of the Data Protection Act 2018 (see section 3(10), (11) and (14) of that Act)."

281 (1) Article 25 (the Council's power to require disclosure of information) is amended as follows.

(2) In paragraph (3), after "enactment" insert "or the GDPR".

(3) In paragraph (6)—
    (a)   for "paragraph (5)," substitute "paragraph (3)—", and
    (b)   at the appropriate place insert—
            ""the GDPR" has the same meaning as in Parts 5 to 7 of the Data Protection Act 2018 (see section 3(10), (11) and (14) of that Act)."

282   In article 39B (European professional card), after paragraph (2) insert—

"(3)   For the purposes of Schedule 2B, "the GDPR" means Regulation (EU) 2016/679 of the European Parliament and of the Council of 27 April 2016 on the protection of natural persons with regard to the processing of personal data and on the free movement of such data (General Data Protection Regulation), read with Chapter 2 of Part 2 of the Data Protection Act 2018."

283   In article 40(6) (Directive 2005/36/EC: designation of competent authority etc), at the appropriate place insert—
            ""the GDPR" means Regulation (EU) 2016/679 of the European Parliament and of the Council of 27 April 2016 on the protection of natural persons with regard to the processing of personal data and on the free movement of such data (General Data Protection Regulation), read with Chapter 2 of Part 2 of the Data Protection Act 2018;".

284 (1) Schedule 2B (Directive 2005/36/EC: European professional card) is amended as follows.

(2) In paragraph 8(1) (access to data) for "Directive 95/46/EC" substitute "the GDPR".

(3) In paragraph 9 (processing data), omit sub-paragraph (2) (deeming the Society to be the controller for the purposes of Directive 95/46/EC).

285 (1) The table in Schedule 3 (functions of the Council under Directive 2005/36) is amended as follows.

(2) In the entry for Article 56(2), in the second column, for "Directive 95/46/EC" substitute "the GDPR".

Data Protection Act 2018 (c. 12)
Schedule 19 − Minor and consequential amendments
Part 2 − Amendments of other legislation

275

(3) In the entry for Article 56a(4), in the second column, for "Directive 95/46/EC" substitute "the GDPR".

286   In Schedule 4 (interpretation), omit the definition of "Directive 95/46/EC".

Electronic Commerce (EC Directive) Regulations 2002 (S.I. 2002/2013)

287   Regulation 3 of the Electronic Commerce (EC Directive) Regulations 2002 (exclusions) is amended as follows.

288   In paragraph (1)(b) for "the Data Protection Directive and the Telecommunications Data Protection Directive" substitute "the GDPR".

289   In paragraph (3) −
   (a) omit the definitions of "Data Protection Directive" and "Telecommunications Data Protection Directive", and
   (b) at the appropriate place insert −
          ""the GDPR" means Regulation (EU) 2016/679 of the European Parliament and of the Council of 27 April 2016 on the protection of natural persons with regard to the processing of personal data and on the free movement of such data (General Data Protection Regulation);".

Data Protection (Processing of Sensitive Personal Data) (Elected Representatives) Order 2002 (S.I. 2002/2905)

290   The Data Protection (Processing of Sensitive Personal Data) (Elected Representatives) Order 2002 is revoked.

Privacy and Electronic Communications (EC Directive) Regulations 2003 (S.I. 2003/2426)

291   The Privacy and Electronic Communications (EC Directive) Regulations 2003 are amended as follows.

292   In regulation 2(1) (interpretation), in the definition of "the Information Commissioner" and "the Commissioner", for "section 6 of the Data Protection Act 1998" substitute "the Data Protection Act 2018".

293 (1) Regulation 4 (relationship between these Regulations and the Data Protection Act 1998) is amended as follows.

   (2) The existing text becomes sub-paragraph (1).

   (3) In that sub-paragraph, for "the Data Protection Act 1998" substitute "the data protection legislation".

   (4) After that sub-paragraph insert −

      "(2) In this regulation −
            "the data protection legislation" has the same meaning as in the Data Protection Act 2018 (see section 3 of that Act);
            "personal data" and "processing" have the same meaning as in Parts 5 to 7 of that Act (see section 3(2), (4) and (14) of that Act).

      (3) Regulation 2(2) and (3) (meaning of certain expressions) do not apply for the purposes of this regulation."

276   *Data Protection Act 2018 (c. 12)*
Schedule 19 — Minor and consequential amendments
Part 2 — Amendments of other legislation

(5) In the heading of that regulation, for "the Data Protection Act 1998" substitute "the data protection legislation".

Nationality, Immigration and Asylum Act 2002 (Juxtaposed Controls) Order 2003 (S.I. 2003/ 2818)

294   The Nationality, Immigration and Asylum Act 2002 (Juxtaposed Controls) Order 2003 is amended as follows.

295   In article 8(2) (exercise of powers by French officers in a control zone in the United Kingdom: disapplication of law of England and Wales) —
    (a)   for "The Data Protection Act 1998" substitute "The Data Protection Act 2018", and
    (b)   for "are" substitute "is".

296   In article 11(4) (exercise of powers by UK immigration officers and constables in a control zone in France: enactments having effect) —
    (a)   for "The Data Protection Act 1998" substitute "The Data Protection Act 2018",
    (b)   for "are" substitute "is",
    (c)   for "section 5" substitute "section 207",
    (d)   for "data controller" substitute "controller", and
    (e)   after "in the context of" insert "the activities of".

Pupils' Educational Records (Scotland) Regulations 2003 (S.S.I. 2003/581)

297   The Pupils' Educational Records (Scotland) Regulations 2003 are amended as follows.

298 (1) Regulation 2 (interpretation) is amended as follows.

(2) Omit the definition of "the 1998 Act".

(3) At the appropriate place insert —
    ""the GDPR" means Regulation (EU) 2016/679 of the European Parliament and of the Council of 27 April 2016 on the protection of natural persons with regard to the processing of personal data and on the free movement of such data (General Data Protection Regulation), read with Chapter 2 of Part 2 of the Data Protection Act 2018;".

299 (1) Regulation 6 (circumstances where information should not be disclosed) is amended as follows.

(2) After "any information" insert "to the extent that any of the following conditions are satisfied".

(3) For paragraphs (a) to (c) substitute —
    "(aa)   the pupil to whom the information relates would have no right of access to the information under the GDPR;
    (ab)   the information is personal data described in Article 9(1) or 10 of the GDPR (special categories of personal data and personal data relating to criminal convictions and offences);".

Data Protection Act 2018 (c. 12)
Schedule 19 – Minor and consequential amendments
Part 2 – Amendments of other legislation

277

(4) In paragraph (d), for "to the extent that its disclosure" substitute "the disclosure of the information".

(5) In paragraph (e), for "that" substitute "the information".

300   In regulation 9 (fees), for paragraph (1) substitute—

"(1A) In complying with a request made under regulation 5(2), the responsible body may only charge a fee where Article 12(5) or Article 15(3) of the GDPR would permit the charging of a fee if the request had been made by the pupil to whom the information relates under Article 15 of the GDPR.

(1B) Where paragraph (1A) permits the charging of a fee, the responsible body may not charge a fee that—

(a)   exceeds the cost of supply, or

(b)   exceeds any limit in regulations made under section 12 of the Data Protection Act 2018 that would apply if the request had been made by the pupil to whom the information relates under Article 15 of the GDPR."

European Parliamentary Elections (Northern Ireland) Regulations 2004 (S.I. 2004/1267)

301   Schedule 1 to the European Parliamentary Elections (Northern Ireland) Regulations 2004 (European Parliamentary elections rules) is amended as follows.

302 (1) Paragraph 74(1) (interpretation) is amended as follows.

(2) Omit the definitions of "relevant conditions" and "research purposes".

(3) At the appropriate places insert—

""Article 89 GDPR purposes" means the purposes mentioned in Article 89(1) of the GDPR (archiving in the public interest, scientific or historical research and statistics);";

""the GDPR" means Regulation (EU) 2016/679 of the European Parliament and of the Council of 27 April 2016 on the protection of natural persons with regard to the processing of personal data and on the free movement of such data (General Data Protection Regulation);".

303   In paragraph 77(2)(b) (conditions on the use, supply and disclosure of documents open to public inspection), for "research purposes" substitute "Article 89 GDPR purposes".

Freedom of Information and Data Protection (Appropriate Limit and Fees) Regulations 2004 (S.I. 2004/3244)

304   In regulation 3(1) of the Freedom of Information and Data Protection (Appropriate Limit and Fees) Regulations 2004, omit "the appropriate limit referred to in section 9A(3) and (4) of the 1998 Act and".

Environmental Information Regulations 2004 (S.I. 2004/3391)

305   The Environmental Information Regulations 2004 are amended as follows.

306 (1) Regulation 2 (interpretation) is amended as follows.

278   *Data Protection Act 2018 (c. 12)*
Schedule 19 – Minor and consequential amendments
Part 2 – Amendments of other legislation

(2) In paragraph (1), at the appropriate places, insert—

        ""the data protection principles" means the principles set out in—

              (a)   Article 5(1) of the GDPR,

              (b)   section 34(1) of the Data Protection Act 2018, and

              (c)   section 85(1) of that Act;";

        ""data subject" has the same meaning as in the Data Protection Act 2018 (see section 3 of that Act);";

        ""the GDPR" and references to a provision of Chapter 2 of Part 2 of the Data Protection Act 2018 have the same meaning as in Parts 5 to 7 of that Act (see section 3(10), (11) and (14) of that Act);";

        ""personal data" has the same meaning as in Parts 5 to 7 of the Data Protection Act 2018 (see section 3(2) and (14) of that Act);".

(3) For paragraph (4) substitute—

    "(4A)   In these Regulations, references to the Data Protection Act 2018 have effect as if in Chapter 3 of Part 2 of that Act (other general processing)—

        (a)   the references to an FOI public authority were references to a public authority as defined in these Regulations, and

        (b)   the references to personal data held by such an authority were to be interpreted in accordance with regulation 3(2)."

307 (1) Regulation 13 (personal data) is amended as follows.

    (2) For paragraph (1) substitute—

    "(1)   To the extent that the information requested includes personal data of which the applicant is not the data subject, a public authority must not disclose the personal data if—

        (a)   the first condition is satisfied, or

        (b)   the second or third condition is satisfied and, in all the circumstances of the case, the public interest in not disclosing the information outweighs the public interest in disclosing it."

    (3) For paragraph (2) substitute—

    "(2A)   The first condition is that the disclosure of the information to a member of the public otherwise than under these Regulations—

        (a)   would contravene any of the data protection principles, or

        (b)   would do so if the exemptions in section 24(1) of the Data Protection Act 2018 (manual unstructured data held by public authorities) were disregarded.

    (2B)   The second condition is that the disclosure of the information to a member of the public otherwise than under these Regulations would contravene—

        (a)   Article 21 of the GDPR (general processing: right to object to processing), or

        (b)   section 99 of the Data Protection Act 2018 (intelligence services processing: right to object to processing)."

Data Protection Act 2018 (c. 12)
Schedule 19 — Minor and consequential amendments
Part 2 — Amendments of other legislation

279

(4) For paragraph (3) substitute—

"(3A) The third condition is that—

(a) on a request under Article 15(1) of the GDPR (general processing: right of access by the data subject) for access to personal data, the information would be withheld in reliance on provision made by or under section 15, 16 or 26 of, or Schedule 2, 3 or 4 to, the Data Protection Act 2018,

(b) on a request under section 45(1)(b) of that Act (law enforcement processing: right of access by the data subject), the information would be withheld in reliance on subsection (4) of that section, or

(c) on a request under section 94(1)(b) of that Act (intelligence services processing: rights of access by the data subject), the information would be withheld in reliance on a provision of Chapter 6 of Part 4 of that Act."

(5) Omit paragraph (4).

(6) For paragraph (5) substitute—

"(5A) For the purposes of this regulation a public authority may respond to a request by neither confirming nor denying whether such information exists and is held by the public authority, whether or not it holds such information, to the extent that—

(a) the condition in paragraph (5B)(a) is satisfied, or

(b) a condition in paragraph (5B)(b) to (e) is satisfied and in all the circumstances of the case, the public interest in not confirming or denying whether the information exists outweighs the public interest in doing so.

(5B) The conditions mentioned in paragraph (5A) are—

(a) giving a member of the public the confirmation or denial—

(i) would (apart from these Regulations) contravene any of the data protection principles, or

(ii) would do so if the exemptions in section 24(1) of the Data Protection Act 2018 (manual unstructured data held by public authorities) were disregarded;

(b) giving a member of the public the confirmation or denial would (apart from these Regulations) contravene Article 21 of the GDPR or section 99 of the Data Protection Act 2018 (right to object to processing);

(c) on a request under Article 15(1) of the GDPR (general processing: right of access by the data subject) for confirmation of whether personal data is being processed, the information would be withheld in reliance on a provision listed in paragraph (3A)(a);

(d) on a request under section 45(1)(a) of the Data Protection Act 2018 (law enforcement processing: right of access by the data subject), the information would be withheld in reliance on subsection (4) of that section;

(e) on a request under section 94(1)(a) of that Act (intelligence services processing: rights of access by the data subject), the information would be withheld in reliance on a provision of Chapter 6 of Part 4 of that Act."

280

Data Protection Act 2018 (c. 12)
Schedule 19 — Minor and consequential amendments
Part 2 — Amendments of other legislation

(7)   After that paragraph insert—

"(6)   In determining for the purposes of this regulation whether the lawfulness principle in Article 5(1)(a) of the GDPR would be contravened by the disclosure of information, Article 6(1) of the GDPR (lawfulness) is to be read as if the second sub-paragraph (disapplying the legitimate interests gateway in relation to public authorities) were omitted."

308   In regulation 14 (refusal to disclose information), in paragraph (3)(b), for "regulations 13(2)(a)(ii) or 13(3)" substitute "regulation 13(1)(b) or (5A)".

309   In regulation 18 (enforcement and appeal provisions), in paragraph (5), for "regulation 13(5)" substitute "regulation 13(5A)".

Environmental Information (Scotland) Regulations 2004 (S.S.I. 2004/520)

310   The Environmental Information (Scotland) Regulations 2004 are amended as follows.

311 (1)   Regulation 2 (interpretation) is amended as follows.

(2)   In paragraph (1), at the appropriate places, insert—

""the data protection principles" means the principles set out in—
(a)   Article 5(1) of the GDPR, and
(b)   section 34(1) of the Data Protection Act 2018;";

""data subject" has the same meaning as in the Data Protection Act 2018 (see section 3 of that Act);";

""the GDPR" and references to a provision of Chapter 2 of Part 2 of the Data Protection Act 2018 have the same meaning as in Parts 5 to 7 of that Act (see section 3(10), (11) and (14) of that Act);";

""personal data" has the same meaning as in Parts 5 to 7 of the Data Protection Act 2018 (see section 3(2) and (14) of that Act);".

(3)   For paragraph (3) substitute—

"(3A)   In these Regulations, references to the Data Protection Act 2018 have effect as if in Chapter 3 of Part 2 of that Act (other general processing)—
(a)   the references to an FOI public authority were references to a Scottish public authority as defined in these Regulations, and
(b)   the references to personal data held by such an authority were to be interpreted in accordance with paragraph (2) of this regulation."

312 (1)   Regulation 11 (personal data) is amended as follows.

(2)   For paragraph (2) substitute—

"(2)   To the extent that environmental information requested includes personal data of which the applicant is not the data subject, a Scottish public authority must not make the personal data available if—
(a)   the first condition set out in paragraph (3A) is satisfied, or

Data Protection Act 2018 (c. 12)
Schedule 19 — Minor and consequential amendments
Part 2 — Amendments of other legislation

281

(b)   the second or third condition set out in paragraph (3B) or (4A) is satisfied and, in all the circumstances of the case, the public interest in making the information available is outweighed by that in not doing so."

(3)   For paragraph (3) substitute—

"(3A)   The first condition is that the disclosure of the information to a member of the public otherwise than under these Regulations—

(a)   would contravene any of the data protection principles, or

(b)   would do so if the exemptions in section 24(1) of the Data Protection Act 2018 (manual unstructured data held by public authorities) were disregarded.

(3B)   The second condition is that the disclosure of the information to a member of the public otherwise than under these Regulations would contravene Article 21 of the GDPR (general processing: right to object to processing)."

(4)   For paragraph (4) substitute—

"(4A)   The third condition is that any of the following applies to the information—

(a)   it is exempt from the obligation under Article 15(1) of the GDPR (general processing: right of access by the data subject) to provide access to, and information about, personal data by virtue of provision made by or under section 15, 16 or 26 of, or Schedule 2, 3 or 4 to, the Data Protection Act 2018, or

(b)   on a request under section 45(1)(b) of that Act (law enforcement processing: right of access by the data subject), the information would be withheld in reliance on subsection (4) of that section."

(5)   Omit paragraph (5).

(6)   After paragraph (6) insert—

"(7)   In determining, for the purposes of this regulation, whether the lawfulness principle in Article 5(1)(a) of the GDPR would be contravened by the disclosure of information, Article 6(1) of the GDPR (lawfulness) is to be read as if the second sub-paragraph (disapplying the legitimate interests gateway in relation to public authorities) were omitted."

Licensing Act 2003 (Personal Licences) Regulations 2005 (S.I. 2005/41)

313   (1)   Regulation 7 of the Licensing Act 2003 (Personal Licences) Regulations 2005 (application for grant of a personal licence) is amended as follows.

(2)   In paragraph (1)(b)—

(a)   for paragraph (iii) (but not the final ", and") substitute—

"(iii)   the results of a request made under Article 15 of the GDPR or section 45 of the Data Protection Act 2018 (rights of access by the data subject) to the National Identification Service for information contained in the Police National Computer", and

(b)   in the words following paragraph (iii), omit "search".

282   *Data Protection Act 2018 (c. 12)*
Schedule 19 – Minor and consequential amendments
Part 2 – Amendments of other legislation

(3) After paragraph (2) insert—

> "(3)   In this regulation, "the GDPR" has the same meaning as in Parts 5 to 7 of the Data Protection Act 2018 (see section 3(10), (11) and (14) of that Act)."

Education (Pupil Information) (England) Regulations 2005 (S.I. 2005/1437)

314   The Education (Pupil Information) (England) Regulations 2005 are amended as follows.

315   In regulation 3(5) (meaning of educational record) for "section 1(1) of the Data Protection Act 1998" substitute "section 3(4) of the Data Protection Act 2018".

316 (1) Regulation 5 (disclosure of curricular and educational records) is amended as follows.

(2) In paragraph (4)—
  (a)   in sub-paragraph (a), for "the Data Protection Act 1998" substitute "the GDPR", and
  (b)   in sub-paragraph (b), for "that Act or by virtue of any order made under section 30(2) or section 38(1) of the Act" substitute "the GDPR".

(3) After paragraph (6) insert—

> "(7)   In this regulation, "the GDPR" means Regulation (EU) 2016/679 of the European Parliament and of the Council of 27 April 2016 on the protection of natural persons with regard to the processing of personal data and on the free movement of such data (General Data Protection Regulation), read with Chapter 2 of Part 2 of the Data Protection Act 2018."

Civil Contingencies Act 2004 (Contingency Planning) Regulations 2005 (S.I. 2005/2042)

317 (1) Regulation 45 of the Civil Contingencies Act 2004 (Contingency Planning) Regulations 2005 (sensitive information) is amended as follows.

(2) In paragraph (1)(d)—
  (a)   omit ", within the meaning of section 1(1) of the Data Protection Act 1998", and
  (b)   for "(2) or (3)" substitute "(1A), (1B) or (1C)".

(3) After paragraph (1) insert—

> "(1A) The condition in this paragraph is that the disclosure of the information to a member of the public—
>   (a)   would contravene any of the data protection principles, or
>   (b)   would do so if the exemptions in section 24(1) of the Data Protection Act 2018 (manual unstructured data held by public authorities) were disregarded.
>
> (1B)   The condition in this paragraph is that the disclosure of the information to a member of the public would contravene—
>   (a)   Article 21 of the GDPR (general processing: right to object to processing), or

Data Protection Act 2018 (c. 12)   283
Schedule 19 — Minor and consequential amendments
Part 2 — Amendments of other legislation

(b)   section 99 of the Data Protection Act 2018 (intelligence services processing: right to object to processing).

(1C)   The condition in this paragraph is that—

(a)   on a request under Article 15(1) of the GDPR (general processing: right of access by the data subject) for access to personal data, the information would be withheld in reliance on provision made by or under section 15, 16 or 26 of, or Schedule 2, 3 or 4 to, the Data Protection Act 2018,

(b)   on a request under section 45(1)(b) of that Act (law enforcement processing: right of access by the data subject), the information would be withheld in reliance on subsection (4) of that section, or

(c)   on a request under section 94(1)(b) of that Act (intelligence services processing: rights of access by the data subject), the information would be withheld in reliance on a provision of Chapter 6 of Part 4 of that Act.

(1D)   In this regulation—

"the data protection principles" means the principles set out in—

(a)   Article 5(1) of the GDPR,

(b)   section 34(1) of the Data Protection Act 2018, and

(c)   section 85(1) of that Act;

"the GDPR" and references to a provision of Chapter 2 of Part 2 of the Data Protection Act 2018 have the same meaning as in Parts 5 to 7 of that Act (see section 3(10), (11) and (14) of that Act);

"personal data" has the same meaning as in Parts 5 to 7 of the Data Protection Act 2018 (see section 3(2) and (14) of that Act)."

(1E)   In determining for the purposes of this regulation whether the lawfulness principle in Article 5(1)(a) of the GDPR would be contravened by the disclosure of information, Article 6(1) of the GDPR (lawfulness) is to be read as if the second sub-paragraph (disapplying the legitimate interests gateway in relation to public authorities) were omitted."

(4) Omit paragraphs (2) to (4).

Register of Judgments, Orders and Fines Regulations 2005 (S.I. 2005/3595)

318   In regulation 3 of the Register of Judgments, Orders and Fines Regulations 2005 (interpretation)—

(a)   for the definition of "data protection principles" substitute—

""data protection principles" means the principles set out in Article 5(1) of the GDPR;", and

(b)   at the appropriate place insert—

""the GDPR" has the same meaning as in Parts 5 to 7 of the Data Protection Act 2018 (see section 3(10), (11) and (14) of that Act);".

284

Data Protection Act 2018 (c. 12)
Schedule 19 — Minor and consequential amendments
Part 2 — Amendments of other legislation

Civil Contingencies Act 2004 (Contingency Planning) (Scotland) Regulations 2005 (S.S.I. 2005/494)

319   The Civil Contingencies Act 2004 (Contingency Planning) (Scotland) Regulations 2005 are amended as follows.

320 (1) Regulation 39 (sensitive information) is amended as follows.

      (2) In paragraph (1)(d) —

        (a) omit ", within the meaning of section 1(1) of the Data Protection Act 1998", and

        (b) for "(2) or (3)" substitute "(1A), (1B) or (1C)".

      (3) After paragraph (1) insert —

    "(1A) The condition in this paragraph is that the disclosure of the information to a member of the public —

        (a) would contravene any of the data protection principles, or

        (b) would do so if the exemptions in section 24(1) of the Data Protection Act 2018 (manual unstructured data held by public authorities) were disregarded.

    (1B) The condition in this paragraph is that the disclosure of the information to a member of the public would contravene —

        (a) Article 21 of the GDPR (general processing: right to object to processing), or

        (b) section 99 of the Data Protection Act 2018 (intelligence services processing: right to object to processing).

    (1C) The condition in this paragraph is that —

        (a) on a request under Article 15(1) of the GDPR (general processing: right of access by the data subject) for access to personal data, the information would be withheld in reliance on provision made by or under section 15, 16 or 26 of, or Schedule 2, 3 or 4 to, the Data Protection Act 2018,

        (b) on a request under section 45(1)(b) of that Act (law enforcement processing: right of access by the data subject), the information would be withheld in reliance on subsection (4) of that section, or

        (c) on a request under section 94(1)(b) of that Act (intelligence services processing: rights of access by the data subject), the information would be withheld in reliance on a provision of Chapter 6 of Part 4 of that Act.

    (1D) In this regulation —

      "the data protection principles" means the principles set out in —

        (a) Article 5(1) of the GDPR,

        (b) section 34(1) of the Data Protection Act 2018, and

        (c) section 85(1) of that Act;

      "data subject" has the same meaning as in the Data Protection Act 2018 (see section 3 of that Act);

      "the GDPR" and references to a provision of Chapter 2 of Part 2 of the Data Protection Act 2018 have the same meaning as in

Data Protection Act 2018 (c. 12)
Schedule 19 — Minor and consequential amendments
Part 2 — Amendments of other legislation

285

Parts 5 to 7 of that Act (see section 3(10), (11) and (14) of that Act);

"personal data" has the same meaning as in Parts 5 to 7 of the Data Protection Act 2018 (see section 3(2) and (14) of that Act).

(1E) In determining for the purposes of this regulation whether the lawfulness principle in Article 5(1)(a) of the GDPR would be contravened by the disclosure of information, Article 6(1) of the GDPR (lawfulness) is to be read as if the second sub-paragraph (disapplying the legitimate interests gateway in relation to public authorities) were omitted."

(4) Omit paragraphs (2) to (4).

Data Protection (Processing of Sensitive Personal Data) Order 2006 (S.I. 2006/2068)

321 The Data Protection (Processing of Sensitive Personal Data) Order 2006 is revoked.

National Assembly for Wales (Representation of the People) Order 2007 (S.I. 2007/236)

322 (1) Paragraph 14 of Schedule 1 to the National Assembly for Wales (Representation of the People) Order 2007 (absent voting at Assembly elections: conditions on the use, supply and inspection of absent vote records or lists) is amended as follows.

(2) The existing text becomes sub-paragraph (1).

(3) For paragraph (a) of that sub-paragraph (but not the final "or") substitute —

"(a) purposes mentioned in Article 89(1) of the GDPR (archiving in the public interest, scientific or historical research and statistics);".

(4) After that sub-paragraph insert —

"(2) In this paragraph, "the GDPR" means Regulation (EU) 2016/679 of the European Parliament and of the Council of 27 April 2016 on the protection of natural persons with regard to the processing of personal data and on the free movement of such data (General Data Protection Regulation)."

Mental Capacity Act 2005 (Loss of Capacity during Research Project) (England) Regulations 2007 (S.I. 2007/679)

323 In regulation 3 of the Mental Capacity Act 2005 (Loss of Capacity during Research Project) (England) Regulations 2007 (research which may be carried out despite a participant's loss of capacity), for paragraph (b) substitute —

"(b) any material used consists of or includes human cells or human DNA,".

National Assembly for Wales Commission (Crown Status) Order 2007 (S.I. 2007/1118)

324 For article 5 of the National Assembly for Wales Commission (Crown Status)

286

Data Protection Act 2018 (c. 12)
Schedule 19 — Minor and consequential amendments
Part 2 — Amendments of other legislation

Order 2007 substitute —

"5 Data Protection Act 2018

(1) The Assembly Commission is to be treated as a Crown body for the purposes of the Data Protection Act 2018 to the extent specified in this article.

(2) The Assembly Commission is to be treated as a government department for the purposes of the following provisions —

(a) section 8(d) (lawfulness of processing under the GDPR: public interest etc),

(b) section 209 (application to the Crown),

(c) paragraph 6 of Schedule 1 (statutory etc and government purposes),

(d) paragraph 7 of Schedule 2 (exemptions from the GDPR: functions designed to protect the public etc), and

(e) paragraph 8(1)(o) of Schedule 3 (exemptions from the GDPR: health data).

(3) In the provisions mentioned in paragraph (4) —

(a) references to employment by or under the Crown are to be treated as including employment as a member of staff of the Assembly Commission, and

(b) references to a person in the service of the Crown are to be treated as including a person so employed.

(4) The provisions are —

(a) section 24(3) (exemption for certain data relating to employment under the Crown), and

(b) section 209(6) (application of certain provisions to a person in the service of the Crown).

(5) In this article, references to a provision of Chapter 2 of Part 2 of the Data Protection Act 2018 have the same meaning as in Parts 5 to 7 of that Act (see section 3(14) of that Act)."

Mental Capacity Act 2005 (Loss of Capacity during Research Project) (Wales) Regulations 2007 (S.I. 2007/837 (W.72))

325 In regulation 3 of the Mental Capacity Act 2005 (Loss of Capacity during Research Project) (Wales) Regulations 2007 (research which may be carried out despite a participant's loss of capacity) —

(a) in the English language text, for paragraph (c) substitute —

"(c) any material used consists of or includes human cells or human DNA; and", and

(b) in the Welsh language text, for paragraph (c) substitute —

"(c) os yw unrhyw ddeunydd a ddefnyddir yn gelloedd dynol neu'n DNA dynol neu yn eu cynnwys; ac".

Data Protection Act 2018 (c. 12)
Schedule 19 — Minor and consequential amendments
Part 2 — Amendments of other legislation

287

Representation of the People (Absent Voting at Local Elections) (Scotland) Regulations 2007 (S.S.I. 2007/170)

326 (1) Regulation 18 of the Representation of the People (Absent Voting at Local Elections) (Scotland) Regulations 2007 (conditions on the supply and inspection of absent voter records or lists) is amended as follows.

(2) In paragraph (1), for sub-paragraph (a) (but not the final "or") substitute —
"(a)   purposes mentioned in Article 89(1) of the GDPR (archiving in the public interest, scientific or historical research and statistics);".

(3) After paragraph (1) insert —
"(2)   In this regulation, "the GDPR" means Regulation (EU) 2016/679 of the European Parliament and of the Council of 27 April 2016 on the protection of natural persons with regard to the processing of personal data and on the free movement of such data (General Data Protection Regulation)."

Representation of the People (Post-Local Government Elections Supply and Inspection of Documents) (Scotland) Regulations 2007 (S.S.I. 2007/264)

327   In regulation 5 of the Representation of the People (Post-Local Government Elections Supply and Inspection of Documents) (Scotland) Regulations 2007 (conditions on the use, supply and disclosure of documents open to public inspection) —
(a)   in paragraph (2), for sub-paragraph (i) (but not the final "or") substitute —
"(i)   purposes mentioned in Article 89(1) of the GDPR (archiving in the public interest, scientific or historical research and statistics);", and
(b)   after paragraph (3) insert —
"(4)   In this regulation, "the GDPR" means Regulation (EU) 2016/679 of the European Parliament and of the Council of 27 April 2016 on the protection of natural persons with regard to the processing of personal data and on the free movement of such data (General Data Protection Regulation)."

Education (Pupil Records and Reporting) (Transitional) Regulations (Northern Ireland) 2007 (S.R. (N.I.) 2007 No. 43)

328   The Education (Pupil Records and Reporting) (Transitional) Regulations (Northern Ireland) 2007 are amended as follows.

329   In regulation 2 (interpretation), at the appropriate place insert —
""the GDPR" means Regulation (EU) 2016/679 of the European Parliament and of the Council of 27 April 2016 on the protection of natural persons with regard to the processing of personal data and on the free movement of such data (General Data Protection Regulation), read with Chapter 2 of Part 2 of the Data Protection Act 2018;".

288

Data Protection Act 2018 (c. 12)
Schedule 19 — Minor and consequential amendments
Part 2 — Amendments of other legislation

330   In regulation 10(2) (duties of Boards of Governors), for "documents which are the subject of an order under section 30(2) of the Data Protection Act 1998" substitute "information to which the pupil to whom the information relates would have no right of access under the GDPR".

Representation of the People (Northern Ireland) Regulations 2008 (S.I. 2008/1741)

331   In regulation 118 of the Representation of the People (Northern Ireland) Regulations 2008 (conditions on the use, supply and disclosure of documents open to public inspection) —

    (a)   in paragraph (2), for "research purposes within the meaning of that term in section 33 of the Data Protection Act 1998" substitute "purposes mentioned in Article 89(1) of the GDPR (archiving in the public interest, scientific or historical research and statistics)", and

    (b)   after paragraph (3) insert —

        "(4)   In this regulation, "the GDPR" means Regulation (EU) 2016/679 of the European Parliament and of the Council of 27 April 2016 on the protection of natural persons with regard to the processing of personal data and on the free movement of such data (General Data Protection Regulation)."

Companies Act 2006 (Extension of Takeover Panel Provisions) (Isle of Man) Order 2008 (S.I. 2008/3122)

332   In paragraph 1(c) of the Schedule to the Companies Act 2006 (Extension of Takeover Panel Provisions) (Isle of Man) Order 2008 (modifications with which Chapter 1 of Part 28 of the Companies Act 2006 extends to the Isle of Man), for "the Data Protection Act 1998 (c 29)" substitute "the data protection legislation".

Controlled Drugs (Supervision of Management and Use) (Wales) Regulations 2008 (S.I. 2008/3239 (W.286))

333   The Controlled Drugs (Supervision of Management and Use) (Wales) Regulations 2008 are amended as follows.

334   In regulation 2(1) (interpretation) —

    (a)   at the appropriate place in the English language text insert —

        ""the GDPR" ("*y GDPR*") and references to Schedule 2 to the Data Protection Act 2018 have the same meaning as in Parts 5 to 7 of that Act (see section 3(10), (11) and (14) of that Act);", and

    (b)   at the appropriate place in the Welsh language text insert —

        "mae i "y GDPR" a chyfeiriadau at Atodlen 2 i Ddeddf Diogelu Data 2018 yr un ystyr ag a roddir i "the GDPR" a chyfeiriadau at yr Atodlen honno yn Rhannau 5 i 7 o'r Ddeddf honno (gweler adran 3(10), (11) a (14) o'r Ddeddf honno);".

335 (1)   Regulation 25 (duty to co-operate by disclosing information as regards relevant persons) is amended as follows.

    (2)   In paragraph (7) —

Data Protection Act 2018 (c. 12)
Schedule 19 — Minor and consequential amendments
Part 2 — Amendments of other legislation

289

     (a)   in the English language text, at the end insert "or the GDPR", and

     (b)   in the Welsh language text, at the end insert "neu'r GDPR".

  (3) For paragraph (8) —

     (a)   in the English language text substitute —

> "(8)   In determining for the purposes of paragraph (7) whether disclosure is prohibited, it is to be assumed for the purposes of paragraph 5(2) of Schedule 2 to the Data Protection Act 2018 and paragraph 3(2) of Schedule 11 to that Act (exemptions from certain provisions of the data protection legislation: disclosures required by law) that the disclosure is required by this regulation.", and

     (b)   in the Welsh language text substitute —

> "(8)   Wrth benderfynu at ddibenion paragraff (7) a yw datgeliad wedi'i wahardd, mae i'w dybied at ddibenion paragraff 5(2) o Atodlen 2 i Ddeddf Diogelu Data 2018 a pharagraff 3(2) o Atodlen 11 i'r Ddeddf honno (esemptiadau rhag darpariaethau penodol o'r ddeddfwriaeth diogelu data: datgeliadau sy'n ofynnol gan y gyfraith) bod y datgeliad yn ofynnol gan y rheoliad hwn."

336 (1) Regulation 26 (responsible bodies requesting additional information be disclosed about relevant persons) is amended as follows.

  (2) In paragraph (6) —

     (a)   in the English language text, at the end insert "or the GDPR", and

     (b)   in the Welsh language text, at the end insert "neu'r GDPR".

  (3) For paragraph (7) —

     (a)   in the English language text substitute —

> "(7)   In determining for the purposes of paragraph (6) whether disclosure is prohibited, it is to be assumed for the purposes of paragraph 5(2) of Schedule 2 to the Data Protection Act 2018 and paragraph 3(2) of Schedule 11 to that Act (exemptions from certain provisions of the data protection legislation: disclosures required by law) that the disclosure is required by this regulation.", and

     (b)   in the Welsh language text substitute —

> "(7)   Wrth benderfynu at ddibenion paragraff (6) a yw datgeliad wedi'i wahardd, mae i'w dybied at ddibenion paragraff 5(2) o Atodlen 2 i Ddeddf Diogelu Data 2018 a pharagraff 3(2) o Atodlen 11 i'r Ddeddf honno (esemptiadau rhag darpariaethau penodol o'r ddeddfwriaeth diogelu data: datgeliadau sy'n ofynnol gan y gyfraith) bod y datgeliad yn ofynnol gan y rheoliad hwn."

337 (1) Regulation 29 (occurrence reports) is amended as follows.

  (2) In paragraph (3) —

     (a)   in the English language text, at the end insert "or the GDPR", and

     (b)   in the Welsh language text, at the end insert "neu'r GDPR".

  (3) For paragraph (4) —

290

Data Protection Act 2018 (c. 12)
Schedule 19 — Minor and consequential amendments
Part 2 — Amendments of other legislation

    (a)   in the English language text substitute—

> "(4)   In determining for the purposes of paragraph (3) whether disclosure is prohibited, it is to be assumed for the purposes of paragraph 5(2) of Schedule 2 to the Data Protection Act 2018 and paragraph 3(2) of Schedule 11 to that Act (exemptions from certain provisions of the data protection legislation: disclosures required by law) that the disclosure is required by this regulation.", and

    (b)   in the Welsh language text substitute—

> "(4)   Wrth benderfynu at ddibenion paragraff (3) a yw datgeliad wedi'i wahardd, mae i'w dybied at ddibenion paragraff 5(2) o Atodlen 2 i Ddeddf Diogelu Data 2018 a pharagraff 3(2) o Atodlen 11 i'r Ddeddf honno (esemptiadau rhag darpariaethau penodol o'r ddeddfwriaeth diogelu data: datgeliadau sy'n ofynnol gan y gyfraith) bod y datgeliad yn ofynnol gan y rheoliad hwn."

Energy Order 2003 (Supply of Information) Regulations (Northern Ireland) 2008 (S.R. (N.I.) 2008 No. 3)

338 (1) Regulation 5 of the Energy Order 2003 (Supply of Information) Regulations (Northern Ireland) 2008 (information whose disclosure would be affected by the application of other legislation) is amended as follows.

    (2) In paragraph (3)—
        (a)   omit "within the meaning of section 1(1) of the Data Protection Act 1998", and
        (b)   for the words from "where" to the end substitute "if the condition in paragraph (3A) or (3B) is satisfied".

    (3) After paragraph (3) insert—

> "(3A)   The condition in this paragraph is that the disclosure of the information to a member of the public—
>   (a)   would contravene any of the data protection principles, or
>   (b)   would do so if the exemptions in section 24(1) of the Data Protection Act 2018 (manual unstructured data held by public authorities) were disregarded.

> (3B)   The condition in this paragraph is that the disclosure of the information to a member of the public would contravene—
>   (a)   Article 21 of the GDPR (general processing: right to object to processing), or
>   (b)   section 99 of the Data Protection Act 2018 (intelligence services processing: right to object to processing)."

    (4) After paragraph (4) insert—

> "(5)   In this regulation—
>   "the data protection principles" means the principles set out in—
>   (a)   Article 5(1) of the GDPR,
>   (b)   section 34(1) of the Data Protection Act 2018, and
>   (c)   section 85(1) of that Act;

Data Protection Act 2018 (c. 12)
Schedule 19 – Minor and consequential amendments
Part 2 – Amendments of other legislation

291

"the GDPR" has the same meaning as in Parts 5 to 7 of the Data Protection Act 2018 (see section 3(10), (11) and (14) of that Act);

"personal data" has the same meaning as in Parts 5 to 7 of the Data Protection Act 2018 (see section 3(2) and (14) of that Act)."

Companies (Disclosure of Address) Regulations 2009 (S.I. 2009/214)

339 (1) Paragraph 6 of Schedule 2 to the Companies (Disclosure of Address) Regulations 2009 (conditions for permitted disclosure to a credit reference agency) is amended as follows.

(2) The existing text becomes sub-paragraph (1).

(3) In paragraph (b) of that sub-paragraph, for sub-paragraph (ii) substitute—

"(ii)   for the purposes of ensuring that it complies with its data protection obligations;".

(4) In paragraph (c) of that sub-paragraph—

(a)   omit "or" at the end of sub-paragraph (i), and

(b)   at the end insert "; or

(iii)   section 144 of the Data Protection Act 2018 (false statements made in response to an information notice) or section 148 of that Act (destroying or falsifying information and documents etc);".

(5) After paragraph (c) of that sub-paragraph insert—

"(d)   has not been given a penalty notice under section 155 of the Data Protection Act 2018 in circumstances described in paragraph (c)(ii), other than a penalty notice that has been cancelled."

(6) After sub-paragraph (1) insert—

"(2)   In this paragraph, "data protection obligations", in relation to a credit reference agency, means—

(a)   where the agency carries on business in the United Kingdom, obligations under the data protection legislation (as defined in section 3 of the Data Protection Act 2018);

(b)   where the agency carries on business in a EEA State other than the United Kingdom, obligations under—

(i)   the GDPR (as defined in section 3(10) of the Data Protection Act 2018),

(ii)   legislation made in exercise of powers conferred on member States under the GDPR (as so defined), and

(iii)   legislation implementing the Law Enforcement Directive (as defined in section 3(12) of the Data Protection Act 2018)."

292

Data Protection Act 2018 (c. 12)
Schedule 19 — Minor and consequential amendments
Part 2 — Amendments of other legislation

Overseas Companies Regulations 2009 (S.I. 2009/1801)

340 (1) Paragraph 6 of Schedule 2 to the Overseas Companies Regulations 2009 (conditions for permitted disclosure to a credit reference agency) is amended as follows.

(2) The existing text becomes sub-paragraph (1).

(3) In paragraph (b) of that sub-paragraph, for sub-paragraph (ii) substitute —

"(ii) for the purposes of ensuring that it complies with its data protection obligations;".

(4) In paragraph (c) of that sub-paragraph —

(a) omit "or" at the end of sub-paragraph (i), and

(b) at the end insert "; or

(iii) section 144 of the Data Protection Act 2018 (false statements made in response to an information notice) or section 148 of that Act (destroying or falsifying information and documents etc);".

(5) After paragraph (c) of that sub-paragraph insert —

"(d) has not been given a penalty notice under section 155 of the Data Protection Act 2018 in circumstances described in paragraph (c)(ii), other than a penalty notice that has been cancelled."

(6) After sub-paragraph (1) insert —

"(2) In this paragraph, "data protection obligations", in relation to a credit reference agency, means —

(a) where the agency carries on business in the United Kingdom, obligations under the data protection legislation (as defined in section 3 of the Data Protection Act 2018);

(b) where the agency carries on business in a EEA State other than the United Kingdom, obligations under —

(i) the GDPR (as defined in section 3(10) of the Data Protection Act 2018),

(ii) legislation made in exercise of powers conferred on member States under the GDPR (as so defined), and

(iii) legislation implementing the Law Enforcement Directive (as defined in section 3(12) of the Data Protection Act 2018)."

Data Protection (Processing of Sensitive Personal Data) Order 2009 (S.I. 2009/1811)

341   The Data Protection (Processing of Sensitive Personal Data) Order 2009 is revoked.

Provision of Services Regulations 2009 (S.I. 2009/2999)

342   In regulation 25 of the Provision of Services Regulations 2009 (derogations

Data Protection Act 2018 (c. 12) 293
Schedule 19 — Minor and consequential amendments
Part 2 — Amendments of other legislation

from the freedom to provide services), for paragraph (d) substitute—

> "(d) matters covered by Regulation (EU) 2016/679 of the European Parliament and of the Council of 27 April 2016 on the protection of natural persons with regard to the processing of personal data and on the free movement of such data (General Data Protection Regulation);".

INSPIRE Regulations 2009 (S.I. 2009/3157)

343 (1) Regulation 9 of the INSPIRE Regulations 2009 (public access to spatial data sets and spatial data services) is amended as follows.

    (2) In paragraph (2)—

        (a) omit "or" at the end of sub-paragraph (a),

        (b) for sub-paragraph (b) substitute—

> "(b) Article 21 of the GDPR (general processing: right to object to processing), or
>
> (c) section 99 of the Data Protection Act 2018 (intelligence services processing: right to object to processing).",

        and

        (c) omit the words following sub-paragraph (b).

    (3) After paragraph (7) insert—

> "(8) In this regulation—
>
> "the data protection principles" means the principles set out in—
>
> (a) Article 5(1) of the GDPR,
>
> (b) section 34(1) of the Data Protection Act 2018, and
>
> (c) section 85(1) of that Act;
>
> "the GDPR" has the same meaning as in Parts 5 to 7 of the Data Protection Act 2018 (see section 3(10), (11) and (14) of that Act);
>
> "personal data" has the same meaning as in Parts 5 to 7 of the Data Protection Act 2018 (see section 3(2) and (14) of that Act).
>
> (9) In determining for the purposes of this regulation whether the lawfulness principle in Article 5(1)(a) of the GDPR would be contravened by the disclosure of information, Article 6(1) of the GDPR (lawfulness) is to be read as if the second sub-paragraph (disapplying the legitimate interests gateway in relation to public authorities) were omitted."

INSPIRE (Scotland) Regulations 2009 (S.S.I. 2009/440)

344 (1) Regulation 10 of the INSPIRE (Scotland) Regulations 2009 (public access to spatial data sets and spatial data services) is amended as follows.

    (2) In paragraph (2)—

        (a) omit "or" at the end of sub-paragraph (a),

        (b) for sub-paragraph (b) substitute—

> "(b) Article 21 of the GDPR (general processing: right to object to processing), or

294   *Data Protection Act 2018 (c. 12)*
Schedule 19 — Minor and consequential amendments
Part 2 — Amendments of other legislation

    (c) section 99 of the Data Protection Act 2018 (intelligence services processing: right to object to processing).",
    and

  (c) omit the words following sub-paragraph (b).

 (3) After paragraph (6) insert—

  "(7) In this regulation—

    "the data protection principles" means the principles set out in—

     (a) Article 5(1) of the GDPR,

     (b) section 34(1) of the Data Protection Act 2018, and

     (c) section 85(1) of that Act;

    "the GDPR" has the same meaning as in Parts 5 to 7 of the Data Protection Act 2018 (see section 3(10), (11) and (14) of that Act);

    "personal data" has the same meaning as in Parts 5 to 7 of the Data Protection Act 2018 (see section 3(2) and (14) of that Act).

  (8) In determining for the purposes of this regulation whether the lawfulness principle in Article 5(1)(a) of the GDPR would be contravened by the disclosure of information, Article 6(1) of the GDPR (lawfulness) is to be read as if the second sub-paragraph (disapplying the legitimate interests gateway in relation to public authorities) were omitted."

Controlled Drugs (Supervision of Management and Use) Regulations (Northern Ireland) 2009 (S.R (N.I.) 2009 No. 225)

345 The Controlled Drugs (Supervision of Management and Use) Regulations (Northern Ireland) 2009 are amended as follows.

346 In regulation 2(2) (interpretation), at the appropriate place insert—

    ""the GDPR" and references to Schedule 2 to the Data Protection Act 2018 have the same meaning as in Parts 5 to 7 of that Act (see section 3(10), (11) and (14) of that Act);"."

347 (1) Regulation 25 (duty to co-operate by disclosing information as regards relevant persons) is amended as follows.

 (2) In paragraph (7), at the end insert "or the GDPR".

 (3) For paragraph (8) substitute—

  "(8) In determining for the purposes of paragraph (7) whether disclosure is prohibited, it is to be assumed for the purposes of paragraph 5(2) of Schedule 2 to the Data Protection Act 2018 and paragraph 3(2) of Schedule 11 to that Act (exemptions from certain provisions of the data protection legislation: disclosures required by law) that the disclosure is required by this regulation."

348 (1) Regulation 26 (responsible bodies requesting additional information be disclosed about relevant persons) is amended as follows.

 (2) In paragraph (6), at the end insert "or the GDPR".

Data Protection Act 2018 (c. 12)
Schedule 19 — Minor and consequential amendments
Part 2 — Amendments of other legislation

295

(3) For paragraph (7) substitute—

"(7)   In determining for the purposes of paragraph (6) whether disclosure is prohibited, it is to be assumed for the purposes of paragraph 5(2) of Schedule 2 to the Data Protection Act 2018 and paragraph 3(2) of Schedule 11 to that Act (exemptions from certain provisions of the data protection legislation: disclosures required by law) that the disclosure is required by this regulation."

349 (1) Regulation 29 (occurrence reports) is amended as follows.

(2) In paragraph (3), at the end insert "or the GDPR".

(3) For paragraph (4) substitute—

"(4)   In determining for the purposes of paragraph (3) whether disclosure is prohibited, it is to be assumed for the purposes of paragraph 5(2) of Schedule 2 to the Data Protection Act 2018 and paragraph 3(2) of Schedule 11 to that Act (exemptions from certain provisions of the data protection legislation: disclosures required by law) that the disclosure is required by this regulation."

Data Protection (Monetary Penalties) (Maximum Penalty and Notices) Regulations 2010 (S.I. 2010/31)

350   The Data Protection (Monetary Penalties) (Maximum Penalty and Notices) Regulations 2010 are revoked.

Pharmacy Order 2010 (S.I. 2010/231)

351   The Pharmacy Order 2010 is amended as follows.

352   In article 3(1) (interpretation), omit the definition of "Directive 95/46/EC".

353 (1) Article 9 (inspection and enforcement) is amended as follows.

(2) For paragraph (4) substitute—

"(4)   If a report that the Council proposes to publish pursuant to paragraph (3) includes personal data, it is to be assumed for the purposes of paragraph 5(2) of Schedule 2 to the Data Protection Act 2018 and paragraph 3(2) of Schedule 11 to that Act (exemptions from certain provisions of the data protection legislation: disclosures required by law) that the disclosure of the personal data is required by paragraph (3) of this article."

(3) After paragraph (4) insert—

"(5)   In this article, "personal data" and references to Schedule 2 to the Data Protection Act 2018 have the same meaning as in Parts 5 to 7 of that Act (see section 3(2) and (14) of that Act)."

354   In article 33A (European professional card), after paragraph (2) insert—

"(3)   In Schedule 2A, "the GDPR" means Regulation (EU) 2016/679 of the European Parliament and of the Council of 27 April 2016 on the protection of natural persons with regard to the processing of personal data and on the free movement of such data (General Data

296

Data Protection Act 2018 (c. 12)
Schedule 19 — Minor and consequential amendments
Part 2 — Amendments of other legislation

Protection Regulation), read with Chapter 2 of Part 2 of the Data Protection Act 2018."

355 (1) Article 49 (disclosure of information: general) is amended as follows.

(2) In paragraph (2)(a), after "enactment" insert "or the GDPR".

(3) For paragraph (3) substitute —

"(3) In determining for the purposes of paragraph (2)(a) whether a disclosure is prohibited, it is to be assumed for the purposes of paragraph 5(2) of Schedule 2 to the Data Protection Act 2018 and paragraph 3(2) of Schedule 11 to that Act (exemptions from certain provisions of the data protection legislation: disclosures required by law) that the disclosure is required by paragraph (1) of this article."

(4) After paragraph (5) insert —

"(6) In this article, "the GDPR" and references to Schedule 2 to the Data Protection Act 2018 have the same meaning as in Parts 5 to 7 of that Act (see section 3(10), (11) and (14) of that Act)."

356 (1) Article 55 (professional performance assessments) is amended as follows.

(2) In paragraph (5)(a), after "enactment" insert "or the GDPR".

(3) For paragraph (6) substitute —

"(6) In determining for the purposes of paragraph (5)(a) whether a disclosure is prohibited, it is to be assumed for the purposes of paragraph 5(2) of Schedule 2 to the Data Protection Act 2018 and paragraph 3(2) of Schedule 11 to that Act (exemptions from certain provisions of the data protection legislation: disclosures required by law) that the disclosure is required by paragraph (4) of this article."

(4) After paragraph (8) insert —

"(9) In this article, "the GDPR" and references to Schedule 2 to the Data Protection Act 2018 have the same meaning as in Parts 5 to 7 of that Act (see section 3(10), (11) and (14) of that Act)."

357 In article 67(6) (Directive 2005/36/EC: designation of competent authority etc.), after sub-paragraph (a) insert —

"(aa) "the GDPR" means Regulation (EU) 2016/679 of the European Parliament and of the Council of 27 April 2016 on the protection of natural persons with regard to the processing of personal data and on the free movement of such data (General Data Protection Regulation), read with Chapter 2 of Part 2 of the Data Protection Act 2018;".

358 (1) Schedule 2A (Directive 2005/36/EC: European professional card) is amended as follows.

(2) In paragraph 8(1) (access to data), for "Directive 95/46/EC" substitute "the GDPR".

(3) In paragraph 9 (processing data) —

Data Protection Act 2018 (c. 12)   297
Schedule 19 – Minor and consequential amendments
Part 2 – Amendments of other legislation

(a)   omit sub-paragraph (2) (deeming the Council to be the controller for the purposes of Directive 95/46/EC), and

(b)   after sub-paragraph (2) insert—

"(3)   In this paragraph, "personal data" has the same meaning as in the Data Protection Act 2018 (see section 3(2) of that Act)."

359   (1)   The table in Schedule 3 (Directive 2005/36/EC: designation of competent authority etc.) is amended as follows.

(2)   In the entry for Article 56(2), in the second column, for "Directive 95/46/EC" substitute "the GDPR".

(3)   In the entry for Article 56a(4), in the second column, for "Directive 95/46/ EC" substitute "the GDPR".

Data Protection (Monetary Penalties) Order 2010 (S.I. 2010/910)

360   The Data Protection (Monetary Penalties) Order 2010 is revoked.

National Employment Savings Trust Order 2010 (S.I. 2010/917)

361   The National Employment Savings Trust Order 2010 is amended as follows.

362   In article 2 (interpretation)—
(a)   omit the definition of "data" and "personal data", and
(b)   at the appropriate place insert—
""personal data" has the same meaning as in Parts 5 to 7 of the Data Protection Act 2018 (see section 3(2) and (14) of that Act)."

363   (1)   Article 10 (disclosure of requested data to the Secretary of State) is amended as follows.

(2)   In paragraph (1)—
(a)   for "disclosure of data" substitute "disclosure of information", and
(b)   for "requested data" substitute "requested information".

(3)   In paragraph (2)—
(a)   for "requested data" substitute "requested information",
(b)   for "those data are" substitute "the information is", and
(c)   for "receive those data" substitute "receive that information".

(4)   In paragraph (3), for "requested data" substitute "requested information".

(5)   In paragraph (4), for "requested data" substitute "requested information".

Local Elections (Northern Ireland) Order 2010 (S.I. 2010/2977)

364   (1)   Schedule 3 to the Local Elections (Northern Ireland) Order 2010 (access to marked registers and other documents open to public inspection after an election) is amended as follows.

(2)   In paragraph 1(1) (interpretation and general)—
(a)   omit the definition of "research purposes", and

298   *Data Protection Act 2018 (c. 12)*
Schedule 19 — Minor and consequential amendments
Part 2 — Amendments of other legislation

(b)   at the appropriate places insert—

> ""Article 89 GDPR purposes" means the purposes mentioned in Article 89(1) of the GDPR (archiving in the public interest, scientific or historical research and statistics);";
>
> ""the GDPR" means Regulation (EU) 2016/679 of the European Parliament and of the Council of 27 April 2016 on the protection of natural persons with regard to the processing of personal data and on the free movement of such data (General Data Protection Regulation);".

(3)   In paragraph 5(3) (restrictions on the use, supply and disclosure of documents open to public inspection), for "research purposes" substitute "Article 89 GDPR purposes".

Pupil Information (Wales) Regulations 2011 (S.I. 2011/1942 (W.209))

365   (1)   Regulation 5 of the Pupil Information (Wales) Regulations 2011 (duties of head teacher - educational records) is amended as follows.

(2)   In paragraph (5)—

(a)   in the English language text, for "documents which are subject to any order under section 30(2) of the Data Protection Act 1998" substitute "information—

> (a)   which the head teacher could not lawfully disclose to the pupil under the GDPR, or
>
> (b)   to which the pupil would have no right of access under the GDPR.", and

(b)   in the Welsh language text, for "ddogfennau sy'n ddarostyngedig i unrhyw orchymyn o dan adran 30(2) o Ddeddf Diogelu Data 1998" substitute "wybodaeth—

> (a)   na allai'r pennaeth ei datgelu'n gyfreithlon i'r disgybl o dan y GDPR, neu
>
> (b)   na fyddai gan y disgybl hawl mynediad ati o dan y GDPR."

(3)   After paragraph (5)—

(a)   in the English language text insert—

> "(6)   In this regulation, "the GDPR" ("*y GDPR*") means Regulation (EU) 2016/679 of the European Parliament and of the Council of 27 April 2016 on the protection of natural persons with regard to the processing of personal data and on the free movement of such data (General Data Protection Regulation), read with Chapter 2 of Part 2 of the Data Protection Act 2018.", and

(b)   in the Welsh language text insert—

> "(6)   Yn y rheoliad hwn, ystyr "y GDPR" ("*the GDPR*") yw Rheoliad (EU) 2016/679 Senedd Ewrop a'r Cyngor dyddiedig 27 Ebrill 2016 ar ddiogelu personau naturiol o ran prosesu data personol a rhyddid symud data o'r fath (y Rheoliad Diogelu Data Cyffredinol), fel y'i darllenir ynghyd â Phennod 2 o Ran 2 o Ddeddf Diogelu Data 2018."

Data Protection Act 2018 (c. 12)
Schedule 19 — Minor and consequential amendments
Part 2 — Amendments of other legislation

299

Debt Arrangement Scheme (Scotland) Regulations 2011 (S.S.I. 2011/141)

366   In Schedule 4 to the Debt Arrangement Scheme (Scotland) Regulations 2011 (payments distributors), omit paragraph 2.

Police and Crime Commissioner Elections Order 2012 (S.I. 2012/1917)

367   The Police and Crime Commissioner Elections Order 2012 is amended as follows.

368 (1) Schedule 2 (absent voting in Police and Crime Commissioner elections) is amended as follows.

   (2) In paragraph 20 (absent voter lists: supply of copies etc) —
      (a)   in sub-paragraph (8), for paragraph (a) (but not the final "or") substitute —

               "(a)   purposes mentioned in Article 89(1) of the GDPR (archiving in the public interest, scientific or historical research and statistics);", and

      (b)   after sub-paragraph (10) insert —

               "(11) In this paragraph, "the GDPR" means Regulation (EU) 2016/679 of the European Parliament and of the Council of 27 April 2016 on the protection of natural persons with regard to the processing of personal data and on the free movement of such data (General Data Protection Regulation)."

   (3) In paragraph 24 (restriction on use of absent voter records or lists or the information contained in them) —
      (a)   in sub-paragraph (3), for paragraph (a) (but not the final "or") substitute —

               "(a)   purposes mentioned in Article 89(1) of the GDPR (archiving in the public interest, scientific or historical research and statistics),", and

      (b)   after that sub-paragraph insert —

               "(4)   In this paragraph, "the GDPR" means Regulation (EU) 2016/679 of the European Parliament and of the Council of 27 April 2016 on the protection of natural persons with regard to the processing of personal data and on the free movement of such data (General Data Protection Regulation)."

369 (1) Schedule 10 (access to marked registers and other documents open to public inspection after an election) is amended as follows.

   (2) In paragraph 1(2) (interpretation), omit paragraphs (c) and (d) (but not the final "and").

   (3) In paragraph 5 (restriction on use of documents or of information contained in them) —
      (a)   in sub-paragraph (3), for paragraph (a) (but not the final "or")

300   *Data Protection Act 2018 (c. 12)*
Schedule 19 — Minor and consequential amendments
Part 2 — Amendments of other legislation

substitute—

"(a)   purposes mentioned in Article 89(1) of the GDPR (archiving in the public interest, scientific or historical research and statistics),", and

(b)   after sub-paragraph (4) insert—

"(5)   In this paragraph, "the GDPR" means Regulation (EU) 2016/679 of the European Parliament and of the Council of 27 April 2016 on the protection of natural persons with regard to the processing of personal data and on the free movement of such data (General Data Protection Regulation)."

Data Protection (Processing of Sensitive Personal Data) Order 2012 (S.I. 2012/1978)

370   The Data Protection (Processing of Sensitive Personal Data) Order 2012 is revoked.

Neighbourhood Planning (Referendums) Regulations 2012 (S.I. 2012/2031)

371   Schedule 6 to the Neighbourhood Planning (Referendums) Regulations 2012 (registering to vote in a business referendum) is amended as follows.

372   (1)   Paragraph 29(1) (interpretation of Part 8) is amended as follows.

(2)   At the appropriate places insert—

""Article 89 GDPR purposes" means the purposes mentioned in Article 89(1) of the GDPR (archiving in the public interest, scientific or historical research and statistics);";

""the GDPR" means Regulation (EU) 2016/679 of the European Parliament and of the Council of 27 April 2016 on the protection of natural persons with regard to the processing of personal data and on the free movement of such data (General Data Protection Regulation);".

(3)   For the definition of "relevant conditions" substitute—

""relevant requirement" means the requirement under Article 89 of the GDPR, read with section 19 of the Data Protection Act 2018, that personal data processed for Article 89 GDPR purposes must be subject to appropriate safeguards;".

(4)   Omit the definition of "research purposes".

373   In paragraph 32(3)(b)(i), for "section 11(3) of the Data Protection Act 1998" substitute "section 122(5) of the Data Protection Act 2018".

374   In paragraph 33(6) and (7) (supply of copy of business voting register to the British Library and restrictions on use), for "research purposes in compliance with the relevant conditions" substitute "Article 89 GDPR purposes in accordance with the relevant requirement".

375   In paragraph 34(6) and (7) (supply of copy of business voting register to the Office of National Statistics and restrictions on use), for "research purposes in compliance with the relevant conditions" substitute "Article 89 GDPR purposes in accordance with the relevant requirement".

Data Protection Act 2018 (c. 12)
Schedule 19 — Minor and consequential amendments
Part 2 — Amendments of other legislation

301

376   In paragraph 39(8) and (97) (supply of copy of business voting register to public libraries and local authority archives services and restrictions on use), for "research purposes in compliance with the relevant conditions" substitute "Article 89 GDPR purposes in accordance with the relevant requirement".

377   In paragraph 45(2) (conditions on the use, supply and disclosure of documents open to public inspection), for paragraph (a) (but not the final "or") substitute—

"(a)   Article 89 GDPR purposes (as defined in paragraph 29),".

Controlled Drugs (Supervision of Management and Use) Regulations 2013 (S.I. 2013/373)

378 (1) Regulation 20 of the Controlled Drugs (Supervision of Management and Use) Regulations 2013 (information management) is amended as follows.

(2) For paragraph (4) substitute—

"(4)   Where a CDAO, a responsible body or someone acting on their behalf is permitted to share information which includes personal data by virtue of a function under these Regulations, it is to be assumed for the purposes of paragraph 5(2) of Schedule 2 to the Data Protection Act 2018 and paragraph 3(2) of Schedule 11 to that Act (exemptions from certain provisions of the data protection legislation: disclosures required by law) that the disclosure is required by this regulation."

(3) In paragraph (5), after "enactment" insert "or the GDPR".

(4) After paragraph (6) insert—

"(7)   In this regulation, "the GDPR", "personal data" and references to Schedule 2 to the Data Protection Act 2018 have the same meaning as in Parts 5 to 7 of that Act (see section 3(2), (10), (11) and (14) of that Act)."

Communications Act 2003 (Disclosure of Information) Order 2014 (S.I. 2014/1825)

379 (1) Article 3 of the Communications Act 2003 (Disclosure of Information) Order 2014 (specification of relevant functions) is amended as follows.

(2) The existing text becomes paragraph (1).

(3) In that paragraph, in sub-paragraph (a), for "the Data Protection Act 1998" substitute "the data protection legislation".

(4) After that paragraph insert—

"(2)   In this article, "the data protection legislation" has the same meaning as in the Data Protection Act 2018 (see section 3 of that Act)."

Criminal Justice and Data Protection (Protocol No. 36) Regulations 2014 (S.I. 2014/3141)

380   In the Criminal Justice and Data Protection (Protocol No. 36) Regulations 2014, omit Part 4 (data protection in relation to police and judicial co-operation in criminal matters).

302

Data Protection Act 2018 (c. 12)
Schedule 19 — Minor and consequential amendments
Part 2 — Amendments of other legislation

Data Protection (Assessment Notices) (Designation of National Health Service Bodies) Order 2014 (S.I. 2014/3282)

381   The Data Protection (Assessment Notices) (Designation of National Health Service Bodies) Order 2014 is revoked.

The Control of Explosives Precursors etc Regulations (Northern Ireland) 2014 (S.R. (N.I.) 2014 No. 224)

382   In regulation 6 of the Control of Explosives Precursors etc Regulations (Northern Ireland) 2014 (applications) —

(a)   in paragraph (9), omit sub-paragraph (b) and the word "and" before it, and

(b)   in paragraph (11), omit the definition of "processing" and "sensitive personal data" and the word "and" before it.

Control of Poisons and Explosives Precursors Regulations 2015 (S.I. 2015/966)

383   In regulation 3 of the Control of Poisons and Explosives Precursors Regulations 2015 (applications in relation to licences under section 4A of the Poisons Act 1972) —

(a)   in paragraph (7), omit sub-paragraph (b) and the word "and" before it, and

(b)   omit paragraph (8).

Companies (Disclosure of Date of Birth Information) Regulations 2015 (S.I. 2015/1694)

384 (1) Paragraph 6 of Schedule 2 to the Companies (Disclosure of Date of Birth Information) Regulations 2015 (conditions for permitted disclosure to a credit reference agency) is amended as follows.

(2) The existing text becomes sub-paragraph (1).

(3) In paragraph (b) of that sub-paragraph, for sub-paragraph (ii) substitute —

"(ii)   for the purposes of ensuring that it complies with its data protection obligations;".

(4) In paragraph (c) of that sub-paragraph —

(a)   omit "or" at the end of sub-paragraph (i), and

(b)   at the end insert "; or

(iii)   section 144 of the Data Protection Act 2018 (false statements made in response to an information notice) or section 148 of that Act (destroying or falsifying information and documents etc);".

(5) After paragraph (c) of that sub-paragraph insert —

"(d)   has not been given a penalty notice under section 155 of the Data Protection Act 2018 in circumstances described in paragraph (c)(ii), other than a penalty notice that has been cancelled."

(6) After sub-paragraph (1) insert —

"(2) In this paragraph, "data protection obligations", in relation to a credit reference agency, means —

Data Protection Act 2018 (c. 12)
Schedule 19 — Minor and consequential amendments
Part 2 — Amendments of other legislation

303

> > (a) where the agency carries on business in the United Kingdom, obligations under the data protection legislation (as defined in section 3 of the Data Protection Act 2018);
> >
> > (b) where the agency carries on business in a EEA State other than the United Kingdom, obligations under—
> >
> > > (i) the GDPR (as defined in section 3(10) of the Data Protection Act 2018),
> > >
> > > (ii) legislation made in exercise of powers conferred on member States under the GDPR (as so defined), and
> > >
> > > (iii) legislation implementing the Law Enforcement Directive (as defined in section 3(12) of the Data Protection Act 2018)."

Small and Medium Sized Business (Credit Information) Regulations 2015 (S.I. 2015/1945)

385   The Small and Medium Sized Business (Credit Information) Regulations 2015 are amended as follows.

386 (1) Regulation 12 (criteria for the designation of a credit reference agency) is amended as follows.

(2) In paragraph (1)(b), for "the Data Protection Act 1998" substitute "the data protection legislation".

(3) After paragraph (2) insert—

> "(3) In this regulation, "the data protection legislation" has the same meaning as in the Data Protection Act 2018 (see section 3 of that Act)."

387 (1) Regulation 15 (access to and correction of information for individuals and small firms) is amended as follows.

(2) For paragraph (1) substitute—

> "(1) Section 13 of the Data Protection Act 2018 (rights of the data subject under the GDPR: obligations of credit reference agencies) applies in respect of a designated credit reference agency which is not a credit reference agency within the meaning of section 145(8) of the Consumer Credit Act 1974 as if it were such an agency."

(3) After paragraph (3) insert—

> "(4) In this regulation, the reference to section 13 of the Data Protection Act 2018 has the same meaning as in Parts 5 to 7 of that Act (see section 3(14) of that Act)."

European Union (Recognition of Professional Qualifications) Regulations 2015 (S.I. 2015/ 2059)

388   The European Union (Recognition of Professional Qualifications) Regulations 2015 are amended as follows.

389 (1) Regulation 2(1) (interpretation) is amended as follows.

(2) Omit the definition of "Directive 95/46/EC".

304   *Data Protection Act 2018 (c. 12)*
Schedule 19 — Minor and consequential amendments
Part 2 — Amendments of other legislation

(3) At the appropriate place insert —

““the GDPR” means Regulation (EU) 2016/679 of the European Parliament and of the Council of 27 April 2016 on the protection of natural persons with regard to the processing of personal data and on the free movement of such data (General Data Protection Regulation), read with Chapter 2 of Part 2 of the Data Protection Act 2018;”.

390   In regulation 5(5) (functions of competent authorities in the United Kingdom) for “Directives 95/46/EC” substitute “the GDPR and Directive”.

391   In regulation 45(3) (processing and access to data regarding the European Professional Card), for “Directive 95/46/EC” substitute “the GDPR”.

392   In regulation 46(1) (processing and access to data regarding the European Professional Card), for “Directive 95/46/EC” substitute “the GDPR”.

393   In regulation 48(2) (processing and access to data regarding the European Professional Card), omit paragraph (2) (deeming the relevant designated competent authorities to be controllers for the purposes of Directive 95/46/EC).

394   In regulation 66(3) (exchange of information), for “Directives 95/46/EC” substitute “the GDPR and Directive”.

Scottish Parliament (Elections etc) Order 2015 (S.S.I. 2015/425)

395   The Scottish Parliament (Elections etc) Order 2015 is amended as follows.

396 (1) Schedule 3 (absent voting) is amended as follows.

(2) In paragraph 16 (absent voting lists: supply of copies etc) —
   (a)   in sub-paragraph (4), for paragraph (a) (but not the final “or”) substitute —

         “(a)   purposes mentioned in Article 89(1) of the GDPR (archiving in the public interest, scientific or historical research and statistics);”, and

   (b)   after sub-paragraph (10) insert —

         “(11) In this paragraph, “the GDPR” means Regulation (EU) 2016/679 of the European Parliament and of the Council of 27 April 2016 on the protection of natural persons with regard to the processing of personal data and on the free movement of such data (General Data Protection Regulation).”

(3) In paragraph 20 (restriction on use of absent voting lists) —
   (a)   in sub-paragraph (3), for paragraph (a) (but not the final “or”) substitute —

         “(a)   purposes mentioned in Article 89(1) of the GDPR (archiving in the public interest, scientific or historical research and statistics);”, and

   (b)   after that sub-paragraph insert —

         “(4) In this paragraph, “the GDPR” means Regulation (EU) 2016/679 of the European Parliament and of the Council of 27 April 2016 on the protection of natural persons with

Data Protection Act 2018 (c. 12)
Schedule 19 — Minor and consequential amendments
Part 2 — Amendments of other legislation

305

regard to the processing of personal data and on the free movement of such data (General Data Protection Regulation)."

397 (1) Schedule 8 (access to marked registers and other documents open to public inspection after an election) is amended as follows.

(2) In paragraph 1(2) (interpretation), omit paragraphs (c) and (d) (but not the final "and").

(3) In paragraph 5 (restriction on use of documents or of information contained in them) —

(a) in sub-paragraph (3), for paragraph (a) (but not the final "or") substitute —

"(a) purposes mentioned in Article 89(1) of the GDPR (archiving in the public interest, scientific or historical research and statistics);", and

(b) after sub-paragraph (4) insert —

"(5) In this paragraph, "the GDPR" means Regulation (EU) 2016/679 of the European Parliament and of the Council of 27 April 2016 on the protection of natural persons with regard to the processing of personal data and on the free movement of such data (General Data Protection Regulation)."

Recall of MPs Act 2015 (Recall Petition) Regulations 2016 (S.I. 2016/295)

398 In paragraph 1(3) of Schedule 3 to the Recall of MPs Act 2015 (Recall Petition) Regulations 2016 (access to marked registers after a petition), omit the definition of "relevant conditions".

Register of People with Significant Control Regulations 2016 (S.I. 2016/339)

399 Schedule 4 to the Register of People with Significant Control Regulations 2016 (conditions for permitted disclosure) is amended as follows.

400 (1) Paragraph 6 (disclosure to a credit reference agency) is amended as follows.

(2) In sub-paragraph (b), for paragraph (ii) (together with the final "; and") substitute —

"(ii) for the purposes of ensuring that it complies with its data protection obligations;".

(3) In sub-paragraph (c) —

(a) omit "or" at the end of paragraph (ii), and

(b) at the end insert —

"(iv) section 144 of the Data Protection Act 2018 (false statements made in response to an information notice); or

(v) section 148 of that Act (destroying or falsifying information and documents etc);"

(4) After sub-paragraph (c) insert —

"(d) has not been given a penalty notice under section 155 of the Data Protection Act 2018 in circumstances described in sub-

306

Data Protection Act 2018 (c. 12)
Schedule 19 — Minor and consequential amendments
Part 2 — Amendments of other legislation

paragraph (c)(iii), other than a penalty notice that has been cancelled."

401   In paragraph 12A (disclosure to a credit institution or a financial institution), for sub-paragraph (b) substitute—

"(b)   for the purposes of ensuring that it complies with its data protection obligations."

402   In Part 3 (interpretation), after paragraph 13 insert—

"14   In this Schedule, "data protection obligations", in relation to a credit reference agency, a credit institution or a financial institution, means—

(a)   where the agency or institution carries on business in the United Kingdom, obligations under the data protection legislation (as defined in section 3 of the Data Protection Act 2018);

(b)   where the agency or institution carries on business in a EEA State other than the United Kingdom, obligations under—

(i)   the GDPR (as defined in section 3(10) of the Data Protection Act 2018),

(ii)   legislation made in exercise of powers conferred on member States under the GDPR (as so defined), and

(iii)   legislation implementing the Law Enforcement Directive (as defined in section 3(12) of the Data Protection Act 2018)."

Electronic Identification and Trust Services for Electronic Transactions Regulations 2016 (S.I. 2016/696)

403   The Electronic Identification and Trust Services for Electronic Transactions Regulations 2016 are amended as follows.

404   In regulation 2(1) (interpretation), omit the definition of "the 1998 Act".

405   In regulation 3(3) (supervision), omit "under the 1998 Act".

406   For Schedule 2 substitute—

"SCHEDULE 2

INFORMATION COMMISSIONER'S ENFORCEMENT POWERS

Provisions applied for enforcement purposes

1   For the purposes of enforcing these Regulations and the eIDAS Regulation, the following provisions of Parts 5 to 7 of the Data Protection Act 2018 apply with the modifications set out in paragraphs 2 to 26—

(a)   section 140 (publication by the Commissioner);

(b)   section 141 (notices from the Commissioner);

(c)   section 142 (information notices);

(d)   section 143 (information notices: restrictions);

Data Protection Act 2018 (c. 12)   307
Schedule 19 — Minor and consequential amendments
Part 2 — Amendments of other legislation

    (e)   section 144 (false statements made in response to an information notice);

    (f)   section 145 (information orders);

    (g)   section 146 (assessment notices);

    (h)   section 147 (assessment notices: restrictions);

    (i)   section 148 (destroying or falsifying information and documents etc);

    (j)   section 149 (enforcement notices);

    (k)   section 150 (enforcement notices: supplementary);

    (l)   section 152 (enforcement notices: restrictions);

    (m)   section 153 (enforcement notices: cancellation and variation);

    (n)   section 154 and Schedule 15 (powers of entry and inspection);

    (o)   section 155 and Schedule 16 (penalty notices);

    (p)   section 156(4)(a) (penalty notices: restrictions);

    (q)   section 157 (maximum amount of penalty);

    (r)   section 159 (amount of penalties: supplementary);

    (s)   section 160 (guidance about regulatory action);

    (t)   section 161 (approval of first guidance about regulatory action);

    (u)   section 162 (rights of appeal);

    (v)   section 163 (determination of appeals);

    (w)   section 164 (applications in respect of urgent notices);

    (x)   section 180 (jurisdiction);

    (y)   section 182(1), (2), (5), (7) and (13) (regulations and consultation);

    (z)   section 196 (penalties for offences);

    (z1)   section 197 (prosecution);

    (z2)   section 202 (proceedings in the First-tier Tribunal: contempt);

    (z3)   section 203 (Tribunal Procedure Rules).

General modification of references to the Data Protection Act 2018

2   The provisions listed in paragraph 1 have effect as if —

    (a)   references to the Data Protection Act 2018 were references to the provisions of that Act as applied by these Regulations;

    (b)   references to a particular provision of that Act were references to that provision as applied by these Regulations.

Modification of section 142 (information notices)

3   (1) Section 142 has effect as if subsections (9) and (10) were omitted.

    (2) In that section, subsection (1) has effect as if —

        (a)   in paragraph (a) —

            (i)   for "controller or processor" there were substituted "trust service provider";

308

Data Protection Act 2018 (c. 12)
Schedule 19 — Minor and consequential amendments
Part 2 — Amendments of other legislation

        (ii)   for "the data protection legislation" there were substituted "the eIDAS Regulation and the EITSET Regulations";

    (b)   paragraph (b) were omitted.

   (3)   In that section, subsection (2) has effect as if paragraph (a) were omitted.

Modification of section 143 (information notices: restrictions)

4   (1)   Section 143 has effect as if subsections (1) and (9) were omitted.

   (2)   In that section —

    (a)   subsections (3)(b) and (4)(b) have effect as if for "the data protection legislation" there were substituted "the eIDAS Regulation or the EITSET Regulations";

    (b)   subsection (7)(a) has effect as if for "this Act" there were substituted "section 144 or 148 or paragraph 15 of Schedule 15";

    (c)   subsection (8) has effect as if for "this Act (other than an offence under section 144)" there were substituted "section 148 or paragraph 15 of Schedule 15".

Modification of section 145 (information orders)

5   Section 145(2)(b) has effect as if for "section 142(2)(b)" there were substituted "section 142(2)".

Modification of section 146 (assessment notices)

6   (1)   Section 146 has effect as if subsection (11) were omitted.

   (2)   In that section —

    (a)   subsection (1) has effect as if —

        (i)   for "controller or processor" (in both places) there were substituted "trust service provider";

        (ii)   for "the data protection legislation" there were substituted "the eIDAS requirements";

    (b)   subsection (2) has effect as if paragraphs (h) and (i) were omitted;

    (c)   subsections (7), (8), (9) and (10) have effect as if for "controller or processor" (in each place) there were substituted "trust service provider.

    (d)   subsection (9)(a) has effect as if for "as described in section 149(2) or that an offence under this Act" there were substituted "to comply with the eIDAS requirements or that an offence under section 144 or 148 or paragraph 15 of Schedule 15".

Modification of section 147 (assessment notices: restrictions)

7   (1)   Section 147 has effect as if subsections (5) and (6) were omitted.

Data Protection Act 2018 (c. 12)
Schedule 19 – Minor and consequential amendments
Part 2 – Amendments of other legislation

309

(2) In that section, subsections (2)(b) and (3)(b) have effect as if for "the data protection legislation" there were substituted "the eIDAS Regulation or the EITSET Regulations".

Modification of section 149 (enforcement notices)

8   (1) Section 149 has effect as if subsections (2) to (5) and (7) to (9) were omitted.

(2) In that section –
  (a) subsection (1) has effect as if –
      (i) for "as described in subsection (2), (3), (4) or (5)" there were substituted "to comply with the eIDAS requirements";
      (ii) for "sections 150 and 151" there were substituted "section 150";
  (b) subsection (6) has effect as if the words "given in reliance on subsection (2), (3) or (5)" were omitted.

Modification of section 150 (enforcement notices: supplementary)

9   (1) Section 150 has effect as if subsection (3) were omitted.

(2) In that section, subsection (2) has effect as if the words "in reliance on section 149(2)" and "or distress" were omitted.

Modification of section 152 (enforcement notices: restrictions)

10   Section 152 has effect as if subsections (1), (2) and (4) were omitted.

Withdrawal notices

11   The provisions listed in paragraph 1 have effect as if after section 153 there were inserted –

"Withdrawal notices

153A   Withdrawal notices
  (1) The Commissioner may, by written notice (a "withdrawal notice"), withdraw the qualified status from a trust service provider, or the qualified status of a service provided by a trust service provider, if –
      (a) the Commissioner is satisfied that the trust service provider has failed to comply with an information notice or an enforcement notice, and
      (b) the condition in subsection (2) or (3) is met.
  (2) The condition in this subsection is met if the period for the trust service provider to appeal against the information notice or enforcement notice has ended without an appeal having been brought.
  (3) The condition in this subsection is met if an appeal against the information notice or enforcement notice has been brought and –

310

Data Protection Act 2018 (c. 12)
Schedule 19 — Minor and consequential amendments
Part 2 — Amendments of other legislation

      (a)   the appeal and any further appeal in relation to the notice has been decided or has otherwise ended, and

      (b)   the time for appealing against the result of the appeal or further appeal has ended without another appeal having been brought.

  (4) A withdrawal notice must—

      (a)   state when the withdrawal takes effect, and

      (b)   provide information about the rights of appeal under section 162."

Modification of Schedule 15 (powers of entry and inspection)

12 (1) Schedule 15 has effect as if paragraph 3 were omitted.

  (2) Paragraph 1(1) of that Schedule (issue of warrants in connection with non-compliance and offences) has effect as if for paragraph (a) (but not the final "and") there were substituted—

    "(a)   there are reasonable grounds for suspecting that—

      (i)   a trust service provider has failed or is failing to comply with the eIDAS requirements, or

      (ii) an offence under section 144 or 148 or paragraph 15 of Schedule 15 has been or is being committed,".

  (3) Paragraph 2 of that Schedule (issue of warrants in connection with assessment notices) has effect as if—

      (a)   in sub-paragraphs (1) and (2), for "controller or processor" there were substituted "trust service provider";

      (b)   in sub-paragraph (2), for "the data protection legislation" there were substituted "the eIDAS requirements".

  (4) Paragraph 5 of that Schedule (content of warrants) has effect as if—

      (a)   in sub-paragraph (1)(c), for "the processing of personal data" there were substituted "the provision of trust services";

      (b)   in sub-paragraph (2)(d)—

      (i)   for "controller or processor" there were substituted "trust service provider";

      (ii) for "as described in section 149(2)" there were substituted "to comply with the eIDAS requirements";

      (c)   in sub-paragraph (3)(a) and (d)—

      (i)   for "controller or processor" there were substituted "trust service provider";

      (ii) for "the data protection legislation" there were substituted "the eIDAS requirements".

  (5) Paragraph 11 of that Schedule (privileged communications) has effect as if, in sub-paragraphs (1)(b) and (2)(b), for "the data protection legislation" there were substituted "the eIDAS Regulation or the EITSET Regulations".

Data Protection Act 2018 (c. 12)
Schedule 19 — Minor and consequential amendments
Part 2 — Amendments of other legislation

311

Modification of section 155 (penalty notices)

13 (1) Section 155 has effect as if subsections (1)(a), (2)(a), (3)(g), (4) and (6) to (8) were omitted.

  (2) Subsection (2) of that section has effect as if —
    (a) the words "Subject to subsection (4)," were omitted;
    (b) in paragraph (b), the words "to the extent that the notice concerns another matter," were omitted.

  (3) Subsection (3) of that section has effect as if —
    (a) for "controller or processor", in each place, there were substituted "trust services provider";
    (b) in paragraph (c), the words "or distress" were omitted;
    (c) in paragraph (c), for "data subjects" there were substituted "relying parties";
    (d) in paragraph (d), for "section 57, 66, 103 or 107" there were substituted "Article 19(1) of the eIDAS Regulation".

Modification of Schedule 16 (penalties)

14   Schedule 16 has effect as if paragraphs 3(2)(b) and 5(2)(b) were omitted.

Modification of section 157 (maximum amount of penalty)

15   Section 157 has effect as if subsections (1) to (3) and (6) were omitted.

Modification of section 159 (amount of penalties: supplementary)

16   Section 159 has effect as if —
    (a) in subsection (1), the words "Article 83 of the GDPR and" were omitted;
    (b) in subsection (2), the words "Article 83 of the GDPR" and "and section 158" were omitted.

Modification of section 160 (guidance about regulatory action)

17 (1) Section 160 has effect as if subsections (5) and (12) were omitted.

  (2) In that section, subsection (4)(f) has effect as if for "controllers and processors" there were substituted "trust service providers".

Modification of section 162 (rights of appeal)

18 (1) Section 162 has effect as if subsection (4) were omitted.

  (2) In that section, subsection (1) has effect as if, after paragraph (c), there were inserted —
    "(ca) a withdrawal notice;".

Modification of section 163 (determination of appeals)

19   Section 163 has effect as if subsection (6) were omitted.

312

Data Protection Act 2018 (c. 12)
Schedule 19 — Minor and consequential amendments
Part 2 — Amendments of other legislation

Modification of section 180 (jurisdiction)

20 (1) Section 180 has effect as if subsections (2)(d) and (e) and (3) were omitted.

(2) Subsection (1) of that section has effect as if for "subsections (3) and (4)" there were substituted "subsection (4)".

Modification of section 182 (regulations and consultation)

21 Section 182 has effect as if subsections (3), (4), (6), (8) to (11) and (14) were omitted.

Modification of section 196 (penalties for offences)

22 (1) Section 196 has effect as if subsections (3) to (5) were omitted.

(2) In that section—
  (a) subsection (1) has effect as if the words "section 119 or 173 or" were omitted;
  (b) subsection (2) has effect as if for "section 132, 144, 148, 170, 171 or 184" there were substituted "section 144 or 148".

Modification of section 197 (prosecution)

23 Section 197 has effect as if subsections (3) to (6) were omitted.

Modification of section 202 (proceedings in the First-tier Tribunal: contempt)

24 Section 202 has effect as if in subsection (1)(a), for sub-paragraphs (i) and (ii) there were substituted "on an appeal under section 162".

Modification of section 203 (Tribunal Procedure Rules)

25 Section 203 has effect as if—
  (a) in subsection (1), for paragraphs (a) and (b) there were substituted "the exercise of the rights of appeal conferred by section 162";
  (b) in subsection (2)(a) and (b), for "the processing of personal data" there were substituted "the provision of trust services".

Approval of first guidance about regulatory action

26 (1) This paragraph applies if the first guidance produced under section 160(1) of the Data Protection Act 2018 and the first guidance produced under that provision as applied by this Schedule are laid before Parliament as a single document ("the combined guidance").

(2) Section 161 of that Act (including that section as applied by this Schedule) has effect as if the references to "the guidance" were references to the combined guidance, except in subsections (2)(b) and (4).

(3) Nothing in subsection (2)(a) of that section (including as applied by this Schedule) prevents another version of the combined guidance being laid before Parliament.

(4) Any duty under subsection (2)(b) of that section (including as applied by this Schedule) may be satisfied by producing another version of the combined guidance.

Interpretation

27 In this Schedule—

"the eIDAS requirements" means the requirements of Chapter III of the eIDAS Regulation;

"the EITSET Regulations" means these Regulations;

"withdrawal notice" has the meaning given in section 153A of the Data Protection Act 2018 (as inserted in that Act by this Schedule)."

Court Files Privileged Access Rules (Northern Ireland) 2016 (S.R. (N.I.) 2016 No. 123)

407 The Court Files Privileged Access Rules (Northern Ireland) 2016 are amended as follows.

408 In rule 5 (information that may released) for "Schedule 1 of the Data Protection Act 1998" substitute "—

(a) Article 5(1) of the GDPR, and

(b) section 34(1) of the Data Protection Act 2018."

409 In rule 7(2) (provision of information) for "Schedule 1 of the Data Protection Act 1998" substitute "—

(a) Article 5(1) of the GDPR, and

(b) section 34(1) of the Data Protection Act 2018."

Money Laundering, Terrorist Financing and Transfer of Funds (Information on the Payer) Regulations 2017 (S.I. 2017/692)

410 The Money Laundering, Terrorist Financing and Transfer of Funds (Information on the Payer) Regulations 2017 are amended as follows.

411 In regulation 3(1) (interpretation), at the appropriate places insert—

""the data protection legislation" has the same meaning as in the Data Protection Act 2018 (see section 3 of that Act);";

""the GDPR" and references to provisions of Chapter 2 of Part 2 of the Data Protection Act 2018 have the same meaning as in Parts 5 to 7 of that Act (see section 3(10), (11) and (14) of that Act);".

412 In regulation 16(8) (risk assessment by the Treasury and Home Office), for "the Data Protection Act 1998 or any other enactment" substitute "—

(a) the Data Protection Act 2018 or any other enactment, or

(b) the GDPR."

413 In regulation 17(9) (risk assessment by supervisory authorities), for "the Data Protection Act 1998 or any other enactment" substitute "—

(a) the Data Protection Act 2018 or any other enactment, or

314

Data Protection Act 2018 (c. 12)
Schedule 19 — Minor and consequential amendments
Part 2 — Amendments of other legislation

      (b)   the GDPR."

414   For regulation 40(9)(c) (record keeping) substitute—

      "(c)   "data subject" has the same meaning as in the Data Protection Act 2018 (see section 3 of that Act);

      (d)   "personal data" has the same meaning as in Parts 5 to 7 of that Act (see section 3(2) and (14) of that Act)."

415 (1) Regulation 41 (data protection) is amended as follows.

   (2) Omit paragraph (2).

   (3) In paragraph (3)(a), after "Regulations" insert "or the GDPR".

   (4) Omit paragraphs (4) and (5).

   (5) After those paragraphs insert—

     "(6) Before establishing a business relationship or entering into an occasional transaction with a new customer, as well as providing the customer with the information required under Article 13 of the GDPR (information to be provided where personal data are collected from the data subject), relevant persons must provide the customer with a statement that any personal data received from the customer will be processed only—

      (a)   for the purposes of preventing money laundering or terrorist financing, or

      (b)   as permitted under paragraph (3).

     (7) In Article 6(1) of the GDPR (lawfulness of processing), the reference in point (e) to processing of personal data that is necessary for the performance of a task carried out in the public interest includes processing of personal data in accordance with these Regulations that is necessary for the prevention of money laundering or terrorist financing.

     (8) In the case of sensitive processing of personal data for the purposes of the prevention of money laundering or terrorist financing, section 10 of, and Schedule 1 to, the Data Protection Act 2018 make provision about when the processing meets a requirement in Article 9(2) or 10 of the GDPR for authorisation under the law of the United Kingdom (see, for example, paragraphs 10, 11 and 12 of that Schedule).

     (9) In this regulation—

      "data subject" has the same meaning as in the Data Protection Act 2018 (see section 3 of that Act);

      "personal data" and "processing" have the same meaning as in Parts 5 to 7 of that Act (see section 3(2), (4) and (14) of that Act);

      "sensitive processing" means the processing of personal data described in Article 9(1) or 10 of the GDPR (special categories of personal data and personal data relating to criminal convictions and offences etc)."

416 (1) Regulation 84 (publication: the Financial Conduct Authority) is amended as follows.

Data Protection Act 2018 (c. 12)
Schedule 19 — Minor and consequential amendments
Part 2 — Amendments of other legislation

315

(2) In paragraph (10), for "the Data Protection Act 1998" substitute "the data protection legislation".

(3) For paragraph (11) substitute —

"(11) For the purposes of this regulation, "personal data" has the same meaning as in Parts 5 to 7 of the Data Protection Act 2018 (see section 3(2) and (14) of that Act)."

417 (1) Regulation 85 (publication: the Commissioners) is amended as follows.

(2) In paragraph (9), for "the Data Protection Act 1998" substitute "the data protection legislation".

(3) For paragraph (10) substitute —

"(10) For the purposes of this regulation, "personal data" has the same meaning as in Parts 5 to 7 of the Data Protection Act 2018 (see section 3(2) and (14) of that Act)."

418 For regulation 106(a) (general restrictions) substitute —
"(a) a disclosure in contravention of the data protection legislation; or".

419 After paragraph 27 of Schedule 3 (relevant offences) insert —

"27A An offence under the Data Protection Act 2018, apart from an offence under section 173 of that Act."

Scottish Partnerships (Register of People with Significant Control) Regulations 2017 (S.I. 2017/694)

420 (1) Paragraph 6 of Schedule 5 to the Scottish Partnerships (Register of People with Significant Control) Regulations 2017 (conditions for permitted disclosure to a credit institution or a financial institution) is amended as follows.

(2) The existing text becomes sub-paragraph (1).

(3) For paragraph (b) of that sub-paragraph substitute —
"(b) for the purposes of ensuring that it complies with its data protection obligations."

(4) After sub-paragraph (1) insert —

"(2) In this paragraph, "data protection obligations", in relation to a relevant institution, means —
(a) where the institution carries on business in the United Kingdom, obligations under the data protection legislation (as defined in section 3 of the Data Protection Act 2018);
(b) where the institution carries on business in a EEA State other than the United Kingdom, obligations under —
(i) the GDPR (as defined in section 3(10) of the Data Protection Act 2018),
(ii) legislation made in exercise of powers conferred on member States under the GDPR (as so defined), and

316   *Data Protection Act 2018 (c. 12)*
Schedule 19 — Minor and consequential amendments
Part 2 — Amendments of other legislation

(iii) legislation implementing the Law Enforcement Directive (as defined in section 3(12) of the Data Protection Act 2018)."

Data Protection (Charges and Information) Regulations 2018 (S.I. 2018/480)

421   In regulation 1(2) of the Data Protection (Charges and Information) Regulations 2018 (interpretation), at the appropriate places insert—

""data controller" means a person who is a controller for the purposes of Parts 5 to 7 of the Data Protection Act 2018 (see section 3(6) and (14) of that Act);";

""personal data" has the same meaning as in Parts 5 to 7 of the Data Protection Act 2018 (see section 3(2) and (14) of that Act);".

National Health Service (General Medical Services Contracts) (Scotland) Regulations 2018 (S.S.I. 2018/66)

422   The National Health Service (General Medical Services Contracts) (Scotland) Regulations 2018 are amended as follows.

423 (1) Regulation 1 (citation and commencement) is amended as follows.

(2) In paragraph (2), omit "Subject to paragraph (3),".

(3) Omit paragraph (3).

424   In regulation 3(1) (interpretation)—
         (a) omit the definition of "the 1998 Act",
         (b) at the appropriate place insert—
                  ""the data protection legislation" has the same meaning as in the Data Protection Act 2018 (see section 3 of that Act);", and
         (c) omit the definition of "GDPR".

425 (1) Schedule 6 (other contractual terms) is amended as follows.

(2) In paragraph 63(2) (interpretation: general), for "the 1998 Act or any directly applicable EU instrument relating to data protection" substitute "—
         (a) the data protection legislation, or
         (b) any directly applicable EU legislation which is not part of the data protection legislation but which relates to data protection."

(3) For paragraph 64 (meaning of data controller etc.) substitute—

"Meaning of controller etc.

64A   For the purposes of this Part—
         "controller" has the same meaning as in Parts 5 to 7 of the Data Protection Act 2018 (see section 3(6) and (14) of that Act);
         "data protection officer" means a person designated as a data protection officer under the data protection legislation;

"personal data" and "processing" have the same meaning as in Parts 5 to 7 of the Data Protection Act 2018 (see section 3(2), (4) and (14) of that Act)."

(4) In paragraph 65(2)(b) (roles, responsibilities and obligations: general), for "data controllers" substitute "controllers".

(5) In paragraph 69(2)(a) (processing and access of data), for "the 1998 Act, and any directly applicable EU instrument relating to data protection;" substitute "—

(i) the data protection legislation, and

(ii) any directly applicable EU legislation which is not part of the data protection legislation but which relates to data protection;".

(6) In paragraph 94(4) (variation of a contract: general) —

(a) omit paragraph (b), and

(b) after paragraph (d) (but before the final "and") insert —

"(da) the data protection legislation;

(db) any directly applicable EU legislation which is not part of the data protection legislation but which relates to data protection;".

National Health Service (Primary Medical Services Section 17C Agreements) (Scotland) Regulations 2018 (S.S.I. 2018/67)

426 The National Health Service (Primary Medical Services Section 17C Agreements) (Scotland) Regulations 2018 are amended as follows.

427 (1) Regulation 1 (citation and commencement) is amended as follows.

(2) In paragraph (2), omit "Subject to paragraph (3),".

(3) Omit paragraph (3).

428 In regulation 3(1) (interpretation) —

(a) omit the definition of "the 1998 Act", and

(b) at the appropriate place insert —

""the data protection legislation" has the same meaning as in the Data Protection Act 2018 (see section 3 of that Act);", and

(c) omit the definition of "GDPR".

429 (1) Schedule 1 (content of agreements) is amended as follows.

(2) In paragraph 34 (interpretation) —

(a) in sub-paragraph (1) —

(i) omit "Subject to sub-paragraph (3),",

(ii) before paragraph (a) insert —

"(za) "controller" has the same meaning as in Parts 5 to 7 of the Data Protection Act 2018 (see section 3(6) and (14) of that Act);

(zb) "data protection officer" means a person designated as a data protection officer under the data protection legislation;", and

318   *Data Protection Act 2018 (c. 12)*
                                        Schedule 19 — Minor and consequential amendments
                                        Part 2 — Amendments of other legislation

(iii)   for paragraph (d) substitute—

"(e)   "personal data" and "processing" have the same meaning as in Parts 5 to 7 of the Data Protection Act 2018 (see section 3(2), (4) and (14) of that Act).",

(b)   omit sub-paragraphs (2) and (3),

(c)   in sub-paragraph (4), for "the 1998 Act and any directly applicable EU instrument relating to data protection" substitute "—

(a)   the data protection legislation, or

(b)   any directly applicable EU legislation which is not part of the data protection legislation but which relates to data protection.", and

(d)   in sub-paragraph (6)(b), for "data controllers" substitute "controllers".

(3)   In paragraph 37(2)(a) (processing and access of data), for "the 1998 Act, and any directly applicable EU instrument relating to data protection;" substitute "—

(i)   the data protection legislation, and

(ii)   any directly applicable EU legislation which is not part of the data protection legislation but which relates to data protection;".

(4)   In paragraph 61(3) (variation of agreement: general)—

(a)   omit paragraph (b), and

(b)   after paragraph (d) (but before the final "and") insert—

"(da)   the data protection legislation;

(db)   any directly applicable EU legislation which is not part of the data protection legislation but which relates to data protection;".

PART 3

MODIFICATIONS

Introduction

430   (1)   Unless the context otherwise requires, legislation described in sub-paragraph (2) has effect on and after the day on which this Part of this Schedule comes into force as if it were modified in accordance with this Part of this Schedule.

(2)   That legislation is—

(a)   subordinate legislation made before the day on which this Part of this Schedule comes into force;

(b)   primary legislation that is passed or made before the end of the Session in which this Act is passed.

(3)   In this Part of this Schedule—

"primary legislation" has the meaning given in section 211(7);

"references" includes any references, however expressed.

General modifications

431 (1) References to a particular provision of, or made under, the Data Protection Act 1998 have effect as references to the equivalent provision or provisions of, or made under, the data protection legislation.

(2) Other references to the Data Protection Act 1998 have effect as references to the data protection legislation.

(3) References to disclosure, use or other processing of information that is prohibited or restricted by an enactment which include disclosure, use or other processing of information that is prohibited or restricted by the Data Protection Act 1998 have effect as if they included disclosure, use or other processing of information that is prohibited or restricted by the GDPR or the applied GDPR.

Specific modification of references to terms used in the Data Protection Act 1998

432 (1) References to personal data, and to the processing of such data, as defined in the Data Protection Act 1998, have effect as references to personal data, and to the processing of such data, as defined for the purposes of Parts 5 to 7 of this Act (see section 3(2), (4) and (14)).

(2) References to processing as defined in the Data Protection Act 1998, in relation to information, have effect as references to processing as defined in section 3(4).

(3) References to a data subject as defined in the Data Protection Act 1998 have effect as references to a data subject as defined in section 3(5).

(4) References to a data controller as defined in the Data Protection Act 1998 have effect as references to a controller as defined for the purposes of Parts 5 to 7 of this Act (see section 3(6) and (14)).

(5) References to the data protection principles set out in the Data Protection Act 1998 have effect as references to the principles set out in —
   (a)   Article 5(1) of the GDPR and the applied GDPR, and
   (b)   sections 34(1) and 85(1) of this Act.

(6) References to direct marketing as defined in section 11 of the Data Protection Act 1998 have effect as references to direct marketing as defined in section 122 of this Act.

(7) References to a health professional within the meaning of section 69(1) of the Data Protection Act 1998 have effect as references to a health professional within the meaning of section 204 of this Act.

(8) References to a health record within the meaning of section 68(2) of the Data Protection Act 1998 have effect as references to a health record within the meaning of section 205 of this Act.

PART 4

SUPPLEMENTARY

Definitions

433   Section 3(14) does not apply to this Schedule.

Provision inserted in subordinate legislation by this Schedule

434   Provision inserted into subordinate legislation by this Schedule may be amended or revoked as if it had been inserted using the power under which the subordinate legislation was originally made.

SCHEDULE 20   Section 213

TRANSITIONAL PROVISION ETC

PART 1

GENERAL

Interpretation

1   (1)   In this Schedule—

"the 1984 Act" means the Data Protection Act 1984;

"the 1998 Act" means the Data Protection Act 1998;

"the 2014 Regulations" means the Criminal Justice and Data Protection (Protocol No. 36) Regulations 2014 (S.I. 2014/3141);

"data controller" has the same meaning as in the 1998 Act (see section 1 of that Act);

"the old data protection principles" means the principles set out in—

(a)   Part 1 of Schedule 1 to the 1998 Act, and

(b)   regulation 30 of the 2014 Regulations.

(2)   A provision of the 1998 Act that has effect by virtue of this Schedule is not, by virtue of that, part of the data protection legislation (as defined in section 3).

PART 2

RIGHTS OF DATA SUBJECTS

Right of access to personal data under the 1998 Act

2   (1)   The repeal of sections 7 to 9A of the 1998 Act (right of access to personal data) does not affect the application of those sections after the relevant time in a case in which a data controller received a request under section 7 of that Act (right of access to personal data) before the relevant time.

(2)   The repeal of sections 7 and 8 of the 1998 Act and the revocation of regulation 44 of the 2014 Regulations (which applies those sections with modifications) do not affect the application of those sections and that regulation after the relevant time in a case in which a UK competent authority received a request under section 7 of the 1998 Act (as applied by that regulation) before the relevant time.

(3)   The revocation of the relevant regulations, or their amendment by Schedule 19 to this Act, and the repeals and revocation mentioned in sub-paragraphs (1) and (2), do not affect the application of the relevant regulations after the relevant time in a case described in those sub-paragraphs.

Data Protection Act 2018 (c. 12)
Schedule 20 — Transitional provision etc
Part 2 — Rights of data subjects

321

(4) In this paragraph—

"the relevant regulations" means—

 (a) the Data Protection (Subject Access) (Fees and Miscellaneous Provisions) Regulations 2000 (S.I. 2000/191);

 (b) regulation 4 of, and Schedule 1 to, the Consumer Credit (Credit Reference Agency) Regulations 2000 (S.I. 2000/290);

 (c) regulation 3 of the Freedom of Information and Data Protection (Appropriate Limit and Fees) Regulations 2004 (S.I. 2004/3244);

"the relevant time" means the time when the repeal of section 7 of the 1998 Act comes into force;

"UK competent authority" has the same meaning as in Part 4 of the 2014 Regulations (see regulation 27 of those Regulations).

Right to prevent processing likely to cause damage or distress under the 1998 Act

3 (1) The repeal of section 10 of the 1998 Act (right to prevent processing likely to cause damage or distress) does not affect the application of that section after the relevant time in a case in which an individual gave notice in writing to a data controller under that section before the relevant time.

 (2) In this paragraph, "the relevant time" means the time when the repeal of section 10 of the 1998 Act comes into force.

Right to prevent processing for purposes of direct marketing under the 1998 Act

4 (1) The repeal of section 11 of the 1998 Act (right to prevent processing for purposes of direct marketing) does not affect the application of that section after the relevant time in a case in which an individual gave notice in writing to a data controller under that section before the relevant time.

 (2) In this paragraph, "the relevant time" means the time when the repeal of section 11 of the 1998 Act comes into force.

Automated processing under the 1998 Act

5 (1) The repeal of section 12 of the 1998 Act (rights in relation to automated decision-taking) does not affect the application of that section after the relevant time in relation to a decision taken by a person before that time if—

 (a) in taking the decision the person failed to comply with section 12(1) of the 1998 Act, or

 (b) at the relevant time—

  (i) the person had not taken all of the steps required under section 12(2) or (3) of the 1998 Act, or

  (ii) the period specified in section 12(2)(b) of the 1998 Act (for an individual to require a person to reconsider a decision) had not expired.

 (2) In this paragraph, "the relevant time" means the time when the repeal of section 12 of the 1998 Act comes into force.

322

Data Protection Act 2018 (c. 12)
Schedule 20 — Transitional provision etc
Part 2 — Rights of data subjects

Compensation for contravention of the 1998 Act or Part 4 of the 2014 Regulations

6   (1)   The repeal of section 13 of the 1998 Act (compensation for failure to comply with certain requirements) does not affect the application of that section after the relevant time in relation to damage or distress suffered at any time by reason of an act or omission before the relevant time.

     (2)   The revocation of regulation 45 of the 2014 Regulations (right to compensation) does not affect the application of that regulation after the relevant time in relation to damage or distress suffered at any time by reason of an act or omission before the relevant time.

     (3)   "The relevant time" means —
- (a)   in sub-paragraph (1), the time when the repeal of section 13 of the 1998 Act comes into force;
- (b)   in sub-paragraph (2), the time when the revocation of regulation 45 of the 2014 Regulation comes into force.

Rectification, blocking, erasure and destruction under the 1998 Act

7   (1)   The repeal of section 14(1) to (3) and (6) of the 1998 Act (rectification, blocking, erasure and destruction of inaccurate personal data) does not affect the application of those provisions after the relevant time in a case in which an application was made under subsection (1) of that section before the relevant time.

     (2)   The repeal of section 14(4) to (6) of the 1998 Act (rectification, blocking, erasure and destruction: risk of further contravention in circumstances entitling data subject to compensation under section 13 of the 1998 Act) does not affect the application of those provisions after the relevant time in a case in which an application was made under subsection (4) of that section before the relevant time.

     (3)   In this paragraph, "the relevant time" means the time when the repeal of section 14 of the 1998 Act comes into force.

Jurisdiction and procedure under the 1998 Act

8   The repeal of section 15 of the 1998 Act (jurisdiction and procedure) does not affect the application of that section in connection with sections 7 to 14 of the 1998 Act as they have effect by virtue of this Schedule.

Exemptions under the 1998 Act

9   (1)   The repeal of Part 4 of the 1998 Act (exemptions) does not affect the application of that Part after the relevant time in connection with a provision of Part 2 of the 1998 Act as it has effect after that time by virtue of paragraphs 2 to 7 of this Schedule.

     (2)   The revocation of the relevant Orders, and the repeal mentioned in sub-paragraph (1), do not affect the application of the relevant Orders after the relevant time in connection with a provision of Part 2 of the 1998 Act as it has effect as described in sub-paragraph (1).

     (3)   In this paragraph —
         "the relevant Orders" means —

Data Protection Act 2018 (c. 12)
Schedule 20 — Transitional provision etc
Part 2 — Rights of data subjects

323

(a) the Data Protection (Corporate Finance Exemption) Order 2000 (S.I. 2000/184);

(b) the Data Protection (Subject Access Modification) (Health) Order 2000 (S.I. 2000/413);

(c) the Data Protection (Subject Access Modification) (Education) Order 2000 (S.I. 2000/414);

(d) the Data Protection (Subject Access Modification) (Social Work) Order 2000 (S.I. 2000/415);

(e) the Data Protection (Crown Appointments) Order 2000 (S.I. 2000/416);

(f) Data Protection (Miscellaneous Subject Access Exemptions) Order 2000 (S.I. 2000/419);

(g) Data Protection (Designated Codes of Practice) (No. 2) Order 2000 (S.I. 2000/1864);

"the relevant time" means the time when the repeal of the provision of Part 2 of the 1998 Act in question comes into force.

(4) As regards certificates issued under section 28(2) of the 1998 Act, see Part 5 of this Schedule.

Prohibition by this Act of requirement to produce relevant records

10 (1) In Schedule 18 to this Act, references to a record obtained in the exercise of a data subject access right include a record obtained at any time in the exercise of a right under section 7 of the 1998 Act.

(2) In section 184 of this Act, references to a "relevant record" include a record which does not fall within the definition in Schedule 18 to this Act (read with sub-paragraph (1)) but which, immediately before the relevant time, was a "relevant record" for the purposes of section 56 of the 1998 Act.

(3) In this paragraph, "the relevant time" means the time when the repeal of section 56 of the 1998 Act comes into force.

Avoidance under this Act of certain contractual terms relating to health records

11 In section 185 of this Act, references to a record obtained in the exercise of a data subject access right include a record obtained at any time in the exercise of a right under section 7 of the 1998 Act.

PART 3

THE GDPR AND PART 2 OF THIS ACT

Exemptions from the GDPR: restrictions of rules in Articles 13 to 15 of the GDPR

12 In paragraph 20(2) of Schedule 2 to this Act (self-incrimination), the reference to an offence under this Act includes an offence under the 1998 Act or the 1984 Act.

Manual unstructured data held by FOI public authorities

13 Until the first regulations under section 24(8) of this Act come into force, "the appropriate maximum" for the purposes of that section is—

324

Data Protection Act 2018 (c. 12)
Schedule 20 — Transitional provision etc
Part 3 — The GDPR and Part 2 of this Act

      (a) where the controller is a public authority listed in Part 1 of Schedule 1 to the Freedom of Information Act 2000, £600, and

      (b) otherwise, £450.

PART 4

LAW ENFORCEMENT AND INTELLIGENCE SERVICES PROCESSING

Logging

14   (1) In relation to an automated processing system set up before 6 May 2016, subsections (1) to (3) of section 62 of this Act do not apply if and to the extent that compliance with them would involve disproportionate effort.

     (2) Sub-paragraph (1) ceases to have effect at the beginning of 6 May 2023.

Regulation 50 of the 2014 Regulations (disapplication of the 1998 Act)

15   Nothing in this Schedule, read with the revocation of regulation 50 of the 2014 Regulations, has the effect of applying a provision of the 1998 Act to the processing of personal data to which Part 4 of the 2014 Regulations applies in a case in which that provision did not apply before the revocation of that regulation.

Maximum fee for data subject access requests to intelligence services

16   Until the first regulations under section 94(4)(b) of this Act come into force, the maximum amount of a fee that may be required by a controller under that section is £10.

PART 5

NATIONAL SECURITY CERTIFICATES

National security certificates: processing of personal data under the 1998 Act

17   (1) The repeal of section 28(2) to (12) of the 1998 Act does not affect the application of those provisions after the relevant time with respect to the processing of personal data to which the 1998 Act (including as it has effect by virtue of this Schedule) applies.

     (2) A certificate issued under section 28(2) of the 1998 Act continues to have effect after the relevant time with respect to the processing of personal data to which the 1998 Act (including as it has effect by virtue of this Schedule) applies.

     (3) Where a certificate continues to have effect under sub-paragraph (2) after the relevant time, it may be revoked or quashed in accordance with section 28 of the 1998 Act after the relevant time.

     (4) In this paragraph, "the relevant time" means the time when the repeal of section 28 of the 1998 Act comes into force.

Data Protection Act 2018 (c. 12)
Schedule 20 — Transitional provision etc
Part 5 — National security certificates

325

National security certificates: processing of personal data under the 2018 Act

18 (1) This paragraph applies to a certificate issued under section 28(2) of the 1998 Act (an "old certificate") which has effect immediately before the relevant time.

(2) If and to the extent that the old certificate provides protection with respect to personal data which corresponds to protection that could be provided by a certificate issued under section 27, 79 or 111 of this Act, the old certificate also has effect to that extent after the relevant time as if —

    (a) it were a certificate issued under one or more of sections 27, 79 and 111 (as the case may be),

    (b) it provided protection in respect of that personal data in relation to the corresponding provisions of this Act or the applied GDPR, and

    (c) where it has effect as a certificate issued under section 79, it certified that each restriction in question is a necessary and proportionate measure to protect national security.

(3) Where an old certificate also has effect as if it were a certificate issued under one or more of sections 27, 79 and 111, that section has, or those sections have, effect accordingly in relation to the certificate.

(4) Where an old certificate has an extended effect because of sub-paragraph (2), section 130 of this Act does not apply in relation to it.

(5) An old certificate that has an extended effect because of sub-paragraph (2) provides protection only with respect to the processing of personal data that occurs during the period of 1 year beginning with the relevant time (and a Minister of the Crown may curtail that protection by wholly or partly revoking the old certificate).

(6) For the purposes of this paragraph —

    (a) a reference to the protection provided by a certificate issued under —

        (i) section 28(2) of the 1998 Act, or

        (ii) section 27, 79 or 111 of this Act,

    is a reference to the effect of the evidence that is provided by the certificate;

    (b) protection provided by a certificate under section 28(2) of the 1998 Act is to be regarded as corresponding to protection that could be provided by a certificate under section 27, 79 or 111 of this Act where, in respect of provision in the 1998 Act to which the certificate under section 28(2) relates, there is corresponding provision in this Act or the applied GDPR to which a certificate under section 27, 79 or 111 could relate.

(7) In this paragraph, "the relevant time" means the time when the repeal of section 28 of the 1998 Act comes into force.

PART 6

THE INFORMATION COMMISSIONER

Appointment etc

19 (1) On and after the relevant day, the individual who was the Commissioner immediately before that day —

(a) continues to be the Commissioner,

(b) is to be treated as having been appointed under Schedule 12 to this Act, and

(c) holds office for the period—

    (i) beginning with the relevant day, and

    (ii) lasting for 7 years less a period equal to the individual's pre-commencement term.

(2) On and after the relevant day, a resolution passed by the House of Commons for the purposes of paragraph 3 of Schedule 5 to the 1998 Act (salary and pension of Commissioner), and not superseded before that day, is to be treated as having been passed for the purposes of paragraph 4 of Schedule 12 to this Act.

(3) In this paragraph—

"pre-commencement term", in relation to an individual, means the period during which the individual was the Commissioner before the relevant day;

"the relevant day" means the day on which Schedule 12 to this Act comes into force.

Accounts

20 (1) The repeal of paragraph 10 of Schedule 5 to the 1998 Act does not affect the duties of the Commissioner and the Comptroller and Auditor General under that paragraph in respect of the Commissioner's statement of account for the financial year beginning with 1 April 2017.

(2) The Commissioner's duty under paragraph 11 of Schedule 12 to this Act to prepare a statement of account for each financial year includes a duty to do so for the financial year beginning with 1 April 2018.

Annual report

21 (1) The repeal of section 52(1) of the 1998 Act (annual report) does not affect the Commissioner's duty under that subsection to produce a general report on the exercise of the Commissioner's functions under the 1998 Act during the period of 1 year beginning with 1 April 2017 and to lay it before Parliament.

(2) The repeal of section 49 of the Freedom of Information Act 2000 (annual report) does not affect the Commissioner's duty under that section to produce a general report on the exercise of the Commissioner's functions under that Act during the period of 1 year beginning with 1 April 2017 and to lay it before Parliament.

(3) The first report produced by the Commissioner under section 139 of this Act must relate to the period of 1 year beginning with 1 April 2018.

Fees etc received by the Commissioner

22 (1) The repeal of Schedule 5 to the 1998 Act (Information Commissioner) does not affect the application of paragraph 9 of that Schedule after the relevant time to amounts received by the Commissioner before the relevant time.

(2) In this paragraph, "the relevant time" means the time when the repeal of Schedule 5 to the 1998 Act comes into force.

23   Paragraph 10 of Schedule 12 to this Act applies only to amounts received by the Commissioner after the time when that Schedule comes into force.

Functions in connection with the Data Protection Convention

24 (1) The repeal of section 54(2) of the 1998 Act (functions to be discharged by the Commissioner for the purposes of Article 13 of the Data Protection Convention), and the revocation of the Data Protection (Functions of Designated Authority) Order 2000 (S.I. 2000/186), do not affect the application of articles 1 to 5 of that Order after the relevant time in relation to a request described in those articles which was made before that time.

    (2) The references in paragraph 9 of Schedule 14 to this Act (Data Protection Convention: restrictions on use of information) to requests made or received by the Commissioner under paragraph 6 or 7 of that Schedule include a request made or received by the Commissioner under article 3 or 4 of the Data Protection (Functions of Designated Authority) Order 2000 (S.I. 2000/186).

    (3) The repeal of section 54(7) of the 1998 Act (duty to notify the European Commission of certain approvals and authorisations) does not affect the application of that provision after the relevant time in relation to an approval or authorisation granted before the relevant time.

    (4) In this paragraph, "the relevant time" means the time when the repeal of section 54 of the 1998 Act comes into force.

Co-operation with the European Commission: transfers of personal data outside the EEA

25 (1) The repeal of section 54(3) of the 1998 Act (co-operation by the Commissioner with the European Commission etc), and the revocation of the Data Protection (International Co-operation) Order 2000 (S.I. 2000/190), do not affect the application of articles 1 to 4 of that Order after the relevant time in relation to transfers that took place before the relevant time.

    (2) In this paragraph—
             "the relevant time" means the time when the repeal of section 54 of the 1998 Act comes into force;
             "transfer" has the meaning given in article 2 of the Data Protection (International Co-operation) Order 2000 (S.I. 2000/190).

Charges payable to the Commissioner by controllers

26 (1) The Data Protection (Charges and Information) Regulations 2018 (S.I. 2018/480) have effect after the relevant time (until revoked) as if they were made under section 137 of this Act.

    (2) In this paragraph, "the relevant time" means the time when section 137 of this Act comes into force.

Requests for assessment

27 (1) The repeal of section 42 of the 1998 Act (requests for assessment) does not affect the application of that section after the relevant time in a case in which the Commissioner received a request under that section before the relevant time, subject to sub-paragraph (2).

(2) The Commissioner is only required to make an assessment of acts and omissions that took place before the relevant time.

(3) In this paragraph, "the relevant time" means the time when the repeal of section 42 of the 1998 Act comes into force.

Codes of practice

28 (1) The repeal of section 52E of the 1998 Act (effect of codes of practice) does not affect the application of that section after the relevant time in relation to legal proceedings or to the exercise of the Commissioner's functions under the 1998 Act as it has effect by virtue of this Schedule.

(2) In section 52E of the 1998 Act, as it has effect by virtue of this paragraph, the references to the 1998 Act include that Act as it has effect by virtue of this Schedule.

(3) For the purposes of subsection (3) of that section, as it has effect by virtue of this paragraph, the data-sharing code and direct marketing code in force immediately before the relevant time are to be treated as having continued in force after that time.

(4) In this paragraph—

"the data-sharing code" and "the direct marketing code" mean the codes respectively prepared under sections 52A and 52AA of the 1998 Act and issued under section 52B(5) of that Act;

"the relevant time" means the time when the repeal of section 52E of the 1998 Act comes into force.

PART 7

ENFORCEMENT ETC UNDER THE 1998 ACT

Interpretation of this Part

29 (1) In this Part of this Schedule, references to contravention of the sixth data protection principle sections are to relevant contravention of any of sections 7, 10, 11 or 12 of the 1998 Act, as they continue to have effect by virtue of this Schedule after their repeal (and references to compliance with the sixth data protection principle sections are to be read accordingly).

(2) In sub-paragraph (1), "relevant contravention" means contravention in a manner described in paragraph 8 of Part 2 of Schedule 1 to the 1998 Act (sixth data protection principle).

Information notices

30 (1) The repeal of section 43 of the 1998 Act (information notices) does not affect the application of that section after the relevant time in a case in which—

(a) the Commissioner served a notice under that section before the relevant time (and did not cancel it before that time), or

(b) the Commissioner requires information after the relevant time for the purposes of—

(i) responding to a request made under section 42 of the 1998 Act before that time,

Data Protection Act 2018 (c. 12)   329
Schedule 20 − Transitional provision etc
Part 7 − Enforcement etc under the 1998 Act

        (ii)   determining whether a data controller complied with the old data protection principles before that time, or

        (iii)   determining whether a data controller complied with the sixth data protection principle sections after that time.

    (2)   In section 43 of the 1998 Act, as it has effect by virtue of this paragraph—

        (a)   the reference to an offence under section 47 of the 1998 Act includes an offence under section 144 of this Act, and

        (b)   the references to an offence under the 1998 Act include an offence under this Act.

    (3)   In this paragraph, "the relevant time" means the time when the repeal of section 43 of the 1998 Act comes into force.

Special information notices

31   (1)   The repeal of section 44 of the 1998 Act (special information notices) does not affect the application of that section after the relevant time in a case in which—

        (a)   the Commissioner served a notice under that section before the relevant time (and did not cancel it before that time), or

        (b)   the Commissioner requires information after the relevant time for the purposes of—

            (i)   responding to a request made under section 42 of the 1998 Act before that time, or

            (ii)   ascertaining whether section 44(2)(a) or (b) of the 1998 Act was satisfied before that time.

    (2)   In section 44 of the 1998 Act, as it has effect by virtue of this paragraph—

        (a)   the reference to an offence under section 47 of the 1998 Act includes an offence under section 144 of this Act, and

        (b)   the references to an offence under the 1998 Act include an offence under this Act.

    (3)   In this paragraph, "the relevant time" means the time when the repeal of section 44 of the 1998 Act comes into force.

Assessment notices

32   (1)   The repeal of sections 41A and 41B of the 1998 Act (assessment notices) does not affect the application of those sections after the relevant time in a case in which—

        (a)   the Commissioner served a notice under section 41A of the 1998 Act before the relevant time (and did not cancel it before that time), or

        (b)   the Commissioner considers it appropriate, after the relevant time, to investigate—

            (i)   whether a data controller complied with the old data protection principles before that time, or

            (ii)   whether a data controller complied with the sixth data protection principle sections after that time.

    (2)   The revocation of the Data Protection (Assessment Notices) (Designation of National Health Service Bodies) Order 2014 (S.I. 2014/3282), and the repeals mentioned in sub-paragraph (1), do not affect the application of that Order in a case described in sub-paragraph (1).

330

Data Protection Act 2018 (c. 12)
Schedule 20 — Transitional provision etc
Part 7 — Enforcement etc under the 1998 Act

(3) Sub-paragraph (1) does not enable the Secretary of State, after the relevant time, to make an order under section 41A(2)(b) or (c) of the 1998 Act (data controllers on whom an assessment notice may be served) designating a public authority or person for the purposes of that section.

(4) Section 41A of the 1998 Act, as it has effect by virtue of sub-paragraph (1), has effect as if subsections (8) and (11) (duty to review designation orders) were omitted.

(5) The repeal of section 41C of the 1998 Act (code of practice about assessment notice) does not affect the application, after the relevant time, of the code issued under that section and in force immediately before the relevant time in relation to the exercise of the Commissioner's functions under and in connection with section 41A of the 1998 Act, as it has effect by virtue of sub-paragraph (1).

(6) In this paragraph, "the relevant time" means the time when the repeal of section 41A of the 1998 Act comes into force.

Enforcement notices

33 (1) The repeal of sections 40 and 41 of the 1998 Act (enforcement notices) does not affect the application of those sections after the relevant time in a case in which—

    (a) the Commissioner served a notice under section 40 of the 1998 Act before the relevant time (and did not cancel it before that time), or

    (b) the Commissioner is satisfied, after that time, that a data controller —

        (i) contravened the old data protection principles before that time, or

        (ii) contravened the sixth data protection principle sections after that time.

(2) In this paragraph, "the relevant time" means the time when the repeal of section 40 of the 1998 Act comes into force.

Determination by Commissioner as to the special purposes

34 (1) The repeal of section 45 of the 1998 Act (determination by Commissioner as to the special purposes) does not affect the application of that section after the relevant time in a case in which—

    (a) the Commissioner made a determination under that section before the relevant time, or

    (b) the Commissioner considers it appropriate, after the relevant time, to make a determination under that section.

(2) In this paragraph, "the relevant time" means the time when the repeal of section 45 of the 1998 Act comes into force.

Restriction on enforcement in case of processing for the special purposes

35 (1) The repeal of section 46 of the 1998 Act (restriction on enforcement in case of processing for the special purposes) does not affect the application of that section after the relevant time in relation to an enforcement notice or information notice served under the 1998 Act—

    (a) before the relevant time, or

Data Protection Act 2018 (c. 12)
Schedule 20 — Transitional provision etc
Part 7 — Enforcement etc under the 1998 Act

331

      (b)   after the relevant time in reliance on this Schedule.

    (2)   In this paragraph, "the relevant time" means the time when the repeal of section 46 of the 1998 Act comes into force.

Offences

36   (1)   The repeal of sections 47, 60 and 61 of the 1998 Act (offences of failing to comply with certain notices and of providing false information etc in response to a notice) does not affect the application of those sections after the relevant time in connection with an information notice, special information notice or enforcement notice served under Part 5 of the 1998 Act—

      (a)   before the relevant time, or

      (b)   after that time in reliance on this Schedule.

    (2)   In this paragraph, "the relevant time" means the time when the repeal of section 47 of the 1998 Act comes into force.

Powers of entry

37   (1)   The repeal of sections 50, 60 and 61 of, and Schedule 9 to, the 1998 Act (powers of entry) does not affect the application of those provisions after the relevant time in a case in which—

      (a)   a warrant issued under that Schedule was in force immediately before the relevant time,

      (b)   before the relevant time, the Commissioner supplied information on oath for the purposes of obtaining a warrant under that Schedule but that had not been considered by a circuit judge or a District Judge (Magistrates' Courts), or

      (c)   after the relevant time, the Commissioner supplies information on oath to a circuit judge or a District Judge (Magistrates' Courts) in respect of—

          (i)   a contravention of the old data protection principles before the relevant time;

          (ii)   a contravention of the sixth data protection principle sections after the relevant time;

          (iii)   the commission of an offence under a provision of the 1998 Act (including as the provision has effect by virtue of this Schedule);

          (iv)   a failure to comply with a requirement imposed by an assessment notice issued under section 41A the 1998 Act (including as it has effect by virtue of this Schedule).

    (2)   In paragraph 16 of Schedule 9 to the 1998 Act, as it has effect by virtue of this paragraph, the reference to an offence under paragraph 12 of that Schedule includes an offence under paragraph 15 of Schedule 15 to this Act.

    (3)   In this paragraph, "the relevant time" means the time when the repeal of Schedule 9 to the 1998 Act comes into force.

    (4)   Paragraphs 14 and 15 of Schedule 9 to the 1998 Act (application of that Schedule to Scotland and Northern Ireland) apply for the purposes of this paragraph as they apply for the purposes of that Schedule.

332

Data Protection Act 2018 (c. 12)
Schedule 20 — Transitional provision etc
Part 7 — Enforcement etc under the 1998 Act

Monetary penalties

38   (1)   The repeal of sections 55A, 55B, 55D and 55E of the 1998 Act (monetary penalties) does not affect the application of those provisions after the relevant time in a case in which—

  (a)   the Commissioner served a monetary penalty notice under section 55A of the 1998 Act before the relevant time,

  (b)   the Commissioner served a notice of intent under section 55B of the 1998 Act before the relevant time, or

  (c)   the Commissioner considers it appropriate, after the relevant time, to serve a notice mentioned in paragraph (a) or (b) in respect of—

    (i)   a contravention of section 4(4) of the 1998 Act before the relevant time, or

    (ii)   a contravention of the sixth data protection principle sections after the relevant time.

  (2)   The revocation of the relevant subordinate legislation, and the repeals mentioned in sub-paragraph (1), do not affect the application of the relevant subordinate legislation (or of provisions of the 1998 Act applied by them) after the relevant time in a case described in sub-paragraph (1).

  (3)   Guidance issued under section 55C of the 1998 Act (guidance about monetary penalty notices) which is in force immediately before the relevant time continues in force after that time for the purposes of the Commissioner's exercise of functions under sections 55A and 55B of the 1998 Act as they have effect by virtue of this paragraph.

  (4)   In this paragraph—

    "the relevant subordinate legislation" means—

    (a)   the Data Protection (Monetary Penalties) (Maximum Penalty and Notices) Regulations 2010 (S.I. 2010/31);

    (b)   the Data Protection (Monetary Penalties) Order 2010 (S.I. 2010/910);

    "the relevant time" means the time when the repeal of section 55A of the 1998 Act comes into force.

Appeals

39   (1)   The repeal of sections 48 and 49 of the 1998 Act (appeals) does not affect the application of those sections after the relevant time in relation to a notice served under the 1998 Act or a determination made under section 45 of that Act—

  (a)   before the relevant time, or

  (b)   after that time in reliance on this Schedule.

  (2)   In this paragraph, "the relevant time" means the time when the repeal of section 48 of the 1998 Act comes into force.

Exemptions

40   (1)   The repeal of section 28 of the 1998 Act (national security) does not affect the application of that section after the relevant time for the purposes of a provision of Part 5 of the 1998 Act as it has effect after that time by virtue of the preceding paragraphs of this Part of this Schedule.

Data Protection Act 2018 (c. 12)
Schedule 20 — Transitional provision etc
Part 7 — Enforcement etc under the 1998 Act

333

(2) In this paragraph, "the relevant time" means the time when the repeal of the provision of Part 5 of the 1998 Act in question comes into force.

(3) As regards certificates issued under section 28(2) of the 1998 Act, see Part 5 of this Schedule.

Tribunal Procedure Rules

41 (1) The repeal of paragraph 7 of Schedule 6 to the 1998 Act (Tribunal Procedure Rules) does not affect the application of that paragraph, or of rules made under that paragraph, after the relevant time in relation to the exercise of rights of appeal conferred by section 28 or 48 of the 1998 Act, as they have effect by virtue of this Schedule.

(2) Part 3 of Schedule 19 to this Act does not apply for the purposes of Tribunal Procedure Rules made under paragraph 7(1)(a) of Schedule 6 to the 1998 Act as they apply, after the relevant time, in relation to the exercise of rights of appeal described in sub-paragraph (1).

(3) In this paragraph, "the relevant time" means the time when the repeal of paragraph 7 of Schedule 6 to the 1998 Act comes into force.

Obstruction etc

42 (1) The repeal of paragraph 8 of Schedule 6 to the 1998 Act (obstruction etc in proceedings before the Tribunal) does not affect the application of that paragraph after the relevant time in relation to an act or omission in relation to proceedings under the 1998 Act (including as it has effect by virtue of this Schedule).

(2) In this paragraph, "the relevant time" means the time when the repeal of paragraph 8 of Schedule 6 to the 1998 Act comes into force.

Enforcement etc under the 2014 Regulations

43 (1) The references in the preceding paragraphs of this Part of this Schedule to provisions of the 1998 Act include those provisions as applied, with modifications, by regulation 51 of the 2014 Regulations (other functions of the Commissioner).

(2) The revocation of regulation 51 of the 2014 Regulations does not affect the application of those provisions of the 1998 Act (as so applied) as described in those paragraphs.

PART 8

ENFORCEMENT ETC UNDER THIS ACT

Information notices

44 In section 143 of this Act—
(a) the reference to an offence under section 144 of this Act includes an offence under section 47 of the 1998 Act (including as it has effect by virtue of this Schedule), and

334

Data Protection Act 2018 (c. 12)
Schedule 20 — Transitional provision etc
Part 8 — Enforcement etc under this Act

    (b)   the references to an offence under this Act include an offence under the 1998 Act (including as it has effect by virtue of this Schedule) or the 1984 Act.

Powers of entry

45   In paragraph 16 of Schedule 15 to this Act (powers of entry: self-incrimination), the reference to an offence under paragraph 15 of that Schedule includes an offence under paragraph 12 of Schedule 9 to the 1998 Act (including as it has effect by virtue of this Schedule).

Tribunal Procedure Rules

46 (1) Tribunal Procedure Rules made under paragraph 7(1)(a) of Schedule 6 to the 1998 Act (appeal rights under the 1998 Act) and in force immediately before the relevant time have effect after that time as if they were also made under section 203 of this Act.

    (2) In this paragraph, "the relevant time" means the time when the repeal of paragraph 7(1)(a) of Schedule 6 to the 1998 Act comes into force.

PART 9

OTHER ENACTMENTS

Powers to disclose information to the Commissioner

47 (1) The following provisions (as amended by Schedule 19 to this Act) have effect after the relevant time as if the matters they refer to included a matter in respect of which the Commissioner could exercise a power conferred by a provision of Part 5 of the 1998 Act, as it has effect by virtue of this Schedule—

    (a)   section 11AA(1)(a) of the Parliamentary Commissioner Act 1967 (disclosure of information by Parliamentary Commissioner);

    (b)   sections 33A(1)(a) and 34O(1)(a) of the Local Government Act 1974 (disclosure of information by Local Commissioner);

    (c)   section 18A(1)(a) of the Health Service Commissioners Act 1993 (disclosure of information by Health Service Commissioner);

    (d)   paragraph 1 of the entry for the Information Commissioner in Schedule 5 to the Scottish Public Services Ombudsman Act 2002 (asp 11) (disclosure of information by the Ombudsman);

    (e)   section 34X(3)(a) of the Public Services Ombudsman (Wales) Act 2005 (disclosure of information by the Ombudsman);

    (f)   section 18(6)(a) of the Commissioner for Older People (Wales) Act 2006 (disclosure of information by the Commissioner);

    (g)   section 22(3)(a) of the Welsh Language (Wales) Measure 2011 (nawm 1) (disclosure of information by the Welsh Language Commissioner);

    (h)   section 49(3)(a) of the Public Services Ombudsman Act (Northern Ireland) 2016 (c. 4 (N.I.)) (disclosure of information by the Ombudsman);

    (i)   section 44(3)(a) of the Justice Act (Northern Ireland) 2016 (c. 21 (N.I.)) (disclosure of information by the Prison Ombudsman for Northern Ireland).

(2) The following provisions (as amended by Schedule 19 to this Act) have effect after the relevant time as if the offences they refer to included an offence under any provision of the 1998 Act other than paragraph 12 of Schedule 9 to that Act (obstruction of execution of warrant) —

    (a) section 11AA(1)(b) of the Parliamentary Commissioner Act 1967;

    (b) sections 33A(1)(b) and 34O(1)(b) of the Local Government Act 1974;

    (c) section 18A(1)(b) of the Health Service Commissioners Act 1993;

    (d) paragraph 2 of the entry for the Information Commissioner in Schedule 5 to the Scottish Public Services Ombudsman Act 2002 (asp 11);

    (e) section 34X(5) of the Public Services Ombudsman (Wales) Act 2005 (disclosure of information by the Ombudsman);

    (f) section 18(8) of the Commissioner for Older People (Wales) Act 2006;

    (g) section 22(5) of the Welsh Language (Wales) Measure 2011 (nawm 1);

    (h) section 49(5) of the Public Services Ombudsman Act (Northern Ireland) 2016 (c. 4 (N.I.));

    (i) section 44(3)(b) of the Justice Act (Northern Ireland) 2016 (c. 21 (N.I.)).

(3) In this paragraph, "the relevant time", in relation to a provision of a section or Schedule listed in sub-paragraph (1) or (2), means the time when the amendment of the section or Schedule by Schedule 19 to this Act comes into force.

Codes etc required to be consistent with the Commissioner's data-sharing code

48 (1) This paragraph applies in relation to the code of practice issued under each of the following provisions —

    (a) section 19AC of the Registration Service Act 1953 (code of practice about disclosure of information by civil registration officials);

    (b) section 43 of the Digital Economy Act 2017 (code of practice about disclosure of information to improve public service delivery);

    (c) section 52 of that Act (code of practice about disclosure of information to reduce debt owed to the public sector);

    (d) section 60 of that Act (code of practice about disclosure of information to combat fraud against the public sector);

    (e) section 70 of that Act (code of practice about disclosure of information for research purposes).

(2) During the relevant period, the code of practice does not have effect to the extent that it is inconsistent with the code of practice prepared under section 121 of this Act (data-sharing code) and issued under section 125(4) of this Act (as altered or replaced from time to time).

(3) In this paragraph, "the relevant period", in relation to a code issued under a section mentioned in sub-paragraph (1), means the period —

    (a) beginning when the amendments of that section in Schedule 19 to this Act come into force, and

    (b) ending when the code is first reissued under that section.

49 (1) This paragraph applies in relation to the original statement published under section 45E of the Statistics and Registration Service Act 2007 (statement of principles and procedures in connection with access to information by the Statistics Board).

(2) During the relevant period, the statement does not have effect to the extent that it is inconsistent with the code of practice prepared under section 121 of this Act (data-sharing code) and issued under section 125(4) of this Act (as altered or replaced from time to time).

(3) In this paragraph, "the relevant period" means the period —

    (a) beginning when the amendments of section 45E of the Statistics and Registration Service Act 2007 in Schedule 19 to this Act come into force, and

    (b) ending when the first revised statement is published under that section.

Consumer Credit Act 1974

50   In section 159(1)(a) of the Consumer Credit Act 1974 (correction of wrong information) (as amended by Schedule 19 to this Act), the reference to information given under Article 15(1) to (3) of the GDPR includes information given at any time under section 7 of the 1998 Act.

Freedom of Information Act 2000

51   Paragraphs 52 to 55 make provision about the Freedom of Information Act 2000 ("the 2000 Act").

52 (1) This paragraph applies where a request for information was made to a public authority under the 2000 Act before the relevant time.

  (2) To the extent that the request is dealt with after the relevant time, the amendments of sections 2 and 40 of the 2000 Act in Schedule 19 to this Act have effect for the purposes of determining whether the authority deals with the request in accordance with Part 1 of the 2000 Act.

  (3) To the extent that the request was dealt with before the relevant time —

    (a) the amendments of sections 2 and 40 of the 2000 Act in Schedule 19 to this Act do not have effect for the purposes of determining whether the authority dealt with the request in accordance with Part 1 of the 2000 Act, but

    (b) the powers of the Commissioner and the Tribunal, on an application or appeal under the 2000 Act, do not include power to require the authority to take steps which it would not be required to take in order to comply with Part 1 of the 2000 Act as amended by Schedule 19 to this Act.

  (4) In this paragraph—

    "public authority" has the same meaning as in the 2000 Act;

    "the relevant time" means the time when the amendments of sections 2 and 40 of the 2000 Act in Schedule 19 to this Act come into force.

53 (1) Tribunal Procedure Rules made under paragraph 7(1)(b) of Schedule 6 to the 1998 Act (appeal rights under the 2000 Act) and in force immediately before the relevant time have effect after that time as if they were also made under section 61 of the 2000 Act (as inserted by Schedule 19 to this Act).

  (2) In this paragraph, "the relevant time" means the time when the repeal of paragraph 7(1)(b) of Schedule 6 to the 1998 Act comes into force.

54   (1)   The repeal of paragraph 8 of Schedule 6 to the 1998 Act (obstruction etc in proceedings before the Tribunal) does not affect the application of that paragraph after the relevant time in relation to an act or omission before that time in relation to an appeal under the 2000 Act.

     (2)   In this paragraph, "the relevant time" means the time when the repeal of paragraph 8 of Schedule 6 to the 1998 Act comes into force.

55   (1)   The amendment of section 77 of the 2000 Act in Schedule 19 to this Act (offence of altering etc record with intent to prevent disclosure: omission of reference to section 7 of the 1998 Act) does not affect the application of that section after the relevant time in relation to a case in which —

            (a)   the request for information mentioned in section 77(1) of the 2000 Act was made before the relevant time, and

            (b)   when the request was made, section 77(1)(b) of the 2000 Act was satisfied by virtue of section 7 of the 1998 Act.

     (2)   In this paragraph, "the relevant time" means the time when the repeal of section 7 of the 1998 Act comes into force.

Freedom of Information (Scotland) Act 2002

56   (1)   This paragraph applies where a request for information was made to a Scottish public authority under the Freedom of Information (Scotland) Act 2002 ("the 2002 Act") before the relevant time.

     (2)   To the extent that the request is dealt with after the relevant time, the amendments of the 2002 Act in Schedule 19 to this Act have effect for the purposes of determining whether the authority deals with the request in accordance with Part 1 of the 2002 Act.

     (3)   To the extent that the request was dealt with before the relevant time —

            (a)   the amendments of the 2002 Act in Schedule 19 to this Act do not have effect for the purposes of determining whether the authority dealt with the request in accordance with Part 1 of the 2002 Act, but

            (b)   the powers of the Scottish Information Commissioner and the Court of Session, on an application or appeal under the 2002 Act, do not include power to require the authority to take steps which it would not be required to take in order to comply with Part 1 of the 2002 Act as amended by Schedule 19 to this Act.

     (4)   In this paragraph —

            "Scottish public authority" has the same meaning as in the 2002 Act;

            "the relevant time" means the time when the amendments of the 2002 Act in Schedule 19 to this Act come into force.

Access to Health Records (Northern Ireland) Order 1993 (S.I. 1993/1250 (N.I. 4))

57   Until the first regulations under Article 5(4)(a) of the Access to Health Records (Northern Ireland) Order 1993 (as amended by Schedule 19 to this Act) come into force, the maximum amount of a fee that may be required for giving access under that Article is £10.

Privacy and Electronic Communications (EC Directive) Regulations 2003 (S.I. 2003/2450)

58 (1) The repeal of a provision of the 1998 Act does not affect its operation for the purposes of the Privacy and Electronic Communications (EC Directive) Regulations 2003 ("the PECR 2003") (see regulations 2, 31 and 31B of, and Schedule 1 to, those Regulations).

(2) Where subordinate legislation made under a provision of the 1998 Act is in force immediately before the repeal of that provision, neither the revocation of the subordinate legislation nor the repeal of the provision of the 1998 Act affect the application of the subordinate legislation for the purposes of the PECR 2003 after that time.

(3) Part 3 of Schedule 19 to this Act (modifications) does not have effect in relation to the PECR 2003.

(4) Part 7 of this Schedule does not have effect in relation to the provisions of the 1998 Act as applied by the PECR 2003.

Health and Personal Social Services (Quality, Improvement and Regulation) (Northern Ireland) Order 2003 (S.I. 2003/431 (N.I. 9))

59 Part 3 of Schedule 19 to this Act (modifications) does not have effect in relation to the reference to an accessible record within the meaning of section 68 of the 1998 Act in Article 43 of the Health and Personal Social Services (Quality, Improvement and Regulation) (Northern Ireland) Order 2003.

Environmental Information Regulations 2004 (S.I. 2004/3391)

60 (1) This paragraph applies where a request for information was made to a public authority under the Environmental Information Regulations 2004 ("the 2004 Regulations") before the relevant time.

(2) To the extent that the request is dealt with after the relevant time, the amendments of the 2004 Regulations in Schedule 19 to this Act have effect for the purposes of determining whether the authority deals with the request in accordance with Parts 2 and 3 of those Regulations.

(3) To the extent that the request was dealt with before the relevant time—
    (a) the amendments of the 2004 Regulations in Schedule 19 to this Act do not have effect for the purposes of determining whether the authority dealt with the request in accordance with Parts 2 and 3 of those Regulations, but
    (b) the powers of the Commissioner and the Tribunal, on an application or appeal under the 2000 Act (as applied by the 2004 Regulations), do not include power to require the authority to take steps which it would not be required to take in order to comply with Parts 2 and 3 of those Regulations as amended by Schedule 19 to this Act.

(4) In this paragraph—
    "public authority" has the same meaning as in the 2004 Regulations;
    "the relevant time" means the time when the amendments of the 2004 Regulations in Schedule 19 to this Act come into force.

Environmental Information (Scotland) Regulations 2004 (S.S.I. 2004/520)

61 (1) This paragraph applies where a request for information was made to a Scottish public authority under the Environmental Information (Scotland) Regulations 2004 ("the 2004 Regulations") before the relevant time.

(2) To the extent that the request is dealt with after the relevant time, the amendments of the 2004 Regulations in Schedule 19 to this Act have effect for the purposes of determining whether the authority deals with the request in accordance with those Regulations.

(3) To the extent that the request was dealt with before the relevant time —

(a) the amendments of the 2004 Regulations in Schedule 19 to this Act do not have effect for the purposes of determining whether the authority dealt with the request in accordance with those Regulations, but

(b) the powers of the Scottish Information Commissioner and the Court of Session, on an application or appeal under the 2002 Act (as applied by the 2004 Regulations), do not include power to require the authority to take steps which it would not be required to take in order to comply with those Regulations as amended by Schedule 19 to this Act.

(4) In this paragraph —

"Scottish public authority" has the same meaning as in the 2004 Regulations;

"the relevant time" means the time when the amendments of the 2004 Regulations in Schedule 19 to this Act come into force.

Printed in Great Britain
by Amazon